THE CRIMINALIZATION
OF MENTAL ILLNESS

THE CRIMINALIZATION OF MENTAL ILLNESS

CRISIS & OPPORTUNITY FOR THE JUSTICE SYSTEM

Risdon N. Slate

and

W. Wesley Johnson

CAROLINA ACADEMIC PRESS

Durham, North Carolina

Library of Congress Cataloging-in-Publication Data

Slate, Risdon N.
Criminalization of mental illness : crisis and opportunity for the justice
system / by Risdon N. Slate, W. Wesley Johnson.
    p. cm.
Includes bibliographical references and index.
ISBN 978-1-59460-268-9 / ISBN 10: 1-59460-268-9 (alk. paper)
1. Insanity (Law)--United States. 2. Mentally ill--Commitment and
detention--United States. 3. Mentally ill offenders--United States. I.
Johnson, W. Wesley. II. Title.

KF9242.S59 2008
364.3'8--dc22

2008008281

Carolina Academic Press
700 Kent Street
Durham, NC 27701
Telephone (919) 489-7486
Fax (919) 493-5668
www.cap-press.com

Printed in the United States of America

DEDICATION

To Claudia and Virginia Slate for your love and support

and

To Dean Shoe for helping me find my voice

and

To Ron Vogel for assisting me in finding the confidence to use it

and

To every person who has ever been knocked down

and

To those, such as Ron Hudson, who have extended a hand to help them up.

Also

To Candy and Arretta Johnson
for riding the roller coaster of life with me and doing it in style

and

To Joe Jacoby, Ben Wright, and Dennis Longmire
who opened doors for me and changed my life

and

To my brothers, Barry and Gerrald and my youngest brother Alan,
who tried his best to fight the demons that haunted his life

and

To the many caring professionals in the mental health and criminal justice
systems that are dedicated to people that are troubled by their own thoughts.

CONTENTS

FOREWORD

By Henry J. Steadman, Ph.D.

In 2008, one in every 100 Americans was in jail or prison. In recent years, U.S. jails booked in approximately 14 million people. Just about five million U.S. citizens were under community correctional supervision in the last U.S. Bureau of Justice Statistics census.

Within these groups, rates of major depression are four times higher than national general population rates for men and 10 times higher for women. For schizophrenia, these rates for justice-involved people are two to three times higher and 10 times higher for bipolar disorders. Further, 75-80% of all these people with serious mental illness have co-occurring substance use disorders.

So what are we going to do? What will provide the groundwork to develop the political will, to equip advocates for the fight, and to frame strategies for adequate response? The answer lies in the content of this comprehensive and timely book by Drs. Slate and Johnson. As the 1999 Surgeon General's Report on Mental Health clearly demonstrated, we have many technologies to effectively respond to the clinical conditions in question. We know much about what makes people better. Getting it to the people in need in a timely manner is what we are bad about.

A roadmap of where we have been and where we need to get is embedded in this book. There are no simple solutions. Law enforcement can be less confrontational and divert to community-based alternatives. Mental health courts can facilitate the reduction of unnecessary jail detentions. Discharge planning can be implemented to help with continuity of care. However, unless there is a greater commitment to provide the comprehensive and appropriate services these justice-involved people need in the community, all the CIT programs, mental health courts, and discharge planning initiatives will be in vain.

With the framework this book provides, the needs are clear. How we got here is apparent. The complexities of the solutions are starkly visible. In the face of these complexities, we cannot afford to be overwhelmed by the challenges. We must move forward. But how?

Again, the thinking encompassed here blazes the way. Responding to headline events makes for bad public policy. Instead, " ... policymakers need to be provided not only with the reasons for implementing policies but also with the numbers to justify their existence" (Slate & Johnson, p. 369). The exceptional, high profile event, while often a catalyst for political action, usually posits the wrong premise on which to build effective policy and practice. The more informed approach, the one taken here by Slate and Johnson, is to look at history and recent data to move towards the thoughtful resolution of competing ideas. As Slate and Johnson emphasize, " ... the cost to 'do it right' will be enormous, but the cost of not doing so, both in terms of human suffering and financially, is even greater" (p. 370).

In the end, doing right for justice-involved persons with mental illness, for the administrators of the systems of care and detention, for the caring clinicians who are all too often overwhelmed by inadequate resources, and for the general public is made much more likely by an understanding of these issues as laid out in this book. What is "right" really does benefit all the relevant parties; this is eminently clear from the ideas and information included in this book. Kudos!

PREFACE

Wesley Johnson and Risdon Slate met in a South Carolina prison in 1985. Wes was a professor bringing students for a tour, and Ris was the prison administrator who served as tour guide. It would be some nine years later in a strip cell in the Richland County South Carolina Jail that the seeds for this book would be planted.

For a myriad of reasons the criminal justice system has become the de facto mental health system, with the three largest inpatient psychiatric institutions in America being jails - not hospitals. This book explores how and why this is the case. Too often crises have driven missives in the interface between the mental health and criminal justice systems. Waiting for sensationalized cases to influence policy can lead to impulsively enacted and misguided interventions.

Persons with mental illnesses are disproportionately coming into contact with the criminal justice system, a system that has been largely ill equipped to deal with such individuals. Many in both the mental health and criminal justice systems don't see it as their job or responsibility to intervene. However, today some criminal justice practitioners, often faced with inadequate treatment resources, are taking the lead in seeking innovative alternatives for linking justice involved persons with mental illnesses to mental health treatment. These initiatives are taking place in both pre and post booking formats and may engage law enforcement, the courts, corrections, and/or probation/parole authorities in collaborative partnerships that often involve persons with mental illnesses, their family members, and mental health treatment providers. Various examples are presented in this book.

Topics covered in the book run the gamut from specialized law enforcement responses, to mental health courts, to jails and prisons, to discharge planning, diversion, re-entry, and outpatient commitment. An examination of criminal justice practitioners who become mentally ill is also considered, and the standard topics of insanity and competency are addressed. The balance between preserving civil liberties and maintaining public safety is emphasized. The need for adequate mental health treatment services and the compilation of outcome data to establish evidence-based practices while maintaining allegiance to the concept of therapeutic jurisprudence is stressed. Real-life illustrative vignettes from professionals engaged in dispensing justice to persons with mental illnesses are included throughout.

It is our belief that this book can serve a multitude of purposes. We hope it educates college students who may one day act as positive change agents in this interface of the mental health and criminal justice systems. We also believe this book can be of benefit to training academies, criminal justice practitioners and mental health providers in identifying and assessing what feasible alternatives are in existence and how to develop comprehensive services. This book also provides guidance for advocates, persons with mental illnesses and their family members to use in their advocacy. Lastly, this book should be used to inform policymakers.

Risdon N. Slate
W. Wesley Johnson

ACKNOWLEDGMENTS

Special thanks are in order for Hank Steadman for his expertise through the years and his willingness to write the insightful foreword. Ron Hudson once said that meeting Jackson Browne must be like meeting Buddha. Hank Steadman writing the foreword was like having Buddha write it. We are also honored to have Xavier Amador provide an endorsement as well. His work has provided profound insight and understanding regarding persons with mental illnesses. We keep waiting for the Dr. X television show, and we hope to be among his first guests.

We would like to thank our friends and colleagues who have provided understanding and/or levity: Pat Anderson, Bruce Darby, Mike Denham, Bill and Melody Gregory, Frank Hodges, Sharon Masters, Ed Plowman, and Pat Smith. Also, a thank you is due to Dean Susan Conner and President Anne Kerr at Florida Southern College and Lisa Nored at the University of Southern Mississippi for their appreciation and support of scholarship. On the home front, Claudia Slate provided comfort and expert editing skills. Thanks also to Rhonda Hickey at USM for hours of work on the index and chores that enabled us to bring the book to print.

We are indebted to the Carolina Academic Press team beginning with Jennifer Whaley and continuing with Karen Clayton, who has done an excellent job with editing, Beth Hall (communications), and Tim Colton (cover design). In particular, we are grateful to Keith Sipe for his appreciation of this project and his willingness to give it a try.

We are pleased to have expert contributions by distinguished professionals, as one chapter was written by Ron Honberg, and Dick Lamb, Anand Pandya, and Suzanne Vogel-Scibilia contributed another chapter. Also, various professionals when asked submitted significant input regarding their personal experiences with the interface of the mental health and criminal justice systems, and we are pleased to include these offerings from Sam Cochran, Ginger Lerner-Wren, Stephanie Rhoades, Angela Cowden, Mark Heath, Michele Saunders, Barbara Lewis, Tony Rolón, John Thomason, Paul Michaud, Kendall Wiley,

Joyce Wilde, Jack Richards, Brian Garrett, Jim Rice, Louise Pyers, Denise Spratt, and Anne Marie Wendel. Stephen Bacallao and Peggy Symons are to be commended for their tenacity and sharing their bureaucratic battle with us. Thanks also to Grady Judd for his commitment to CIT and willingness to explore alternatives to the incarceration of persons with mental illnesses. Two fellow travelers who know something about turning crisis into opportunity, Jack Gillen and Bob Carolla, are recognized for all their good works.

Larry Thompson thankfully early on provided research documents from his archives, and John Petrila provided information as well. Friends who have offered encouragement before, during, and/or after this project include Carl Reed, Jacki Buffington-Vollum, Mike Mathes, Steve Leifman, Mike Thompson, Arlene Stoltz, Dennis Longmire, Randy Garner, and David Lauterbach. Thanks are also in order to the entire NAMI family. Terry Wells would have likely been involved in this project if he were still with us, but in many ways his presence was felt.

Risdon N. Slate—Lakeland, Florida
W. Wesley Johnson—Hattiesburg, Mississippi
— Huntsville, Texas
or somewhere between

THE CRIMINALIZATION
OF MENTAL ILLNESS

CHAPTER 1

INTRODUCTION

"The world breaks every one and afterward many are strong at the broken places."

Ernest Hemingway

The gates to the criminal justice system are open 24 hours a day, and the police typically serve as the gatekeepers. Furthermore, law enforcement officers are often the first point of contact for persons with mental illnesses in crisis. There are a myriad of reasons that will be explored in this book as to why this is the case. The harsh reality is that police officers usually equipped with a vast amount of discretion, particularly when dealing with minor offenses, often times find themselves with a lack of alternatives or a lack of awareness of those alternatives when handling persons with mental illnesses in crisis.

With that as the reality, the three largest inpatient psychiatric facilities in the United States are jails, with each of these jails housing more persons with mental illnesses than any state hospital in the United States; of course, we also continue to close state hospitals across the country. As you read this, the largest inpatient psychiatric institution in your home state is very likely a jail or a prison.

Prisoners have been perceived as toxic waste (see Simon & Feeley, 1995), and jails have traditionally served a cleansing role of social sanitation—sweeping the unsightly rabble off the streets and putting them out of sight and out of mind. Historically, researchers have tried to differentiate criminals from law abiding citizens by physical characteristics [i.e., phrenology—the study of bumps on the head to identify malformations of the brain that might be linked to crime and aberrant behavior; physiognomy—judging character by facial features; body type theories—suggesting that certain physical types were more prone to certain types of criminality—(Vold, Bernard, & Snipes, 1998). Likewise, persons with mental illnesses have been portrayed as physically different, atavistic in nature—throwbacks to an earlier evolutionary stage (see Wahl, 2003).

Many citizens like to think there are significant basic differences between those in prison and themselves; that prisoners are underdeveloped human beings. It would certainly simplify treatment and punishment if there were a set of genetic characteristics that facilitated the identification of criminals. How comforting to be able to feel a sense of superiority by believing one is physically and mentally more evolved than those maladaptive beings institutionalized in prisons, jails, and asylums. Also, such a perspective is palatable to the powers that be, the lawmakers and the policymakers. If the problem with mental illness is an inherently biological, genetic, hereditary, malady, how can lawmakers and policymakers be considered responsible or blamed for a mental health crisis in America?

For the very same reason that Cesare Lombroso is considered the Father of the Positive School of Criminology, as opposed to Guerry and Quetelet (see Vold et al., 1998), biological explanations for aberrant behavior resonate more so with lawmakers and policymakers than an examination of how their own social policies may be contributing to the mental health crisis in America. Today, there is no conclusive evidence that physical type theories have any substantive relationship to crime causation (Vold et al., 1998). Similarly, although portrayed in the media as being physically different in terms of appearance, persons with mental illnesses are not actually physically different in their appearance (Wahl, 2003).

As noted in the Surgeon General's Report on Mental Health, over the span of a year it is estimated that one in five individuals in the United States has a diagnosable mental illness (U.S. Department of Health and Human Services, 1999). Think about this the next time that you are on a commercial airline flight as you look at the individuals sitting on your row: the probability is that one of you is likely mentally ill. Of course, unless it is you, you will probably never know whom you encounter in your daily life that is mentally ill. Indeed, people with mental illnesses are not physically different, and most people with mental illnesses do not exhibit abnormal behavior. While there are a number of success stories of persons with mental illnesses, including those of psychiatrists, lawyers, and even professors, the stigma imposed by our society upon persons with mental illnesses often prevents them from publicly acknowledging their diagnosis.

This book addresses the historical handling of persons with mental illnesses, including religious exorcisms, up to today's remaining contributions to stigma. The closing of state hospitals, with the best of intentions and for the right reasons, is considered in light of the abysmal establishment of community mental health treatment and lack of linkage of persons with mental illnesses to treatment in the community. In turn, a trans-institutionalization has occurred, as persons with mental illnesses have fallen through the cracks and had their health induced aberrant behaviors criminalized, resulting in encounters with criminal justice authorities and often incarceration in the nation's jails and prisons.

The traditional criminal justice system tends to look backward, finding fault, assessing blame, and meting out a punishment with little if any thought about the future consequences wrought by the imposition of a sanction on the perpetrator or society (Slate, 2003). One needs to look no further than our system's high recidivism rates to discern this approach. In most instances we could merely flip a coin and do just as well, if not better, at preventing recidivism.

Typically, attorneys are in tune with their clients' desires when embroiled in the adversarial process (Miller, 1997) and have a tendency to ignore what transpires as a result of their decisions for both clients and society, as usually the long range consequences of a legal decision are not considered (Finkelman and Grisso, 1994). In fact, Winick (1997) has maintained that the traditional criminal defense model does not promote the effective assessment of treatment needs for persons with mental illnesses and is in fact anti-therapeutic. As noted by Winick (1997, p. 187):

> Therapeutic jurisprudence seeks to apply social science to examine law's impact on the mental and physical health of the people it affects. It recognizes that, whether we realize it or not, law functions as a therapeutic agent, bringing about therapeutic or nontherapeutic consequences.

Therapeutic jurisprudence decisions are rendered with concern for the future impact on individuals, relationships, and the community at large long after an individual's contact with the criminal justice system has ended (Slate, 2003).

In the spirit of therapeutic jurisprudence, various law enforcement agencies across the country have developed and implemented programs in an attempt to divert persons with mental illnesses from the criminal justice system and link them to treatment in the community. Regardless of whether these programs involve specialized police training or pairing mental health professionals with police to assist them in responding to crisis calls, the primary goals are ensuring officer, individual, and community safety and preventing persons with mental illnesses from recycling over and over through the criminal justice system.

Likewise, specialty courts, such as mental health courts and drug courts, are armed with the therapeutic jurisprudence philosophy as well as the use of "therapeutic leverage" and "caring coercion" to link persons with mental illnesses to treatment in the community in an attempt to divert these individuals from further involvement with the criminal justice system. In addition to efforts at diverting persons with mental illnesses from the criminal justice system, protocols for handling incarcerated persons with mental illnesses in the jail and prison systems will be delineated.

Prevalence estimates for the number of persons with mental illnesses who are incarcerated in jails and prisons will be discussed, as will problems in ascertaining accurate estimates. The ability to identify co-occurring disorders (i.e. mental illness combined with a substance abuse disorder) can be a critical aspect in ensuring linkage to an appropriate treatment regimen. All too often untrained criminal justice practitioners are too prone to hone in on symptoms of substance abuse and may miss an underlying mental illness that is being masked by the self-medicating reliance upon alcohol or drugs. On the other hand, specially trained clinicians are able to sort out such distinctions.

All too often persons with mental illnesses returning to society after encounters with the criminal justice system are not adequately linked to treatment in the community. Time and again persons with mental illnesses are set up to fail upon their release from custody and perpetually recycle through the system to the point that they are often known as "frequent fliers" due to their repeated contact with the criminal justice system. However, some jurisdictions and agencies are taking innovative, progressive means to try to ensure the successful re-entry of persons with mental illnesses from the criminal justice system back into the community, with the goal of preventing returns to the criminal justice system. Examples of these programs will be discussed.

Traditionally, criminal justice practitioners have been largely untrained and ill-equipped to deal with persons with mental illnesses in crises. As such, criminal justice professionals, often the first responders to crises, may find themselves outside their locus of control and beyond their training in such situations which may result in criminal justice professionals becoming overwhelmed and symptomatic, succumbing to the manifestation of mental illnesses themselves. There is much that can be done to help alleviate the burden placed on criminal justice practitioners, and there is much that they can learn from mental health professionals and vice versa. However, too often avenues of communication are blocked, and one group blames the other for deficiencies without knowing the other side's perspective. There is enough blame to go around, and, while the criminal justice system receives a significant brunt of that criticism, many of the factors that contribute to persons with mental illnesses being in crises are simply not the fault of the criminal justice system.

For a myriad of reasons the criminal justice system has become the de facto mental health system. Factors that contribute to the criminal justice system being the de facto mental health system will be discussed, as will possible solutions. Collaborations between criminal justice and mental health professionals, plus consumers of mental health services and their family members, are essential for informing and influencing reasonable decisions to correct this trend. As will be discussed, cross training between mental health and criminal justice professionals can serve to knock down barriers to communication and establish common ground as well.

A crucial consideration in navigating the handling of persons with mental illnesses is striking the balance between public safety and individual civil liberties. Trying to ensure a harmonious balance between the two can be like opening a Pandora's box. With seemingly the best of intentions, state hospitals have been largely emptied, and restrictive limits have been placed on civil commitment requirements. This brings to the forefront the police power of the state paired with the *parens patriae*, protective nature of the state while trying to guarantee the civil liberties of those persons with mental illnesses in need of help who come into contact with authorities. It has been said that it is all right for one to perceive one's self as Napoleon, as long as the individual does not declare war (Levine, 2007). What boundaries can one's behavior cross before intervention is warranted? A review of the civil commitment process will flesh out legal and ethical considerations in providing treatment to persons with mental illnesses who encounter the criminal justice system.

From the Council of State Government's Justice Center (2007), Figure 1 (see next page) depicts the complexity of processing that offenders with mental illnesses face when they are arrested. The ability to assist an arrested family member or friend whose current mental state is decompensating through the legal maze of the criminal justice system is daunting. The ability of the offender with mental illness alone to do so presents even greater challenges.

Most people with mental illnesses who come into contact with the criminal justice system are not violent, do not plead guilty or not guilty by reason of insanity, or end up on death row. We will, of course, consider those few who do conversely find themselves in one of the above categories and who come to the public's attention via the media, but we will also examine persons with mental illnesses who come to the attention of criminal justice authorities and never make the headlines. This latter group comprises the bulk of where the work is done with persons with mental illnesses who encounter the criminal justice system and is an area that is seldom illuminated.

Figure 1.

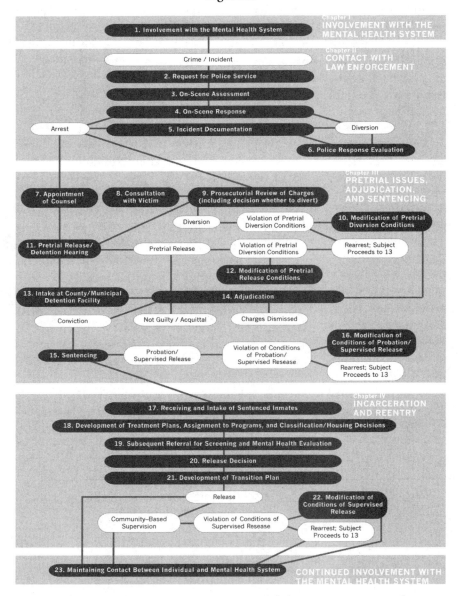

Reprinted with permission from the Council of State Governments Justice Center (2007).
Navigate by a Flowchart of Select Events Experienced by a Person with Mental Illness
in the Criminal Justice System. Retrieved from the World Wide Web on February 29, 2008:
http://consensusproject.org/the_report/flowchart/

According to modern interpretation, two characters, one symbolizing danger and the other opportunity, represent the word crisis in Mandarin Chinese.[1]

Chinese character wēi danger

**Chinese character jī
(in simplified form) opportunity**

Indeed, in any crisis there is danger, but there is also, often unrealized, the opportunity for positive change. Many persons with mental illnesses who reach the breaking point, if given the chance, may come to realize what Ernest Hemingway meant when he said, "The world breaks every one and afterward many are strong at the broken places."[2] Just as individuals can recover from crises, the criminal justice system can also recuperate.

As Samuel Walker (2006) has noted, sensationalized, celebrated cases tend to drive policy within the criminal justice system. These cases are often the exception rather than the rule. Nevertheless, these aberrations can affect change. In other words, crisis drives policy.

As we shall see, this has certainly been the case as tragedies involving persons with mental illnesses have been instrumental in initiating outpatient commitment statutes, in establishing and implementing police responses to persons in crises with mental illnesses, in creating mental health courts, and in instituting re-entry procedures for persons with mental illnesses returning to the community after being in the custody of the criminal justice system. Such tragedies can result in opportunities for the criminal justice system to develop meaningful solutions. Influential criminal justice professionals have stepped to the forefront in making the most of crises involving persons with mental illnesses to drive policy, hopefully for the good of all and the reduction of future tragedies while balancing civil liberties.

---

1. Mair, V.H. (2007). danger + opportunity = crisis: How a misunderstanding about Chinese characters has led many astray. A guide to the writing of Mandarin Chinese in romanization. Retrieved from the World Wide Web on June 7, 2007: http://www.pinyin.info/chinese/crisis.html

2. Chapter 34, p. 249, of Ernest Hemingway's 1929 novel, *A Farewell to Arms*.

It is a shame that crises have played such an integral role in driving policies in this area. This book is a search for a more reasoned approach.

Lastly, means for enhancing public policy in this interface between the mental health and criminal justice systems will be explored. In particular, emphasis will be placed on the importance of the establishment of informed, strategic, meaningful collaborations and partnerships for influencing policy in this area and the accumulation of outcome data to support the development of evidence-based practices.

References

Council of State Governments Justice Center. (2007). *Criminal Justice/Mental Health Consensus Project*, New York. Retrieved from the World Wide Web October 31, 2007: http://consensusproject.org/the_report/flowchart/.

Finkelman, D., & Grisso, T. (1994). Therapeutic jurisprudence: From idea to application. *New England Journal on Criminal and Civil Confinement* 20, pp. 243–257.

Levine, A. (2007). Institutional madness: As South Florida's mental health system spirals out of control, troubled minds are meeting tragic, preventable ends. Retrieved from the World Wide Web on July 13, 2007: http://artlevine.blogspot.com/articles/Institutional%20Madness.htm.

Miller, R. D. (1997). Symposium on coercion: An interdisciplinary examination of coercion, exploitation, and the law: III. Coerced confinement and treatment: The continuum of coercion: Constitutional and clinical considerations in the treatment of mentally disordered persons. *Denver University Law Review* 74, pp. 1169–1214.

Simon, J., & Feeley, M. (1995). True crime: The new penology and public discourse on crime. In T. Blomberg & S. Cohen (Eds.), *Punishment and social control*, New York: Aldine de Gruyter.

Slate, R. N. (2003). From the jailhouse to capitol hill: Impacting mental health court legislation and defining what constitutes a mental health court. *Crime & Delinquency* 49(1), pp. 6–29.

U.S. Department of Health and Human Services. (1999). *Mental health: A report of the surgeon general*. Rockville, MD: U.S. Department of Health and Human Services, Substance Abuse and Mental Health Services Administration, Center for Mental Health Services, National Institute of Health, National Institute of Mental Health.

Vold, G. B., Bernard, T. J., & Snipes, J. B. (1998). *Theoretical criminology, 4th ed.*, New York: Oxford University Press.

Wahl, O. F. (2003). *Media madness: Public images of mental illness.* New Brunswick, NJ: Rutgers University Press.

Walker, S. (2006). *Sense and non-sense about crime and drugs: A policy guide,* 6th ed. Belmont, California: Thomson Wadsworth.

Winick, B. J. (1997). The jurisprudence of therapeutic jurisprudence. *Psychology, Public Policy and Law* 3, pp. 184–206.

CHAPTER 2

THE HISTORY OF MAINTAINING ORDER WITH PERSONS WITH MENTAL ILLNESSES

"There's always the chance that justice will be done."

Attorney Richard "Racehorse" Haynes[1]

Introduction

Mental wellness or illness may be best understood when viewed on a continuum. Some of us are more or less mentally well/ill than others. Like our physical health our mental health fluctuates. Very few individuals reach a perfect balance point in their lives where they are physically and mentally healthy. The maintenance of order in society can be correlated with the difficulty in maintaining order in one's own life. Like the maintenance of order and balance in our lives, the maintenance of order in society is a dynamic, organic process involving numerous social, political, and economic factors. The tenuous process of maintaining order in society is impacted by the morale, vitality, and mental health of communities and individuals. It can also be argued that the manner in which order is maintained impacts the morale, vitality, and mental health of communities; they are interactive, reciprocal processes. Certainly, the various less-privileged classes of American citizens (women, racial minorities, children, immigrants, and persons with mental illnesses) suffer severe mental and emotional distress from repressive justice practices. This chapter provides an examination of the evolution of the handling and processing of persons with mental illnesses.

---

1. Friedman, K. (2001). Guide to Texas Etiquette. New York: Harper Collins, p. 102.

The institutionalization of a human being is the most intrusive form of state intervention, second only to capital punishment. For centuries societies have struggled with the care, treatment and control of persons with mental illnesses. This struggle has been exacerbated by the difficulty in discerning who is a criminal, who is a person with mental illness, and who is a criminal with mental illness. Mental institutions house criminals and prisons house persons with mental illnesses. These systems overlap and have been shaped by advancements in the fields of science, medicine, and psychology. A history of mental illness must include the treatment of criminality in its discourse and vice versa. The two histories are intertwined and cannot be sufficiently disaggregated. From a policy standpoint it is difficult to determine what should be considered a proper balance between the two separate but overlapping systems. An examination of this history reveals that the criminalization of mental illness is not a new phenomena.

Pre-Civilization Era

Early accounts of tribal life document the use of herbal and spirit-based approaches to treat illness by medicine men. Such practices are based upon the assumption that the soul and body are distinct entities. These are issues discussed in the works of Descartes, St. Augustine and St. Thomas Aquinas. A philosophical position which accepts such a duality provides the basis for treatment responses that go beyond the treatment of just the body, accepting treatments that include a psychological or mental component.

Attempts to treat the mind/brain are as old as civilization. Examination of skulls by anthropologists indicate that cranial trephining was used approximately 7,000–8,000 years ago to treat brain/mind dysfunction. Trephination, as practiced in ancient times, involved removing a piece of the skull to expose the dura mater. It is thought that such procedures would release evil spirits. There is evidence that trephining is still practiced today by tribal groups in South America and Africa. Trephining has become a much more sophisticated medical procedure in modern hospitals and is used to relieve pressure on the brain due to head trauma and swelling of the brain (Prioreschi, 1991).

Hippocrates (460–377 BC), the father of modern medicine, also professed the brain as the center of mental processes.[2] Hippocrates identified a number

---

2. Retrieved June 26, 2007 from http://allpsych.com/timeline.html.

of mental illnesses including phobias, mania, depression and anxiety. From *The Genuine Works of Hippocrates* (1849),

> as long as the brain is at rest, the man enjoys his reason, but disorder of the brain arises from phlegm and bile, either of which you may recognize in this manner: Those who are mad from phlegm are quiet, and do not cry out nor make a noise; but those from bile are vociferous, malignant, and will not be quiet, but are always doing something improper. If the madness be constant, these are the causes of it.[3]

From Hippocrates's science, mental illness was a result of disturbed physiology, an imbalance in the body's fluids. Remedies based on his line of reasoning involved laxatives and surgery to cleanse the body of impurities.

As early as 387 BC, Plato proposed the brain was the center of mental processes. Aristotle, Plato's student, proposed the heart was the foundation for mental processes. There are many today that believe the brain is the last frontier (Restak, 1980).

Controversies regarding the role of brain functioning in determining individual accountability under criminal law haunt global jurisprudence systems. One of the earliest judicial responses to mental and physical illness was exclusion. Those threatening the order and well being of social groups prior to the development of urban areas were subject to banishment. Considering the need to function as a group for purposes of eating and defense from other forces, banishment equated to death. Institutions of confinement function as modern forms of exclusion.

Prior to the development of structured governments as we know them today, the management of deviants was a family/clan responsibility. The management of clans was usually the responsibility of elder relatives. As a result, governing bodies developed first along blood lines. Over time, families became less involved in the care, treatment, and control of persons with mental illnesses. At the same time, possibly in response to changes in family functioning, governments have become more involved in the care of the mentally ill. Where individuals refused or were incapable of being normalized, governments assumed responsibility (Ebert, 1999).

---

3. Adapted from *The Genuine Works of Hippocrates*, translated from the Greek by Francis Adams, Robert E. Krueger Publishing Co, Huntington, N.Y. 1972 (from 1946 reprint of 1849 original).

During the middle ages (476 BC to early 1400s) demonology re-emerged as an explanation for abnormal behavior, mental illness, and criminality. Laws reinforced notions of salvation, spiritual conversion, and allegiance to the rituals of the church with an emphasis on execution or torture. The Egyptians attributed certain diseases and various other evils to demons and believed in the efficacy of magical charms and incantations for banishing or dispelling them. During this time, spots on the skin, *stigmata diablo* (devil spots), were examined to identify individuals that were possessed by demonic spirits. Hindus historically practiced exorcism rituals through such means as blowing cow dung smoke, burning pig excreta, beating or pulling the victim's hair, reciting prayers or mantras, and offering gifts of candy and other presents to get the evil spirits to depart from persons so afflicted. One of the best known Judaic rituals, cited in Judaism rabbinical literature dating from the first century AD, involves the *dybbuk*, an evil or doomed spirit which possesses a victim and brings about mental illness and a personality change. The *dybbuk* is expelled through the victim's small toe, and then is either redeemed or sent to hell. Jesus is said to have sought out those who suffered with mental illnesses, to have healed the spirit, and restored such individuals to full community membership. In Islamic tradition, Avicenna (980–1037, a Persian physician from the Golden Age of Islam) established what may be considered the first mental hospital. Avicenna records the account of how he dealt with a prince who thought he was a cow (Suich, 2005).

Reference by physicians and priests to *Malleus Maleficarum*, Latin for *The Hammer of Witches*, was used as a diagnostic manual to identify witches. Identification and punishments of witches was used to reaffirm the power of the State and the Church to maintain social order. Fear of being labeled a witch and suffering torture and/or execution motivated citizens to express allegiance to the State and the Church. At this time, monarchies and churches were closely aligned, possessed great wealth, and controlled the implementation of policies regulating human behavior (White, 1888).

Beginning in the late 1300s, the growth of a new philosophy of humanism fueled the birth of the Italian Renaissance. The Renaissance was a time of creativity and change and reflected a move away from the moral and religious orientations of the Middle Ages. This new focus on humanism emphasized life in the present, individual expression and concern for others (Israel, 2006).

The Italian Renaissance's focus on personal development and humanism influenced changes in the care of persons with mental illnesses. In the 1400s, England began the custodial confinement of "lunatics" at Bethlem. While modern day critics claim the conditions at Bethlem were inhumane, the confinement of persons with mental illnesses was an attempt to mitigate previous practices of execution, torture, and attempts to exorcise demons from the body of the condemned.[4] For over 400 years those confined at Bethlem, later called Bedlam, were kept in chains (Andrews, Briggs, & Waddington, 1997).

Johann Weyer (1515–1588), a Dutch medical doctor, was considered by some to be the first psychiatrist. Weyer provided scientific evidence to refute the claims of witchcraft and demon possession made in the *Malleus Malefi-carum*. He is proclaimed to be the first person to use the term mentally ill and the first physician to sustain a challenge to the Catholic Church's Inquisition, asserting that psychopathy was not the work of demon forces and was treatable (Zilboorg, 1935). His persistent criticism of the Catholic Church was possible only by his protection from Dutch royalty.

The Era of Enlightenment

Beginning in the 1600s and into the 1700s a movement of self criticism emerged fueled by the writings of Isaac Newton (natural science), Thomas Hobbes (social contract) John Locke (empirical psychology), Blaise Pascal and René Descartes.[5] René Descartes' (1596–1650) writings mark what has been called the beginning of modern psychology. He believed, like the early Greeks, in the concept of dualism, that a separate nonmaterial soul existed that expressed itself in a physical body. While the physical body needed no proof of its existence, the soul did. Descartes, using epistemology (the study of the na-

---

4. Furthermore, the use of exorcisms to remove demons is not so far removed today when the following case is considered, *Lambert v. New York State Office of Mental Health*, 2000 WL 863461 (E.D.N.Y., June 2000). In this case, a Reverend envisioned six inhabitants of the Kingsboro Psychiatric Center to be possessed by demons and offered a discount rate for the expulsion of the demons. The court concluded that no responsible jury could perceive the hiring of the Reverend as an exorcist as reasonable medical care [Cohen, F. (2000 September/October) "Hiring discount exorcist to treat delusional forensic patient leads to executive's dismissal," Correctional Mental Health Report p. 41]; The mother of Seung Hui Cho (Seung Hui Cho is the individual who inflicted the massacre on the Virginia Tech University campus), realizing her son had problems, actually sought out the assistance of Presbyterian church members at One Mind Church in Woodbridge, Virginia to heal him of "demonic power" but before the intervention could take place Cho had to return for his senior year of school late last summer [Gardner, A. & Cho, D. (2007, May 6). Isolation defined Cho's senior year. *Washington Post*, p. A01].

5. See Hans Toch (1979) The psychology of crime, and criminal justice, Waveland Press, Inc. Prospect Heights, p. 149.

ture and grounds of knowledge with reference to its limits and validity) as his proof, contended that the acceptance of his now famous principle, *cogito ergo sum*, "I reflect, therefore I am," was necessary to understand the relationship between the mind and the body. According to Descartes' rationale, man could not doubt the existence of his/her own self (mind/soul) unless there was a self to do the doubting (Custance, 1997). The writing of Descartes and others' writings spawned a new enlightened way of thinking about the relationship between man and society and man and government. During the Middle Ages, ruling monarchies capitalized on being able to bring order to societies ravaged by plagues and warring tribes. They developed complex systems of political patronage and accumulated great sums of wealth. Beginning in the late 1600s, a new age philosophy emerged, seeded by the Era of Enlightenment, which questioned the arbitrariness of decision making in monarchial systems and argued for more democratic forms of government and a more humanistic view toward man. During the early 1700s, punishment was the primary form of social control. At that time there were over 100 crimes punishable by death (McLynn, 1989).

Foucault (1965) labels the move to institutionalize offenders *The Great Confinement*. This change in social control policy was (is) a product of moral, philosophical, or economic forces. Arguments over which social forces are responsible for the maintenance of institutional responses to deviance remain today. Undeniably, Era of Enlightenment philosophers such as Cesare Beccaria (1738–1794) had an impact on policymakers of the time. In *Homo Criminalis*, Cesare Bonesana, the Marquis of Beccaria, proposed a new science of man (circa, 1760). Beccaria, associated with the Classical School of writers, proposed that laws should be based upon the notion that man has free will, is rational and thus is able to be deterred from crime. From Beccaria's rational, scientific approach, public and private attempts at individual normalization would approach the mind and soul, not just the body (Staples, 1977).

The philosophical and moral reasoning behind the introduction of confinement in the 17th Century as a "new solution" is reflected in the notion that institutions were inclusive and were designed to provide a modicum of custodial services: food, shelter, and at some level, security. From a practical perspective, the need for government intervention and confinement was responsive to an economic crisis that was affecting the entire Western world: "reduction of wages, unemployment, scarcity of coin ..." (Foucault, 1965, p. 49). The institutionalization of deviants became the first of many attempts to provide a panacea to social ills of modern life.

Shortly thereafter, Franz Mesmer (circa 1774) proposed a cure for some mental illnesses. His cure, once called mesmerism, is now referred to as hypnosis. In 1793, Philippe Pinel released patients from confinement in mental institutions. This can be characterized as the first deinstitutionalization movement and reflects the movement of the time toward more humane treatment of persons with mental illnesses. In 1808, Franz Gall, a Viennese physician, attempted to popularize phrenology, the notion that a person's skull shape and placement of bumps on the head can reveal personality traits and determine one's propensity for deviant behavior. While many find humor in Gall's diagnostic approach, phrenology helped introduce the notion of a possible link between brain functioning and personality.

Cesare Lombroso, an Italian physician, was among the first to use empirical-based research to explain mental abnormality and criminality. Although his focus would change over time, Lombroso (1835–1909) initially asserted a theory of atavism where criminality was an inherited trait and criminals possessed body characteristics similar to previous generations of humans. While Lombroso's research was refuted based on methodological and analytical errors, his work is important for two primary reasons: his work led to more sophisticated and valid research, and it paved the way for biological explanations for deviance. Advancements in the understanding of the biological bases for aggression and violence owe some allegiance to the work of Cesare Lombroso. Lombroso's work could also be considered important because it challenged popular theories (i.e. Jeremy Bentham and Cesare Beccaria) of the time espousing rationality, self-determination, and deterrence (Wilson and Hernstein, 1985).

The post-enlightenment period (late 1700s to late 1800s) was one of "increasing domination masked in a guise of emancipation and humanitarianism" (Staples, 1977, p. 18). According to Foucault, the focus of reformers changed in the late 18th century from trying to dominate the world around them to applying emerging disciplinary technologies. The human body (mind) became the object of attention. During this time definitions of what could be called normal behaviors became increasingly narrow. The operationalization of such definitions was made possible by systems aimed at classifying, regulating, excluding, and eliminating particular human behaviors (Foucault, 1965).

The Reform Era

Dorothea Dix (1802–1887), a socially active nurse practitioner during the mid 1800s, after visiting jails and prisons throughout the United States, protested the criminalization of persons with mental illnesses. She argued that such persons would be better served in hospitals. Mrs. Dix was successful in garnering support for publicly supported mental hospitals. As a result many state supported hospitals were built and thousands of criminals who were mentally ill were diverted from prisons and jails to state mental hospitals. The rationale for this move was that punishment would be replaced with healing that focused on the root cause of the deviant behavior (Gilligan, 2001).

The first psychiatric hospital in America, the Eastern Lunatic Asylum in Williamsburg, Virginia, opened in 1773 with 20 beds. In 1816 a second psychiatric hospital opened in Baltimore and was soon followed by others in Philadelphia, Boston, and New York, and the era of hospital confinement for the mentally ill had begun. It would last for 150 years (Torrey, 1997).

The acceptance of Mrs. Dix's plans would not have been possible without the acceptance of the work being done by Dr. Benjamin Rush. Dr. Rush proposed the radical notion that mental illness was a disease of the mind rather than a result of possession by demons. He emphasized recreational and occupational therapies and experimented with various alternative treatments. Dr. Rush is considered by many to be the father of American Psychiatry. Dr. Rush was among the first to study mental illness in the Americas and directed the psychiatric ward at the Pennsylvania Hospital in Philadelphia (Gilligan, 2001).

During the last decades of the 19th century, scientists began to understand how the human mind and behavior were linked to the various parts of the brain. The case of Phineas Gage brought wide spread public attention to the connection between brain dysfunction and aggression. Gage, the victim of a construction accident, was lobotomized after an explosion sent a steel rod through his skull disconnecting his frontal lobes from the rest of his brain. Miraculously Gage survived but suffered from significant changes in his personality characterized by fits of violence, irreverence and profanity. While the accidental lobotomization of Phineas Gage resulted in long term negative consequences for Mr. Gage, physicians and scientists concluded that frontal lobotomies might actually be beneficial, especially for patients with mental illnesses and with excessive anxiety disorders (Peterson, 1999).

Friederich Golz, a German scientist, conducted experiments in 1890 on the neocortex of dogs. He claimed that when the temporal lobe was removed the dogs became more docile than the dogs who had not received the operation. Gottlieb Burkhardt, a Swiss physician and supervisor of an insane asylum, in 1892 performed an operation to remove parts of the cortex of six schizophrenic patients. He claimed his operations were successful in calming the behavior of his patients. Two of his patients died not long after the surgery, and Burkhardt became the object of intense criticism by the medical community. As a result very few psychosurgeries were carried out in the next 40 years or so (Sabbatini, 1997).

At the turn of the 20th Century, a new industrial age, combined with advances in science and a volatile global political climate, led to two World Wars. Use of weapons of mass destruction left behind enumerable physically and emotionally scarred victims of war and repression. Soldiers returned home to families and communities with limited resources to cope with the psychological effects of war. Soldiers suffering with what was later labeled PTSD (post traumatic stress disorder) were often left to work their problems out alone. Many self medicated, using alcohol or street drugs. The social costs were enormous (Favaro, Tenconi, Colombo, & Santonastaso, 2006).

Harvard anthropologist E.A. Hooton advocated for the elimination of the mentally unfit (Vold & Bernard, 1986), and both the United States and German governments have sordid histories of sterilizing persons considered mentally defective. The often eloquent United States Supreme Court Justice Oliver Wendell Holmes, in his majority opinion in *Buck v. Bell* (1927), stated "Three generations of imbeciles is enough" (p. 207) upon upholding the forced sterilization of institutionalized females. Such persons were considered a burden on society, and Holmes likened the sacrifice of sterility to that of a soldier putting his needs aside for his country. In Germany, a law was passed in 1933 authorizing the sterilization of persons considered to be mentally ill. The Third Reich referred to such individuals as "unfit," " life unworthy of life," and "useless eaters." The Nazis would extend their handling of the mentally ill beyond sterilization to actual systematic elimination of persons considered mentally ill by lethal injection or gas via an order from Adolf Hitler in October 1939. This secret "euthanasia" operation was code-named T4, for Tiergartenstrasse 4, the street address of the program's coordinating office in Berlin (Nazi Persecution of the Disabled, 2007; Education for Teachers, 2007).

In the 1930s, the treatment of mental illness was radically changed by the introduction of four therapies: insulin coma therapy, metrazol-convulsive shock, electric shock, and frontal lobotomy (Valenstein, 1986). Frontal lobotomies quickly became the new panacea in the treatment of persons with mental illnesses who exhibited violent behavior. In 1935, Carlyle Jacobsen, a Yale University scientist, performed lobotomies on chimpanzees. Jacobsen claimed the surgery was successful in reducing aggression without the loss of memory or intelligence. Further work at Yale University by experimental neurologist John Fulton on primates popularized the potential use of lobotomies in humans.

Dr. Antônio Egas Moniz, a Portuguese neuropsychiatrist, performed lobotomies in attempts to alleviate some of the severe mental symptoms of patients with intractable psychoses. Moniz contended that lobotomies would break the recurrent thought patterns that haunted patients with paranoia and obsessive-compulsive disorder. He reported mixed results from his experiments and urged that the procedure he called leukotomy, the cutting of white matter, be used as a last resort. Dr. Antônio Egas Moniz was awarded the Nobel Prize for Medicine and Physiology in 1949 for his creation of the prefrontal leukotomy. As a result, more lobotomies were performed in the ensuing three years than in all previous years (Sabbatini, 1997).

Walter Freeman, a clinical neurologist and physician, performed the first leukotomy in America in 1936. In 1945, Freeman introduced a "refined" process using a local anesthetic, a common ice pick, and a hammer that he called frontal lobotomy. Freeman claimed the procedure was less messy, could be performed in a matter of minutes, and could be performed on an out-patient basis. Freeman performed approximately 3,500 lobotomies.

While there were over 40,000 lobotomies performed between 1939 and 1980, many veteran neurosurgeons were upset by the primitive nature of this new procedure and expressed ethical concerns regarding the potential misuses of the procedure. Unlike the current world of consent and liability, government states prior to the 1960s often made decisions to lobotomize individuals based on management rather than health interests. Evidence of abuses of the procedure occurred throughout the world. In Japan, "problem" children made up most of the lobotomies. It was not uncommon for the criminally insane to be operated on without their, or their families', consent. Records show that families trying to get rid of difficult relatives submitted them to lobotomy. In Russia, rebels and political opponents were treated as mentally deranged by authorities and operated on. Amateur surgeons would often perform hundreds of lobotomies without even doing a systematic psychiatric evaluation (Sabbatini, 1997).

In the Soviet Union, lobotomy was outlawed in the 1940s, not because it was not useful to suppress opponents of the Communist régime (they used other methods, such as forced hospitalization), but because there was an ideological stance against it (Sabbatini, 1997). Opposition to lobotomies grew between 1950 and 1960 and was translated into law in the 1970s. Much of the opposition was fueled by introduction of scientific research which questioned the cost/benefit of the operation to the individual and to society. Today, there are less than 300 hundred brain operations conducted worldwide to treat psychiatric disorders. While the new procedures are not called lobotomies, they use lasers to target regions of the brain most closely implicated in obsessive-compulsive disorders (El-Hai, 2005). Japan, Australia, Sweden and India are among the countries that still accept the use of psychosurgery (Sabbatini, 1997). During the 1950s and 1960s in America, overcrowded and under funded mental hospitals produced deplorable living conditions for thousands of patients, as did institutions for persons with mental retardation.

Conclusion

Public support for state supported mental hospitals waned fueled by several factors including the popularization of introspective therapies (i.e. Freudian, Gestalt, Adlerian, etc.), the use of psychoactive drugs such as Thorazine, the acceptance of electric shock therapy, and the institutionalization of new immigrants and ethnic minorities. As state funding for mental hospitals dwindled and institutional living conditions deteriorated, legal, medical, and mental health professionals turned to community mental health treatment as the primary response to what some termed a mounting crisis in mental health. This social experiment was called "deinstitutionalization" (Gilligan, 2001).

Current research indicates that more than half of individuals in jails and prisons have a mental health problem [although methodological concerns with this study will be addressed later] (James & Glaze, 2006). Beyond those arrested and processed by the justice system there is a much larger population of persons suffering from various forms of mental illnesses that present management problems for hospitals, schools, and public transportation. Virtually every aspect of public life presents security issues that are affected by how mental illness is managed (Staples, 1977). Quality of life at both the individual and community level will be determined by how mental illness is managed. The next chapter will focus on how the handling of persons with mental illnesses has digressed instead of evolving after the implementation of deinstitutionalization and other detrimental factors.

References

Andrews, J., Briggs, A., & Waddington, K. (1997). History of Bethlem. London, England: Routledge.

Buck v. Bell, 274 U.S. 200 (1927).

Custance, A. (1997). The mysterious matter of mind. Retrieved from the World Wide Web on October 19, 2007: http://custance.org/old/mind/ ch2m.html.

Ebert, T. G. (1999). *Mental Illness and Its Treatment in the Late 19th and Early 20th Century*. Wyndham Hall Press: Lima, OH.

Education for Teachers (2007). Teaching about the Holocaust. United States Holocaust Memorial Museum. Retrieved from the World Wide Web on October 19, 2007: http://www.ushmm.org/education/foreducators/.

El-Hai, J. (2005). *The lobotomist: A maverick medical genius and his tragic quest to rid the world of mental illness*. John Wiley and Sons, Inc.: Hoboken, NJ.

Favaro, A., Tenconi E., Colombo, G., & Santonastaso, P. (2006). Full and Partial Post-Traumatic Stress Disorder among World War II Prisoners of War. *Psychopathology* 39, 187–191.

Foucault, M. (1965). *Madness and Civilization: A History of Insanity in the Age of Reason*, trans. Richard Howard, New York: Pantheon.

Gilligan, J. (2001). The last mental hospital, *Psychiatric Quarterly* 2, 45–77.

Israel, J. I. (2006). *Enlightenment Contested: Philosophy, Modernity, and the Emancipation of Man 1670–1752*. Oxford University Press: England.

James, D., & Glaze, L. (2006). Mental Health Problems of Prison and Jail Inmates. Washington, DC: Bureau of Justice Statistics, U.S. Department of Justice.

McLynn, F. L. (1989). *Crime and Punishment in Eighteenth-century England*. Routledge: London.

Nazi Persecution of the Disabled (2007). Murder of the "unfit." United States Holocaust Memorial Museum. Retrieved from the World Wide Web on October 19, 2007: http://www.ushmm.org/museum/exhibit/focus/disabilities_02/.

Peterson, G. (1999). The humanizing brain: Where religion and neuroscience meet. Retrieved June 27, 2007 from http://www.gpc.edu/~bbrown/psyc1501/brain/psychosurg.htm.

Prioreschi, P. (1991). *Trephining, Perspect Biol Med*, Winter 34, 296–303.

Restak, R. (1980). *The Brain: The last frontier*. NY: Warner Books.

Sabbatini, R. M. E. (1997). The history of psychosurgery, Brain & Mind Magazine. Retrieved June 27, 2007 from http://www.cerebromente.org.br/n02/historia/psicocir_i.htm.

Staples, W. (1977). *Culture of surveillance*. NY: St. Martin's Press, Inc.

Suich, P. (2006, September 27). Mental illness: The role of the faith community. The Florida Center for Science and Religion, Lakeland, Florida.

Torrey, E. F. (1997). *Out of the shadows: Confronting America's mental illness crisis*. NY: John Wiley & Sons.

Valenstein, E. S. (1986). *Great and desperate cures: The rise and decline of psychosurgery and other radical treatments for mental illness*. Basic Books: New York.

Vold, G. B., & Bernard, T.J. (1986). *Theoretical criminology*, 3rd ed. New York: Oxford University Press.

White, E. (1888). *The Great Controversy Between Christ and Satan: The Conflict of the Ages in the Christian Disposition.* Mountain View, CA: Pacific Press Publishing Association.

Wilson, J. Q., & Hernstein, R. (1985). *Crime and Human Nature: The definitive study of the causes of crime.* New York: Simon & Schuster, Inc.

Zilboorg, G. (1935). *The Medical Man and the Witch During the Renaissance.* Baltimore: Johns Hopkins.

CHAPTER 3

THE CRIMINALIZATION
OF PERSONS WITH
MENTAL ILLNESSES

If you are to punish a man, you must injure him. If you are to reform
a man, you must improve him, and men are not improved by injuries.

—George Bernard Shaw[1]

Surely punishing persons with mental illness via incarceration in jail or
prison for conduct for which they are not responsible, often with inadequate
treatment and no follow-up on re-entry into the community, is a recipe for
failure. Often, in efforts to do the right thing, we do more harm than good.
The recycling of persons with mental illnesses through the criminal justice system is an example of this phenomenon. How did it get this way, how bad is it,
and how might we improve the process?

The civil rights movement of the 1960s in America went beyond striving for
equality in race relations, hotel accommodations, public transit opportunities,
restaurant accessibility, and access to restroom facilities. The wave of the movement led to the extension of due process rights to juveniles, and, seemingly with
the best of intentions and sometimes for the right reasons, due to abuse and horrific conditions in state hospitals, the mental health system came under scrutiny.

In 1972, Abramson first coined the phrase "the criminalization of the mentally ill" after passage of more restrictive criteria for civil commitment proceedings in California in the form of the Lanterman-Petris-Short Act (Abramson,
1972; Lamb & Weinberger, 1998; Miller, 1992). In addition to stringent civil
commitment requirements, Lamb, Weinberger, and Gross (2004) cite deinsti-

---

1. Kittrie, N.N. (1978). *The right to be different: Deviance and enforced treatment.* P. 1–2
Baltimore: John Hopkins University Press.

tutionalization and the lack of access to intermediate and long-term acute care beds for persons with chronic and severe mental illnesses; inadequate community support service and difficulty accessing mental health treatment upon re-entering society from jail or prison; a belief that has been ingrained in the psyche of some law enforcement personnel that they can more expeditiously and efficiently process persons with mental illnesses within the criminal justice system as opposed to within the mental health system as factors contributing to the criminalization of persons with mental illnesses.

Within our society there is sometimes a tendency to blame the victim which can be much easier than digging beneath the surface and trying to determine who or what the real culprits are that may be propelling persons with mental illnesses, not of their own volition, into the criminal justice system. In addition to the factors listed above leading to the criminalization of persons with mental illnesses, other factors contributing to this phenomenon include homelessness, stigma, co-occurring disorders, lack of insight into one's illness, negative side effects of medications, and actions/omissions/mistakes by treatment providers.

Deinstitutionalization

At the beginning of the twentieth century there were approximately 145,000 patients in state mental hospitals (Earley, 2006). By 1955, that number had reached its highest point in America with 559,000 persons institutionalized in state hospitals (Lamb et al., 2004). From 1960 to 1980 this number plunged to less than 100,000 (Earley, 2006); as we enter the twenty first century, approximately 55,000 persons with mental illnesses are housed in state mental hospitals (Lamb et al., 2004). Some even suggest that number may be as low as 40,000 persons being housed today in state psychiatric hospitals (Transforming Florida's Mental Health System, 2007). This mass exodus from the residential mental health system has been labeled deinstitutionalization. Lamb and Bachrach (2001) characterize deinstitutionalization as theoretically being comprised of several processes: the establishment of specialized community treatment services for persons with mental illnesses who are not institutionalized and the movement of psychiatric hospital patients and the diversion of potential new admittees to alternative community facilities and treatment. As noted by Lamb and Bachrach (2001), the development of treatment services for the care of persons with mental illnesses in the community has lagged far behind the dumping of persons with mental illnesses from psychiatric hospitals into the community and the prevention of persons with mental illnesses from being housed in those hospitals. In other words, thousands of individuals have been thrust into the streets, with many remaining homeless, while adequate community treatment and care have not been established.

Former investigative reporter Peter Earley (2006) indicates that the convergence of several factors led to the deinstitutionalization movement in America. These factors included: attorneys influenced by the civil rights movement who were willing to file class-action lawsuits against states for mistreating persons in state hospitals, the discovery of the drug Thorazine (Cournos & Le Melle, 2000), the exposure via the media of inhumane conditions and abuses in state hospitals, the evolution of the anti-psychiatry counter-culture, and President John F. Kennedy's initiative for creating an infrastructure of community mental health centers (CMHCs) throughout the country.

Litigation

In *Wyatt v. Stickney* (1972) it was argued that persons with mental illnesses who were hospitalized had a right to treatment. However, the ulterior motive was allegedly to deliver patients from their confinement to mental institutions, and this case, along with *O'Connnor v. Donaldson* (1975) dealing with involuntary commitment, failed to establish a right to treatment but served to set the deinstitutionalization process into motion (White, 1995).[2]

Thorazine

In 1952, chlorpromazine, which would come to be known as Thorazine, was discovered in Paris; this is at a time that French and even American psychiatrists were skeptical of the pharmaceutical treatment of mental illnesses, largely believing that Freudian psychoanalysis and behavior modification were the most promising methods for treating persons with mental illnesses (Earley, 2006). According to Earley, the pharmaceutical company Smith Kline took over development of Thorazine and was pretty much stonewalled by the French and American psychiatric communities which were skeptical of the benefits of such a drug; in turn, Smith Kline sent their representatives to talk with state legislators. The con-

---

2. The U.S. Supreme Court in *Estelle v. Gamble* (1976) determined that deliberate indifference to an inmate's medical needs could constitute a violation of the 8th Amendment's prohibition against cruel and unusual punishment.

tention was that Thorazine would improve the conditions of persons with mental illnesses who were currently institutionalized so that they could be released into the community, thereby saving millions of tax dollars for state legislators. Thorazine was even touted as a cure for mental illness, and in its first eight months of use it was administered to more than two million individuals; in the next ten years, over 50 million patients worldwide were given the drug. Thanks to Thorazine, Smith Kline's revenues doubled three times in 15 years (Earley, 2006).

As noted by Earley (2006), in the end it was money that motivated the dispensing of the drug Thorazine on the market. It was not some great concern and compassion for the institutionalized. Just as humanitarian ideals did not bring about the shift in correctional policy allowing inmates to communicate with each other while working, as the Pennsylvania prison system was discarded and the Auburn system of confinement was embraced, the ability to produce more and make a profit was the catalyst (Welch, 2004). Likewise, it was money that could be saved by lawmakers and profits to be made that motivated changes in mental health policy and management; Thorazine did not turn out to be the wonder drug it was thought to be (Earley, 2006).

Negative Publicity

In 1943, in Ohio, newspaper headlines such as "Mental Patients Here Beaten and Shackled" and "Mental Patients Given Bad Food, Little Meat" were combined with a story of a mental patient dying and having his face eaten off by rats while in a makeshift morgue in the basement of a mental hospital. These events led to a grand jury investigation and ultimately a national reform movement of state hospitals; in 1946 the horrors of the state asylum system were exposed in the popular media by Life magazine in a twelve page article entitled "Bedlam 1946: Most U.S. Hospitals are a Shame and a Disgrace" (Torrey, 1997). The state of living conditions in mental hospitals was also made public by the publication of *Snake Pit* by Mary Jane Ward in 1946 and the subsequent movie by the same name starring Olivia de Havilland in 1948 (Ward, 1946).[3] The atrocities long hidden behind the walls were now out in the open for the public to see.

---

3. The title stems from an ancient practice of dealing with the mentally ill where they were thrown into a pit of snakes. The theory was that such a practice would make a normal person insane; therefore it must work in reverse. Of course, there is no evidence such a strategy works.

Anti-Psychiatry Movement

Traditionally, the anti-psychiatry movement which emerged in the 50s and 60s can be traced to efforts by psychiatrists and intellectuals both inside and outside of the U.S. till today where it is primarily dominated by former patients fighting against medications, forced hospitalizations, and authoritarian psychiatrists. Some of the activists aligned with this movement see psychiatry as a means of providing a crutch or scapegoat via invented diagnoses for people who want to avoid personal responsibility for their actions (Savodnik, 2006). According to Rissmiller and Rissmiller (2006), the anti-psychiatry movement and its founders, Michel Foucault (France), R.D. Laing (Great Britain), and Thomas Szasz (America), contributed immensely to the deinstitutionalization movement. Also helpful were judges such as David Bazelon, who detested dictatorial psychiatric practices and established in *Lake v. Cameron* (1966) that the least restrictive environment possible standard should guide all psychiatric treatment decisions, and attorneys like Bruce Ennis, who founded the "Mental Health Bar" aimed at ending involuntary commitments. Rissmiller and Rissmiller (2006) discuss Foucault, Laing, and Szasz below.

Michel Foucault—*Madness and Civilization: A History of Insanity in the Age of Reason*—emphasized that economic and cultural interests have always defined mental illness and that psychiatry had become a third order of repression in a jurisdiction disallowing appeals situated between law enforcement and the judiciary.

R.D. Laing—*The Divided Self: An Existential Study in Sanity and Madness*, which became a college bestseller in Great Britain and the United States—posited the idea that mental illness was due to social causes, with the implication that mental illness could be eradicated through social remedies.

Thomas Szasz, psychoanalyst—*"The Myth of Mental Illness"*—shortly after joining the faculty at the State University of New York, wrote the aforesaid article. Over the course of three years, six psychiatric journals rejected his manuscript; until it was ultimately published in the *American Psychologist* journal. The article led to a best-selling book by the same name. The thesis was that the state via psychiatric coercion was able to fulfill its need to silence nonconformists, the rabble, and dissidents. Szasz equated the collusion between psychiatry and the government with the Spanish Inquisition and referred to it as the most destructive force to impact American society in the last fifty years.

Counterculture icon Timothy Leary, prior to being terminated from Harvard, wrote to Szasz informing him that *The Myth of Mental Illness* was the most important book in the history of psychiatry and maybe even the most important work published in the twentieth century (Rissmiller & Rissmiller, 2006). This of course was long before the demise of Mr. Leary, the proponent of mind-altering drugs, and the blast off of his ashes via a Pegasus rocket into space (CNN, 1997).

Szasz, relying upon the principle of separation of church and state, maintained that the state and psychiatry should also be separated—otherwise the state for its own desires, like in Nazi Germany and the Soviet Union, would corrupt psychiatry to control the minds of recalcitrants. Science fiction writer and founder of scientology L. Ron Hubbard co-founded with Szasz the Citizens Commission on Human Rights which advocated for the prosecution and imprisonment of psychiatrists for crimes against humanity. In fact, Hubbard was so disdainful of psychiatry that he indicated, "'There is not one institutional psychiatrist alive who could not be arraigned and convicted of extortion, mayhem, and murder" (Rissmiller & Rissmiller, 2006, p. 864). His followers, including the actor Tom Cruise, remain dismissive of psychiatry. Cruise, on NBC's Today Show, stood by his previous criticism of actress Brooke Shields for seeking therapy and taking anti-depressants for postpartum depression, informing host Matt Lauer that there was no such thing as a chemical imbalance in the body and that vitamins and exercise would be an appropriate treatment for depression. Cruise went on to tell host Matt Lauer that neither Lauer nor Shields understands the history of psychiatry, but he does (Leiby, 2005). Of course, Cruise possesses no medical degree; in fact he doesn't have a college education, as the actor's education is listed as having attended seminary at age 14 for one year (Stritof & Stritof, 2007). Apparently, according to Lerma (2005), scientologists aren't big on formal education, as introduction to the scientific method and critical thinking skills can interfere with indoctrination into their system. In sizing up Cruise's medical opinion, "Since when would a celebrity have expertise in medicine? Would you go to your doctor and ask him about movie roles?" (Leiby, 2005). More recently CNN's Gary Tuchman (2007) has reported on a landing spot prepared by scientologists in the desert outside Las Vegas, New Mexico, to guide reincarnated scientologists to earth from outer space. Thus, it appears that many of those opposed to psychiatry have a fascination with science fiction and outer space.

Inadequate Community Support: Where are the CMHCs?

The Joint Commission on Mental Illness and Health, created in 1955, issued its final report in 1961 and provided the evidence and rationale for the passage of the Community Mental Health Act (Grob, 2000). As a result, tens of thousands of patients were released from mental hospitals to receive community care. Such care was premised on the assumption that minimal institutionalization was best for the individual, allowed patients to be (re)integrated into their communities, was cheaper, and placed accountability for the care of the mentally ill back in the hands of local authorities. In 1963, the Community Mental Health Centers (CMHCs) Construction Act was passed to provide CMHCs; however, these centers tended to focus on higher-functioning clientele and ignored the needs of the severely and persistently mentally ill that had been served by state hospitals. These centers were largely under-funded—with all federal monies received by CMHCs from 1963 to 1981 amounting to less than the estimated total disbursement in 1981 alone of all Supplemental Security Income and Social Security Disability Insurance payments to persons with mental illness (Cournos & Le Melle, 2000).

Two task forces of the American Psychiatric Association have determined that the concept of deinstitutionalization itself is not the problem; the conundrum has been the lack of implementation of all facets of the plan (Lamb & Bachrach, 2001). Gilligan (2001) has maintained that with the advent of deinstitutionalization money was actually appropriated for adequate community treatment programs; however, the money was never allocated because of a not in my back yard (NIMBY) mentality. As has often been seen with prison construction, community residents want prisoners and persons with mental illnesses out of sight and out of mind and are therefore resistant to facilities in their communities.

Plans for establishment of half-way houses, community residences, out patient clinics, in home psychiatric providers, and other alternatives to mental hospitals never materialized. Those that were either turned out of mental hospitals, or were never allowed to enter, were forced into the streets of America, where they were arrested and incarcerated, or died (Gilligan, 2001). Spitzer (1976) labeled the untreated as "social junk." Feeley and Simon (1992) reported that the untreated and the untreatable have been described as "toxic waste" reflective of social control policies of the 1970s–90s that emphasized massive warehousing and human storage.

Lack of Access to Long-Term Care

As early as 1939, Penrose found that as prison populations increase mental hospital populations decrease and vice versa (Lamb & Weinberger, 1998). While there is debate about whether deinstitutionalization has caused the criminalization of persons with mental illnesses (Fisher, 2003; Hogan, 2000), there is some evidence that deinstitutionalization has indeed contributed to the criminalization of persons with mental illnesses (Lamb et al., 2004; Lamb & Weinberger, 1998). Moreover, Raphael (2000) maintains that a strong inverse, causal relationship exists between deinstitutionalization and incarceration rates, as state hospitals are downsized or closed, more and more individuals with mental illnesses are drifting into the streets and encountering the criminal justice system—a system that is often ill-quipped to deal with their needs (Butterfield, 1998; Kerle, 1998). This phenomenon is captured in the editorial cartoon by Englehart (2000) on the following page.

Michael Hogan (2000), the Chairman of the President's New Freedom Commission on Mental Health, has cautioned that the belief that deinstitutionalization has caused the criminalization of persons with mental illnesses may wrongly imply that somehow reinstitutionalization is the answer. Lamb and Bachrach (2001) believe that most persons with mental illnesses, including those who are homeless or inappropriately incarcerated, with the provision and implementation of adequate community resources, can realize their potential and function within society. However, Hogan (1995) and Lamb (1992) acknowledge that the closure of state hospitals should be predicated on the provision of appropriate inpatient facilities for that small percentage of forensic and acute patients who may need more extensive hospital care.

Indeed, the important function of state hospitals remains, as there is a need for intermediate and long-term twenty four hour structured care for that minority of chronically ill patients that require such services (Fisher et al., 2001; Lamb & Shaner, 1993), and Emery (2006) argues that access to twenty-four hour-acute psychiatric care is a necessity in communities with the possibility of median stays of thirty or less days. Likewise, Lamb and Weinberger (2005) maintain that there is a requirement for the expansion of twenty-four-hour hospitalization even in lock up facilities for some, a need that few in the mental health system discuss or advocate.

Both deinstitutionalization and reduced hospital stays have been identified as factors increasing the number of persons with mental illnesses who encounter the criminal justice system (Greenberg, Shah, & Seide, 1993). Trudel and Lesage (2006), in a Canadian study, even suggested that long-term residential services should be available to community inhabitants ranging from ten to 40

beds per 100,000 in the population, contingent upon whether an area is metropolitan and/or socially deprived.

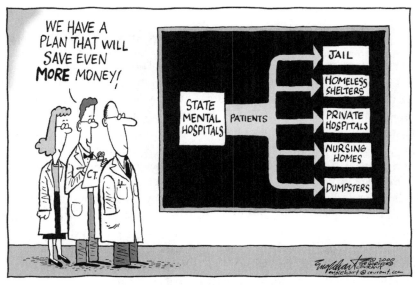

© Bob Englehart, Hartford (CT) Courant

Difficulty Accessing Mental Health Treatment and Cost Shifting

Further evidence of money driving public policy is seen with congressional
passage of various laws that allow eligibility for persons with mental illnesses
in federal assistance programs such as housing, Medicaid, Medicare, disability insurance, supplemental income, and food stamps (Earley, 2006; Goldman, Adams, & Taube, 1983; Torrey, 1997). With the initiation of these federal
programs, state legislators, in the face of mounting class-action litigation and
increasing public scrutiny of horrific conditions in state hospitals, seized upon
this as an opportunity to unload the costs of caring for persons with mental
illnesses from the states to the federal government (Earley, 2006; Goldman et
al., 1983). Cournos and Le Melle (2000) note one means of doing this was by
treating persons with mental illnesses in homes for the aged and dependent
instead of state hospitals, as states used federal matching money for nursing homes,
and the percentage of institutionalized persons in mental hospitals from 1950

to 1980 shifted from 40 percent to 10 percent while the percentage of institutionalized persons in nursing homes increased from 20 to more than 50 percent.

Managed Care and Medicaid Reform

The bottom line for managed care is to produce profits, and the question becomes to what extent will agencies go to save money by cutting services. Managed care typically refers to a health care delivery system that includes means for monitoring and authorizing use of services, with traditional fee for service schemas being erased and replaced with negotiated, capitated payment plans for all enrollees (Mowbray, Grazier, & Holter, 2002). According to Sodaro and Ball (1999), psychiatric managed care corporations can and do deny needed care to ensure huge profits. They also report that universal single payer systems like Canada or multi-payer systems as seen in Germany (by law non-profit) have an overhead of approximately five percent, while managed care agencies in the United States have an overhead commonly in the range of fifty percent.[4] In other words, 95 cents on the dollar goes to patient care in Canada and Germany, with only about 50 cents on the dollar going there in the United States. Sodaro and Ball (1999) also cite specific incidences of managed care cost cutting. For example, they report that a large insurer in Rhode Island was fined for paying incentives to the company's psychiatrist to deny treatment coverage for mental illness and maximize profits; in Iowa, each denial of hospital admission for inpatient psychiatric care was awarded with an $880.00 commission to the responsible party who ensured the denial of the coverage. As of 2002, two-thirds of the states in the U.S. have implemented some type of managed care program to oversee Medicaid benefits for persons seeking mental health services (Kaye, 2005).

Today, Medicaid is the main provider of funding for persons with severe and persistent mental illness in the U.S., with Medicaid covering 50 percent of all public mental health allocations; it is expected Medicaid's dominance of funding in this area will increase to 60 percent of all public mental health spending by 2010 (NAMI, 2005).[5] Via the Deficit Reduction Act of 2006, the

---

4. Brink, S. (1998, January 19). I'll say I'm suicidal: The mentally ill struggle through the maze of managed care. *U.S. News Online*, Retrieved from the World Wide Web on May 16, 2007: http://www.redandgreen.org/Medical/Suicidal/19mana.htm actually reports on a managed mental health care company where 67 percent of the money went to profits and overhead, a fact that employers are often not aware of.

5. The National Alliance on Mental Illness' stance on managed care can be accessed via the internet, see: Managed care: A national overview. Policy Topics. The National Alliance

president signed into law a mechanism that would allow Medicaid to become more like privately managed plans, providing an estimated savings of 6.9 billion dollars to the federal government and a shifting of costs to the states, with potentially horrendous consequences in terms of access to mental health services for the most vulnerable (Koyanagi, 2006). This push to the privatization of mental health services emerged and continues even in light of the fact that state and federal oversight of such programs becomes more problematic under private control (Bloom, Williams, Land, McFarland, & Reichlin, 1998).

Kane (1995) cautions that the false promises of deinstitutionalization—a system with efficient provision of prevention services, coupled with early intervention and continuity of care—sound very much like the alleged offerings of managed care and health maintenance organizations (HMOs). In a comparison of the pitfalls of deinstitutionalization with managed care Mowbray et al. (2002) conclude that managed behavioral health care should be closely monitored and, with its profit motive, may actually result in limited choice for consumers, can result in decreased access to care, deficiencies in quality, appropriateness, and outcomes of care, and may not be the right model for persons with mental illnesses depending on their employment status. It is also argued that, structurally, managed care parallels the restrictions placed on civil commitment laws during the 1970s, as managed care initiatives of pre-certification and concurrent review mirror the restricted admission procedures and limited involuntary commitment stays with the same results (SAMHSA, 1996). With more restrictive commitment laws it is expected that the police will utilize the criminal code more often on less serious offenses with persons with mental illnesses to remove them from the community (Bonovitz & Bonovitz, 1981). In essence, the very processes that seemingly were enacted to protect the rights of persons with mental illnesses—restrictive civil commitment statutes—are today actually resulting in greater deprivation of liberties in the criminal justice system, as there is evidence of the migration of clients from the mental health system to the criminal justice system. Also, managed care, with its cost-saving measures may cut corners, denying services, resulting in cost shifting instead of cost saving.

Thus, there is the strong possibility that upon the implementation of managed care into the Medicaid arena there is likely to be an increase in Medicaid recipients being ushered into the criminal justice system; therefore, it is imperative that measures be put in place to evaluate whether savings in one area merely

on Mental Illness. Arlington, Virginia. Retrieved from the World Wide Web on May 22, 2007: http://www.nami.org/Template.cfm?Section=Issue_Spotlights&template=/Content-Management/ContentDisplay.cfm&ContentID=34786.

results in costs being shifted to another area (SAMHSA, 1996). As noted in NAMI's (2006) Grading the States report, in which no state received an A and the average grade for state public adult mental health care systems was a D, "the long-run costs of Medicaid 'reforms' often run higher than short-term savings. Costs are only shifted elsewhere. Cuts shift costs to hospital emergency departments[6].... Inadequate treatment leads to relapses. Relapses lead to hospitalizations. Medicaid 'reforms' come with a price. Inadequate treatment can also lead to jail or prison" (p. 9).

According to Cordner (2006), the introduction of private for profit corporations into the mental health arena can simply be driven by greed, as to cut costs minimal staff are provided and wages are low, resulting in the police being engaged in the management of community facilities. The profit motive of managed care taking priority over societal and treatment interests can result in decisions by providers with horrific consequences. This will be discussed in Chapter 7 on civil commitment regarding the matter of Andrew Goldstein. Other problems caused from decisions made by treatment providers will be addressed in Chapter 5 on mental health courts via information provided by Miami Public Defender Howard Finkelstein and in congressional testimony contained in Chapter 12.

Difficulty Accessing Treatment upon Community Re-entry from Incarceration

The ability to access Medicaid benefits and to have a seamless flow from custody to free society to ensure continuity of care and access to psychotropic medications for persons with mental illnesses upon return to the community is essential to the prevention of persons with mental illnesses from continuing to recycle through the criminal justice system and being labeled as recidivists or "frequent fliers" as criminal justice practitioners often refer to them. In most areas throughout the United States, persons who have been detained in jails lose access to their Medicaid benefits upon re-entry into the community; this does not have to be the case, as federal law does not dictate that Medicaid benefits

---

6. After implementation of managed care, Claassen, C.A., Kashner, T.M., Gilfillan, S.K., Larkin, G.L., & Rush, A.J. (2005), Psychiatric emergency service use after implementation of managed care in a public mental health system, *Psychiatric Services*, 56(6), p. 691–698, found police-accompanied visits with persons with mental illness to a psychiatric emergency department to increase from 32 percent to 56 percent of all visits.

cease upon being confined in jail or that the cessation of benefits needs to transpire at all (GAINS/SAMHSA, 2002). While states may have policies in place for disenrolling persons' Medicaid benefits upon being incarcerated in jails, in an analysis of two urban jail systems, researchers found that the longer persons were detained in jail (90 to 150 days compared to half a month to a month) the more likely they were to have had their Medicaid benefits terminated while locked up and not to have access to those benefits upon return to the community (Morrissey et al., 2006a). Indeed, researchers examining the two metropolitan jail systems referred to above have found that the assurance of Medicaid enrollment at the time of release from jail enhances access to and actual obtainment of mental health services after release from custody (Morrissey et al., 2006b). Further barriers to treatment and solutions for persons with mental illnesses returning to the community from the criminal justice system will be discussed in Chapter 6.[7]

Preferred Drug Lists/Restricted Formularies

Cost shifting can be seen today as states seek to reform Medicaid[8] and implement preferred drug lists/restricted formularies, which can ultimately result in financial burdens being shifted from states to counties. Preferred drug

---

7. Also, brochures are available that provide guidance on how to ensure that benefits are restored upon return from incarceration to the community (Bazelon Center for Mental Health Law. (2001, March). Finding the key to successful transition from jail to community: An explanation of Federal Medicaid and disability program rules. Washington, DC.; Koyanagi, C. (2004, March). Arrested? What happens to your benefits if you go to jail or prison?: A guide to the federal rules on SSI, SSDI, Medicaid, Medicare and veterans benefits for adults with disabilities. Bazelon Center for Mental Health Law: Washington, DC.; *Social Security Administration.* (2003, October).*What prisoners should know about Social Security. Social Security Online: Electronic fact sheet. SSA Publication No. 05-10133, Washington, DC.* Retrieved from the World Wide Web on May 22, 2007: http://www.ssa.gov/pubs/10133.html.

8. Medicaid is a program of health coverage administered by the states in partnership with the federal government whereby federal matching funds can be provided to states for specific persons with extremely high medical expenses or low incomes and depends on age, disability, or family status and on an individual's or family's ability to pay-based on income and available resources, with benefits directly payable to providers not consumers — GAINS/SAMHSA, 2002; Medicare Advocacy, (2006), What's the difference between Medicare and Medicaid? Retrieved from the World Wide Web on February 10, 2006: http://www.medicareadvocacy.org/Medicaid_Diff.Vs.Medicare.htm.

lists have been imposed by state legislatures as a cost saving measure, whereby Medicaid recipients have restricted access to medications. These restrictive limitations require individuals to obtain generic drugs in lieu of brand-name medications; if no generic drugs for a particular condition are in existence, the least expensive brand-name medication will be made available as an alternative; states, in situations where two or more brand-name alternative drugs that are comparable in expense exist, may still be able to save money by negotiating a quantity discount for a single drug with a pharmaceutical company with projected savings into the millions of dollars (Gudrais, 2006). Unfortunately, unlike many prescribed drugs, psychotropic medications are not readily replaced with reliable, effective substitutes, and there is an extreme danger that without appropriate treatment individuals will decompensate and relapse with horrific consequences (Levine, 2006).[9]

The problem with the projected short-term savings such schemes offer is that the Therapeutic Jurisprudence ideal, discussed in Chapter 1, of looking to the long-range future ramifications of such decisions is not considered. While a few dollars will be saved in the short term, what are the long-term consequences of the implementation of such policies? While appeal processes are often in place for physicians to request that their patients be maintained on medications that have proven to be effective in the past, appeals are often denied, and, instead, fail first policies implemented—meaning that a patient will have to fail first on the cheaper medication before possibly being returned to the medication that has worked previously (Adams, 2006).[i] The effects of failure can be irreversible and result in permanent damage, even death, for persons with mental illnesses as well as having potentially harmful ramifications for the citizenry.

i. Here is an example of a letter demonstrating just how frustrating the bureaucratic appeals process can be as evinced in this correspondence by Stephen Bacallao, designated representative for Peggy Symons, a woman with schizophrenia, who has served as a CIT trainer for law enforcement officers (S. Bacallao, personal communication, October 3, 2007). Note, how impersonal the process is and how unaccountable the matter is as the letter is not even sent to a person. The name of private provider has been removed from the letter, as no response was obtained from the provider. This matter was ultimately referred to U.S. Senator Bill Nelson's office, and, only after inquiries from his office, did the private corporate provider agree to allow coverage for this dosage of medication for one year. Shortly thereafter the provider contacted Ms. Symons offering to switch her to a small co-pay for future provision of medication. Ms. Symons agreed, but the provider never sent a representative to

9. See the reference to Keith Howard from reporter Stephen Hudak in the concluding chapter of this book.

sign her up. This provider has since ended its relationship with Medicare in Florida, and Ms. Symons has been automatically transferred to another provider with no problems so far (S. Bacallao, personal communication, April 24, 2008). How many others without such resilience, contracts and networking ability would have succumbed to the corporate beast and given up?

October 3, 2007
Medicare Region 4
61 Forsythe St. S.W.
Suite 4T20
Atlanta, Ga. 30303
RE: Peggy Symons
Dear Region 4 Medicare Office,

I am an advocate for people with psychiatric disabilities. My wife and I are past co-presidents of The National Alliance on Mental Illness of Greater Orlando. In addition, I am also serving as the Chair of the Area 7 Florida Medicaid Behavioral Health Managed Care Advisory Group.

Peggy Symons has authorized me to act as her representative.

Peggy was auto enrolled by the State of Florida as a duel eligible in _____ Medicare Part D Prescription Plan.

Since the very beginning _____ has been denying her prescription for Seroquel, 100 milligram tablets, the only antipsychotic medicine at the only dosing schedule that has ever worked for her. In addition, from the very first day coverage began _____ even refused to authorize a 30 day supply as required by law.

In 20 months of coverage by _____ Part D, Peggy's prescription has been denied more often than honored.

In 1998, after months of balancing multiple medicines at multiple doses, her psychiatrist of 25 years, Dr.Walter J. Muller finally found the medicines that have saved her life and kept her out of hospitals.

Florida Medicaid Medically Needy Catastrophic Costs coverage never dishonored, denied or overrode Dr. Muller's clinical judgment or long term experience with Peggy's illness.

Throughout 20 months of denials, the Group for Psychiatry and Peggy have filed numerous expedited appeals, multiple Prior Authorizations, severe adverse reaction reports, plea after desperate plea for her life and her medicine.

The following information has been provided to _____'s Clinical Pharmacy Review Committee and Grievance and Appeals Department in nearly every one of these appeals and contacts.

Peggy Symons:

1) Has been stabilized on this medicine at this dose since 1998.
2) Prior to this medication regime she was hospitalized 16 times.
3) She has failed on over 30 medicines and alternative doses.
4) She failed to improve even after a series of shock treatments.
5) She survived several serious suicide attempts even with a gun and slashed wrists.
6) She lives with a chronic disease of the brain that requires daily doses of her medication taken on time.

For months _____ has received urgent warnings and red flags warning that the denial of this critically necessary medicine has created a huge risk of relapse, re hospitalization and suicide. These warnings came from the Group for Psychiatry, Medicare, and from Peggy. For 20 months _____ has turned deaf ears and blind eyes to these desperate pleas for life and justifiably prescribed medication.

On August 14, 2007, in a call referenced telephone communication, _____ denied that Medicare had sent red flags and warnings on August 7, 2007 that Peggy was out of medication and that there were life threatening consequences. _____ stated that prior to receiving a "life threatening" message from Medicare on August 14, 2007 (second complaint filed) "they never knew there was an issue of suicide relevant to their denials" of Peggy's medication.

On August 15, 2007, Peggy's illness blew up in her face; she began to hear voices, started to engage in behaviors to out run the devil, and made suicide threats. This was a previously stable psychotic illness. The Group for Psychiatry saw her in an emergency appointment, gave her more sample medicine and had to make the decision of whether or not to re-hospitalize her. The denials continued.

On September 24, 2007 Peggy brought a new prescription to the pharmacy, once again she was turned away by _____ without her medicine. The Group for Psychiatry finally threw up their hands and told Peggy that after 20 months and hours of fruitless paperwork, appeals and Prior Authorizations that, there was nothing more they could do to help her access her prescription. This was treatment time being taken from Peggy and other patients.

Over the years that I have been an advocate for the mentally ill, I have trained police officers, taught advocacy to college students and guided many families through severe mental illnesses. I have never seen an appropriately prescribed antipsychotic medicine denial go this far.

Although Peggy speaks and writes with a fair fluency she cannot follow even the most basic sequence of directions or instructions. Peggy Symons doesn't know the difference between left and right. This is the very nature of psychiatric disabilities.

A review of _____'s denials and appeals processes reveals that they are so complicated and time consuming even a PhD would have endless trouble complying with all the terms and conditions.

A 20 month and very well documented paper trail shows that Peggy has put up a good fight, but as of the last denial of her prescription on October 2, 2007 it is very clear that she is completely and totally unable to navigate this company's procedures for her prescription, (we have copies of all denials, appeals, certified letters, Prior Authorizations; call reference numbers, appeal file numbers, detailed records from the Group for Psychiatry, pharmacy denial printouts, records of sample medications, we have names, dates, call center locations etc.).

In addition to these unjust and dangerous denials of a life sustaining medicine _____ has:

1) Refused to comply with three requests sent by certified mail to provide a history of "complaints, grievances and appeals filed against _____ by other members in the past". _____ is required by law to provide this information on request.

2) Failed to respond to expedited appeals within the 24 to 72 hour required time frame.

3) _____ refused three requests sent by certified mail to provide information in numbered appeal files that contain the clinical criteria and rationale that were relied on to deny appeals for Peggy's medicine. By law _____ must comply with this request.

Peggy continues to live with significant deficits caused by a lifelong battle with Schizophrenia and bipolar disorder but with the constant support of the Group for Psychiatry and the love of her family she has tried very hard to build up a life of meaning and purpose.

This company has had 20 months to make choices between honoring a profound responsibility to their weakest and sickest customers or to dishonor it in pursuit of profit and profit alone. _____ has withheld an expensive antipsychotic medicine to their cost advantage, leaving a customer who has no ability to fight back as good as dead. At the very least, _____ Medicare Part D Prescription Plan would have left Medicare holding the bag for numerous hospitalizations at $1,300 a day. Without the intensive assistance of the Group for Psychiatry, her family and sample medication Peggy would have died.

Peggy and her family survived 25 years of a daily fight with severe mental illness and potential suicide. Every single denial issued to her by _____ Medicare Part D Prescription Plan has been a potential death sentence. For the corporate equivalent of a pocketful of change a very fragile individual is being forced to return to a chronic and severe mental illness, hospitals and a daily battle against suicide.

If this is happening to Peggy it is also happening to other Medicare Part D customers with schizophrenia and bipolar disorder (Peggy has both). No doubt, like Peggy, they are being turned away from pharmacies without appropriately prescribed and critically necessary antipsychotic medicines. With no medicine and no hope of help, some maybe falling ill or dying with the first denials.

These are invisible Medicare Part D customers who have the very least ability to stand up. They are being taken advantage of by a globally wealthy corporation. They are losing their lives behind a corporate curtain of privacy laws and no accountability. These abuses will remain hidden and entrenched unless they are shaken out, investigated and made visible.

Hopefully, Medicare will act to protect these powerless and profoundly ill people with specific laws and regulations that will allow them access to their medications without having to navigate impossible "cost containment" strategies that are potentially costing lives.

In addition, a close look reveals that there may be even wider civil rights issues involving discrimination against people with severe mental illnesses.

A review of Peggy Symons pharmacy records show that in 20 months of _____ coverage, prescriptions have been filled for 11 medical conditions as well as for an anticonvulsant drug. None of them were in any way restricted or denied. The only medicine _____ Medicare Part D Prescription Plan has consistently refused to cover is her prescription for Seroquel, at the 100mg per dosing level prescribed by her doctor, a modern antipsychotic medicine used to treat her schizophrenia and bipolar disorder.

In closing, I appreciate any assistance you can provide me in resolving this on-going and despicable situation. Peggy Symons has turned to me as her last hope of accessing her medicine. Please respond to this request, in writing, in as timely a manner as possible.

Sincerely,
Stephen Bacallao,
CC: Peggy Symons

As previously indicated in Chapter 1, crises often drive policies within the criminal justice system (Walker, 2006), but, sometimes policies can drive crises. The imposition of preferred drug lists can be costly in terms of human suffering for persons on psychotropic medication and for the community. In testimony before the Florida Senate Committee on Health Care, Slate (2005) informed lawmakers that implementation of such policies would lead to crises. Unfortunately, such failures on improvised medications instituted by such a policy can be traumatic with horrific, potentially tragic, consequences. As noted by Stone (1997), there is a causal relationship between the manifestation of serious, persistent mental illness and restrictive insurance regulations. In other words, more adequate insurance coverage for persons with mental illnesses would result in more of these individuals receiving adequate treatment and medication and fewer of them being transported to jail for aberrant behavior upon becoming symptomatic when their access to medication and/or treatment is restricted or prohibited financially. Such restrictions, for example as those imposed by Medicaid, can serve as another means for states to shift costs, albeit to counties, particularly when those denied access to benefits wind up in jail. Is it any wonder that Linda Teplin, professor of psychiatry at Northwestern University lamented that "Jails have become the poor person's mental hospitals" (Butterfield, 1999, p. A10,).

The Haves and the Have Nots

As suggested by Gilligan (2001), economics permeates the punitiveness of our society (see Messner & Rosenfeld, 2007). Specifically, Gilligan (2001) contends that the most influential factor in determining the homicide rate throughout the world and the degree of punitiveness directed toward those labeled as criminals is the magnitude of the chasm between the rich and the poor in a society. Additionally, Gilligan notes that increased punitiveness is the most powerful known cause of violent crime (which can in a somewhat circuitous relationship serve to lead to increased punitiveness), and neglect of persons with mental illnesses also leads to punitiveness and criminalization, which can be overwhelming for those who are impoverished and lack resources. Miller (1992) maintains that patients in need of mental health services are often shifted to inappropriate sites for treatment, including the criminal justice system, solely for economic reasons. From 1980 to 1992, there was a 154 percent increase in the reported number of persons with mental illnesses in jails (Watson, Hanrahan, Luchins, & Lurigio, 2001). From 1992 to 2003, according to the Centers for Disease Control, a 56 percent increase (from 2,381,000 to 3,718,000) in the number of persons with a primary diagnosis of mental illness visited emergency departments across the country; these emergency rooms, in the absence of acute care facilities, were often overcrowded, shorthanded, under funded, and lacking connections for referral to more adequate services, resulted in more persons with mental illness becoming enmeshed with the criminal justice system (Emery, 2006). Likewise, Coleman (1997) reports that one study found that two-thirds of U.S. hospitals dump patients with mental illnesses who are unable to pay.[10]

Markowitz (2006) found a predominance of private psychiatric hospital beds in cities to be significantly associated with increases in both arrest and crime rates, suggesting that when the mental health system is privatized police have fewer referral options to mental health treatment and are more likely to make an arrest. The resulting criminalization of persons with mental illnesses is a concern worthy of consideration as more and more states have moved to managed mental health care plans with stringent restrictions on expenditures for inpatient care. Thus, private psychiatric hospitals and care providers have been able to dodge treating indigent persons with mental illnesses, and some psy-

---

10. Anderson Cooper opened his *60 Minutes* segment entitled Dumped on Skid Row on May 17, 2007 by saying, "The first rule in medicine is do no harm." He then commences to show a homeless woman on videotape being dropped off at Los Angeles' Skid Row upon release from the hospital. In another instance, a paraplegic man is dropped off on the street, without a wheelchair, via a van from Hollywood Presbyterian Hospital four blocks from the Midnight Mission on Skid Row. When Cooper asked one of the Skid Row regulars about the dumping, the man replied, "It's nothing new.... It just got noticed because they [sic] been bringing 'em [sic] down in their hospital gowns." Chief of Hollywood Presbyterian Kaylor "Shemberger points out that hospital care for the homeless is only a part of a much larger problem. In Los Angeles County, about 88,000 people don't have a roof over their heads on any given day. He says there simply aren't enough shelters and clinics to care for them. 'When these people are discharged from a medical facility, they need a place to go, and we need a place to take them to that can accommodate their needs. Those resources are, you know, just lacking in this community,' Shemberger says. Asked if he thinks the hospitals are just an easy target, Shemberger says, 'I think we're being unfairly pursued in these particular cases. After all, you know, we're here to take care of their medical needs, not their housing needs.'" Retrieved from the World Wide Web on June 6, 2007: http://www.cbsnews.com/stories/2007/05/17/60minutes/main2823079.shtml.

chiatrists have faced the possibility of being terminated or potentially facing malpractice suits due to inadequate treatment because of managed behavioral health care penalties aimed at them for excessive referrals (Miller, 1997).

Homelessness

Decreased public hospital capacity for persons with mental illnesses has been found to be associated with increased homelessness, while increased homelessness has been determined to be directly related to higher crime rates and arrests for violent crime (Markowitz, 2006). Thus, according to McGuire and Rosenheck (2004), lack of housing becomes an integral avenue for pushing one's actions into the crime category when long-term psychiatric inpatient care is not available. With treatment beds non-existent and friends and family as caretakers unavailable, the aberrant behavior of homeless persons with mental illnesses is pushed into the streets where it is more likely to come to the attention of the authorities and result in criminal justice sanctions.

In the first national census of the homeless in a decade, it is estimated that there are 744,000 homeless people in America (A Snapshot of Homelessness, 2007). Furthermore, it is believed that one-third to one-half of homeless persons in the U.S. have a severe mental illness (McQuistion, Finnerty, Hirschowitz, & Susser, 2003).

While veterans constitute approximately one-third of the adult male population in the United States, they are overrepresented in the homeless population, with roughly forty percent of homeless males being veterans (Homeless Veterans, 2008). It is estimated that at some time in 2006, 336,000 U.S. veterans were homeless, with 1,500 of these homeless veterans having emerged from the conflicts in Iraq and Afghanistan (McClam, 2008). Among the causes associated with this recent cadre of homeless veterans are mental illness (which often manifests itself in the form of post traumatic stress disorder [PTSD], repetitive and extended tours of duty in hazardous areas, and the heightened dimension of the use of improvised explosive devices making everywhere a potential combat zone (McClam, 2008). While the plight of many veterans is dismal, the adjustment for enlisted troops returning from Iraq is less than story book as well, as the stigma of mental health treatment in the military precludes many troops from seeking treatment. In a recent Department of Defense study, approximately seventeen percent of troops responding admitted symptoms of mental illness, such as PTSD, yet sixty percent of these respondents would be reluctant to reveal such symptoms to superiors or peers because they believed that they would be treated differently (Welch, 2008).

The treatment received by enlistees who exhibit signs and symptoms of mental illnesses won't make it into military recruiting brochures or be boasted about at recruiting depots. For example, Lt. Elizabeth Whiteside, a 25-year-old University of Virginia graduate and Army reservist, purportedly during a psychotic break, tried to kill herself while serving in Iraq, pointed her weapon at a superior and fired two shots into a ceiling; her commander indicated that mental illness was merely being used as an excuse for her actions, recommending court martial. Court martial and a dishonorable discharge could prevent Lt. Whiteside from having medical benefits provided by the Army to treat her severe depression, which culminated after seven years of impeccable service in her breakdown after constant harassment by a superior in an Iraqi prison and being overcome by efforts to quell disturbances at that prison following the execution of Saddam Hussein. An Army hearing officer ultimately recommended that the charges against Whiteside should be dismissed; however, she languished as higher ups went for weeks without approving the hearing officer's recommendation of dismissal, which resulted in a second suicide attempt by Lt. Whiteside in the confines of her room at Walter Reed Army Medical Center on January 28, 2008 (Priest, 2008).

> Suicides among active-duty soldiers in 2007 reached their highest level since the Army began keeping such records in 1980…. Last year, 121 soldiers took their own lives, nearly 20 percent more than in 2006. At the same time, the number of attempted suicides or self-inflicted injuries in the Army has jumped sixfold since the Iraq war began … from approximately 350 soldiers in 2002 to around 2100 soldiers last year… From a suicide rate of 9.8 per 100,000 active-duty soldiers in 2001…, the Army reached an all-time high of 17.5 suicides per 100,000 active-duty soldiers in 2006 (Priest, 2008, A01).

The aforesaid figures do not reflect suicides involving veterans, and the Department of Veteran Affairs (VA) has been accused of covering up those numbers. In fact, an e-mail from December 2007, uncovered from Dr. Ira Katz, who is in charge of mental health at the VA, reveals that " 'there are 18 suicides per day' among all vets and '4-5 suicides per day' among those being treated by the VA" (Malbran, 2008).

While the condition of being homeless has been linked to crime—making the aberrant actions of homeless persons more visible to law enforcement officers in the streets—some caution that it might not be so much that mental illness leads to homelessness, but that an extraneous variable such as poverty may exacerbate problems associated with both mental illness and homelessness (Draine, Salzer, Culhane, & Hadley, 2002). As noted by Piers Anthony (An Interview with Piers Anthony, 2004), the rich are considered eccentric, while the poor are viewed as crazy. One's lot in life and potential caregivers may very well determine what options, if any, are available when crises emerge.

America has demonstrated a strong desire to banish from its midst the social rabble, the undesirables and problematic persons with mental illnesses (Austin & Irwin, 2001; Rothman, 1971). Such exclusion can come in the form of geographic displacement, institutionalization in asylums, and incarceration within the criminal justice system; said banishment can even be cloaked in humanitarian terms. Those banished traditionally to total institutions were treated in hospitals and are now housed in prisons (Gilligan, 2001). In fact, clinicians familiar with the characteristics of hospitalized patients with mental illnesses prior to deinstitutionalization have acknowledged the similarity in make-up with those persons with mental illnesses who are now incarcerated (Lamb & Weinberger, 1998).

Daytona Beach, Florida, a beachside city, renowned for its tourism, expansive beaches, enticing year-round climate, and the Daytona 500 NASCAR race, has also attracted a homeless population. Daytona Beach Police Chief Michael Chitwood wants to help the homeless out via a little cost-shifting banishment measure of his own, by offering each homeless person a one-way Greyhound bus ticket to anywhere but Daytona. He alleges that this would give them an opportunity to reconnect with family and friends. However, experts contend that these are ties that have likely been severed long ago and are no longer existent (Ma, 2006; Editorial, 2006). The editors of the *Orlando Sentinel* newspaper chide Chief Chitwood for his quick-fix mentality, suggesting that he should step up and take a leadership role in an informed collaborative community process as opposed to promoting a Wizard of Oz solution—ruby red slippers would work as well as bus tickets (Editorial, 2006). Steve Feinstein (personal communication, January 1, 2007) maintains similar practices of "Greyhound therapy" have been tried with state hospital providers in the past, with little success, by busing people out of catchment areas with a few dollars for food so that services would be obtained on someone else's dime.[11]

---

11. Greyhound therapy was employed with Russell Weston who was hospitalized in Montana after making a threat against then President Clinton; upon release, Weston was provided with a one way ticket to Illinois whereby he decompensated and ultimately ended up in a hallway of the nation's Capitol shooting and killing two law enforcement officers before being detained (Butterfield, F. (1998, July 28). Treatment can be illusion for violent mentally ill. *The New York Times*. Retrieved from the World Wide Web on June 16, 2007:

Other Florida law enforcement agencies have been covered in recent press accounts for encounters with the homeless as well. An incident in St. Petersburg, Florida is another example of crisis driving policy. St. Petersburg police received negative press attention about the slashing of tents by their police officers caught on videotape during a raid at a homeless camp (Raghunathan, 2007) that led to the unveiling of a strategy for alleviating immediate needs of the homeless and plans for a shelter (Sharockman, 2007).[12]

Stigma

According to the Surgeon General's report (1999), stigma is "the most formidable obstacle to future progress in the arena of mental illness and health" (Chapter 1). The word stigma has roots in Middle English (stigme—meaning brand), Latin (stigma, stigmat—tattoo indicating slave or criminal status), and Greek (tattoo mark, from stizein, stig—to prick). Its archaic meaning is a mark burned into the skin of a criminal or slave; a brand. Today "stigma" refers to a mark or token of infamy, disgrace, or reproach, with a synonym being stain. In medicine, stigma is considered a mark or characteristic indicative of a history of disease or abnormality.[13] Other synonyms of stigma include: a mark of discredit or disgrace, black eye, blemish, blot, onus, shame, spot, stain, taint, tarnish, and archaic—attaint.[14] Antonyms of stigma include: credit, honor, and pride.[15]

http://query.nytimes.com/gst/fullpage.html?res=950CEFDA1638F93BA15754C0A96E958260&sec=health&spon=&pagewanted=print Editorial. (1998, August 3). From tragedy, new hope. *Los Angeles Times*. Retrieved from the World Wide Web on June 16, 2007: http://www.desertpacific.mirecc.va.gov/news/lps-reform/LATimes-8-3-98.html.

12. In another police encounter with a homeless individual, a Bradenton, Florida police officer, Nicolas Evans, was heralded by advocates for the homeless for pulling a shopping cart containing a homeless woman's belongings alongside his police car as he made his way to jail to book her for violating a court order; however, a second encounter the following night, with the same shopping cart transportation service provided, resulted in a recommendation by Evans' supervisor that he be terminated, instead, the police chief imposed a thirty-day suspension. Anderson, J. (2007, February 5). Bradenton officer punished for insubordination. *Bay News 9*. Retrieved from the World Wide Web on May 5, 2008: http://www.baynews9.com/content/36/2007/2/1/220206.html.

13. The American Heritage Dictionary (2007) Retrieved from the World Wide Web on May 26, 2007 from: http://www.answers.com/topic/stigma.

14. Houghton Mifflin and Company (2007) Retrieved from the World Wide Web on May 26, 2007 from: http://www.answers.com/topic/stigma.

15. Answers.com (2007) Retrieved from the World Wide Web on May 26, 2007 from: http://www.answers.com/topic/stigma.

Erving Goffman (1968) describes those who are stigmatized as being unable to gain full social acceptance because they are not able to adhere to standards that society has deemed as normal. As such, those unable to conform are cast off as outsiders (Becker, 1963).

Historically, we have tried to differentiate criminals from law-abiding citizens by physical characteristics. With the failure of those experiments, the second most common way that we have attempted to distinguish criminals from law-abiding citizens has been by mental deficiency. How placating for upstanding members of society to self-righteously pat themselves on the back and to believe that they are somehow superior to those miscreants who have been institutionalized. Of course, if we can't separate criminals by physical and/or mental characteristics, maybe we can put a mark on them. So historically, in an effort to set criminals apart and to shame them, we have indeed stigmatized them by branding them (e.g. a "T" branded to the forehead of a thief) or, after locking one's head and hands in the pillory, nailing the criminal's ears to the pillory so that the earlobes would have to be ripped at the cessation of the publicly displayed punishment leaving a permanent mark that upstanding citizens would readily recognize as that of a criminal (see Welch, 2004).

The ultimate status degradation ceremony is the application of the criminal process to individuals, commencing with arrest (Vold, Bernard, & Snipes, 1998); we know that researchers estimate that roughly fifty percent of persons with mental illnesses have been arrested at least once (Frankle et al., 2001; Solomon & Draine, 1995a; Walsh & Bricourt, 1997), with most of these individuals having been arrested more than once (Borum, Swanson, Swartz, & Hiday, 1997). For persons with mental illnesses who have experienced the humiliation of arrest, it is as if a double whammy occurs. They are stigmatized for their mental illnesses and they are stigmatized for being processed by the criminal justice system. However, persons with mental illnesses are not only stigmatized for their actions that lead to encounters with both mental health and criminal justice authorities, they are also branded when others who are alleged to be mentally ill or are mentally ill act out, particularly when those actions are of a violent nature.[16]

---

16. Gusfield maintains that we as a society have a tendency to push the actions of individuals who commit such unconventional acts as mass murder into the sick deviant category because law-abiding citizens cannot fathom the possibility of a rational person engaging in such reprehensible behavior, and it helps conventional society to better cope with such atrocities (Williams, F.P. & McShane, M.D. (2004). *Criminological theory, 4th ed.*, Upper Saddle River, NJ: Prentice Hall).

Most Persons with Mental Illnesses Are Not Violent

Most people who are mentally ill are not violent. Brekke, Prindle, Bae, and Long (2001) found persons with schizophrenia living in the community to be fourteen times more likely to be victims of a violent crime than to be charged for one. According to McCampbell (2001), less than one percent of persons with mental illnesses ever exhibit violent behavior. Friedman (2006) reports that the attributable risk of being victimized by someone with serious mental illness is somewhere between a three to five percent chance, with an individual seven times more likely to be violently assaulted by someone who is not mentally ill but is abusing substances. Current research, including the U.S. Surgeon General's Report on Mental Health (1999), overwhelmingly demonstrates that the vast majority of persons with mental illnesses are not violent.

While Stuart and Arboleda-Florez (2001) did not find substance use disorders to be significant contributors to the perpetration of violence by persons with mental illnesses that came to the attention of the police, substance abuse coupled with homelessness for persons with mental illnesses has been found to substantially increase the chances of them being criminally victimized (Hiday, Swartz, Swanson, Borum, & Wagner, 1999). Others have concluded that small subset of persons with mental illnesses may have increased risk for violence when certain factors are present. Included among these factors potentially leading to an increased risk of violence on the part of persons with mental illnesses is abuse of substances, past incidences of violence, and noncompliance with treatment/medication or lack of treatment (Borum et al., 1997; Honberg, 2007; Monahan & Arnold, 1996; Steadman, et al., 1998; Swanson et al., 1997). Swanson et al. (2006), in a national study involving persons with schizophrenia, found that violence was more likely to be escalated when accompanied by "positive" psychotic symptoms, such as persecutory ideation, signs of depression, childhood conduct problems and victimization. Borum, Fein, Vossekuil, and Berglund (1999) contend "[M]ental illness per se does not have a strong association with violent behavior. Rather, any association between mental illness and violence appears primarily to be related to substance abuse and/or specific psychotic symptoms" (p. 333).

The United States Secret Service, which is involved in threat assessments at the highest levels in this country, has indicated the following: "[M]ental illness is not critical to determining dangerousness; the ability and capacity to develop and execute a plan is much more significant" (United States Secret Service,

2006). Fein and Vossekuil (1998; 1999) in a study of 83 assassins or attempted assassins of public officials or figures in the United States from 1949 to 1996 concluded that while mental health histories are relevant in conducting threat assessments rarely does mental illness play a role in assassinations.

Further, Dedman (2000) reports that the United States Secret Service's evaluation of 41 school shooters involved in 37 school shooting incidents in the United States found that very few of the shooters had been determined to suffer from a mental illness. We now turn our focus to the Virginia Tech shootings.

Virginia Tech and Its Aftermath

Almost two weeks after Seung-Hui Cho's rampage, police remained at a loss as to why Cho shot and killed thirty-two fellow college students and professors at Virginia Tech University (Williams & Morrison, 2007). Still today there is no consensus as to what his motive was on that day. The problem may very well be trying to apply rationality to irrational behavior. The reason for Cho's killing spree, which has been characterized as "the deadliest shooting rampage in American history" (Hauser, 2007), may be as simple as the mantra he went into on his televised videotaped manifesto shown on NBC television. It could be that Cho had succumbed to the pressure to achieve the American Dream that criminologists Robert Merton, Richard Cloward, Lloyd Ohlin, Scott Messner, and Richard Rosenfeld have elaborated on (Messner & Rosenfeld, 2007; Vold et al., 1998), and Cho, in so many ways, had fallen short. Perhaps his heritage, as suggested by Thomas (2007), had heightened the strain on him to attain material success and acquire the trappings that come with it in America. This could be reflected in Cho's diatribe as he seemingly compares his suffering with Christ's and disdainfully assails those who have everything, saying, "You had everything you wanted. Your Mercedes wasn't enough, you brats. Your golden necklaces weren't enough, you snobs. Your trust fund wasn't enough. Your vodka and Cognac weren't enough. All your debaucheries weren't enough. Those weren't enough to fulfill your hedonistic needs. You had everything" (Chicago Tribune, 2007). In terms of rationality, it did not matter that most students at Virginia Tech, as pointed out by Thomas (2007), are not very wealthy. What mattered was that Cho in his own mind did not measure up and felt persecuted. How ironic it might be that the very thing that possibly motivated Cho, the drive for money, permeates the delivery or lack thereof of mental health services in this country.[17]

Whatever the possible motive for his onslaught, it is a sad day in America if a focus on violence is the means by which the problems with mental health make it to the forefront of policymakers' desks and get addressed. Like it or not, violence has become the "elephant in the room," and Cho's actions at Virginia Tech University may serve as an opportunity to liberate the mental health system, increasing access to treatment, and freeing the criminal justice system to focus more on the work it is intended to do. However, Cho's conduct on that fateful morning may set the treatment of mental illnesses back a hundred and fifty years. Although, some would argue that we are already there, suggesting that we are where Dorothea Dix found us, with our lack of access to mental health treatment and criminalization of persons with mental illnesses (Geller, 2002; Sharfstein, 2000).

> Historian James Truslow Adams in 1929 indicated, 'We must rule or be ruled,' … because unless the crime problem is brought under control, social order will sooner or later give way to chaos, opening the way for 'the dictator who inevitably 'saves society' when social insubordination and disintegration have become intolerable'[;] he recognized the genuine vulnerability of democratic rights and freedoms to demagogic appeals for law and order (Messner & Rosenfeld, 2007, p.101–102).

As noted by former U.S. Senator Sam Ervin, "In a free society you have to take some risks. If you lock everybody up, or even if you lock up everybody you think might commit a crime, you'll be pretty safe, but you won't be free" (Neubauer, 1992, p. 21). Indeed, crisis drives policy. Commissions have been formed rapidly, with hearings transpiring in the wake of the Virginia Tech tragedy.[18] It remains to be seen whether a savior for the mental health prob-

---

17. See Michael Winerip's article entitled "Bedlam on the streets: Increasingly, the mentally ill have nowhere to go. That's their problem and ours," as he describes the ordeal of Andrew Goldstein trying to get treatment and the denial of that treatment resulting in the death of Kendra Webdale in *The New York Times Magazine*, May 23, 1999, p. 42–49, 56, 65–66, and 70; will be discussed in Chapter 7.

18. See Ron Honberg's (2007) congressional testimony on gun control after the Virginia Tech tragedy; Virginia Governor Kaine quickly assembled a commission to investigate the Virginia Tech tragedy and the response to it (Smith, L. 2007, April 20). Virginia Governor names 6 experts to panel that will review tragedy and responses. *The Chronicle of Higher Education*, Retrieved from the World Wide Web on June 6, 2007: http://chronicle.com/free/2007/04/2007042001n.htm; Florida Governor Crist has formed a committee to identify best practices to implement to ward off such tragedies (see Van der Werf, M. 2007, June 6). Florida

lem in America will emerge from the ashes and whether that salvation will come in the form of liberation or dictatorship.

Representatives of the Treatment Advocacy Center (TAC), major proponents of assisted treatment or involuntary outpatient commitment—which will be discussed in Chapter 7, have been criticized for their over reliance on violence to try to drive their missives with lawmakers across the country. One of the individuals affiliated with TAC, D.J. Jaffee, has indicated, "Laws change for a single reason, in reaction to highly publicized incidences of violence. People care about public safety. I am not saying it is right. I am saying this is the reality ... So, if you're changing your laws in your state, you have to understand that" (Corrigan, Watson, Warpinski, & Gracia, 2004, p. 577). Jaffee also said, " 'Once you understand that it means that you have to take the debate out of the mental health arena and put it in the criminal justice/public safety arena[;] ... [i]t may be necessary to capitalize on the fear of violence' " (Vine, 2001).

Examples of some of the information that Dr. E. Fuller Torrey, President of TAC, and TAC members have been reportedly disseminating are his assertion that persons with untreated schizophrenia and bipolar disorders commit 20 murders a week, adding up to 1,000 in a year (Arnold, 2004; Vine 2001) and that persons with mental illnesses are five and one half times as likely to shoot and kill a law enforcement officer (Dawdy, 2006a;b).

Media Influence

Jonathan Stanley (2004) of TAC, in defense of allegedly playing the violence card, indicates that a search of a database of leading newspapers only produced 71 items with the keywords "violence" and "Treatment Advocacy Center" in the past five years, and a search with the keywords "violence" and mental illness" revealed 536 pieces in the past month. Stanley (2004) contends that "people can't see what doesn't happen and newspapers can't print it (p. 834)." Even

---

panel, appointed after Virginia Tech tragedy, recommends sharing information about troubled students, *The Chronicle of Higher Education,* Retrieved from the World Wide Web on June 6, 2007: http://chronicle.com/daily/2007/05/2007052502n.htm?rss. The verdict is till out on where all of these reform efforts will lead, but it would be wise to tread cautiously. Sometimes rushed decisions do not make for good workable policies; see the Jessica Lunsford Act for example (Bowen, C.T. 2005, July 1) Well-intentioned law results in a nightmare for schools, *St. Petersburg Times,* Retrieved from the World Wide Web on June 6, 2007: http://www.sptimes.com/2005/07/01/news_pf/Pasco/Well_intentioned_law_.shtml.

so, Corrigan et al. (2004) report that from their research inculcating individuals with stories of linkages between mental illness and violence is not likely to result in urges for increased funding for mental health treatment programs, instead it is likely to generate attitudes that result in the withholding of such help and further segregation of persons with mental illnesses form society. With stigma seen as the foremost barrier to treatment, E. Fuller Torrey (2002) maintains that the primary cause of stigma is the fear of violence, and unless violence is addressed, stigma will continue in an unabashed fashion; however, Perlick and Rosenheck (2002) retort by noting that violence and misconceptions about violence among persons with mental illnesses contribute to unwarranted stigmatization.

When it comes to this age of media sensationalism it is indeed the tendency of the media to report on the planes that crash and burn, the aberrant exceptions. We don't hear about all the planes that make it day after day successfully, nor do we hear about all the persons with mental illnesses (psychiatrists, psychologists, lawyers, legislators, and even professors) who got up today and went to work, performed exceptionally and returned home safely only to do it again tomorrow and the next day and the next day and the next.... [19] Research confirms that the citizenry's primary source of information on mental illness is the media (Edney, 2004). Thus, media sensationalism can have a significant impact on public perceptions and opinion regarding mental illness.[20]

---

19. See for example NAMI's (2007) *People with mental illness enrich our lives,* Retrieved from the World Wide Web on June 6, 2007: http://www.nami.org/PrinterTemplate.cfm?Section=Helpline1&template=/ContentManagement/ContentDisplay.cfm&ContentID=4858 which includes Abraham Lincoln, Lionel Aldridge, Ludwig Beethoven, Leo Tolstoy, Tennessee Williams, Vincent Van Gogh, Issac Newton, Ernest Hemingway, Michelangelo, Winston Churchill, Patty Duke, and Charles Dickens.

20. The National Alliance on Mental Illness (NAMI) has established a StigmaBusters network, headed by Stella March, smarch@nami.org, who have advocates throughout the country and around the world who fight against electronic and print media misrepresentations and hurtful messages regarding mental illnesses Retrieved from the World Wide Web on June 2, 2007: http://www.nami.org/PrinterTemplate.cfm?section=fight_stigma.

Also, Vickers (2006), a mental health advocate and attorney by training with bipolar disorder, believes that education is the key to overcoming the stigma of mental illnesses. In particular, she advocates for educating the legal profession where she is aware of other attorneys with mental illnesses who will not come to the aid of other colleagues with mental illnesses for fear that by such associations they themselves might be outed; she tells of a judge who may be exhibiting signs and symptoms of mental illness but is afraid to see a psychologist or psychiatrist for an evaluation that might negatively impact his judicial career, as he would be required to report the contact to the judicial qualifying commission;

As previously indicated, the vast majority of persons who are violent are not mentally ill (American Psychiatric Association, 1994). However, Wahl (2003), reporting on seventeen years of research monitoring television content, indicated that 72 percent of all mentally ill characters in prime-time dramas were depicted as violent, with 21 percent of these characters portrayed as murderers; this same study analyzed daytime soap operas and concluded that approximately 66 percent of mentally ill characters in this venue were depicted as criminal and violent. Other research on such portrayals has found less focus on linking mental illness to violence,[21] but the message is still inaccurate, with approximately one-third of such depictions reportedly focusing on dangerousness among persons characterized as mentally ill; this translates into roughly half of all citizens perceiving persons who have mental illnesses as being more violent than individuals who do not (Violence and Mental Illness, 2007). As noted by Stuart and Arboleda-Florez (2001), "Public perceptions of mentally ill persons as criminally dangerous appear to be greatly exaggerated" (p. 654). This is particularly true when it is considered that Szmukler (2000) reported that the probability of being murdered by a psychotic stranger is about the odds of being struck by lightning and dying from the strike, about a one in a million chance. In fact, one is four hundred times more likely to die from influenza than from a patient with mental illness (Dobson, 1998; Violence and Mental Illness, 2007).

there is the judge that believes that mental illnesses are the result of being possessed by the devil, and an exorcism by the church would more readily cast out the demon than anything doctors and drugs could do; there was the attorney that stated that all persons with mental illnesses should be sterilized or put behind bars. Vickers, A.D. (2006). Brain bondage: The delay in mental illness recovery. Jacksonville, Florida: The Hartley Press, Inc.

21. Dietrich, S., Heider, D., Matschinger, H., & Angermeyer, M.C. (2006). Influence of newspaper reporting on adolescents' attitudes toward people with mental illness' *Social Psychology and Psychiatric Epidemiology,41,* p. 318–322, in a study of the impact of newspaper reports stated that the majority of media stories on mental illness selectively and almost exclusively focus on violence and dangerousness. Levin (2005) reports that in a recent study of over three thousand articles in seventy major outlets it was determined that approximately forty percent of the newspaper stories associated mental illness with crime and dangerousness. Wahl (2003) notes that purposeful misrepresentations are not uncommon by the media. For example, casting for One Flew Over the Cuckoo's Nest, a darling of the antipsychiatry counterculture movement (Rissmiller and Rissmiller, 2006), was reportedly suspended until the producers could locate actors who looked distinctively unusual enough to portray the perceived image of mental patients. Although the movie was filmed at the Oregon State Hospital and actual hospital patients were considered for parts in the movie, the producers declined because the actual patients did not look bizarre enough in line with misinformed expectations to play such a role on the big screen.

The reality, contrary to media misrepresentations, is that persons with se-vere mental illnesses are more likely to be victims of crime, including violent crime, than perpetrators of crime. A Northwestern University study shows that when compared with the general population persons with severe mental illnesses are eleven times more likely to be violent crime victims; eight times more likely to be robbed; 140 times more likely to have property stolen from their person; fifteen more times likely to be victims of assault, and twenty-three times more likely to be a rape victim (Teplin, McClelland, Abram, & Weiner, 2005).

Less Stigma Improves Treatment Opportunities

Less stigmatization can also affect the attitudes of persons about seeking treatment for mental illnesses. Mojtabai (2007) has found that in the last decade Americans have reportedly become more willing to seek mental health treat-ment (less than 50 percent of those surveyed), and this may have a significant impact on the demand for mental health services in the future. It is even hoped that the very public and publicized police-escorted involuntary commitments twice within a month's time of Britney Spears can prove to be educable mo-ments by using her celebrity to further de-stigmatize a diagnosis of mental ill-ness and the receipt of treatment for such an illness (Blankstein, Gold, & Winton, 2008). As will be discussed in Chapter 12, it is believed that parity in insur-ance coverage whereby mental illnesses are covered and treated on par with physical illnesses would go a long way toward educating the general public on the fact that mental illnesses are no different from physical illnesses. We don't treat someone with diabetes, caused by a chemical imbalance, as if they are to blame for their illness, nor should we blame someone with a mental illness. Parity could go a long way towards tearing down the walls of stigma that have been built up and surround mental illness in America today. This would in turn provide greater access to mental health treatment and would ensure that more individuals, with stigma diminished, would more readily seek treatment.

Negative Side Effects of Medications and Anosognosia

Some individuals refuse or discontinue taking their medication for mental illness due to the adverse side effects associated with the medications that vary from person to person. Negative side effects can include dry mouth, weight gain, tiredness, and depression. Using antipsychotic medications may also cause Akathisia, Dystonia, Parkinsonianism, Tardive dyskinesia, and agranulocytosis. These terms are defined below:

> **Akathisia**—subjective feelings of distress and discomfort, agitation, restlessness, frequent arm and leg movements, non-localized pain.
> **Dystonia**—sudden involuntary muscle contractions, bizarre and uncontrolled movements of face, neck, tongue and back, oculogyric crisis—often mistaken as seizure activity.
> **Parkinsonianism**—slowed movement, expressionless face, shuffling gait, tremors
> **Tardive dyskinesia**—'late appearing movement disorder'—most devastating side effect of therapy. Jerking muscle movements, body rocking, and tic-like movements of face and tongue —can progress to the entire body or remain mild. It is seldom reversible. Increases with age and duration of drug use.
> **Agranulocytosis**—(a severe adverse side effect involving the loss of white blood cells that fight infection), requires that ... [individuals] taking [the particular drug] be monitored with blood tests every one to two weeks. (New York State Office of Mental Health, 2006).

In addition to the reasons for discontinuing or refusing medication cited above, there is another condition called anosognosia which parallels the condition sometimes found in stroke victims who may wrongly sense that they are moving their extremities when in actuality they are not. Amador (2006) refers to this phenomenon as a lack of insight into one's mental illness. Although everyone around the person with mental illness is blatantly aware of the individual's erratic behavior, the individual with mental illness is not aware of their actions and does not recognize a problem with their behavior. This adds to the importance of seeking input from family members and friends regarding past history and customary behavior when interventions with persons with mental illnesses occur.

Restricting Civil Commitment

"It would indeed be ironic if the Magna Carta of the mentally ill ... led to their criminal stigmatization and incarceration in jails and prisons, where little or no mental health treatment is provided."

—Abramson

Another factor identified as contributing to the criminalization of persons with mental illnesses is perhaps an unintended consequence of the Civil Rights movement which provided a stimulus for uncovering abuses of civil liberties in the operation of state hospitals. Often, with the best of intentions, civil commitment statutes were modified across the United States—making it more difficult to civilly commit someone and force treatment upon them. Such imposed, restrictive, civil commitment criteria in the name of civil liberties prompted Abramson (1972) to remark "It would indeed be ironic if the Magna Carta of the mentally ill ... led to their criminal stigmatization and incarceration in jails and prisons, where little or no mental health treatment is provided." A California study comparing arrests in San Mateo County from three and one-half years before implementation of the Lanterman-Petris-Short Act, aimed at making civil commitment requirements more restrictive, to four and one-half years after passage of the act found that the arrest rate for persons with mental illnesses had increased four and one-half times since implementation of the civil commitment reform (Sosowsky, 1978). Some believe the more difficult it is to civilly commit an individual the more likely that person will become entangled in the criminal justice system (Lamb & Weinberger, 1998). There appears to be support for this theory.

The Criminal Justice System Has Evolved into the de Facto Mental Health System

There is no more complicated or intractable a problem within criminal justice than that posed by the needs of persons with severe mental disorders, and ... the failure to rationally respond to the issues raised by the incarceration of persons with severe mental disorders results in the unfair and disproportionate criminalization of persons with severe disorders (Stone, 1997, p. 286).

The three largest inpatient psychiatric facilities in the country are jails, with the Los Angeles County Jail, Rikers Island Jail in New York City, and the Cook County Jail in Chicago each individually housing more persons with mental illnesses than any psychiatric institution in the United States.

—Council of State Governments, 2007

Whatever the causes, we know that approximately five percent of the U.S. population has a serious mental illness; those with mental illnesses are significantly more likely to come into contact with the criminal justice system (Council of State Governments, 2002). While some researchers have assessed the percentage of persons with mental illnesses who are incarcerated in the United States to be from five to eight times larger than the percentage of persons with mental illnesses in free society (Panzer, Broner, & McQuistion, 2001; Stone, 1997; Watson et al., 2001), according to the President's New Freedom Commission on Mental Health (2003), the rate of serious mental illness for persons in jail in the U.S. is 3 to 4 times more than that of the general, non-inmate population.

More persons with mental illnesses are residing in prisons and jails today than in public psychiatric hospitals (Lamb & Bachrach, 2001). Also, jails and prisons in the U.S. hold approximately three to five times more individuals with mental illnesses than state psychiatric hospitals do across the country (Fellner, 2006; Leifman, 2001; Lerner-Wren, 2000). In fact, with the downsizing and closing of hospitals for the mentally ill, the three largest inpatient psychiatric facilities in the country are jails, with the Los Angeles County Jail, Rikers Island Jail in New York City, and the Cook County Jail in Chicago each individually housing more persons with mental illnesses than any psychiatric institution in the United States (Council of State Governments, 2007). Is it any wonder that funding efforts, in terms of pursuit of grants, for re-entry of persons with mental illnesses from prisons and jails back into the community has been led on a three to one basis by criminal justice agencies over mental health providers as reported by one study? (Wilson & Draine, 2006)

Persons with mental illnesses have been found to be almost twice as likely as individuals without any known mental illness to be arrested for their behavior in similar situations (Teplin, 1984). Contrary to media sensationalism, persons with mental illnesses, when arrested, are usually arrested on minor charges, with approximately half of all persons with mental illnesses having been arrested at least once (Cuellar, Snowden, & Ewing, 2007; Solomon & Draine, 1995a; Walsh & Bricourt, 1997); some of these individuals recycle dozens and even hundreds of times in and out of custody within the criminal justice system (Osher, Steadman, & Barr, 2003). Once arrested, individuals with mental illnesses have a tendency to remain in custody for longer periods of time than those persons who are not mentally ill who have been brought in on similar charges (Solomon & Draine, 1995b). For example, persons who are delusional or psychotic as a result of their illness, who are tossed into the bowels of the criminal justice system, may lack the ability to understand and comprehend directives issued to them by detention or corrections officers, much less have the ability to comport themselves accordingly. The inability to act as an automaton and follow the institutionalized rules can result in disciplinary infractions, imposed isolation, and even new charges for prosecution in the court system. In essence, without treatment, the condition of persons with mental illnesses who are incarcerated within the criminal justice system deteriorates (Stone, 1997), and such persons are prone to victimization in such settings, including assaults, rapes, and suicides (Kondo, 2000). Furthermore, it has been found that less than 50 percent of individuals with mental illnesses housed in county jails actually receive mental health services while in custody (Perez, Leifman, & Estrada, 2003; Teplin, Abram, & McClelland, 1997; Veysey, Steadman, Morrissey, & Johnsen, 1997; Walsh & Holt, 1999).

Thus, custodial settings within the criminal justice system may not be environments conducive to mental health, and mental health treatment within those settings may often be questionable or even nonexistent (Kerle, 1998). While this may be so, the reality is that for many, such as homeless and uninsured persons, due to lack of access and linkages to treatment in the community, their only receipt of mental health services is via the criminal justice system (Osher et al., 2003). Gilligan (2001) contends that jails, prisons, and the prison mental hospital are the last mental hospital in operation. The continued treatment of the mentally ill by the criminal justice system reflects both constructive and destructive trends. A constructive trend, if it can be so labeled, is that prisons are sometimes providing at least a modicum of mental health treatment. As in Dorothea Dix's time, there is a destructive trend. Large numbers of individuals with major mental illnesses are being diverted to jails and prisons, an environment that tends to create rather than alleviate the signs and symptoms of mental illness.

Prevalence

Ditton (1999) found that approximately 16 percent of persons incarcerated in jails and prisons reported having a mental illness. The reliability of self-report data is often suspect, especially when dealing with a sensitive matter such as mental illness. Unfortunately, the stigma surrounding mental illness within our society may make individuals reluctant to acknowledge that they have such an illness, particularly in a jail or prison setting where trust is often lacking and vulnerability is to be avoided. Thus, it is very possible that the percentage of persons with mental illnesses incarcerated within the criminal justice system is actually higher than Ditton's findings, and this is especially true when co-occurring disorders are considered. A co-occurring disorder results when an individual has both a Diagnostic and Statistical Manual of Mental Disorders IV (DSM IV) Axis I major psychiatric disorder (e.g., psychotic, bipolar, and depressive disorders) and a drug and/or alcohol use disorder (Peters & Hill, 1997). Research indicates that seventy-two percent of persons with severe mental illnesses in jails in the United States are also suffering from a substance abuse disorder (GAINS, 2005). With the war on drugs and the heightened scrutiny given by the police to ordinance infractions and quality of life violations, the criminal justice system has been thrust into the unenviable role of becoming the social system of last resort (Goldkamp & Irons-Guynn, 2000).

The problem, of course, is that it is a role the criminal justice system is ill prepared to assume. Criminal justice practitioners are somewhat adept at determining when someone is high on alcohol or drugs and have a certain protocol with various responses to rely upon for identification during such encounters. However, criminal justice professionals are not as seasoned at recognizing the signs and symptoms of mental illnesses. Persons who are mentally ill may knowingly or unknowingly mask their mental illness by using drugs or alcohol. For example, a person who has bipolar disorder may drink alcohol, which acts as a depressant and lessens his/her mania. Therefore, to the untrained eye the substance abuse problem is observed but the underlying mental illness goes unidentified and untreated, resulting in an increased likelihood for the person who has encountered the criminal justice system, without appropriate intervention, to return again to the system. This inability to appropriately identify and consider co-occurring disorders within the criminal justice system also adds to the possibility that Ditton's findings regarding the percentage of persons with mental illnesses in the criminal justice system are less than the actual percentage of persons with mental illnesses incarcerated in the United States.

In fact, a recent Bureau of Justice Statistics study reports that more than half of all prison and jail inmates have a mental health problem, which includes 64 percent of jail inmates, 45 percent of federal inmates, and 56 percent of persons confined in state prisons (James & Glaze, 2006). While the findings of James and Glaze are encouraging from an advocacy standpoint of arguing for the diversion of persons with mental illnesses from the criminal justice system and linking them to treatment, there are questions about the reliability of their study.[22] In actuality, the true percentage of persons with

---

22. In a personal communication on May 22, 2007 from Dr. Henry J. Steadman of Policy Research Associates, he provides a critique of the James and Glaze report. As indicated by Dr. Steadman, "The B[ureau of] J[ustice] S[tatistics'] data radically overestimate the actual rates of serious mental illness and less serious forms of mental illness in jails and prisons. What [Glaze and James] have done is measure a construct they have called 'mental health problems.' They have done this in a way that has no basis in research or clinical prac-

mental illnesses incarcerated in the United States likely lies somewhere between the percentages reported by Ditton and James and Glaze (probably closer to Ditton's); whatever the actual figures, the numbers of persons with mental illness housed in the criminal justice system in this country is unacceptable.

Conclusion

While acknowledging that it is hard to determine, Lamb and Bachrach (2001) indicate an increase in the jail and prison population has occurred as the result of deinstitutionalization and the restrictions placed on civil commitment criteria; a large percentage of these persons with mental illnesses incarcerated in the criminal justice system today are similar in characteristics to the long-term residents of state hospitals that were observed prior to deinstitutionalization (Lamb & Weinberger, 1998). This movement of persons with mental illnesses from psychiatric facilities to custody in criminal justice institutions has been referred to as transcarceration (Lowman & Menzies, 1986) or transintitutionalization (Lurigio & Swartz, 2000). Many persons with mental illnesses, without adequate access to treatment, ultimately make their way into the criminal justice system (Lamb, 1998: Lamb & Weinberger, 1998; Lee-Griffin, 2001; Sigurdson, 2000; Lamb, Weinberger, Marsh, & Gross, 2007) recently found over three-fourths of persons with severe mental illnesses in the Los Angeles County Jail to have received their mental health treatment from the criminal justice system and not the mental health system. They argue that the mental health system needs to expand the scope of its coverage and prioritize treatment for those in the criminal justice system who are on the verge of entering the system.

On June 11, 2002, the U.S. Senate Judiciary Committee held hearings to discuss the "criminalization of mental illness." They listened to police and prosecutors, local officials and mental health professionals, and advocates for peo-

---

tice. They have an unnamed scale that has a wide range of mental illness symptoms which, when properly weighted, can arrive at summary scores for levels of mental illness. That is not what they did. Instead, they reported on the proportion of inmates in each category who endorsed each individual item. If they said 'yes' to any item, they were defined as having a 'mental health problem.' If one examines those individual items, e.g. 'Insomnia or hypersomnia,' 'Thoughts of revenge,' or 'Persistent anger or irritability,' in the context of a person residing in a jail and prison, they would seem to be rather common feelings one might expect rather than individually indicating a mental health problem. Accordingly, these exceedingly high figures are nearly worthless for purposes of estimating the need for mental health and substance abuse services for inmates in jails and prisons."

ple with mental illnesses. It is very rare for representatives from groups with such wide-ranging points of view to agree on an issue. But on this day, everyone was in agreement. All those who spoke echoed the sentiments of Chris Koyanagi from the Bazelon Center for Mental Health Law who said:

> Our country is punishing people with mental illnesses for the failure of the mental health system. We used to warehouse people with mental disorders in large state institutions. Today, increasingly, we simply incarcerate them in jail. We must reverse this trend. This means forging new and continuing coordination between criminal justice and mental health agencies. It will also require improved training of law enforcement officials to recognize and respond appropriately to people with mental illnesses, expanded options for jail diversion and adequate planning and community support for inmates with mental illnesses when they are released. In the long term, we must slow the tide of people with mental illnesses who end up in the criminal justice system. We can do this only if we ensure access to mental health treatment, adequate housing, vocational help and the other forms of social support necessary for someone with a mental illness to lead an independent and dignified life (Jordan, 2002).

As noted by the Human Rights Watch (2003) organization, there is a direct connection between the increasing number of persons with mental illnesses who are incarcerated and the lack of adequate mental health services in the community. In fact, the Council of State Governments (2002) in its Criminal Justice/Mental Health Consensus Project observed:

> Law enforcement officers, prosecutors, defenders, and judges—people on the front lines every day—believe too many people with mental illness(es) become involved in the criminal justice system because the mental health system has somehow failed. They believe that if many of the people with mental illness(es) received the services they needed, they would not end up under arrest, in jail, or facing charges in court. Mental health advocates, service providers, and administrators do not necessarily disagree. Like their counterparts in the criminal justice system, they believe that the ideal mechanism to prevent people with mental illness(es) from entering the criminal justice system is the mental health system itself—if it can be counted on to function effectively. They also know that in most places the current system is overwhelmed and performing this preventive function poorly (p.26).

Multi-system collaboration is a key to solving the problems facing the mental health and criminal justice systems today. In the chapters that follow, we will endeavor to explore innovative strategies for bolstering the mental health system and striving to alleviate the criminal justice system from further becoming a dumping ground for persons with mental illnesses.

The history of the treatment of persons with mental illnesses represents a struggle of individuals, groups, communities, and policymakers. Advancements in technology, science, and treatment will continue to change what is "the right thing to do." The successful treatment of persons with mental illnesses will depend on the ability of policymakers to adapt and do what they know is right. Treating persons with mental illnesses in pathological environments (jails, prisons, etc.) is not morally right or, in the long term, the best economic decision.

As previously noted, often times law enforcement officers, perhaps lacking options or not being aware of them, come to perceive the criminal justice process of arrest and jail as preferable in terms of efficiency and expediency to seeking treatment for persons with mental illnesses who they encounter in crises. Isaac and Armat (1990) acknowledge that the work of Thomas Szasz and the anti-psychiatry movement in tightening up civil commitment standards has made it easier to put a person with mental illness in jail than it is to secure treatment for them. One mental health advocate describes it this way, "'It's harder to get into Bellevue [State Hospital] than Harvard'" (Closing the Hospitals, 2002).

Law enforcement officers need to navigate the murky, impersonal, red tape of mental health bureaucracies by establishing collaborations and enhancing communication, not only with mental health providers and other members of the justice system but also with persons with mental illnesses and their families. Such relationships can serve to identify alternatives to the criminal justice system, prevent unnecessary suffering, reduce the potential for tragedy, and thwart the implementation of policies that are not well reasoned. The next chapter will explore ways of improving law enforcement encounters with and responses to persons with mental illnesses who are in crisis.

References

A Snapshot of Homelessness (2007). Washington, DC: National Alliance to End Homelessness. Retrieved from the World Wide Web on June 6, 2007: http://www.endhomelessness.org/section/tools/tenyearplan/snapshot.

Abramson, M. F. (1972). The criminalization of mentally disordered behavior: Possible side-effect of a new mental health law. *Hospital & Community Psychiatry* 23(4), pp. 101–105.

Adams, R. W. (2006, July 12). Depression takes financial toll in Florida. *The Ledger*, Retrieved from the World Wide Web on June 4, 2007: http://www.the ledger.com/apps/pbcs.dll/article?Date=20060712&Category=NEWS&ArtNo=6 07120355&SectionCat=&Template=printart.

Amador, X. (2006). *I am not sick. I don't need help! How to help someone with mental illness accept treatment.* Peconic, NY: Vida Press.

American Psychiatric Association (1994). *Fact Sheet: Violence and mental illness.* Washington, DC: American Psychiatric Association.

An Interview with Piers Anthony (2004, June 26). Retrieved from the World Wide Web on June 6, 2007: http://www.angelfire.com/film/rings/interviews/piers. html.

Arnold, J. (2004). Stigma and public education about mental illness: To the editor. *Psychiatric Services* 55(7), p. 833.

Austin, J., & Irwin, J. (2001). It's about time: America's imprisonment binge, 3rd ed. Belmont, CA: Wadsworth.

Becker, H. (1963). *Outsiders: Studies in the sociology of deviance.* New York: Free Press.

Blankstein, A., Gold, S., & Winton, R. (2008, February 1). Precision teamwork in Spears operation. *Los Angeles Times.* Retrieved from the World Wide Web on February 3, 2008: http://www.latimes.com/entertainment/news/celebrity/la-me-britney1feb01,0,7795736.story.

Bloom, J. D., Williams, M. H., Land, C., McFarland, B., & Reichlin, S. (1998). Changes in public psychiatric hospitalization in Oregon over the past two decades. *Psychiatric Services* 49(3), pp. 366–369.

Bonovitz, J. C., & Bonovitz, J. S. (1981). Diversion of the mentally ill into the criminal justice system: The police intervention perspective. *American Journal of Psychiatry* 138(7), pp. 973–976.

Borum, R., Fein, R., Vossekuil, B., & Berglund, J. (1999). Threat assessment: Defining an approach for evaluating risk of targeted violence. *Behavioral Sciences and the Law* 17, pp. 323–337.

Borum, R., Swanson, J., Swartz, M., & Hiday, V. (1997). Substance abuse, violent behavior and police encounters among persons with severe mental disorder. *Journal of Contemporary Criminal Justice* 13(3), pp. 236–250.

Brekke, J. S., Prindle, C., Bae, S. W., & Long, J. D. (2001). Risks for individuals with schizophrenia who are living in the community. *Psychiatric Services* 52(10), pp. 1358–1365.

Butterfield, F. (1998, March 5). Prisons replace hospitals for the nation's mentally ill. *The New York Times*, 1A, 18A.

Closing the Hospitals (2002). *Part Two of Dangerous Minds*, Treatment Advocacy Center. Arlington, Virginia. Retrieved from the World Wide Web on June 30, 2002: www.psychlaws.org.

Coleman, B. C. (1997, December 10). Study: Most hospitals dump mental patients. *The Ledger* A4.

Cordner, G. (2006). People with mental illness. Problem-Oriented Guides for Police, Guide No. 40. Washington, DC: Office of Community Oriented Policing Services, U.S. Department of Justice.

Corrigan, P.W., Watson, A.C., Warpinski, A.C., & Gracia, G. (2004). Implications of educating the public on mental illness, violence, and stigma. *Psychiatric Services* 55(5), pp. 577–580.

Council of State Governments (2007). People with mental illness in the criminal justice system: About the problem. *Criminal Justice / Mental Health Consensus Project*, New York. Retrieved from the World Wide Web on May 23, 2007: http://consensusproject.org/resources/fact-sheets/factsheet.

Council of State Governments, Police Executive Research Forum, Pretrial Services Resource Center, Association of State Correctional Administrators, Bazelon Center for Mental Health Law, and the Center for Behavioral Health, Justice, and Public Policy (2002). Criminal Justice / Mental Health Consensus Project. New York: Council of State Governments.

Cournos, F., & Le Melle, S. (2000). The young adult chronic patient: A look back. *Psychiatric Services* 51, pp. 996–1000.

Butterfield, F. (1999, July 12). Prisons brim with mentally ill, study finds. *New York Times*, A10.

CNN (1997, April 20). Space final frontier for Timothy Leary: Ashes of LSD guru, 'Star Trek' creator to rocket into orbit. Retrieved from the World Wide Web on June 6, 2007: http://www.cnn.com/TECH/9704/20/space.ashes/.

Cuellar, A.E., Snowden, L.M., & Ewing, T. (2007). Criminal records of persons served in the public mental health system. *Psychiatric Services* 58(1), 114–120.

Dawdy, P. (2006a, May 15). Fuller Torrey is dangerous. Retrieved from the World Wide Web on June 4, 2007: http://www.furiousseasons.com/archives/2006/05/fuller_torrey_is_dangerous.html.

Dawdy, P. (2006b, May 16). Pete Earley now has a problem. Retrieved from the World Wide Web on June 4, 2007: http://www.furiousseasons.com/archives/2006/05/pete_earley_now_has_a_problem_1.html.

Dedman, B. (2000, October 15). School shooters: Secret service findings. *Chicago Sun-Times*, Retrieved from the World Wide Web on June 18, 2007: http://www.secretservice.gov/ntac/chicago_sun/find15.htm.

Ditton. P. M. (1999). *Mental health and treatment of inmates and probationers: Special report* . Washington, DC: U.S. Department of Justice, Bureau of Justice Statistics.

Dobson, R. (1998, July). Are schizophrenics the lepers of our time? *Independent Review* 21, p. 11.

Draine, J., Salzer, M., Culhane, D. P., & Hadley, T. R. (2002). 'Role of social disadvantage in crime, joblessness, and homelessness among persons with a serious mental illness', Psychiatric Services 53(5), pp. 565–573.

Earley, P. (2006). *Crazy: A father's search through America's mental health madness.* New York: G.P. Putnam's Sons.

Editorial (2006, December 30). No solution. *Orlando Sentinel,* Orlando, Florida. Retrieved from the World Wide Web on June 6, 2007: http://www.highbeam.com/doc/1G1-156509865.html.

Edney, D.R. (2004, January). Mass media and mental illness: A literature review. Canadian Mental Health Association, Ontario, Canada. Retrieved from the World Wide Web on June 4, 2007: www.ontario.cmha.ca/content/ about_mental_illness/mass_media.asp.

Emery, B.D. (2006, November). The crisis in acute psychiatric care: Report of a focus group meeting held on June 19–20. National Association of State Mental Health Program Directors, Washington, D.C.

Feeley, M.M., & Simon, J. (1992). The new penology: Notes on the emerging strategy of corrections and its implications. *Criminology* 30, pp. 449–474.

Fein, R.A., & Vossekuil, B. (1998). Protective intelligence and threat assessment investigations: A guide for state and local law enforcement officials. Office of Justice Programs. National Institute of Justice. Washington, DC: U.S. Department of Justice.

Fein, R.A., & Vossekuil, B. (1999). Assassination in the United States: An operational study of recent assassins, attackers, and near-lethal approachers. *Journal of Forensic Sciences* 44(2), pp. 321–333.

Fellner, J. (2006). A corrections quandary: Mental illness and prison rules. *Harvard Civil Rights-Civil Liberties Law Review* 41, pp. 391–412.

Fisher, W.H. (2003). *Community based interventions for criminal offenders with severe mental illness* . Oxford, England: Elsevier, Ltd.

Fisher, W.H., Barreira, P.J., Geller, J.L., White, A.W., Lincoln, A.K., & Sudders, M. (2001). Long-stay patients in state psychiatric hospitals at the end of the 20th century. *Psychiatric Services* 52(8), pp. 1051–1056.

Frankle, W.G., Shera, D., Berger-Hershkowitz, H., Evins, A. E., Connolly, C., Goff, D. C., et al. (2001). Clozapine-associated reduction in arrest rates of psychotic patients with criminal histories. *American Journal of Psychiatry* 158, pp. 270–274.

Friedman, R.A. (2006) Violence and mental illness—*How strong is the link? New England Journal of Medicine*, 355, pp. 2064–66.

GAINS/SAMHSA (2005, Summer). Fact Sheet: The prevalence of co-occurring mental illness and substance use disorders in jails. Delmar, New York: GAINS Center.

GAINS/SAMHSA (2002). Fact Sheet: Maintaining Medicaid benefits for jail detainees with co-occurring mental health and substance use disorders. Delmar, New York: GAINS Center.

Geller, J. L. (2002). Not a joking matter: In reply. *Psychiatric Services, 53*(3), 346.

Gilligan, J. (2001) The Last Mental Hospital. *Psychiatric Quarterly* 72(1), pp. 45–77.

Goffman, E. (1968). Asylums: Essays on the social situation of mental patients and other inmates. (Harmondsworth: Penguin, 1968)

Goldkamp, J. S., & Irons-Guynn, C. (2000). *Emerging judicial strategies for the mentally ill in the criminal caseload: Mental health courts in Fort Lauderdale, Seattle, San Bernardino, and Anchorage.* Washington, DC: U.S. Department of Justice, Office of Justice Programs, Bureau of Justice Assistance.

Goldman, H. H., Adams, N. H., & Taube, C. A. (1983). Deinstitutionalization: The data demythologized. *Psychiatric Services* 34, pp. 129–134.

Greenberg, W. M., Shah, P. J., & Seide, M. (1993). Recidivism on an acute psychiatric forensic service. *Hospital and Community Psychiatry* 44(6), pp. 583–585.

Grob, G. N. (2000). Mental health policy in 20th-century America in *Mental Health, United States.* Substance Abuse and Mental Health Services Administration, U.S. Department of Health and Human Services. Retrieved from the World Wide Web on June 2, 2007: http://mentalhealth.samhsa.gov/publications/allpubs/SMA01-3537/chapter2.asp.

Gudrais, E. (2006, July 27). New Medicaid law on generic drugs draws criticism. The Providence Journal. Retrieved May 16, 2007 from the World Wide Web: http://www.projo.com/news/content/projo_20060727_drugs24.3541833.html.

Hauser, C. (2007, April 17). Virginia gunman identified as a student. *The New York Times.* Retrieved from the World Wide Web on May 5, 2008: http://www.nytimes.com/2007/04/17/us/17virginia.html?_r=1&pagewanted=print&oref=slogin.

Hiday, V. A., Swartz, M. S., Swanson, J. W., Borum, R., & Wagner, H. R. (1999). Criminal victimization of persons with severe mental illness. *Psychiatric Services* 50(1), pp. 62–68.

Hogan, M. F. (2000, September 21). *Testimony before the Subcommittee on Crime of the Committee on the Judiciary, U.S. House of Representatives.* Retrieved May 18, 2002 from www.house.gov/judiciary/hoga0921.htm.

Hogan, M. F. (1995). Letters: Deinstitutionalization. *Psychiatric Services* 46(10), pp. 1078–1079.

Homeless Veterans (2007). NCH Fact Sheet # 14. National Coalition for the Homeless. Washington, DC. Retrieved from the World Wide Web on February 4, 2008: http://www.nationalhomeless.org/publications/facts/veterans.pdf.

Honberg, R.S. (2007, May 10). Federal gun reporting requirements and their application to people with mental illness. *Testimony before the Domestic Policy Subcommittee of the House Oversight and Government Reform Committee,* received via personal communication.

Human Rights Watch. (2003). U.S. prisons and offenders with mental illness. New York. Retrieved from the World Wide Web on June 9, 2007: http://www.hrw.org/reports/2003/usa1003/3.htm#_Toc51489447

Isaac, R. J., & Armat, V. C. (1990). *Madness in the Streets: How Psychiatry and the Law Abandoned the Mentally Ill.* New York: Macmillan, Free Press.

James, D. and Glaze, L. (2006). Mental Health Problems of Prison and Jail Inmates. Bureau of Justice Statistics, U.S. Department of Justice, Washington, DC.

Jordan, P. (2002). Jailing people with mental illness. Retrieved from the World Wide Web on April 30, 2008: http://www.wpas-rights.org/Envoy%20Archives/jailing_people_with_medical_illness.htm.

Kane, C. F. (1995). Deinstitutionalization and managed care: deja vu? *Psychiatric Services* 46, pp. 883–884.

Kaye, N., (2005, June). Medicaid managed care: Looking forward, looking back. National Academy for State Health Policy. The Association of Community Affiliated Plans. Retrieved from the World Wide Web on May 22, 2007:http://209.85.165.104/search?q=cache:gRclmiesA58J:www.nashp.org/Files/mmc_guide_final_draft_6–16.pdf+managed+care+and+medicaid&hl=en&ct=clnk&cd=3&gl=us.

Kerle, K. E. (1998). *American jails: Looking to the future.* Boston: Butterworth-Heinemann.

Kondo, L. L. (2000). Therapeutic jurisprudence: Issues, analysis and applications: Advocacy of the establishment of mental health specialty courts in the provision of therapeutic justice for mentally ill offenders. *Seattle University Law Review* 24, pp. 373–464.

Koyanagi, C. (2006). Economic grand rounds: The deficit reduction act: Should we love it or hate it? *Psychiatric Services* 57(12), pp. 1711–1712.

Koyanagi, C. (2002, June 20). Jailing people with mental illness: Senate panel holds hearings on the "criminalization of mental illness" by Phil Jordan. Retrieved from the World Wide Web on June 4, 2007: http://www.wpas-rights.org/Envoy_Online/Envoy%20Archives/jailing_people_with_mental_illness.htm.

Lamb, H. R., & Weinberger, L. E. (1998). Persons with severe mental illness in jails and prisons: A review. *Psychiatric Services* 49(4), pp. 483–492.

Lamb, H. R., & Bachrach, L. L. (2001). Some perspectives on deinstitutionalization. *Psychiatric Services* 52(8), pp. 1039–1045.

Lamb H. R., & Shaner, R. (1993). When there are almost no state hospitals left. *Hospital and Community Psychiatry* 44(10), pp. 973–976.

Lamb, H. R., & Weinberger, L. E. (2005). The shift of psychiatric inpatient care from hospitals to jails and prisons. *Journal of the American Academy of Psychiatry and the Law* 33, pp. 529–534.

Lamb, H. R., Weinberger, L. E., & Gross, B. H. (2004). Mentally ill persons in the criminal justice system: Some perspectives. *Psychiatric Quarterly* 75(2), pp. 107–126.

Lamb, H. R., Weinberger, L. E., Marsh, J. S., & Gross, B. H. (2007). Treatment prospects for persons with mental illness in an urban county jail. *Psychiatric Services* 58, pp. 782–786.

Lee-Griffin, P. A. (2001). The criminalization of individuals suffering from symptoms of mental illness: An exploratory study. *Dissertation Abstracts International: Section B: The Sciences & Engineering* 62(1-B), pp. 156.

Leiby, R. (2005, June 25). A couch Tom Cruise won't jump on: Actor lambastes psychiatry on 'Today.' *Washington Post*, p. C01.

Leifman, S. (2001, August 16). Mentally ill and in jail. *Washington Post*, p. A25.

Lerma, A. (2005, March 28). The secret life of Beck Hansen—A guide for the professional journalist. Retrieved from the World Wide Web on June 2, 2007: http://www.lermanet.com/beck/.

Lerner-Wren, G. (2000). Broward's mental health court: An innovative approach to the mentally disabled in the criminal justice system. *Community Mental Health Report* 1(1), 5–6, 16.

Levin, A. (2005). When mental illness makes news, facts often missing in action. *Psychiatric News* 40(12), p. 18.

Levine, S. (2006, February 6). Stability of mentally ill shaken by Medicare drug plan problems. *Washington Post*, p. A01.

Lowman, J. and Menzies, R. (1986). Out of the fiscal shadow: Carceral trends in Canada and the United States, *Crime and Social Justice* 26, pp. 95–115.

Lurigio, A. J., & Swartz, J. A. (2000). *Changing the contours of the criminal justice system to meet the needs of persons with serious mental illness.* Washington, DC: National Institute of Justice.

Ma, K. (2006, December 28). Daytona chief: Bus homeless out of city. *Orlando Sentinel.* Retrieved from the World Wide Web on June 6, 2007: http://lists.co.alachua.fl.us/cgi-bin/wa.exe?A2=ind0612e&L=rodney-j-long&P=660

Malbran, P. (2008, April 25). Despite e-mails, A boss denies cover up. *CBS News.* Retrieved from the World Wide Web on April 26, 2008: http//www.cbsnews.com/stories/2008/04/25/cbsnews_investigates/printable40443999.shtml.

Markowitz, F.E. (2006). Psychiatric hospital capacity, homelessness, and crime and arrest rates. *Criminology* 44(1), pp. 45–72.

McCampbell, S.W. (2001). Mental health courts: What sheriffs need to know. *Sheriff,* 53(2), pp. 40–43.

McClam, E. (2008, January 20). New generation of homeless vets emerges. Washingtonpost.com. Retrieved from the World Wide Web on January 28, 2008: http://www.washingtonpost.com/wp-dyn/content/article/2008/01/20/AR2008012000568_p.

McGuire, J. F., & Rosenheck, R. A. (2004). Criminal history as a prognostic indicator in the treatment of homeless people with severe mental illness. *Psychiatric Services* 55, pp. 42–48.

McQuistion, H. L., Finnerty, M., Hirschowitz, J., & Susser, E. S. (2003). Challenges for psychiatry in serving homeless people with psychiatric disorders. *Psychiatric Services* 54, pp. 669–676.

Messner, S. F., & Rosenfeld, R. (2007). *Crime and the American dream,* 4th ed., Belmont, CA: Thomson Wadsworth.

Miller, R. D. (1997). Symposium on coercion: An interdisciplinary examination of coercion, exploitation, and the law: III. Coerced confinement and treatment: The continuum of coercion: Constitutional and clinical considerations in the treatment of mentally disordered persons. *Denver University Law Review* 74, pp. 1169–1214.

Miller, R. D. (1992). Economic factors leading to diversion of the mentally disordered from the civil to the criminal commitment systems. *International Journal of Law and Psychiatry* 15, pp. 1–12.

Morrissey, J. P., Dalton, K. M., Steadman, H. J., Cuddeback, G. S., Haynes, D., & Cuellar, A. (2006a). Assessing gaps between policy and practice in

Medicaid disenrollment of jail detainees with severe mental illness. *Psychiatric Services* 57(6), pp. 803–808.

Morrissey, J., Steadman, H. J., Dalton , K. M., Cuellar, A., Stiles, P. & Cuddeback, G. S. (2006b). Medicaid enrollment and mental health service use following release of jail detainees with severe mental illness. *Psychiatric Services* 57(6), pp. 809–815.

Mojtabai, R. (2007). Americans' attitudes toward mental health treatment seeking: 1990–2003. *Psychiatric Services* 58, pp. 642–651.

Mowbray, C. T., Grazier, K. L., & Holter, M. (2002). Managed behavioral health care in the public sector: Will it become the third shame of the states? *Psychiatric Services* 53(2), pp. 157–170.

NAMI (2006). *Grading the States: A Report on America's Health Care System for Serious Mental Illness.* The National Alliance on Mental Illness. Arlington, Virginia.

NAMI (2005, January). Medicaid funding of mental illness treatment. The National Alliance on Mental Illness. Arlington, Virginia. Retrieved from the World Wide Web on May 22, 2007: http://www.nami.org/Template.cfm?Section=Issue_Spotlights&template=/ContentManagement/ContentDisplay.cfm&ContentID=43405.

New York State Office of Mental Health (2006, January 20). Medication: What types of antipsychotic medications are there? Retrieved from the World Wide Web on May 25, 2007 from: http://www.omh.state.ny.us/omh-web/ebp/adult_medication.htm#Healthcenterwebsite.

Neubauer, D. W. (1992). *America's courts and the criminal justice system.* Pacific Grove, California: Brooks/Cole Publishing Company.

O'Connnor v. Donaldson, 422 U.S. 563(1975).

Osher, F., Steadman, H. J., & Barr, H. (2003). A best practice approach to community reentry from jails for inmates with co-occurring disorders: The APIC model. *Crime & Delinquency* 49(1), pp. 79–96.

Panzer, P. G., Broner, N., & McQuistion, H. L. (2001). Mentally ill populations in jails and prisons: A misuse of resources. *Psychiatric Quarterly,* 72(1), 41–43.

Perez, A., Leifman, S., & Estrada, A. (2003). Reversing the criminalization of mental illness. *Crime & Delinquency* 49(1), pp. 62–78.

Perlick, D. A., & Rosenheck, R. R. (2002). Stigma and violence: In reply. *Psychiatric Services* 53(9), p. 1179.

Peters, R. H., & Hill, H. A. (1997, December). Intervention strategies for offenders with co-occurring disorders: What works? University of South Florida in conjunction with the GAINS Center: Delmar, New York.

President's New Freedom Commission on Mental Health (2003) *Achieving the Promise: Transforming Mental Health Care in America. Final Report.* DHHS Pub. No. SMA-03-3832. Rockville, MD.

Priest, D. (2008, January 31). Soldier suicides at record level. *Washington Post*, A01.

Raghunathan, A. (2007, February 2). Homeless fight back with high tech. *St. Petersburg Times*, Retrieved from the World Wide Web on June 6, 2007: http://www.sptimes.com/2007/02/02/Southpinellas/Homeless_fight_back_w.sh tml.

Raphael, S. (2000, September). The deinstitutionalization of the mentally ill and growth in the U.S. prison populations 1971 to 1996. *Working Papers*. Retrieved May 16, 2007 from the World Wide Web: http://socrates. berkeley.edu/~raphael/raphael2000.pdf.

Rissmiller, D. J., & Rissmiller, J. H. (2006). Evolution of the antipsychiatry movement into mental health consumerism. *Psychiatric Services, 57*(6), 863–866.

Rothman, D. J. (1971). *The discovery of the asylum: Social order and disorder in the new republic.* Boston: Little Brown.

SAMHSA, Substance Abuse and Mental Health Services Administration, (1996, December). Community Support: An Overview of Evaluations of the Massachusetts Medicaid Managed Behavioral Health Care Program U.S. Department of Health and Human Services, Washington DC, Retrieved from the World Wide Web on May 22, 2007: http://mentalhealth. samhsa.gov/ cmhs/communitysupport/research/publications/pn23ch7.asp.

Savodnik, I. (2006, January 1). Psychiatry's sick compulsion: turning weaknesses into diseases. *Los Angeles Times*, Retrieved from the World Wide Web on June 6, 2007: http://www.latimes.com/news/opinion/sunday/editorials/la-op-psych1jan01,0,1868753.story?coll=la-home-sunday-opinion

Sharfstein, S. . (2000). Whatever happened to community mental health? *Psychiatric Services* 51(50), pp. 616–620.

Sharockman, A. (2007, February 1). St. Pete unveils plan to help the homeless. *The Ledger*, Lakeland, Florida. Retrieved from the World Wide Web on June 6, 2007: http://www.theledger.com/apps/pbcs.dll/article?AID=/ 20070201/NEWS/702010447/1004.

Sigurdson, C. (2000). The mad, the bad and the abandoned: The mentally ill in prisons an jails. *Corrections Today*, 62(7), pp. 70–78.

Slate, R. N. (2005, April 12). Medicaid Reform, Preferred Drug Lists, and Allowing Open Access to Psychotropic Medications. *Testimony before the Florida Senate Committee on Health Care*, Tallahassee, Florida.

Sodaro, E. R., & Ball, J. (1999, January) Neglected adolescent mental Illness: Managed care at its worst. Coalition Report. The national coalition of mental health professionals and consumers. Retrieved May 22, 2007 from the World Wide Web: http://www.thenationalcoalition.org/neglect.html.

Solomon, P., & Draine, J. (1995a). Issues in serving the forensic client." Social Work 40(1), pp. 25–33.

Solomon, P., & Draine, J. (1995b). Jail recidivism in a forensic case management program. Health and Social Work 20(3), pp. 167–173.

Sosowsky, L. (1978). Crime and violence among mental patients reconsidered in view of the new legal relationship between the state and the mentally ill. American Journal of Psychiatry 135(1), pp. 33–42.

Spitzer, S. (1976). Toward a Marxian Theory of Deviance. Social Problems 22: 638–651.

Stanley, J. (2004). Stigma and public education about mental illness: To the editor. Psychiatric Services 55(7), pp. 833–834.

Stone, T. H. (1997). Therapeutic implications of incarceration for persons with severe mental disorders: Searching for rational health policy. American Journal of Criminal Law 24, pp. 283–358.

Stritof, S., & Stritof, B. (2007). Tom Cruise and Katie Holmes marriage profile. Retrieved from the World Wide Web on June 6, 2007: http://marriage.about.com/od/entertainmen1/p/tomcruise.htm.

Stuart, H. L., & Arboleda-Florez, J. E. (2001). A public health perspective on violent offenses among persons with mental illness. Psychiatric Services 52, pp. 654-659.

Swanson, J., Estroff, S., Swartz, M., Borum R., Lachiotte, W., Zimmer, C., et al. (1997). Violence and severe mental disorder in clinical and community populations: The effects of psychotic symptoms, comorbidity, and lack of treatment. Psychiatry 60, pp. 1–22.

Swanson, J. W., Swartz, M. S., Van Dorn, R. A., Elbogen, E. B., Study of violent behavior in persons with schizophrenia. Archives of General Psychiatry 63, pp. 490–499.

Szmukler, G. (2000). Homicide enquiries: what sense do they make? Psychiatric Bulletin 24, pp. 6–10

Teplin, L. A. (1984). Criminalizing mental disorder: The comparative arrest rate of the mentally ill. American Psychologist 39, pp. 794–803.

Teplin, L., Abram, K., & McClelland, G. M. (1997). Mentally disordered women in jail: Who receives services? American Journal of Public Health 87(4), pp. 604–609.

Teplin, L. A., McClelland, G. M., Abram, K. M., & Weiner, D. A. (2005). Crime victimization in adults with severe mental illness: Comparison with the national crime victimization survey. *Archives of General Psychiatry* 62, pp. 911–921.

Thomas, E. (2007, April 30). Making of a massacre: Quiet and disturbed, Cho Seung-Hui seethed, then exploded. His odyssey. Newsweek. Retrieved from the World Wide Web on May 15, 2007: http://en.wikipedia.org/wiki/Seung-Hui_Cho.

Torrey, F. T. (1997). *Out of the shadows: Confronting America's mental illness crisis.* New York: John Wiley & Sons, Inc.

Torrey, F. T. (2002). Stigma and violence. *Psychiatric Services*, 53(9), p. 1179.

Transforming Florida's Mental Health System (2007). Constructing a Comprehensive and Competent Criminal Justice System/Mental Health/Substance Abuse Treatment System: Strategies for Planning, Leadership, Financing, and Service Development. Florida Supreme Court. Retrieved from the World Wide Web on January 30, 2008: http://www.floridasupreme-court.org/pub_info/documents/11-14-2007_Mental_Health_Report.pdf.

Trudel, J. F., & Lesage, A. (2006). Care of patients with the most severe and persistent mental illness in an area without a psychiatric hospital. *Psychiatric Services*, 57(12), 1765–1770.

Tuchman, G. (2007, May 14). Report on CNN Anderson Cooper 360. Retrieved from the World Wide Web on June 6, 2007 http://transcripts. cnn.com/TRANSCRIPTS/0705/14/acd.01.html.

U.S. Department of Health and Human Services (1999). *Mental health: A report of the surgeon general.* Rockville, MD: U.S. Department of Health and Human Services, Substance Abuse and Mental Health Services Administration, Center for Mental Health Services, National Institute of Health, National Institute of Mental Health.

United States Secret Service (2006). National threat assessment center. Washington, DC: United States Secret Service. Retrieved from the World Wide Web on June 14, 2007: http://www.secretservice.gov/ntac.shtml.

Veysey, B. M., Steadman, H. J., Morrissey, J. P., & Johnsen, M. (1997). In search of the missing linkages: Continuity of care in U.S. jails. *Behavioral Science Law* 15, pp. 383–397.

Violence and Mental Illness: The Facts (2007). Open Minds Open Doors Fact Sheet. Mental Health Association in Pennsylvania, Harrisburg, PA. Retrieved from the World Wide Web on June 4, 2007: http://www.open-mindsopendoors.com/documents/FACTSHEETViolenceMyth_000.doc.

Vine, P. (2001, May/June). Mindless and deadly: Media hype on mental illness and violence. Retrieved from the World Wide Web on June 4, 2007: http://www.narpa.org/media.hype.htm.

Vold, G. B., Bernard, T. J., & Snipes, J. B. (1998). *Theoretical criminology, 4th ed.* New York: Oxford University Press.

Wahl, O. F. (2003). Media madness: Public images of mental illness. New Brunswick, NJ: Rutgers University Press.

Walsh, J., & Bricourt, J. (1997). Services for persons with mental illness in jail: Implications for family involvement. *Families in Society: The Journal of Contemporary Human Services* (Jul.–Aug.), pp. 420–428.

Walsh, J., & Holt, D. (1999). Jail diversion for people with psychiatric disabilities: The sheriffs' perspective. *Psychiatric Rehabilitation Journal* 23(2), pp. 153–160.

Walker, S. (2006). Sense and nonsense about crime and drugs: A policy guide, 6th ed. Belmont, CA: Wadsworth.

Ward, M. J. (1946). *The snake pit.* New York: Random House.

Watson, A., Hanrahan, P., Luchins, D., & Lurigio, A. (2001). Mental health courts and the complex issue of mentally ill offenders. *Psychiatric Services* 52(4), pp. 477–481.

Welch, W. M. (2008). Trauma of Iraq war haunting thousands returning home. *USA Today.* Retrieved from the World Wide Web on February 3, 2008: http://usatoday.printthis.clickability.com/pt/cpt?action=cpt&title=USATO-DAY.com+-+Trauma+of+Iraq+war+haunting+thousands+returning+home&expire=&urlID=13378250&fb=Y&url=http%3A%2F%2Fwww.usatoday.com%2Fnews%2Fworld%2Firaq%2F2005-02-28-cover-iraq-injuries_x.htm&partnerID=1660.

Welch, M. (2004). *Corrections: A critical approach, 2nd ed.* New York: McGraw-Hill.

White, Jr., R. W. (1995). Mental patients' rights should be limited. In W. Barbour (Ed.), *Mental illness: Opposing viewpoints* (195–203). San Diego, CA: Greenhaven Press.

Williams, R., & Morrison, S. (2007, April 26). Police: No motive found. The Roanoke Times. Retrieved from the World Wide Web on May 6, 2008: http://www.roanoke.com/vtshootingaccounts/wb/114655.

Wilson, A. B., & Draine, J. (2006). Collaborations between criminal justice and mental health systems for prisoner reentry. *Psychiatric Services* 57(6), pp. 875–878.

Wyatt v. Stickney, 325 F. Supp. 781 (M.D. Ala. 1971), 334 F. Supp. 1341. (1971), 344 F. Supp. 373, and 344 F. Supp. 385 (1972); see also, *Wyatt v. Ader-holt*, 503 F. 2d 1305 (1974).

CHAPTER 4

THE LAW ENFORCEMENT RESPONSE TO PERSONS WITH MENTAL ILLNESSES IN CRISES

"Mental illness is not a ... choice; it is a medical disease."

—Greenberg, 2001, p. 43

Law enforcement officers are accustomed to issuing directives and gaining compliance to their commands, often with a good guys versus bad guys mindset, equipped with techniques to ratchet up a situation or encounter with enough force necessary to gain the cooperation of reluctant, recalcitrant, or defiant suspects. However, what happens when subjects are not compliant with officers' demands, not because they are bad guys, in a desperate situation to elude capture, with a disdain and lack of respect for authority, but because they are ill, confused, and unable to comport their behavior to the officer's and society's expectations?

We all come to each encounter as a culmination of our past experiences, which serve to influence our expectations about how to resolve problems that we are confronted with on a daily basis. Unfortunately, the traditional tactics, i.e., to quell disturbances and subdue bad guys may serve to escalate police encounters with persons with mental illnesses, sometimes resulting in tragedy.[1]

---

1. For example, see the "Preventable Tragedies" database maintained by the Treatment Advocacy Center in Arlington, Virginia at: http://www.treatmentadvocacycenter.org/ep.asp. Certainly included within these tragedies are what has been referred to as "suicide by cop" (sbc) or "victim-precipitated homicide" (vph). Mental illnesses can be a contributor to sbc or vbh; Lord (2004) offers definitions of sbc, " 'Incidents in which individuals bent on self-destruction, engage in life-threatening and criminal behavior to force the police to kill them," (p. 4) and vph, " 'the suicidal person confronting an assailant, with a real or perceived lethal weapon, forcing the assailant to respond with deadly force' " (p. 5)—in Lord,

Furthermore, the implementation of specialized police training in handling encounters with persons with mental illnesses has often been precipitated by nearly tragic or deadly events.[2] Even so, contrary to media sensationalism, as previously discussed, most persons with mental illnesses are not violent individuals. Unfortunately, as discussed in Chapter 1, it often seems to take crises to influence policy within the criminal justice system.

V.B. (2004). Suicide by cop: Inducing officers to shoot. Flushing, New York: Looseleaf Law Publications.

2. Louise Pyers founded the Connecticut Alliance to Benefit Law Enforcement (CABLE) after her son, in a suicide by cop encounter, was shot in the abdomen. Thankfully, her son lived, and the officer who shot him was not permanently traumatized. CABLE is a grassroots organization comprised of mental health providers, police professionals and family members. CABLE coordinates and provides all crisis intervention trainaing (CIT) training in the state in partnership with the National Alliance on Mental Illness (NAMI), and Louise's son has participated in some of the trainings (L.C. Pyers, personal communication, June 24, 2006). CIT was implemented in 1988 following a police shooting of a person with mental illness (Cochran, 2004; Dupont & Cochran, 2000); Two incidents, one resulting in death of a person with mental illness and another that took too long to resolve and inconvenienced the citizenry which would have preferred a quicker resolution by police, led to the establishment of CIT in Seattle based on the Memphis model (Jamieson & Wilson, 2000); The Louisville Metropolitan Police Department implemented CIT training after officers were involved in the fatal shooting of a man with mental illness (D. Spratt, personal communication, May 8, 2007), as did the Polk County Sheriff's Office in Bartow, Florida (B. Garrett, personal communication, June 8, 2007), and a modified version of CIT was implemented at the St. Petersburg Police Department, in St. Petersburg, Florida, after an officer shot a man with mental illness in 1997 (T. Rolón, personal communication, February 22, 2007). NAMI Board Member Dave Lushbaugh (personal communication, June 19, 2007) indicates what could have been a tragic encounter with a loved one of his and the police has led to CIT training in Georgia and the support of Director Vernon M. Keenan of the Georgia Bureau of Investigation. Joyce Wilde, CIT Program Administrator, of the Ventura County Sheriff's Office informs us that: In the summer of 1997, Camarillo State Hospital closed its doors. The state hospital was a fixture in Ventura County, California, for decades—serving thousands of severely mentally ill individuals. Ventura County is a beach community; over time, many of the individuals from the State Hospital were released to the community and continued to live in the local area. In 1998, Ventura County law enforcement experienced seven lethal use-of-force incidents; five of the individuals were considered mentally ill. Local law enforcement experienced another higher than usual lethal use-of-force year in 2001, with seven incidents; four of the individuals were considered mentally ill. In 2001, Ventura Police Department (VPD) began to research a way to increase safe encounters with emotionally disturbed individuals. In December 2001, the first 40-hour CIT Academy was conducted in Ventura County and includes countywide training for five police agencies and a sheriff's department. (J. Wilde, J. Frank, & M. Zabarsky, personal communication, May 1, 2007).

After crises sometimes agencies rush to quell community disruption by implementing agency wide training programs, however, that may not sufficiently address the problem (Bunch, 2005). Jim Fyfe, former director of training for the New York City Police Department stated, "[A]ll officers can be trained in a couple of days to follow some basic rules: To initially keep a safe distance away and clear away bystanders; to designate one officer as the 'talker' and for the other police on the scene to 'shut up and listen;' and— most importantly— to take as much time as necessary, even it runs into hours or days" (Bunch, 2005, p. 1).

Of course, the resolution of a law enforcement encounter with a person with mental illness in crisis can vary from agency to agency, individual to individual, and situation to situation. Less experienced officers, for example, have been found to be more likely to make an arrest than more seasoned officers (Watson & Angell, 2007). This may be because they lack awareness of other alternatives and aren't hardened enough to simply walk away without taking action. Also, compliance is more likely obtained and escalation least likely to occur when one officer is dispatched to the scene of a person with mental illness in crisis, perhaps due to being more careful and attentive to detail when encountering a person with mental illness in crisis without back up; in fact, injuries to officers and persons with mental illnesses are more likely to occur when two or more officers are on the scene as opposed to one (Watson & Angell, 2007). Fear from both sides can certainly be a factor in this equation, especially for the person who is to be brought under control, and can contribute to the potential escalation of violence (Ruiz & Miller, 2004; Watson, Corrigan, & Ottati, 2004).

The public nature of an event may often serve to influence officer discretion (Cooper, McLearen, & Zapf, 2004). Patch and Arrigo (1999) note that when calls to such crises are made by the citizenry officers feel less leeway in their decision making ability and will often proceed with an arrest. Thus, the more public an event, the more likely an arrest will follow in a law enforcement officer's encounter with a person with mental illness.[3] With the public's influence on the behavior of police officers in mind, the need for public education and de-stigmatization regarding mental illness is of paramount concern. A

---

3. Officers are apparently highly concerned about negative publicity, as Slate, Johnson & Colbert (2007) recently found in a study that the number one stressor for law enforcement officers is concern about negative press accounts of police actions (Slate, R.N., Johnson, W.W., & Colbert, S. Police stress: A structural model, *Journal of Police and Criminal Psychology* 22, pp. 102–112.

community generally receives the type of law enforcement it desires (Wilson, 1978), even if those desires are misguided. A misinformed public can in turn influence self-serving and self-aggrandizing policymakers to enact misguided policies.

Police Encounters with and Perceptions of Persons with Mental Illnesses

"Mental illness is not a ... choice; it is a medical disease" (Greenberg, 2001, p. 43). As noted by Cordner (2006), there is a tendency to blame persons with mental illnesses for their behavior. However, as discussed in the previous chapter on criminalization, there are a myriad of factors that serve to make the behavior of persons with mental illnesses not truly volitional.[4] Lamb, Weinberger, and DeCuir (2002) maintain that inadequate training of law enforcement officers can contribute to the criminalization of persons with mental illnesses. Many officers have difficulty in recognizing the signs and symptoms of mental illnesses, as, without proper training, they are essentially laypersons (Lamb, Weinberger, & Gross, 2004). Unless officers have experienced interactions with family members or friends with mental illnesses and/or equipped with ade-

---

4. An example provided by Lt. Brian Garrett (personal communication, June 8, 2007), of the Polk County Sheriff's Office in Bartow, Florida, is illustrative of an individual not freely choosing mental illness: "A CIT deputy who finished training less than two weeks before responds to a call of a woman hearing voices from under her front porch. Upon arrival he makes contact with the woman who has previously been diagnosed with schizophrenia but is not currently taking her medications because she cannot afford them. She recognizes she is in crisis and is worried about her two young children because she has no local support system. The CIT deputy involuntarily commits her for mental health stabilization and is forced to place the children in the custody of the state child welfare agency because there are no family members or friends available to care for them. The CIT deputy later re-contacted her to determine her wellbeing and learns she is still not medicine compliant because she was released from the mental health treatment facility with a prescription for her medicine that she could not afford and still be able to care for her two children. She was even further depressed after having to battle the welfare agency to get her children back home The deputy then spent most of his next day off researching sources for low or no cost medicines for indigent persons in need. He was able to find a local pharmacy participating in the program and then paid for the two prescriptions out of his own pocket and delivered them to the subject who willingly accepted them. She stayed medicine compliant and had no further involuntary commitments until she moved from our service area due to her transitory nature. She has since been committed several times for not being medicine compliant."

quate specialized training for such encounters such escalations can result in unnecessary injury and even death to both persons with mental illnesses and officers. According to Borum (2000), encounters with persons with mental illnesses are more likely to escalate to uses of force when officers' stress levels are heightened, when officers lack training and self-confidence and are unable to control the situation; situations are least likely to escalate to uses of force when officers are able to communicate and utilize negotiation skills, maintain a positive attitude and employ anger management skills.

Citizens rarely kill police officers, and "[l]ess than 1/20 of one percent of all police-citizen encounters result in a fatal shooting by a police officer" (Borum, 2000, p. 334). However, when a fatal shooting does happen and it involves a person with mental illness heightened scrutiny and sensationalism occur. In actuality, persons with mental illnesses are more likely to be harmed by the police than are the police to be injured by persons with mental illnesses, with persons with mental illnesses four times more likely to be killed by the police (Cordner, 2006).

Previous research has reported that on average officers have six encounters per month with a person with mental illness in crisis, and Borum, Deane, Steadman, and Morrissey (1998) found 92 percent of officers in their study had encountered a person with mental illness in crisis in the past month, with 84 percent having had more than one such encounter in the past month. Cooper et al. (2004) reported that arrest rates did not differ on the basis of race when encounters with persons with mental illnesses transpired, but officers were more likely to civilly commit whites for treatment rather than blacks.

The police generally do not have negative views of persons with mental illnesses (Watson & Angell, 2007); the police have actually been found to be more empathetic toward persons with mental illnesses than the general public (Price, 2005). Panzarella and Alicea (1997), in a study of Special Weapons and Tactics (SWAT) team members in a large metropolitan police department, did find that officers stereotypically believed that it was not possible to have a meaningful conversation with a mentally disturbed person. As noted by Ruiz and Miller (2004), the two most common misperceptions held by the police about persons with mental illnesses are that they are all incapable of reasoning and violent. Of course, having preconceived notions about someone being violent increases the likelihood that more aggressive approaches will be taken by law enforcement when encounters with persons with mental illnesses in crises occur and increases the potential for ratcheting up a situation. What is needed is education and training to increase opportunities for officer interactions with persons with mental illnesses in an attempt to debunk stereotypes and seek positive solutions.

Police Training and Preparedness for Dealing with Persons with Mental Illnesses in Crises

The police are often the first responders when dealing with persons with mental illnesses in crises and serve as gatekeepers[5] to either the mental health or the criminal justice system, a role they are typically neither trained for or prepared to deliver (Borum et al., 1998; Lamb et al., 2002; Lamb et al., 2004; Panzarella & Alicea, 1997; Patch & Arrigo, 1999; Price, 2005; Vermette, Pinals, & Appelbaum, 2005). In a survey of Massachusetts law enforcement officers, Vermette et al. (2005) found ninety percent of respondents indicated that training on the topic of mental illness was either fairly or very important to their jobs, yet Ruiz and Miller (2004) and Cooper et al. (2004) report that a common theme among officers is that they do not feel properly trained or qualified when dispatched to crisis calls involving persons with mental illnesses.

In a 1975 literature review, Teese and Wormer (1975) found no references to mental health consultation with the police. Lamb et al. (2004) indicate that some level of training regarding interactions with persons with mental illnesses in crises is needed for all sworn law enforcement officers, not just for those officers assigned to specialized response teams or units. They maintain that types of training topics recommended for all officers includes recognition of mental illness, how to handle and de-escalate violence, identification of suicide warning signs and handling of suicidal persons, when to bring in a specialized response team, available community resources and how to access them, who to divert to the mental health system and who to process through the criminal justice system.

In a study of the training curricula of twenty eight police academies around the country, Greenberg (2001) reports that the average amount of time dedicated to police interactions with persons with mental illnesses is four hours, with only one agency providing up to 28 hours. Hails and Borum (2003) indicate that today almost all officers receive some training related to mental health crises but the breadth and extent of that training remains largely narrow and limited in focus. Such training may even be limited to the civil commitment process.

Most law enforcement agencies do not provide specialized training for officers on how to deal with and process mental health crises or have a formal-

---

5. In this role as gatekeeper in dealing with persons with mental illnesses, the police have been referred to as "amateur social workers," "forensic gatekeepers," "psychiatric medics" and "streetcorner psychiatrists" (see Green, 1997; Sellers, Sullivan, Veysey, & Shane, 2005; Teplin, 2000).

ized policy for doing so (Greenberg, 2001; Price, 2005). While most departments may not have formal policies governing encounters with persons with mental illnesses in crises, Sergeant Kendall Wiley (personal communication, May 21, 2007) of the Las Vegas Metropolitan Police Department shares pertinent sections of her agency's policy.

Las Vegas Metropolitan Police Department CIT Policy

6/005.01 CRISIS INTERVENTION TEAM (C.I.T.); A.S. 41.2.7, 46.2.1

It is the policy of this department to handle incidents involving the mentally ill and those in crisis with care and expertise, ensuring that such persons receive a response which is appropriate to the needs of the individual involved. The diversion of certain persons away from the criminal justice system and toward treatment, whenever available and appropriate, is a desirable option. Whenever possible, patrol officers with specialized skills will be dispatched to provide direction and guidance during the initial patrol response to events involving persons who are in crisis, showing signs and symptoms of excited delirium (see 6.005.00) or who are believed to be mentally ill (see 5/105.12).

All contacts made by officers who are dealing with persons who may be suffering from mental illness will be thoroughly investigated for adherence to procedures and policies. The results of these contacts as well as other related analyses will be the foundation for updating procedures and training.

General

Crisis Intervention Team (CIT) officers are on-duty, uniformed patrol division officers who perform all normal patrol-related services, including routine response to calls for service. They will be dispatched to certain events involving persons who are known to have a diagnosed mental illness or who are in a volatile emotional crisis. CIT officers are not SWAT officers or hostage/crisis negotiators. CIT Officers are trained to:

- Interact with persons who are mentally ill, in an emotional crisis, (including suicidal persons, subjects experiencing signs and symptoms of excited delirium, Alzheimer/dementia victims when violent and the developmentally disabled)

- De-escalate crisis events and move them away from violent outcomes whenever possible
- Fully utilize the resources/services available for the mentally ill in southern Nevada

During the initial patrol response to an event involving a person believed to be mentally ill or who is experiencing a volatile emotional crisis, the senior CIT officer on the scene has the authority to direct police activities during the event unless relieved by a field supervisor. CIT officers are accountable for actions and outcomes relative to such events. CIT officers will be dispatched to:

- Disturbances involving persons known to have a reported or diagnosed mental illness (including domestic events reported by family members, crimes involving the mentally ill, etc.)
- Events involving persons threatening suicide under violent/volatile circumstances (individual armed and threatening/holding weapon/firearm/other instrument, threatening to jump from life-threatening height, etc.)
- Persons who are experiencing the signs and symptoms of excited delirium [see 6/005.00] (Wiley, 2007).

Communication

Effective communication skills are a key to successfully resolving police encounters with persons who have mental illnesses. Of course, there is verbal communication and nonverbal cues. Mastery of both forms of expression is extremely important to ensure de-escalation of situations as opposed to escalation of encounters. As Curtis (1975) has noted, a lack of verbal skills can be a precursor to violence. When people run out of things to say in a heated confrontation that may be the point at which they are so emotionally balled up that they may resort to a knife, a gun, a bat, or other implement that is handy to express themselves. This can be particularly true when a subject is irrational and paranoid during an encounter with police. Being willing to take the time and being able to establish a rapport with persons who are mentally ill is critical to successful resolutions of police interactions with persons who are mentally ill and in crisis.

The primary role of communication skills in law enforcement work is reflected in the following comments. Lt. Paul Michaud (personal communication, May 6, 2007) of the Fulton County Georgia Police Department in Atlanta observes, "In my training, I talk about the 'Force Continuum,' and we devote a lot of training hours to firearms and defensive tactics. What is the percentage of time that officers discharge their weapons on duty? Please don't get me wrong. It's very important training, but my point is how much time is devoted to the 90% of what we do (officer presence or verbal and non-verbal communication)?"

The first few seconds of a police encounter with a person with mental illness is considered to be the most critical (Reuland, 2004). A sizeable minority of law enforcement officers have a tendency to believe that it is best to resolve mental health calls quickly (Ruiz & Miller, 2004); however, if there is a rush to force compliance early on in an encounter, escalation into violence may very well result. If an officer spends the first few moments talking with the person in crisis, establishing rapport, and utilizing de-escalation skills, the chances of resolving the interaction successfully without violence are greatly improved (Watson & Angell, 2007).

Police Options

According to Rolón (personal communication, February 22, 2007), "some officers do not hold themselves to any standard when it comes to dealing with the mentally ill. They tend to answer the question 'custody or no custody' and then find themselves taking action or removing themselves from the circumstance." Police options when encountering a person with mental illness in crisis include handling the matter informally, making an arrest, civilly committing or involuntarily hospitalizing someone, or doing nothing (Cooper et al., 2004; Sellers, Sullivan, Veysey, & Shane, 2005). Of course, the availability or feasibility of some of these options in particular jurisdictions may often be limited or at least perceived as limited by officers.

Cooper et al. (2004), for example, in a survey of police officers' attitudes regarding the interface of the mental health and criminal justice systems, found the lowest rated item to be the supportiveness of local mental health facilities. Likewise, Husted, Charter, and Perrou (1995) state that the majority of law enforcement agencies report being dissatisfied with their interactions with mental health agency personnel. Borum et al. (1998) and Cooper et al. (2004) indicate that the mental health system is often viewed as unavailable to less than helpful when considered by the police for assistance in resolving conflicts with persons with mental illnesses. Due to the rigidity of time consuming civil commitment requirements and practices, with prior referrals by police to the mental health system viewed as botched and the futility of persons with mental illnesses rapidly re-emerging in the same or worse condition on the street after police referral to mental health clinicians, arrest and utilization of the criminal justice process is often times perceived as a more expedient option than referral to the mental health system (Borum et al., 1998; Borum, Swanson, Swartz, & Hiday, 1997; Dempsey & Forst, 2008; Greenberg, 2001; Panzarella & Alicea, 1997; Price, 2005; Sellers et al., 2005).

The constriction of available mental health options via civil commitment restrictions, among other things, results in service delivery for the mental health system coming from the criminal justice system, as social sanitation is still the rule; it is just easier to unlock the gates to the criminal justice system and herd persons with mental illnesses in. This has prompted some to refer to the criminal justice system as "the system 'that can't say no'" (Lamb et al., 2002, p. 1267).

Arrest may even be perceived as a more beneficial alternative than the mental health system, with law enforcement officers engaging in what are termed mercy bookings (Greenberg, 2001; Lamb et al., 2002; Sargeant, 1992). The use of a mercy booking implies that the officer feels that by getting a person with mental illness booked into jail that individual will at least have basic needs met with the provision of food, shelter, a bed, and the opportunity to bathe. Therein, at least, persons with mental illnesses won't return immediately to the community to cause more unrest, and officers can get on with the crime fighting roles for which they have been trained. Since 1965, the trend has been toward a higher rate of arrest for former mental health patients (Patch & Arrigo, 1999). Bernstein and Seltzer (2003) report that persons with mental illnesses are almost twice as likely to be arrested by police during encounters on the street as opposed to police contacts with persons without mental illnesses; Teplin (2000) in one study found the likelihood of arrest of persons exhibiting signs and symptoms of mental illnesses to be 67% greater than those who did not appear to be mentally ill.

Evidence of law enforcement frustration with the provision or lack thereof of mental health services is seen in the declaration of a police chief in a small town in Florida. Avon Park Chief Frank Mercurio put workers at a crisis stabilization unit (CSU) in Bartow, Florida, on notice that he would arrest them for obstructing justice the next time one of his officers made a medically necessary long haul transport to their CSU facility only to be turned away. Furthermore, providing persons with mental illnesses are accepted for treatment, complaints were registered against mental health personnel due to quick releases from the unit. The mental health provider, on the other hand, maintains that they are handcuffed by budget cuts, and different protocols for handling persons abusing substances versus persons who have mental illnesses, and policymakers continue to close state hospitals, creating greater burdens on both the mental health and criminal justice systems (Saenz, 2002).

To ensure clear delineation of and adherence to responsibilities in partnerships between the mental health and criminal justice systems, entities should enter into interagency agreements specified in memorandums of understanding [MOUs] (Sellers et al., 2005). Teplin (2000) has also discussed the importance of negotiated "no-decline" agreements between law enforcement agencies and treatment providers specifying responsibilities so that providers do not, as is sometimes the case, skirt their duties by refusing to treat individuals because of a history of violence, frequent hospitalizations, abuse of substances, and/or inability to pay for services.

Conflicting Police Roles

With the attention on terrorism these days, both domestically and internationally, concern is expressed about the protection of society versus violation of individual rights. This dilemma regarding societal protection and civil liberties is often present when police encounter persons with mental illnesses in crises. Police decisions about whether, when, and how to intervene in such situations is not an exact science and can be very subjective while trying to balance public safety and civil liberties. A number of factors can enter in to the resolution of such encounters.

As stated by Miller (1997, p. 1173), "The state has a legitimate interest under its parens patriae powers in providing care to its citizens who are unable because of emotional disorders to care for themselves; the state also has authority under its police power to protect the community from the dangerous tendencies of some who are mentally ill" (Green, 1997; Lamb et al., 2002; Lamb et al., 2004). Sometimes the lines between this paternalistic protection by the state on the one hand and the awesome power to protect the citizenry on the other may become so blurred and murky that it is difficult to discern which function is of primary concern to the authorities.

Adams (2006), for example, in an article on law enforcement officers in Lakeland, Florida following up after previous contact with persons with mental illnesses to check on their welfare and ensure that they are compliant with their medications, refers to these officers as "compassionate enforcers." Likewise, police in Ithaca, New York, have been featured for their efforts at prevention and revisits to persons with mental illnesses while accompanied by mental health personnel (Goodstein, 2000). However, it is not always readily discernable whose interests are primarily being considered. As indicated by "Henry J. Steadman, the president of Policy Research Associates, 'There is a potential invasiveness there for individuals who would feel coerced into mental health services because the police are still checking up on them in the role of police officers.... If the person is simply seen as in need of treatment, then why should the police be hanging around forcing the person into treatment?' Ron Honberg, director of legal affairs at [the National Alliance on Mental Illness (NAMI)], said, 'I think it's great that Ithaca cares enough to do something creative. I just worry that if it's done the wrong way it conjures up images of Big Brother at its worst'" (Goodstein, 2000).

There are those that do not believe that the police should be involved in the treatment of persons with mental illnesses (Boyd, 2006; Weathersbee, 2006). The police would agree (Borum, 2000), but it's not like they have had a choice. During the past 15 to 20 years, law enforcement agencies have increasingly implemented practices or programs to deal with persons with mental illnesses, and although there has been reluctance by law enforcement agencies to intervene in this area, partially due to a mentality that if they step in it will become their problem, the reality is that it is already their problem (Reuland, 2005).

According to Panzarella and Alicea (1997), "American police function least well in paramilitary situations. To the extent that situations involving mentally disturbed persons are approached as paramilitary operations, they are likely to remain the bane of police work" (p.337). They suggest that a specialized unit designed to specifically handle crises with persons with mental illnesses would likely work better than a paramilitary SWAT unit to successfully resolve such situations and not escalate them.

Police, even with current emphases on community oriented policing and problem oriented policing, prefer their role as crime fighters to that of service providers (Perrott & Taylor, 1995). Some caution that specialized programs to divert persons with mental illnesses from the criminal justice system may actually result in net widening (Sellers et al., 2005), bringing more people under control of the system than prior to implementation of such diversion programs. However, the ultimate goal is to link individuals with mental illnesses to treatment to stop their incessant recycling through the criminal justice system. Providing law enforcement officers with the knowledge, skills, and training to more efficiently resolve encounters with persons with mental illnesses in crises can indeed serve to free officers up to spend more of their time as crime fighters. Commander Barbara Lewis (personal communication, July 13, 2007) of the Orange County Sheriff's Office in Orlando,

Florida, provides an example of freeing an officer up for tending to crime fighting.

> I have a deputy that responded almost every shift to a residence of a single mother who had a very difficult son approximately eight years old. He would not listen to her, wouldn't go to school, do his homework, go to bed, etc. Sometimes the call would be that the child was fighting her. She would call 911 requesting a deputy for a family disturbance. Upon arrival the deputy would tell the child to do what ever it was the mother wanted and the boy would comply. This was very frustrating for the deputy as it was not really a law enforcement function to parent the child for the mother. However, he still had to respond to the disturbance. After CIT training, the deputy responded again to this residence. During his assessment of the situation, using his newly required skills from CIT, he saw possible signs of mania in the child. After resolving the issue he was called there for, the deputy gave the mom a NAMI brochure. He explained the family-to-family program and that she might be eligible to attend and that they might be able to teach her how to better handle her son. He also told her that there were services through NAMI to help identify if there was more going on with her son other than just bad behavior. The deputy said within a month he was no longer responding to the house. He believes the referral to NAMI (which he had no knowledge of previous to CIT) assisted the mother and connected her to services for her son. He believes the boy was likely bipolar and with proper diagnosis by a mental health professional, he was able to get help, thereby reducing interaction with law enforcement and preventing a negative contact (arrest or injury) for the child.
>
> The reduction of calls to this residence allowed the deputy to handle true law enforcement duties instead of parental duties of the mother. This was a major benefit to the agency (B. Lewis, personal communication, July 13, 2007).6

---

6. Law enforcement officers often establish strong relationships with NAMI affiliates, and NAMI can serve as a great resource for officer referrals. Deputy Sharon Clark of the Orange County Sheriff's Office was recently cited as CIT Deputy of the Year for her agency, and she raised more money for NAMI Walks [see http://www.nami.org/template.cfm?section=namiwalks] in 2005 than all other officers combined for her agency (B. Lewis, personal communication, July 13, 2007). Lt. Brian Garrett of the Polk County Sheriff's Office was recently elected president of his local NAMI affiliate.

Three types of specialized responses for dealing with persons with mental illnesses in crises are identified and examined.

Specialized Police/Mental Health Responses to Persons with Mental Illnesses in Crises

Diversion programs generally fall into the pre-booking category or the post-booking category, and police-based diversion programs are considered to be pre-booking in nature, prior to arrest and charges being filed (Steadman, Deane, Borum, & Morrissey, 2000). In a survey of 174 metropolitan police departments in 42 states, it was determined that seven percent of all police contacts involved encounters with persons believed to be mentally ill, yet the majority of these departments reported no specialized response in place for handling such contacts (Deane, Steadman, Borum, Veysey, & Morrissey, 1999). Specialized responses identified by the researchers could be categorized as (1) a police-based specialized police response with 3% of the departments reporting this model, which fits in with the community policing concept; (2) a police-based specialized mental health response with 12% of the departments reporting this approach; and (3) a mental health-based specialized mental health response with 30% of the departments reporting this method. In the spirit of therapeutic jurisprudence, as discussed in Chapter 1, the goal of each of these specialized responses is to take a problem solving approach, linking individuals to treatment, not merely temporarily incapacitating them, to try to prevent future recycling through the system (Borum et al., 1997). Of course, varying community characteristics may influence which type of specialized response is best for a particular community (Borum et al., 1998). Examples of specialized police responses follow.

Mobile Crisis Team—Mental Health-Based Specialized Mental Health Response

Mobile crisis teams are housed separately form law enforcement agencies, do not have arrest powers, and operate in conjunction with law enforcement. "A mobile crisis team [MCT] is an interdisciplinary team of mental health professionals [that can be comprised of various combinations of clinicians] (e.g., nurses, social workers, psychiatrists, psychologists, mental health technicians, addiction specialists, peer counselors). Teams [can] operate under the auspices of voluntary agencies and municipal hospitals" (Mobile Crisis Team, 2004). MCTs can operate in partnership with law enforcement as evidenced in such areas as Knoxville, Tennessee, Middletown, Connecticut (Reuland, 2005), Anne Arundel County (Council of State Governments, 2002) and Montgomery County, Maryland (Crisis Center, 2007).

Among other things, Lamb et al. (2004) advocate for increased training for law enforcement, better mental health services after arrest and the need for better mental health treatment in the community. They also tend to lean toward collaborations between mental health and law enforcement, favoring the mobile crisis team approach to provide safety and reduce fears of mental health professionals and provide information and expertise to law enforcement officers in crisis situations with persons with mental illnesses. An advantage of mobile crisis teams comprised of mental health personnel and sworn law enforcement officers is that this can allow for the complete mental health history of a person in crisis to be available to mental health clinicians on the team, not just prior information, if available, from prior police contacts, as mental health professionals employed by mental health agencies on such teams may legally obtain such information (Lamb et al., 2002).

PERT, MET, SMART, & CSOs — Police-Based Specialized Mental Health Responses

There are a number of variations of police-based specialized mental health response programs across the country:

> [I]n San Diego County, Psychiatric Emergency Response Team (PERT) officers receive 40 hours of training as well as 7 hours of ongoing training on a monthly basis. The training includes modules on assessment of mental illnesses, resource networks, and the role of the clinician. The training team includes mental health professionals and police personnel (Reuland, 2005, p. 11).

Police and clinicians respond jointly to mental health crisis situations, with clinicians typically not being the first responder to the scene (Reuland, 2005).

The Long Beach, California Police Department employs a Mental Evaluation Team (MET) that couples an officer with a graduate education with a mental health professional as co-responders to mental health crisis calls. Los Angeles has crisis intervention teams (see *Police-Based Specialized Police Response* below) and also utilizes a Systemwide Mental Assessment Response Team (SMART) that pairs a law enforcement officer with a clinician from the Los Angeles County Department of Mental Health as co-responders/evaluators, and officers are to have access via hotline around the clock to clinicians (Reuland, 2005).

Burnett et al. (2000) describe Community Service Officers (CSOs) employed by the Birmingham, Alabama Police Department. These CSOs provide a social service component for persons with mental illnesses in crises. A typical day for a CSO involves networking, brokering services and acting as an advocate for persons with mental illnesses. CSOs must have at least a bachelor's degree in social work and usually at least a year of work experience as a social worker or some other equivalent combination of education and experience. CSOs have certain specified hours to work and are otherwise on call. CSOs can make follow-up visits with or without an officer's presence depending on the circumstances. CSOs have their own separate vehicles and can be called to the scene to assist and advise officers. CSOs are not sworn officers, but if circumstances warrant, police can leave them at a scene to resolve non-criminal matters. Individuals do not have to be in psychiatric crises to receive services from CSOs.

CIT — A Police-Based Specialized Police Response

Crisis intervention team (CIT) training involves specialized training of police officers for responding to persons with mental illnesses in crises. As will be discussed, the Memphis Police Department has the prototypical CIT model. Other police agencies have developed modified CIT approaches, such as the one utilized by the Florence, Alabama Police Department, whereby they employ an officer as a Community Mental Health Officer (Reuland, 2005). This officer is to be available for responses around the clock and is to have had approximately 100 hours of mental health training; this individual is also involved in monitoring logs for and conducting follow-ups on individuals with mental illnesses in crises who encounter the criminal justice system, as well as maintaining outcome data (Council of State Governments, 2003).

Comparisons of the Law Enforcement
Response Models

There have been several comparative studies of law enforcement response models to persons with mental illnesses in crises. Although the significance of this study by Deane, Steadman, Borum, Veysey, and Morrissey (1999) was limited by self-perceptions within police departments, the researchers concluded that the mobile crisis team approach [mental health-based specialized mental health response] was rated higher in terms of effectiveness [82%] than either of the police involved responses, CIT [67%, police-based specialized police response] or for example CSOs [70%, police-based specialized mental health response]. Perhaps this was due at the time to a perception on the part of law enforcement that persons with mental illnesses in crises should be the responsibility of the mental health system, with officers resenting involvement in the process. However, today, many in the law enforcement community have come to realize that if they don't responsibly step up and become involved in establishing accountability and confronting these crises no one else will.

Three specific sites, each using a different response to persons with mental illnesses in crises, were examined in one study. In this comparative study a police-based specialized police response [Memphis CIT], a police-based specialized mental health response [Birmingham, CSOs], and a mental health-based specialized mental health response [Knoxville, mobile crisis unit] were analyzed. Memphis CIT and non-CIT officers were found to be more likely to perceive their agency as more effective in each of the following areas than were Birmingham or Knoxville officers: minimizing the amount of time spent on mental health related crisis calls, fulfilling the needs of persons with mental illnesses in crisis situations, avoiding jail for persons with mental illnesses in crises, and providing safety for the community (Borum et al., 1998). The researchers found that Memphis CIT officers felt better prepared to handle mental disturbance calls.

Memphis was much more likely to link individuals to treatment via transport than the other two sites. Birmingham was much more likely to resolve matters on the scene, though there were staffing problems with Birmingham, with limited availability on nights and weekends. Knoxville police found response times excessive and frequently opted for jail. Arrest rates were highest in Birmingham, but all programs indicate that such police diversion programs are a good way to avoid the inappropriate use of jails to house persons with mental illnesses. Recidivism rates for those handled on scene or arrested versus those referred for treatment were not monitored or compared (Steadman et al., 2000). Arrest rates for encounters with persons with mental illnesses in crisis were lowest in Memphis where officers were quicker on the scene and more likely to transport to treatment instead of merely making a referral (Cochran, Deane, & Borum, 2000).

Regardless of the model in place, essential ingredients have been identified to heighten the success rate in encounters with persons with mental illnesses. Steadman et al. (2001) examined police-based diversion programs in Memphis, Tennessee, Montgomery County, Pennsylvania, and Multnomah County, Oregon; the Multnomah program is modeled after the Memphis police crisis intervention team concept, and Montgomery County's program provides for the dispatch of psychiatric crisis counselors out into the field. They found crucial elements that contributed to the success of each of these programs: the availability of an around the clock centralized single point of entry crisis receiving facility, with streamlined intake to minimize officer down time and a no refusal policy for law enforcement drop offs to free officers up to get back on the street and tend to crime fighting duties. "[T]he arrest rate in mental health crisis situations in cities with specialized police responses has been found to be only 6.7 percent [in mental health crises]. This rate is a third of that reported [in mental health crises in another study] for nonspecialized police responses" (Steadman, et al., 2001, p. 222).

Memphis is unique in that it does have one centralized receiving facility, likely contributing to over one-half of the Memphis officers evaluating their CIT program as highly effective in reducing the amount of time spent on calls involving persons with mental illnesses in crisis (Borum et al., 1998). Availability and utilization of a crisis receiving facility to efficiently ease the transfer of persons with mental illnesses from law enforcement personnel to mental health clinicians has been found to be an integral component in enhancing the perceived effectiveness by law enforcement personnel of processing persons with mental illnesses who they encounter in crises (Deane et al., 1999). As noted by Steadman et al. (2001), a single point of entry, with streamlined intake for police responses and a no-refusal policy, serves to make the services police friendly. Reducing turnaround time for officers increases the probability that some action will be taken and the mental health system will be relied upon, while lessening the likelihood of arrest (Borum et al., 1998).

Reuland (2005) examined 28 law enforcement agencies using either police-based police responses such as the Memphis CIT Model (22 agencies) or police-based-mental health responses (6 agencies) with the goal of diversion and improved treatment. Police-based responses could be combined with a mobile crisis team, but mobile crisis teams alone were not included in Reuland's analysis, as modifications in law enforcement training and protocol is not as pronounced under such circumstances. She reports that CIT seems to have emerged as the more popular specialized program among the police because they are typically the first on the scene, and in those first few crucial moments whether a crisis escalates or de-escalates tends to revolve around their actions.

Of the three specialized responses, the Memphis Police Department's CIT program is the most well known of all police diversion programs in the country (Steadman et al., 2000). Memphis CIT is the most often replicated specialized response model (Greenberg, 2001), and it is considered to be the most effective in successfully resolving mental health crises (Sellers et al., 2005).

The Procedural Fairness of CIT

Cooperation is more likely to be garnered when persons view the interaction with authorities as procedurally fair as opposed to perceiving the actions of authorities as coercive. According to Watson and Angell (2007), the CIT model clearly incorporates elements of procedural justice to ensure that persons are treated with respect and dignity and establishes trust while expressing concern for one's well being. Watson and Angell (2007) offer the admonition that,

> [O]veremphasizing procedural justice concerns...could, if unchecked, lead to substantively unjust outcomes being obscured by seemingly fair procedures. Absent genuine concern, procedural justice techniques are simply a form of manipulation in the moment, which may backfire on officers in subsequent contacts with the individuals.... [I]n training police officers, the importance of substantively fair treatment, not simply the appearance of fair treatment [must be emphasized] (p. 792).

Persons with mental illnesses can remember their encounters and the outcomes of those interactions with the police. Therefore, it is important that they be treated fairly so as to better ensure that the next contact will be a positive one.

It is also noted that one's level of perceived status may influence the amount of their need to focus on procedural fairness. For example, if one's status has been eroded and diminished by the stigma of mental illness, a person's self-worth and self-respect may be bolstered or further diminished by interaction with police. The quality of police interactions with the mentally ill will have repercussions for future encounters with authorities. Thus, how law enforcement officers treat individuals that they encounter has both an immediate and long range effect; it has been shown that disrespectful actions on the part of law enforcement officers diminishes the probability of citizen cooperation in the future. Researchers have substantiated the accuracy of persons with mental illnesses while symptomatic and in crises to accurately determine whether an encounter was coercive (Watson & Angell, 2007).

Key components of procedural justice include having a voice; participation and input into decisions that impact one's self; to be listened to by the decider; to be treated with dignity, respect and politeness, acknowledging one's rights and trusting that the arbiter is concerned with one's well being (Watson & Angell, 2007). Regardless of the outcome of the decision, individuals want to feel that they were treated with respect. Individuals who perceive that they have been treated fairly are more like to be cooperative with requests from authorities.

An example of treating a person with compassion, respect and dignity and establishing trust while expressing concern for one's well being is seen in the following example involving St. Petersburg, Florida police officer Tony Rolón (personal communication, February 22, 2007) as presented in officer Rolón's own words:

> I met Stella at Publix supermarket. She had been caught shoplifting again. The manager wanted me to arrest her and give her a trespass warning. I looked with a heavy heart upon the little old lady who could be my grandmother. I took the time to talk with her before I did anything. I saw she was paying for some items and stealing others, bread, oranges. I detected something in Stella. I gave her a little cognitive test, you know, "who is the president ..." She didn't do so well. I spoke to the manager and asked if I could take Stella. I pled her case. I told him that I believed that she was suffering from the infirmities of aging as well as a social security check which was way too small. He relented. and I took Stella home. Stella thanked me and unlocked her door. I walked in with her. She got mad. I went to the cupboards and fridge. Stella had next to nothing in food or belongings. She had notes everywhere to remind her to do this and do that. I knew what was going on. I told her I had to leave but would be back. It was check off. My sergeant asked about the little old lady and what I had done with her. I explained the circumstances to him. He gave me $5. I went to Publix Supermarket and bought the things Stella had tried to boost. I called the Department of Children and Families (the agency in Florida entrusted to look out for the public welfare of its citizens), blah, blah ... not a risk ... have to be in the criminal justice system to help ... blah. I was now on a crusade! I contacted the Little Old Lady League, an informal group of retired ladies who help other little old ladies out. Imagine that! I got some real clothes for Stella. One of the lady's sons is a podiatrist. Stella got her hammertoes fixed and got real shoes, and now she would not have to cut the sides out. I got her some real cookware. And, I finally found her daughter in Chicago. Gina wanted nothing to do with her mom. Stella was too much trouble, that's why she sent her to Florida. I tried to charge Gina criminally ... I couldn't find a crime which fit. We watched over Stella for several years until her health got to such a point that she needed a supported living environment. Stella went to a nursing home. After Stella met me she was never arrested for shoplifting again (Rolón, 2007).

Results of CIT

There are a number of reasons that have been articulated as to why CIT has been singled out as the premiere model for responding to persons with mental illnesses in crises. CIT has been identified as the best of the three specialized responses for lowering arrest rates and generating a greater perception of effectiveness on the part of the police (Borum et al., 1998; Honberg, 2005; Steadman et al., 2000). CIT has been touted for its effectiveness in diminishing injuries to both persons with mental illnesses and police officers, reducing arrests while increasing transports and access of mental health treatment services (Bunch, 2005; Dupont & Cochran, 2000; Honberg, 2005; Reuland & Cheney, 2005; Skeem & Bibeau, 2008; Thompson & Borum, 2006), and reducing jail suicides (Honberg, 2005).

Steadman et al. (2000), for example, found an arrest rate of 6.7% in cases involving CIT police encounters with persons with mental illnesses, while the estimated national average non-CIT arrest rate for such confrontations is 20% (Strauss et al., 2005). Similarly, Skeem and Bibeau (2008) found that CIT officers in Las Vegas were four times less likely than non-CIT officers to make arrests in crisis encounters. Referrals in Memphis to treatment by officers doubled within four years of implementation of the CIT program there, and within one year of the establishment of a CIT program in Louisville, Kentucky, the average number of referrals by police to mental health treatment increased from 500 to 600 persons a month (Strauss et al., 2005).

Not all studies have reported a reduction in arrests as a result of the implementation of CIT. An exception to CIT induced reductions of arrest rates was found in one study in Ohio. Teller, Munetz, Gil, and Ritter (2006), with the implementation of CIT in Akron, Ohio, found that CIT trained officers were more prone to transport persons for treatment than they had been prior to CIT training. However, while CIT is touted as a pre-arrest jail diversion program, the researchers actually discovered that CIT-trained officers were more likely, though not statistically significant, to arrest persons with mental illnesses than those officers on the force who had not received CIT training. This phenomenon may have coincided with the establishment of a mental health court that could assist in ensuring linkages to treatment in the community via the criminal justice system.

CIT training has also been found to potentially reduce law enforcement officers' stigmatizing attitudes toward persons with mental illnesses (Comptom, Esterberg, McGee, Kotwicki, & Oliva, 2006). Honberg (2005) noted that CIT results in improved relationships between law enforcement and advocates. CIT also translates into fewer shootings of persons with mental illnesses by police

(Watson & Angell, 2007), fewer deaths for persons with mental illnesses and police (Honberg, 2005), and deployment of SWAT teams have reportedly decreased considerably from 50 to almost 60 percent after implementation of CIT (Council of State Governments, 2007). CIT has been found to also reduce use of force incidents (Thompson & Borum, 2006), and injuries to persons with mental illnesses decreased by 40 percent shortly after implementation of CIT in Memphis (Council of State Governments, 2007).

Strauss et al. (2005) projects that in addition to reducing officer injuries and uses of force that de-criminalization of persons with mental illnesses may be realized resulting in cost savings and reductions in psychiatric morbidity by linking persons with mental illnesses to appropriate treatment. If so, the expectation would be that over time CIT contacts and referrals to emergency treatment providers would diminish. In other words, if operated efficiently and with the necessary mental health infrastructure in place, CIT operations may hopefully ultimately put themselves out of business, as mental health treatment will eventually take place where it should have been taking place all along— within the mental health system.[7]

CIT Training

First and foremost, the goal of CIT training is to ensure officer safety. Successful resolutions of crises with persons with mental illnesses cannot be achieved without maintaining officer safety. Borum (2000) also categorizes the goals of CIT training as improving the understanding of the signs and symptoms of mental illnesses; identifying community resources and alternative dispositions; and enhancing crisis communication skills so de-escalation can take place without physical confrontations. CIT officers are specially trained to respond to mental health crises and when not on those calls perform the general duties of any other patrol officer (Reuland, 2005).

Typical CIT training curriculum components include a history of how the criminal justice system became the de facto mental health system; why the actions of persons with mental illnesses who have encounters with law enforce-

---

7. Even prosecutors have been impressed with the results rendered by CIT training. Commander Barbara Lewis (2007) reports that Vance Voyles of the Orange County Sheriff's Office was recently praised by an assistant intake prosecutor for his insight in diverting a person with mental illness to treatment instead of arresting her.

ment are not truly volitional; signs and symptoms of mental illnesses; types of mental illnesses;[8] varieties of psychotropic medications; civil commitment process; pertinent laws and regulations; co-occurring disorders; suicide; departmental policies; identification of community resources, such as site visits of emergency rooms, mental health facilities, receiving facilities, drop-in centers, clubhouses, assisted living facilities, and the like; discussion of special programs, such as assertive community treatment[9]; interaction with consumers of mental health services and family members; role-playing, videos, training in de-escalation techniques. Other CIT training components may address cultural differences, developmental disabilities, substance abuse, and dementia/Alzheimer's disease.

---

8. Comptom and Kotwicki, (2007) recommend that the following disorders be covered in CIT training: "schizophrenia and other psychotic disorders, mood disorders, anxiety disorders, personality disorders, childhood and emotional disorders, posttraumatic stress disorder, neurological disorders" (p. 37)] Comptom and Kotwicki (2007) also spend a lot of time in their book describing in detail the types of mental illnesses. This information can also be gleaned from the American Psychiatric Association (1994) *Diagnostic and Statistical Manual of Mental Disorders—Fourth Edition* (DSM-IV), Washington D.C.: American Psychiatric Association. However, it should be cautioned that the goal in CIT training is not to make law enforcement officers in to quasi-psychiatrists. The goal is for them to recognize that a mental health problem exists and safely get the person in crisis to a mental health clinician for evaluation and diagnosis. Officers in CIT training should be instructed that all they need to be able to do is to realize, "Houston, there's a problem!" While it may help to articulate some of the symptoms they have observed to a clinician, they don't have to know specifically what the problem is; they just need to link the individual to a professional to recognize and fix it.

9. Knowing what community resources are available to assist persons with mental illnesses in crises is extremely beneficial for law enforcement officers. Lt. Anne-Marie Wendel of the Lakeland Police Department (LPD) in Lakeland, Florida describes engagement of an assertive community treatment (ACT) team counselor in the treatment process. The ACT concept will be discussed in the chapter on diversion and re-entry. Lt. A.M. Wendel (personal communication, April 30, 2007) relates the following story: "An ACT client came to LPD to try and check out computer equipment to stop the people stalking him through the television set. A CIT officer made contact with him in the lobby and worked with him for over an hour to include contacting his ACT counselor. The CIT officer did civilly commit him but had everything coordinated with the ACT counselor. The officer even took the extra step to take his bicycle (only mode of transportation) back to his apartment and lock it inside and then take the keys back to the hospital. Follow-up contacts have been successful. The individual continues to contact the CIT Officer to talk with the officer when things are not going too well thus receiving more assistance."

Some CIT training formats, such as Polk County and Sarasota County, Florida, have also incorporated a simulation experience entitled "Hearing Disturbing Voices." This involves utilization of an audio compact disc developed by Dr. Patricia Deegan who actually has schizophrenia (Fasshauer & Garrett, 2006). CIT trainees are asked to complete a number of tasks while hearing voices via their headsets. Audio/visual simulators have also been devised based on input from persons with schizophrenia and have been used in police CIT training for example in Brown County, Ohio (Lee, 2007). It should be noted that CIT has been adapted to meet the needs of rural areas, such as Brown County, Ohio, and urban areas. Lt. Jeff Murphy of the Chicago Police Department reported that the Chicago Police Department hopes to provide CIT training to fifteen to seventeen percent of its patrol division, training 1,000 officers by 2008 (J. Murphy, personal communication, August 30, 2007), with the ultimate goal of training approximately 1400 officers in Chicago (Lushbaugh, 2007).

Generally, officers are advised in training not to play to a delusion that someone is experiencing unless they have to do so. However, officer Tony Rolón (personal communication, February 22, 2007), of the St. Petersburg Police Department in St. Petersburg, Florida, provides an example of where such actions may facilitate resolution of a recurring problematic encounter.

> A little old lady began to call the police on a regular basis. Her complaint was always the same; Arnold Schwarzenegger was in her attic and could not get out. Patrol officers would just try to calm her and tell her that he was not really there. Obviously this did not work so well and the lady would call back. Finally, I was dispatched to talk with her. I took the time to learn that Arnold was stuck in the attic because that is where he went to hide. You see she and Arnold were having an affair. When her husband would come home and almost catch them, Arnold would hide in the attic and then could not get out.
>
> We must realize that sometimes there are resolutions which do not hurt and can act as calming agents. I showed the lady how to get Arnold out of the attic. I was completely serious as I explained how to do this so she could continue her affair. In this case her delusion is harmless and my solution is just as harmless. However, my solution acted as a calming agent for her. We have not gotten a return call from her (T. Rolón, personal communication, February 2007).

With an emphasis on officer safety, policies on use of force should be clearly delineated for CIT officers. Watson and Angell (2007) maintain that law enforcement officers need to know when to use force and guidelines should be developed on how much force is necessary under specified circumstances. Comptom and Kotwicki (2007) devote a chapter in their book to de-escalation techniques that includes the stages of the escalation of a crisis as devised by the Memphis Police Department. Those officers who do well in de-escalating situations are empathetic, have good listening skills, remain calm, show patience, are flexible, have the ability to think on their feet and exhibit assertiveness and control (Comptom & Kotwicki, 2007). Good communication skills, both verbal and non-verbal, with simple requests, using a non-threatening approach [the officer may introduce him/herself by first name] and stance, while calmly assessing an encounter with a person with mental illness, can serve to facilitate a successful resolution.

CIT trained officers should also have access to less than lethal munitions. Cordner (2006) recommends use of less lethal weapons, such as, pepper sprays, stun guns, and beanbag rounds, to employ the least amount of force necessary. Munetz, Fitzgerald, and Woody (2006) suggest that tasers might be issued to officers in communities that have established effective partnerships between the police and mental health providers and reported use of the taser 35 times in the first 18 months of utilization in the Akron, Ohio police department, with no serious injuries, and 27 of the 35 incidents involved a person with mental illness.

Cooper et al. (2004) contend that the mental health system owes it to the criminal justice system to familiarize criminal justice practitioners on the roles and responsibilities of mental health workers. Typically, CIT training engages clinicians from the local community as instructors to discuss their areas of expertise, such as signs and symptoms of mental illnesses and psychotropic medications, with law enforcement officers. This provides a good starting place for beginning and fostering a professional dialogue between the mental health and criminal justice systems. Healthy partnerships and alliances can be formed, and CIT training can help identify viable options and link names and faces from one system to the other to facilitate expedient and efficient resolution of future conflicts between the two systems. Individuals who previously failed to communicate and pointed fingers of blame at each other can now work together collaboratively.

Memphis CIT training includes eight hours of police consumer interaction (Cochran, 2004). Family members of persons with mental illnesses can also prove to be a valuable resource for police when crises occur, and family members should be engaged as CIT trainers. Since more and more responsibility for persons with mental illnesses is shifted from mental health authorities to families, as noted by

Dempsey and Forst (2008), frequently it is family members who make the initial call to police for assistance with their loved one with mental illness in crisis.

Lt. John Thomason (personal communication, July 25, 2007) of the Lakeland Police Department in Florida discusses the importance of the reliance upon family members to ascertain valuable information when dealing with a distraught individual in crisis. He also notes in the following discussion that not all officers are suited for dealing with persons in crisis.

Dealing with the mentally ill can be a challenge. The situation may be totally abnormal and the circumstances and conditions may add to the difficulty. I remember several years ago being contacted in regards to a suicidal person. The call came at around 3 AM on the coldest day of that winter. A suicidal male had climbed to nearly the top of an electric company substation and was clinging around poles and hanging on in the midst of an extremely powerful electrical substation. Officers had tried to talk him down to no avail, and he had been up there for an hour or so in the nearly freezing temperatures. I responded to the scene and assessed the situation. Police, Fire and EMS units were present as well as electric company employees. I saw a W/M subject in his early 30s, hanging onto a power substation tower in only his underwear. His arms were tightly wrapped around the poles. Below I could see a lot of wires and electrical equipment that if the fall didn't kill him then the electrical shock surely would. We took immediate action by having portions of the electrical substation shut down. This caused a power shut down for a section of the city so we knew we couldn't keep the power off for long. Family members were contacted and arrived at the scene. A debrief of the family revealed that our suicidal man had been diagnosed with AIDS, had just had a break up in a relationship, and was struggling with drug and alcohol issues as well as financial problems.

By the time you have read the previous paragraph, you would likely say that you understand why he is having issues. Yet we have a job to do and we need to try and help him. Our strategy was to talk straightforward with him and discuss the fact that he has a family who loves him and he might work out his issues with his relationship or find someone new. We could mention that there are all types of drugs now being used that are prolonging the lives of those with AIDS. Lastly, we would mention the pain and anguish he could suffer and possibility of major injury and not death and then having to live with those injuries. We mentioned a variety of assistance and options that he had. It was also mentioned as to how cold it was.

I don't know that we had to mention that one, but sometimes it is good to remind someone of the conditions they are in. Needless to say, we were able to talk the gentleman down, actually by way of an electric truck, and he was Baker Acted and given assistance. While some would say you should do this or not do that when dealing with these types of situations, it is more art than it is science.

Experience, understanding, and negotiations training will help most people. Hostage negotiation or crisis response teams aren't for everyone or every officer, but if you are interested in that specialty, you have the opportunity to handle some extreme situations that can prove to be a great adventure as well as a rewarding one (J. Thomason, personal communication, July 25, 2007).

Crisis intervention team training is a way of breaking down barriers by bringing law enforcement officers and persons with mental illnesses and their family members together to establish rapport and enhance future interactions. It is important to get a buy-in from consumers and family members for mental health/criminal justice partnerships, and this lends credibility to programs and training. Consumers and family members should be engaged in the planning stages of specialized programs and involved as trainers, evaluators, and ambassadors of such programs as well. Typically, the best and most influential presenters are those that have had previous contact with the police while in crisis. The key is that both family members and consumers of mental health services involved in such training and collaborations need to be emotionally past the critical incidents and over any resentments from these prior contacts to be able to make a significant and meaningful contribution. Often times officers, unless they have a friend or family member with mental illness, have never to their knowledge had an encounter with a person with mental illness without that person being in crisis. It is amazing to watch the transformations that take place, for all involved, as consumers and family members share their compelling stories with law enforcement officers. Relationships are fostered that go beyond a training classroom.[10]

---

10. It is not uncommon to see police officers drop by assisted living facilities and drop-in centers to check in with persons with mental illnesses, persons that they would have never taken time out for before except in a crisis. This type of behavior prompted one person at a drop-in center to remark, "In the past we used to duck under tables here anytime

There are a number of places that agencies that want to engage consumers and family members in these kinds of productive partnerships can go to identify those willing to participate, NAMI Speaker's Bureau, Peer to Peer, Peer specialists, Program for Assertive Community Treatment (PACT), In Our Own Voice (IOOV), the Depression and Bipolar Support Alliance (http://www.ndmda.org/ June 14, 2007), local clinicians, advocacy centers for person with disabilities, drop-in-centers, club houses, National Alliance on Mental Illness (NAMI) consumer council, student disability services and counseling centers. The GAINS Center is also great at inclusiveness (http://gainscenter.samhsa.gov/html/ June 14, 2007).

NAMI has established a CIT Technical Assistance Resource Center to act as a clearinghouse for information and provide policymakers, law enforcement agents, mental health personnel, consumers of mental health services and family members with up to date information on CIT and related jail diversion initiatives (Dailey et al., 2006). The Center is engaged in the expansion of CIT via networking nationally and is able to provide assistance to advocates in locales interested in implementing CIT programs adaptable to their particular jurisdictions. The critical role of involving consumers of mental health services and family members is also addressed by the Center.

In Our Own Voice (IOOV) is a program that originated in 1996 to empower persons with mental illnesses to speak publicly about their illnesses and journeys to recovery to a vast array of community and professional groups; this program can be a natural resource for any law enforcement agencies looking for consumer trainers or college classes desirous of exploring this subject (Sultan, O'Brien, Farinholt, & Talley, 2006).[11] Local NAMI affiliates can be reached

---

the police showed up, as there was always a crisis when they pulled up. Now, we sit down across the table and have a cup of coffee and chat with them." Just as the media can sensationalize and negatively portray persons with mental illnesses, it can also do the same to police officers. However, supposedly hardened, calloused, law enforcement officers have been seen taking up offerings to pay a speeding ticket for one CIT presenter who received a ticket while running late for a CIT presentation and to provide funds to purchase medication for a consumer presenter with schizophrenia who had lost his benefits because he was earning too much money from his service station job and was unable to afford his psychotropic medication.

11. The previously mentioned Montgomery County Emergency Service (MCES) in Pennsylvania offers a provider run police school that emerged in 1974 and is considered to be the first systematic attempt to familiarize law enforcement with issues pertaining to mental illnesses in the nation. (MCES Quest, 2005). In provider training of police officers in Pennsylvania, MCES has engaged NAMI's "In Our Own Voice" presenters to share their personal struggles with mental illnesses and their recovery with officers (MCES Quest, 2005). [*See MCES Quest (2005, September). MCES crisis intervention specialist (CIS) training: Enhanc-*

to ascertain contact information via nami.org. The IOOV program when presented to audiences has been found to promote the concept of recovery and contribute to the de-stigmatization of persons with mental illnesses (Wood & Wahl, 2006).

NAMI has endorsed the 40 hour CIT training standard of the Memphis Model and encourages and supports the implementation of this model to the degree practicable nationwide (Honberg, 2005). In addition to training state, university, and local sworn law enforcement personnel, others reportedly trained in various jurisdictions included dispatchers, emergency medical technicians, fire personnel, paramedics, hospital/emergency room staff, probation officers, security officers, judges, and detention/correctional officers (Honberg, 2005).

Major Sam Cochran of the Memphis Police Department is considered the guru of CIT training. He is an internationally sought after speaker and has assisted numerous jurisdictions in initiating their own CIT programs. In his own words, Major Cochran outlines the essence of CIT and informs us that CIT is more than just training.

The Essence of CIT

The Crisis Intervention Team

The Crisis Intervention Team is about uniting community partnerships, such as, law enforcement; advocacy groups (NAMI); mental health providers; family members and consumers of mental health services.

CIT is committed to quality of services that are directed to those who struggle and cope with mental illnesses and other co-occurring disorders. CIT offers leadership to encourage and promote the accomplishments of community goals: Safety, Understanding and Compassion.

In promoting CIT it is important to acknowledge and visualize the "CIT model as more than just training." Yes, CIT Training is important, but the framing of CIT should be in collaboration with community partnerships/relationships. It is these attributes (necessary components) that manifest a change of "hearts" within people. A change to accommodate quality of life issues and the building of hope:

• Community collaboration/Partnerships to the Model

---

ing police effectiveness in the community, 5(1), 1–8. Montgomery County, Pennsylvania: Montgomery County Emergency Service, Inc.]

- Developing and maintaining community ownership and advocacy to the Model
- Selecting, building and nurturing community anchors (leaders, team members and services)
- Creating and Infusing of systems/infrastructures to accommodate appropriate and workable solutions/ services
- Uncompromising and relentless approach to defeating stigma (mental illnesses).

The people of whom I speak are **not** just law enforcement officers. A more inclusive understanding of the word "people" should be considered within terms of **all people** — within communities, counties and states. It is important to bring forth a mindset of fairness and openness by which to understand and to acknowledge that we must not embrace nor deny the encroachment by which **"stigma"** has harmed us all.

This may sound as if I am speaking only in terms of training. Not so, CIT is the "flagship" by which people of communities, counties and states work together within partnerships to better address and accommodate appropriate crisis services.

CIT has been proclaimed and noted as a model which is "more than just training." Again, training is important and indeed brings about attributes of stability and structure within the overall intent and purpose of community crisis services. The pursuit of the CIT model should be undertaken with honorable attributes of passion and service and should be viewed carefully within the context of the following points:

(1) Some law enforcement officers are not ready, nor suited for the role as a CIT Officer (leadership). Please understand, that this concept holds true in consideration of individual placement within any "specialized" program/service.

(2) Communities that are careless by minimizing efforts of not advocating or seeking the implementation of other appropriate systems and infrastructures so as NOT to inappropriately/unnecessarily criminalize people with mental illnesses; are in effect, performing on a fragile stage exhibiting little or no leadership standards by which to promote community safety, services and hope.

(3) Training is essential, but utilizing a training only approach, will significantly adversely impact and marginalize the overall intent and purpose of the CIT model. Failing to consider or act on the fragmentation of systems and services undermines the CIT potential, pro-

jecting instead a quick-fix or "band-aid" or cosmetic approach in addressing very real and very complex community crisis issues. By default the intended paradigm becomes the truism: stigma of mental illnesses harms us all.

CIT is about changing the hearts of America. The Crisis Intervention Team; it's more than just training (S. Cochran, personal communication, January 4, 2007).

"The family members and the consumers: they're the people who inspire us. They're the people we need to address our attention and service to. With passion, we ask, "Who are 'the mentally ill'?" They're our fathers, our mothers, our sons and daughters, our cousins, aunts and uncles. They're us.... Persons with mental illnesses are "deserving of special care and services" (Cochran, 2004).

Types of CIT Encounters with Persons with Mental Illnesses

Suicidal ideations appear to be a common reason for dispatching CIT trained officers to encounters with persons with mental illnesses (B. Lewis, personal communication, July 13, 2007; T. Rolón, personal communication, February 22, 2007; Skeem & Bibeau, 2008; D. Spratt, personal communication, May 8, 2007). Commander Barbara Lewis (personal communication, July 13, 2007) of the Orange County Sheriff's Office in Orlando, Florida relays the following story of Officer Peter Hernandez that was shared with her by Lt. James A. Como of the Ocoee Police Department in Ocoee, Florida. This story is indicative of how CIT training can thwart suicide attempts and save lives.

On April 5, 2006, a young gentleman approached Officer Hernandez outside the Ocoee Police Department. The gentleman related to Officer Hernandez his worry about his former girlfriend and mother of their children because of unsettling behavior she exhibited. The gentleman indicated how he attempted to speak with the woman but because of their inability to resolve anything without arguing he left. Although the gentleman had second thoughts about his concern and told Officer Hernandez not to worry about it after all, Officer Hernandez asked him where the woman lived and said he would like to go by and check on her anyway.

Officer Hernandez then went to the address he had been given and met with the woman, Jane Doe. Though Ms. Doe tried to assure Officer Hernandez that all was well and there was nothing to worry about, Officer Hernandez detected in her voice an uneasy calm that suggested otherwise. He felt something just wasn't right.

Officer Hernandez spent quite awhile speaking with Ms. Doe, studying her body language and voice stress and was gradually able to break down emotional barriers that Ms. Doe had erected. Finally, Ms. Doe began to open up and confess to Officer Hernandez that on this evening she planned to take the lives of her daughter, age 4, and son, age 3, by suffocating them and then take her own life by an overdose of medication that she had already called into the pharmacy but did not have the chance to pick up because of the arrival of Officer Hernandez at her door. Officer Hernandez earned Ms. Doe's trust and was able to bring her to the Crisis Center where she was admitted. The two children were placed with their grandparents.

Officer Hernandez had insisted on checking on Ms. Doe, even after her former boyfriend recanted. His intuition and instincts as a Crisis Intervention Team Officer enabled him to intervene before Ms. Doe had the chance to carry out the unspeakable act of taking the lives of her innocent young children and herself. Because of Officer Hernandez, these three lives were saved. Officer Hernandez received a commendation from the Ocoee Police Department and an award from the American Society for Industrial Security for his compassionate intervention (Lewis, 2007).

Lt. Denise Spratt (personal communication, May 8, 2007) of the Louisville Metro Police Department, in Louisville, Kentucky, describes some of the unusual encounters her department has had with persons with mental illnesses:

A female called stating her cat was "demonized." On arrival, the woman appeared quite calm and was looking down at the cat. However, she had stabbed herself in the throat and was bleeding profusely. The woman seemed almost unaware and stated that would stop the demons. She was in and out of reality during the dialogue.

A man whose brother worked at the sanitation plant walked in and tried to jump in the incinerator.

> We've had several CIT runs that involve patients being nude in pub-
> lic. One man was naked on the sidewalk walking around "preaching"
> incoherently with his hand in his anus.[12]
>
> We have several bridges that go over the Ohio River between Ken-
> tucky and Indiana. We get several bridge jumpers or attempted
> jumpers.
>
> A man put his head on the railroad tracks to commit suicide but
> changed his mind at the last second and pushed himself off with his
> hands. Both of his arms were severed.
>
> Man stabbed himself in the heart with an ink pen. The pen was
> approximately ½ inch deep in his chest.
>
> A homeless female living in a viaduct, after multiple encounters
> with a CIT officer is now living in government subsidized housing.
> She is compliant with her treatment (D. Spratt, personal communi-
> cation, May 8, 2007).

Commander Barbara Lewis (personal communication, July 13, 2007) of
the Orange County Sheriff's Office in Orlando, Florida, shares the following story:

> An encounter with an intoxicated heavily armed [with access to four
> loaded weapons] veteran suffering from Post Traumatic Stress Dis-
> order and believing that he was back in Vietnam was successfully re-
> solved by using Navy jargon. The deputy even got the compliant
> subject to march into the crisis receiving center by chanting in ca-
> dence, "left, right, left … (Lewis, 2007).

---

12. Nudity is indeed a common theme that is observed among persons with mental illnesses when symptomatic. For example, a Hamilton, Ohio prosecutor, who reportedly suf-
fers from bipolar disorder and was under stress, was charged with public indecency for
being spotted on security cameras walking around at night nude in a county office building [see CBS News (2006, October 11), Camera catches prosecutor naked, Retrieved from
the World Wide Web on July 20, 2007: http://www.cbsnews.com/stories/2006/10/11/na-
tional/main2083758.shtml] This phenomenon is also exhibited in the case of Andrew Mar-
tinez who was referred to as "the naked guy" during his days as a student at the University
of California at Berkeley. Believing that the CIA was after him and using a shopping buggy
to transport rocks to intersections to unload and block traffic, he was ultimately diagnosed
as schizophrenic. He eventually committed suicide while incarcerated in solitary confinement by placing a plastic bag over his head and tying a bed sheet tightly around the bag to
prevent ventilation [see Zengerle, J. (2006, December 31), The naked guy, *The New York Times*,
Retrieved from the World Wide Web on July 20, 2007: http://www.nytimes.com/
2006/12/31/magazine/31naked.t.html?ex=1185076800&en=d74f23a98bc549f6&ei=5070].

Delusions are false beliefs, and religious ideations are common among persons with mental illnesses when symptomatic (Torrey, 2006). Perceiving one's self as Jesus, for example, is not an uncommon theme for persons who are delusional (see Buchanan, 2007; Staik, 2007). Officer Tony Rolón (personal communication, February 22, 2007) of the St. Petersburg Police Department relates the following encounter replete with religious overtones.

I was called to a first floor condo in a nice neighborhood to check the welfare of the man who lived there. I was surprised to find a smallish 30 something meek looking soft-spoken man. We spoke at the door and I told him of my call. He assured me that there was nothing wrong. I learned that he had lived in the complex for several years. After I left I checked and found that there were no prior police reports for this man.

I was called back to the apartment several weeks later. The caller advised that there were loud noises coming from within the apartment. I spoke with the meek man again. Just from looking at him and hearing him speak one would never think he would be capable of violence. He allowed me into the apartment on this day, but only the entry hallway.

The apartment was dark and I could see that a light fixture was pulled out of the hallway wall and hanging from the wires. I told the man that I had a number of hobbies and asked about his. He told me that he liked to shoot his hand gun. I asked to see it but he declined. He told me that everything was Ok.

I was called out again to the condo a couple of weeks later. I spoke with the man and he allowed me into the apartment again. I stepped inside a little further than I had the first time. I saw that the rear sliding glass doors had been shattered and glass was outside on the patio. Also on the patio was a loveseat. I asked what had happened. The man said that he had thrown the loveseat through the door. He said he had lost his job in the past months and was running out of money. I was able to see the handgun and convinced him to allow me to "hold onto it" for safekeeping.

I was called out several days later. The caller said the man was burning something. We had a good rapport and he allowed me into the apt. He allowed me to take a tour of the condo on this occasion. I found that every light fixture had been pulled from the wall or ceiling and was hanging. The stereo was in the middle of the living room floor and was tuned to a local Christian talk radio show. In the kitchen I found that there were burn marks on the counters.

I got the man to explain the state of his home. He told me that everything was alright since he lost his job. He told me that God had begun to talk to him through the radio, that's why it had a prominent place in the living room. He needed to pull the light fixtures from the drywall to ensure that no evil spirits were behind them. The burn marks were burnt offerings to God. He was only doing as commanded.

I realized the potential for violence and began to inquire more about the commands and what God was telling him. He told me that his task on this world was to cleanse the lesbians. He believed that lesbians were evil and had to be cleansed. He would not tell me what the cleansing was.

I was able to get some help for the man. He was without funds so he was appointed a counselor to assist him. He got back on his medication, which stopped when he was fired. And he began to see a mental health professional on an out patient basis. I was terribly afraid of his potential for violence, so I visited him almost daily. I enlisted the aid of another officer so we did not miss seeing him on any day. We both made sure the man took his medications while we were present.

Regardless of the assistance the man was getting, he fell into crisis. One evening he turned the radio up very loud and left his unit. He walked to the second floor where two college girls lived. He hacked at the door violently with a large knife. He then took a fire extinguisher and attempted to break the door open. Officers arrived on scene while he was still beating on the door and yelling unintelligibly. When the man saw the officers he calmed down and obeyed all of their commands (Rolón, personal communication, February 22, 2007).

Of course, as discussed, most persons with mental illnesses are not violent. The importance of CIT programs is that they can provide appropriate interventions to de-escalate violence. As we shall see, a number of those programs and CIT trained officers are emerging across the country.

The Number of CIT Programs

It is difficult to estimate the total number of CIT programs currently in operation in the country. Just because someone has undergone specialized police-based response training does not ensure that fidelity to the core components of the CIT model have been maintained. Just because a few officers from an agency attended a week of training does not mean that they returned to their department and started a CIT program. Providing less than 40 hours specialized training on how to deal with persons with mental illnesses in crisis has been referred to as CIT-Lite, or providing 40 hours training to all members of a police department, not just select members, has been called bastardizing CIT (Turnbaugh, Remolde, & Slate, 2004). As noted by Thompson and Borum (2006), the Memphis CIT Model requires that at least 15 to 20 percent of the sworn patrol force be CIT trained to ensure around the clock coverage for mental health crises, and with the majority of law enforcement agencies across the country employing less than 10 full-time sworn officers, adjustments to the program would need to occur to facilitate implementation of CIT with small departments and in rural areas.

As of 2004, Cochran (2004) indicated roughly 50 to 80 jurisdictions had implemented CIT, and Teller et al. (2006) estimated that seventy law enforcement agencies nationwide had developed CIT programs. In a survey with 251 respondent law enforcement agencies, NAMI determined that 168 (67 percent) of the agencies reported having a CIT program in their communities; the majority of these programs (61 percent) reflected some aspect of consumer and family member involvement (Honberg, 2005).

CIT appears to be rapidly growing in popularity, and the third annual national CIT conference was held in Memphis in August 2007, with the next conference slated for Atlanta in November 2008. Currently, Steadman (2007), while acknowledging questions of total fidelity to the model, estimates that there are 500 to 600 jurisdictions with CIT programs in place across the country.

Some states [Colorado, Connecticut, Florida, Georgia, Illinois, and Ohio] of late have initiated efforts for implementation of the CIT training program statewide (Munetz, Morrison, Krake, Young, & Woody, 2006). However, there are concerns that if such training becomes too centralized at the state or federal level adaptation to the nuances and proclivities of a particular local jurisdiction may be lost. As noted by Thompson and Borum (2006), local jurisdictions may be hesitant to relinquish CIT training to state authorities whereby centralized, rigid state mandated curricula and training plans may not be readily adaptable to all jurisdictions that have significant differences in mental health and criminal justice resources.

Although, as noted above, Florida is attempting to initiate a statewide training initiative, it is being driven from the grassroots, not via a centralized state training academy. Florida's first forty hour crisis intervention training took place in March of 1999 (Turnbaugh, 1999). Since then, it is estimated that 2000 officers in the state of Florida have received CIT training from close to 200 jurisdictions; of course, this is a far cry from saying that there have been 200 CIT programs developed and operational in Florida (Thompson, 2007).

Again exemplifying questions of fidelity to the Memphis CIT model, Jamieson and Wilson (2000) note that the Seattle Police Department has adopted the Memphis CIT model but has fewer less lethal weapons than Memphis, with access only to pepper spray and batons. A Seattle firearms instructor, Ken Saucier, counters, "You don't take a bean bag gun to a gunfight" and expresses concern that if officers lessen their guard when encountering persons with mental illnesses in crises they may do so at their peril (Jamieson & Wilson, 2000). A trained CIT officer on the scene of a crisis with a person with mental illness can be designated to take charge of a situation regardless of the rank of the other officers (Watson & Angell, 2007), but this is not the case in Seattle. Seattle allows pretty much all its officers to participate in CIT training, while Memphis is much more selective, identifying those officers that appear to best suited for this innovative approach (Jamieson & Wilson, 2000). As indicated by Cochran (2004), Memphis is selective because some officers can't write a traffic citation without getting into a confrontation, much less if interacting with someone in a psychiatric crisis.

Agency Costs and Community Benefits

The primary agency allocation for implementing and carrying out CIT training is simply allowing officers time to attend the training sessions. Other than that, the costs are minimal, as instructors from the local community often donate their time. Of course, photocopying costs can be anticipated for the production of training manuals and compilation of community resource guides which specify ready reference contact information for local mental health resources. Access to appropriate space for the training is also necessary.

Most agencies signify that an officer has been CIT trained by design of a special pin that is worn on the police uniform. Persons with mental illnesses and their family members often look for such pins and find them to symbolize a source of comfort in crises. Lt. Brian Garrett (personal communication, June 8, 2007) of the Polk County Sheriff's Office, Bartow, Florida, describes one family's attachment to CIT.

A request came in for a CIT deputy to respond to a report of a 13-year-old child out of control in his home. Upon arrival the CIT deputy found the child barricaded in his room threatening to harm himself. The child had been diagnosed with bipolar disorder but was not medicine compliant. The subject then left the house through the bedroom window and attempted to flee the area. The deputy, concerned for the child's safety, gave chase and was able to take him into protective custody down the street after a brief physical struggle. The deputy recognized the child was in need of emergency mental health intervention and declined to charge him criminally for resisting a law enforcement officer. During the car ride to the local mental health receiving center, the young CIT deputy established a rapport with the child and consistent with CIT protocol told him he would come by the house to see him once he received treatment.

The deputy did make re-contact once the child got home and they had the time to discuss video games and other interests they had in common; the deputy used the encounter to urge the child to stay on his medicines and agree to go to counseling, something he had refused to do previously.

The deputy then gave the child his cell phone number and told him he could call anytime he needed someone to talk to and said he would return after the child's first counseling session. The child stabilized and is much improved in school and at home due to the intervention of a caring CIT deputy. The mother and I had actually spoken about her son after I gave a CIT presentation at the local NAMI meeting about a month prior to this incident. I had told her to specifically request that a CIT deputy respond if she needed help with her son in the future and she remembered to do so.

The mother later called me, in my capacity as the CIT coordinator, to thank the deputy for his efforts and to tell me what a difference it made in her son's life. She told me she was so impressed with the CIT deputy and the program in general that for several months when the family went out to eat or to other social activities they would only go to places in the county because the nearby city did not have a CIT program and would not have anyone to respond if her son was in crisis. She was very relieved when I told her we would send a CIT deputy anywhere in the county if she called needing help. She told me that immediately after the deputy told her son he would come back after he had been to counseling, her son began wanting to know when he would be seeing the counselor. He continued to ask her to take him in spite of the fact it was spring break from school and it took several days to get an appointment. She also related that the CIT deputy's work schedule was on her calendar and his cell phone number in her speed dial list. The mother told me living with her son's illness was not perfect but it was one thousand percent better than before the CIT intervention. We recruited this mother to speak from the family perspective during the 40-hour CIT training class, and she has done so regularly, becoming a popular presenter (B. Garrett, personal communication, June 8, 2007).

Typically, agencies have CIT graduation ceremonies and sometimes have banquets where distinguished officers, mental health providers, consumers of mental health services, and their family members can be recognized. Financial support for these and other costs may be obtained from grants, pharmaceutical companies, community organizations, and law enforcement academies (Saunders, Slate, Judd, & Brown, 2006).

Confidentiality

There appears to be a lot of misconceptions and down right ignorance about federal confidentiality laws that serve to inhibit communications regarding persons with mental illnesses. As noted by Husted et al. (1995), confidentiality laws may prohibit mental health clinicians from sharing information with law enforcement personnel about specific persons with mental illnesses. Similarly, Petrila (2007) reports that the Health Insurance Portability and Accountability Act (HIPAA) governs some communications regarding treatment of persons with mental illnesses. However, Petrila (2007) notes that

contrary to myth, HIPAA-covered entities do not include the courts, court personnel, ... law enforcement officials such as police or probation officers; [t]here are special rules for correctional facilities.... HIPAA ... permits [some] disclosures without the individual's consent. Those relevant here include disclosures for public health activities; judicial and administrative proceedings; law enforcement purposes; disclosures necessary to avert a serious threat to health of safety; and disclosures mandated under state abuse and neglect laws.... HIPAA incorporates the principle that in general disclosures should be limited to the 'minimal necessary' to accomplish the purpose for which disclosure is permitted.

So, for example, protected health information could be given by a treating agency whereby the agency could notify police of release of an arrestee, as "HIPAA permits a covered entity to disclose protected health information to a law enforcement official's request for 'information for the purpose of identifying or locating a suspect, fugitive, material witness, or missing person'" (Petrila, 2007). Petrila offers the caveat that state confidentiality laws may be more stringent than the HIPAA federal law, and he suggests that uniform consent/waiver forms like the one referenced below should be developed for release of information to ensure multi-agency cooperation. An example of a form for the disclosure of confidential information can be accessed via the Internet: http://www.gainscenter.samhsa.gov/html/resources/presentation_materials/pdfs/Un iformPermission.pdf

Another means for law enforcement to circumvent confidentiality requirements is to have consumers of mental health services voluntarily identify themselves to law enforcement. Residents of Orange, Seminole, Lake, Osceola, and Brevard counties in central Florida with mental health disabilities may register with the "Medical Security Program." Registrants will be issued a picture identification card and an identifiable bracelet recognizable to law enforcement personnel indicating that one is a voluntary enrollee in the program. This program is touted as a means of ensuring ready identification of persons with mental illnesses should crises occur and the initiation of a different tact in safely handling these individuals in such situations (Beary, 2005).

Cordner (2006) also maintains that HIPAA does not apply to police personnel and communications amongst themselves; therefore, tracking repeat calls, counting incidents, mapping locations, days/times of calls and hot spots are perfectly acceptable by law enforcement officers. Certainly, specialized training to properly address the avoidance of labeling and stigmatization by the police should be undertaken, and Cordner cites an example in Charlotte, North Carolina, where officers were summoned to the same residence over 100 times on mental disturbance calls. This is certainly not indicative of therapeutic jurisprudence in action. Proper tracking and flagging of such calls and sharing of information should serve to reduce unnecessary utilization of law enforcement resources.

Even so, most law enforcement agencies do not maintain a record of calls for service involving persons with mental illnesses, with many agencies believing such logs would be in violation of the rights of persons with disabilities (Greenberg, 2001). However, even if HIPAA violations resulted, the repercussions for such violations are miniscule. Since the adoption of HIPAA in 2003, as of November 1, 2006, there had been 22,664 complaints lodged within the U.S. Department of Health and Human Services with no penalties imposed, and individuals cannot bring suit for alleged violations, as HIPAA is monitored through regulatory agencies (Petrila, 2007). For obvious reasons, discussions on the topics of confidentiality laws and regulations should be included in any specialized police training concerning interactions with persons with mental illnesses,[13] and memorandums of understanding (MOUs) should be entered into by both mental health and criminal justice agencies to clearly delineate agreements and responsibilities.

Liability

There is an increased likelihood of liability for law enforcement agencies and officers for police encounters with persons with mental illnesses. These types of encounters can result in misuse of force, civil rights violations, and wrongful death claims (Borum, 2000).

> Sergeant Kendall Wiley (personal communication, May 21, 2007), CIT Coordinator of the Las Vegas Metropolitan Police Department, reports that in the past few years her Department has had some major incidents with persons with mental illnesses that resulted in use of deadly force with serious injuries to officers and/or consumers, and sometimes resulted in litigation. She provides the following examples:
>
> Le Menn died Jan. 4 while in custody on three misdemeanor charges at the Clark County Detention Center. Police said Le Menn, a 33-year-old French citizen, yelled that he was Satan and Jesus Christ. When guards were removing Le Menn from his cell, a struggle ensued in which the inmate was pepper sprayed. The fight ended with the Frenchman collapsing and dying on the cell floor from asphyxiation, according to Coroner Ron Flud.
>
> *Review Journal June 8, 2000*
> *Metro Paid $500,000*
> *Review Journal June 8, 2003*
>
> Gavigan, who has a history of mental illness, ran into the house after the officers tried to persuade her to drop the knife. Gavigan

---

13. For example, Lisa Yanku, Manager of Emergency Services, with the Kent Center in Warwick, Rhode Island, includes the topic of permitted disclosures to law enforcement under HIPAA in specialized training for police responding to persons with mental illnesses (A. Stoltz, personal communication, October 10, 2007).

then apparently hurt herself with the knife, then moved toward the officers, police said. The other officer backed up until hitting a wall in the house. The officer fired one shot when Gavigan continued to advance toward the officers, police said.

March 01, 2002 Review Journal

Police fatally shot Herrera, a 27-year-old schizophrenic man, outside his home Jan. 17 after he threatened police. Five officers responded to the call and unsuccessfully tried to subdue the knife-wielding Herrera with pepper spray and beanbag rounds fired from a shotgun. When Herrera came within five feet of the officer with a knife, the officer fired his handgun five times, striking Herrera four times.

Herrera v. Las Vegas Metropolitan Police;
298 F. Supp. 2d 1043 (D. Nev. 2004).

The case of a mentally ill man, shot and killed by police officers after use of bean bag pelletsz and pepper spray failed to subdue him, presented a genuine issue of fact as to whether officers had been inadequately trained in dealing with mentally ill persons and in the use of impact projectiles and whether the alleged inadequate training caused his death. Department settled (Undisclosed) (Wiley, 2007).

As pointed out by del Carmen (1998), in the law, duty follows knowledge (City of Canton v. Harris, 1989). In this same case, Hill and Logan (2001) note that the U.S. Supreme Court established that deliberate indifference can result "where the need for additional training is 'so obvious' and the failure to provide the additional training is 'so likely' to result in a constitutional violation" (p. 30–31).

Mental health providers and clinicians are also not immune from liability for their actions or failure to act in their dealings with persons with mental illnesses. For example, the family of a person with mental illness in New Haven, Connecticut, has filed a lawsuit against doctors and a hospital for negligently allowing their loved one to decompensate to the point that he was placed in a position to be shot and killed by police (Mills, 2006).

Saunders et al. (2006) maintain that CIT can reduce police liability and avoid media/community scrutiny with minimal expenditures on the part of the criminal justice system, as expertise in local communities can be tapped to support training initiatives. Thus, implementation of specialized police training for dealing with persons with mental illnesses in crises won't prevent lawsuits but may very well increase the possibility of the dismissal of such suits.

Collection of Outcome Data

More meaningful outcome data needs to be collected to demonstrate the benefits of police-based diversion programs. This compilation of information should contain data associated with officer and citizen safety, reductions in persons with mental illnesses going to jail, and improved police community/mental health relations (Reuland & Cheney, 2005). Economics should not be the primary concern, but cost-savings should be shown when such calculations are possible. The accumulation of accurate, useable outcome data is essential for developing and establishing best practices. The GAINS Center in Delmar, New York, can be of assistance in providing guidance for the appropriate methods for data collection, preservation, and presentation.

Examples of compilation of data regarding CIT outcomes can be seen below from the Las Vegas Metropolitan Police Department, which initiated their CIT training based on the Memphis model in 2002, provided by Sergeant Kendall Wiley (personal communication, May 21, 2007).

(CIT) Crisis Intervention Team
Statistics (Outcomes)
March 2003 through December 2006

	2003	2004	2005	2006	Total	Percent
CoConsumers Assisted	308	298	365	456	1427	
Arrests	**5**	**10**	**29**	**29**	**73**	**5.12%**
WESTCARE (CTC) Voluntarily Went to CTC	50	51	16	14	131	9.18%
Legal-2000 Emergency Psychiatric Exam	186	188	183	307	864	60.15%
Monte Vista (Private Hospital)	17	6	7	3	33	2.31%
Southern Nevada Adult Mental Health	10	7	4	4	25	1.75%
Follow-up Care Voluntarily Went to Hospital	38	34	123	98	293	20.53%
Suicides & Excited Delirium	2	2	3	1	8	0.56%
Revised 01/10/07 (K. Wiley, personal communication, May 21, 2007)						

Data compiled by the Ventura County Sheriff's Office in Ventura, California on CIT reveals the following information. The statistical information is based on data sets derived from CIT Event Summary cards and is compared to the previous year.

CIT trained officers were over 2.5 times more likely to encounter a mentally ill person in possession of a weapon, yet no more likely to use force to resolve the incident than non-CIT trained officers from January 2005–December 2005. CIT trained officers were 1.65 times more likely to encounter a mentally ill person in possession of a weapon and slightly less likely to use force to resolve the incident than non-CIT trained officers from January 2006–December 2006.

The CIT technique of making proactive contacts and developing rapport with mentally ill individuals appears effective in mitigating potential crisis situations as CIT officers were two to five times more likely to have a "contact only" disposition from January 2005–December 2005; CIT officers were 1.5 to 2.5 times more likely to have a "contact only" disposition from January 2006–December 2006. This statistically significant data suggests that CIT trained officers are more effective in managing and de-escalating crisis situations, thus utilizing mental health services less often.

The amount of time jail was used as a disposition was 2.5% or less overall from January 2005–December 2005; the amount of time jail was used as a disposition was 1.5% or less overall from January 2006–December 2006. These percentages are significantly less than the national average that varies between 8–15% and as high as 20%. The time period analyzed below was January 2006–December 2006, and there were no differences with the previous year in terms of outcomes. The rate of use-of-force in managing mentally ill individuals remains low overall, with "verbalization only" techniques used up to 95% of the time (no difference from 2005). Leg restraints, chemical agents, baton, and other less lethal equipment were used slightly more than 2 % of the time. (This year, use of the TASER gun was expanded countywide.)

There has been a correlation over time between a decrease in the number of lethal shootings and an increase in the number of CIT trained officers (no difference from 2005). The amount of injuries that occurred to mentally ill individuals during police involvement was very low overall—less than 1.5% (no difference from 2005). Neither the average disposition time nor the average response time have been adversely affected as a result of the CIT program [no difference from previous year] (J. Wilde, J. Frank, & M. Zabarsky, personal communication, May 1, 2007).

Lt. Denise Spratt (personal communication, May 8, 2007) of the Louisville Metropolitan Police Department provides the following information for the year 2006 regarding the Louisville CIT program that began in 2002. In 2006, the Louisville Metro Police Department made 3,237 CIT runs. Only 75 of those runs involved any level of force by officers. This is less than 2 _ %. Of the 75, over half, 38, involved the use of empty hand control only to gain compliance. The other 37 involved other less-lethal uses of force. Anytime officers can gain voluntary compliance from a person with mental illness who is in crisis to go to a treatment center, it is a win/ win for everyone. Safety is improved for the officer, the patient and the general public. The police department's response to persons with mental illness has improved due to the fact that we are now trained to take them for treatment and not to jail (Spratt, 2007).

Conclusion

Individual jurisdictions should decide if a pre-booking diversion program such as those described above is suitable for their community and identify key stakeholders to become involved in considering such options. Locals may even want to identify a model program and send representatives to observe the program and/or training in operation. The Memphis Police Department's CIT program has served as a model visited by a number of jurisdictions around the country [such as the Orange County Sheriff's Office in Orlando, Florida (B. Lewis, personal communication, July 13, 2007) and the Fulton County Police Department in Atlanta, Georgia (P. Michaud, personal communication, May 6, 2007)].

Community stakeholders that might be considered along with law enforcement at the table for planning and perhaps training purposes include mental health providers, jail administrators, prosecutors, public defenders/defense attorneys, judges, consumers of mental health services, family members of persons with mental illnesses and community organizations such as NAMI. Some jurisdictions, such as evidenced in Connecticut, have developed "CIT Plus" programs whereby officers are trained to partner with special CIT clinicians.

These licensed clinical social workers and state employees are assigned to individual police departments' CIT programs and pick up where the officers leave off. The clinician works with the person in crisis to assess needs and to connect him or her to the proper, available community-based services (L.C. Pyers, personal communication, June 24, 2006).

Law enforcement interventions when coupled with assistance from the courts can prove promising. The next chapter focuses on mental health courts. However, all the planning, coordination and training in the world may not be enough. As noted by Cochran (2004), no amount of police training can compensate for an insufficient infrastructure of services and care.

References

Adams, R. W. (2006, May 1). Compassionate enforcers— Police's new role. *The Ledger* A1; 8; 9.

Beary, K. (2005). Identification bracelet programs. Orlando, Florida: Orange County Sheriff's Office. Retrieved from the World Wide Web on June 14, 2007: http://www.ocso.com/LinkClick.aspx?link=ID+BRACELET+PRO-GRAMS.pdf&tabid=115&mid=510.

Bernstein, R., & Seltzer, T. (2003). The role of mental health courts in system reform. *University of the District of Columbia Law Review* 7, pp. 143–162.

Borum, R. (2000). Improving high risk encounters between people with mental illness and the police. *The Journal of the American Academy of Psychiatry and the Law* 28, pp. 332–337.

Borum, R., Deane, M. W., Steadman, H. J., & Morrissey, J. (1998). Police perspectives on responding to mentally ill people in crisis: Perceptions of program effectiveness. *Behavioral Sciences and the Law* 16, pp. 393–405.

Borum, R., Swanson, J., Swartz, M., & Hiday, V. (1997). Substance abuse, violent behavior and police encounters among persons with severe mental disorder. *Journal of Contemporary Criminal Justice* 13(3), pp. 236–250.

Boyd, E. (2006). Appropriate use of police officers? *Psychiatric Services* 57(12), p. 1811.

Buchanan, D. (2007). Commitment to recovery. Arlington, Virginia: Treatment Advocacy Center. Retrieved from the World Wide Web on July 20, 2007: http://www.psychlaws.org/GeneralResources/pa10.htm.

Bunch, K. (2005, January 30). When cops confront mental illness: Policing mental illness. Medicine.Net.com. Retrieved from the World Wide Web on June 14, 2007: http://www.medicinenet.com/script/main/art.asp?articlekey=51068.

Burnett, V. B., Henderson, B. C., Nolan, S. D., Parham, C. M., Tucker, L. G., & Young, C. (2000). How Birmingham's community service officers unit works. *Community Mental Health Report* 1(1), pp. 1–2; 13.

City of Canton v. Harris, 489 U.S. 378 (1989).

Cochran, S. (2004, Winter). Fighting stigma in law enforcement: The message has to come from the heart. Resource Center to Address Discrimination and Stigma. Washington, DC: U.S. Department of Health and Human Services, Substance Abuse and Mental Health Services Administration, Center for Mental Health Services,. Retrieved from the World Wide Web on June 12, 2007: http://www.stopstigma.samhsa.gov/memoranda/indexwinter2004.htm.

Cochran, S., Deane, M. W., & Borum, R. (2000). Improving police response to mentally ill people. *Psychiatric Services* 51(10), p. 1315.

Cooper, V. G., McLearen, A. M., & Zapf, P. A. (2004). Dispositional decisions with the mentally ill: Police perceptions and characteristics. *Police Quarterly*, 7(3), pp. 295–310.

Comptom, M. T., Esterberg, M. L., McGee, R., Kotwicki, R. J., & Oliva, J. R. (2006). Crisis intervention team training: Changes in knowledge, attitudes, and stigma related to schizophrenia. *Psychiatric Services* 57(8), pp. 1199–1202.

Comptom, M. T., & Kotwicki, R. J. (2007). *Responding to individuals with mental illnesses.* Boston: Jones & Bartlett.

Cordner, G. (2006) People with mental illness. Problem-Oriented Guides for Police, Guide No. 40. Washington, DC: Office of Community Oriented Policing Services, U.S. Department of Justice.

Council of State Governments (2007). Fact sheet: Law enforcement and people with mental illness. *Criminal Justice/Mental Health Consensus Project.* New York. Retrieved from the World Wide Web on June 13, 2007: http://consensusproject.org/resources/fact-sheets/factsheet_law.

Council of State Governments (2003). Community mental health officer. *Criminal Justice/Mental Health Consensus Project.* New York. Retrieved from the World Wide Web on June 16, 2007: http://consensusproject.org/ programs/one?program_id=77&searchlink=%2fprograms%2fsearch%3f%26sho w_p%3dt%26consensus_op%3dge%26order_by%3dtitle%26dir%3dasc.

Council of State Governments. (2002). Contact with law enforcement. Retrieved from the World Wide Web on June 16, 2007: http://consensusproject.org/down loads/Chapter_II.pdf.

Crisis Center (2007). Mobile Crisis Team (MCT) Department of Health and Human Services Montgomery County, Maryland. Retrieved from the

World Wide Web on June 16, 2007: http://www.montgomerycoun-tymd.gov/hhstmpl.asp?url=/content/hhs/crisis_center/mct.asp.

Curtis, L. A. (1975). *Violence, race, and culture*. Lexington, MA: D.C. Heath.

Dailey, J., Daley, G., Lushbaugh, D., White, E., Slate, R. N., & Sultan, B. (2006, September 26). The critical role of consumers and families in advocating for CIT and jail diversion. Orlando, Florida: 2nd Annual Crisis Interven-tion Team (CIT) Conference.

Deane, M. W., Steadman, H. J., Borum, R., Veysey, B. M., & Morrissey, J. P. (1999). Emerging partnerships between mental health and law enforce-ment. *Psychiatric Services* 50(1), pp. 99–101.

del Carmen, R. V. (1998). *Criminal procedure: Law and practice, 4th ed.*. Bel-mont, CA: Wadsworth.

Dempsey, J. S., & Forst, L. S. (2008). *An introduction to policing, 4th ed.*, Bel-mont, CA: Thomson Wadsworth.

Dupont, R., & Cochran, S. (2000). Police response to mental health emer-gencies— barriers to change. *Journal of the American Academy of Psychi-atry and Law* 28, pp. 338–344.

Fasshauer, K. D., & Garrett, B. (2006, September 27). Hearing disturbing voices TM— A program developed by the national empowerment center. Florida Council for Community Mental Health, Hope and Recovery Con-ference, Orlando, Florida. Retrieved from the World Wide Web on July 18, 2007: www.fccmh.org/docs/FCCMH_conf_program.pdf.

Goodstein, L. (2000, September, 6). Trying to prevent the next killer ram-page. *The New York Times*, Retrieved from the World Wide Web on June 11, 2007: http://query.nytimes.com/gst/fullpage.html?res=9A00E3DF1739F 935A 3575AC0A9669C8B63&sec=health&spon=&pagewanted=2.

Green, T. M. (1997). Police as frontline mental health workers. *International Journal of Law and Psychiatry* 20(4), pp. 469–486.

Greenberg, S. F. (2001). Police response to people with mental illness. In M. Reuland, C.S. Brito, & L. Carroll (Eds.), *Solving crime and disorder prob-lems: Current issues, police strategies and organizational tactics* (43–58) Washington, DC: Police Executive Research Forum.

Hails, J., & Borum, R. (2003). Police training and specialized approaches to re-spond to people with mental illnesses. *Crime & Delinquency* 49(1), pp. 52–61.

Hill, R., & Logan, J. (2001, June). Civil liability and mental illness: A proac-tive model to mitigate claims. *The Police Chief*, pp. 29–32.

Honberg, R. (2005, May 12). A national snapshot of CIT programs. Colum-bus, Ohio: 1st National Crisis Intervention Team Conference.

Husted, J. R., Charter, R. A., & Perrou, B. (1995). California law enforcement agencies and the mentally ill offender. The *Bulletin of the Academy of Psychiatry and the Law* 23(3), pp. 315–329.

Lamb, H. R., Weinberger, L. E., & DeCuir, Jr., W. J. (2002). The police and mental health. *Psychiatric Services* 53(10), pp. 1266–1271.

Lamb, H. R., Weinberger, L. E., & Gross, B. H. (2004). Mentally ill persons in the criminal justice system: Some perspectives. *Psychiatric Quarterly* 75(2), pp. 107–126.

Lee, R. (2007, July 5). Sympathy through technology: Virtual reality experience mimics schizophrenia to teach health professionals about their patients. New York: ABC News. Retrieved from the World Wide Web on July 18, 2007: http://www.abcnews.go.com/WN/story?id=3348856.

Lushbaugh, D. (2007, August 30). Awards Banquet. Memphis, Tennessee: National CIT Conference.

Jamieson Jr., R. L., & Wilson, K. A. C. (2000, May 25). Mental illness frequently deepens tragedy of police shootings. *Seattle Post-Intelligencer*, Retrieved from the World Wide Web on June 12, 2007: http://seattlepi.nwsource.com/local/shot252.shtml.

Miller, R. D. (1997). Symposium on coercion: An interdisciplinary examination of coercion, exploitation, and the law: III. Coerced confinement and treatment: The continuum of coercion: Constitutional and clinical considerations in the treatment of mentally disordered persons. *Denver University Law Review* 74, pp. 1169–1214.

Mills, J. (2006, November 21). Lawsuit: Cop shooting was hospital's fault. *The Health Care Connecticut Online Journalism Project*. Retrieved from the World Wide Web on June 16, 2007: http://www.newhavenindependent.org/HealthCare/archives/2006/11/lawsuit_cop_sho.html.

Mobile Crisis Team (2004, June). New York Department of Health and Mental Hygiene, New York. Retrieved from the World Wide Web on June 16, 2007: http://www.nyc.gov/html/doh/html/cis/cis_mct.shtml.

Munetz, M. R., Fitzgerald, A., & Woody, M. (2006). Police use of the taser with people with mental illness in crisis. *Psychiatric Services* 57(6), p. 883.

Munetz, M. R., Morrison, A., Krake, J., Young, B., & Woody, M. (2006). Statewide implementation of the crisis intervention team program: The Ohio model. *Psychiatric Services* 57(11), pp. 1569–1571.

Panzarella, R., & Alicea, J.O. (1997). Police tactics in incidents with mentally disturbed persons. *Policing: An International Journal of Police Strategies & Management* 20(2), pp. 326–338.

Patch, P. C., & Arrigo, B. A. (1999). Police officer attitudes and use of discretion in situations involving the mentally ill: The need to narrow the focus. *International Journal of Law and Psychiatry* 22(1), pp. 23–35.

Perrott, S. B., & Taylor, D. M. (1995). Crime fighting, law enforcement and service provider role orientations in community-based police officers. *American Journal of Police* 14(3/4), pp. 173–195.

Petrila, J. (2007, February). Dispelling the myths about information sharing between the mental health and criminal justice systems. Delmar, New York: The National GAINS Center, Retrieved from the World Wide Web on July 19, 2007: http://gainscenter.samhsa.gov/text/integrated/Dispelling_Myths.asp.

Price, M. (2005). Commentary: The challenge of training police officers. *The Journal of the American Academy of Psychiatry and the Law* 33, pp. 50–54.

Reuland, M. (2004). A guide to implementing police-based diversion programs for people with mental illness. Delmar, NY: GAINS Technical Assistance and Policy Analysis Center for Jail Diversion.

Reuland, M. (2005). A guide to implementing police-based diversion programs for people with mental illness. (Rev. ed.) Delmar, NY: National GAINS Technical Assistance and Policy Analysis Center for Jail Diversion.

Reuland, M., & Cheney, J. (2005). Enhancing success of police-based diversion programs for people with mental illness. Delmar, NY: National GAINS Technical Assistance and Policy Analysis Center for Jail Diversion.

Ruiz, J., & Miller, C. (2004). An exploratory study of Pennsylvania police officers' perceptions of dangerousness and their ability to manage persons with mental illness. *Police Quarterly* 7, pp. 359–371.

Saenz, T. J. (2002, May 1) AP police chief threatens crisis unit with arrest. *Highlands Today*, pp. 1–2.

Sargeant, G. (1992, December). Back to bedlam: Mentally ill often jailed without charges. *Trial*, pp. 96–98.

Saunders, M., Slate, R.N., Judd, G., & Brown, G. (2006, June 20). "Law Enforcement/Mental Health: Partnerships and Initiatives for Change." Orlando, Florida: National Sheriffs' Association Conference.

Sellers, C. L., Sullivan, C. J., Veysey, B. M., & Shane, J. M. (2005). Responding to persons with mental illnesses: Police perspectives on specialized and traditional practices. *Behavioral Sciences and the Law* 23, pp. 647–657.

Skeem, J., & Bibeau, L. (2008). How does violence potential relate to crisis intervention team responses to emergencies? *Psychiatric Services* 59(2), pp. 201–204.

Staik, T. (2007, June 27). Man claiming to be Jesus surrenders after five-hour standoff. *Charlotte Sun Herald*. Retrieved from the World Wide Web on July 20, 2007: http://www.sun-herald.com/Newsheadline.cfm?headline=8838.

Steadman, H.J. (2007, June 21). Treatment not jails: New leadership and promising practices. San Diego, California: National Alliance on Mental Illness Annual Convention.

Steadman, H.J., Stainbrook, K. A., Griffin, P., Draine, J., Dupont, R., & Horey, C. (2001). A specialized crisis response site as a core element of police-based-diversion programs. *Psychiatric Services* 52(2), pp. 219–222.

Steadman, H. J., Deane, M. W., Borum, R., & Morrissey, J. P. (2000). Comparing outcomes of major models of police responses to mental health emergencies. *Psychiatric Services* 51(5), pp. 645–649.

Strauss, G., Glenn, M., Reddi, P., Afaq, I., Podolskaya, A., Rybakova,T., et al. (2005). Psychiatric disposition of patients brought in by crisis intervention team police officers. *Community Mental Health Journal* 41(2), pp. 223–228.

Sultan, B., O'Brien, S., Fairnholt, K. S., & Talley, S. (2006, September 26). CIT and in our own voice: A natural partnership. Orlando, Florida: 2nd Annual Crisis Intervention Team (CIT) Conference.

Teplin, L. A. (2000, July). Keeping the peace: Police discretion and mentally ill persons. *National Institute of Justice Journal*, Washington, DC: U.S. Department of Justice, pp. 8–15.

Teese, C. F., & Van Wormer, J. (1975). Mental health training and consultation with suburban police. *Community Mental Health Journal* 11(2), pp. 115–121.

Teller, J. L. S., Munetz, M. R., Gil, K. M., & Ritter, C. (2006). Crisis intervention team training for police officers responding to mental disturbance calls. *Psychiatric Services* 57(2), pp. 232–237.

Thompson, L. (2007, February 5). *Personal communication.* Florida Mental Health Institute, University of South Florida, Tampa, Florida.

Thompson, L., & Borum, R. (2006). Crisis intervention teams (CIT): Considerations for knowledge transfer. *Law Enforcement Executive Forum* 6(3), pp. 25–36.

Torrey, E. F. (2006). Surviving schizophrenia, 5th ed. New York: Harper Collins.

Turnbaugh, D. G., Remolde, M.L., & Slate, R.N. (2004, November 5). The future of crisis intervention team training. Jacksonville, Florida: NAMI Florida Annual Conference.

Turnbaugh, D. G. (1999, August). Crisis intervention training (CIT) for law enforcement officers. *The Florida Police Chief*, pp. 9–11.

Vermette, H. S., Pinals, D.A., & Appelbaum, P.S. (2005). Mental health training for law enforcement professionals. *The Journal of the American Academy of Psychiatry and the Law* 33, pp. 42–46.

Watson A. C., & Angell, B. A. (2007). Applying procedural justice theory to law enforcement's response tp persons with mental illness. *Psychiatric Services* 58(6), pp. 787–792.

Watson, A. C., Corrigan, P. W., & Ottati, V. (2004). Police officers' attitudes toward and decisions about persons with mental illness. *Psychiatric Services* 55(1), pp. 49–53.

Weathersbee, T. (2006, February 20). Treatment of mentally ill should not be police duty. *Florida Times-Union*, Jacksonville.com, Retrieved from the World Wide Web June 10, 2007: http://www.jacksonville.com/tu-on-line/stories/022006/new_21145923.shtml.

Wilson, J. Q. (1978). *Varieties of police behavior.* Cambridge, MA: Harvard University Press.

Wood, A. L., & Wahl, O. F. (2006). Evaluating the effectiveness: Of a consumer-provided mental health recovery education presentation. *Psychiatric Rehabilitation Journal* 30(1), pp. 46–53.

CHAPTER 5

MENTAL HEALTH COURTS

"Success is not measured so much by the position that one has attained
in life as by the obstacles that one overcomes while trying to succeed."

—Booker T. Washington

History

Specialized mental health courts are playing a crucial role in reducing the needless suffering for many persons with mental illnesses who encounter the criminal justice system. The development of mental health courts was preceded by implementation of the nation's first drug court in 1989 in Dade County, Florida (Denckla & Berman, 2001; Hasselbrack, 2001). To date there are a thousand or more drug courts across the country (Denckla & Berman, 2001; Petrila, 2006). In some jurisdictions mental health courts have emerged under the auspices of a drug court (Goldkamp & Irons-Guynn, 2000; Lurigio, Watson, Luchins, & Hanrahan, 2001). Actually, due to the high correlation between substance abuse and mental disorders [co-occurring disorders], there appears to be a logical relationship between drug and mental health courts (Denckla & Berman, 2001; Osher, Steadman, & Barr, 2003) and, as will be discussed, both types of courts rely upon the principles of therapeutic jurisprudence (Steadman, Davidson, & Brown, 2001). Of course, mental health courts can be distinguished from drug courts in that possession and use of drugs constitutes a crime, whereas being mentally ill and not complying with treatment protocols is not a crime (Haimowitz, 2002).

Mental health courts initially drifted away from the punitive inclinations of drug courts. Drug courts typically utilize punishment, and some mental health courts are generally reluctant to use punishment because of an acknowledgement that persons with mental illnesses may be prone to relapse, and punishment would result in punishing someone because of their status of being mentally ill (Petrila, 2002). Mason (2005) concurs by indicating, "The drug court with coercive sanctions for noncompliance as the model for the mental health court is both problematic and in the long term offers little for persons with mental illness[es] who already walk daily with coercion as a constant companion" (p. 7). As such, mental health courts generally vary in terms of the point of intervention, pre or post booking, and the use of sanctions from drug courts (Poythress, Petrila, McGaha, & Boothroyd, 2002).

Prior to the establishment of the nation's first mental health court, Lamb, Weinberger, and Reston-Parham (1996) recommended that courts in certain cases, such as misdemeanors, consult with psychiatrists when considering treatment and should mandate and monitor such treatment when warranted. The nation's first mental health court originated in 1997 in Broward County Florida (Denckla & Berman, 2001; Elwell, 1998; Lurigio et al., 2001; McGaha, Boothroyd, Poythress, Petrila, & Ott, 2002; Mikhail, Akinkunmi, & Poythress, 2001; Poythress et al., 2002; Ridgeley et al., 2007; Slate, 2000), a neighboring county to the location of the first drug court. As with the development of police-based diversion programs, tragedy often drives policy, and so it was with the nation's first mental health court.[1]

Mental health courts continue to develop. In a survey of mental health courts the Council of State Governments (2005a) reports that "in 1997, only four mental health courts existed in the country; by January 2004, 70 courts were known to be in operation; as of June 2005, there [were] approximately 125 operational courts in 36 states[,]" and today there are an estimated 150 mental health courts in operation across the nation (Steadman, 2007). There

---

1. As related by then Chief Public Defender Howard Finkelstein (who is now the Public Defender), an individual who had suffered a traumatic head injury, upon hearing voices in a grocery store, ran outside and into a little old lady, knocking her and her bag of groceries to the ground. Witnesses observed him trying to put her groceries back into the bag and believed he was trying to rob her, according to Finkelstein. The lady ultimately died from injuries sustained in the fall, and the fellow with the head injury was indicted for manslaughter. Finkelstein essentially told the grand jury that if they were going to indict his client that they should indict the mental health and criminal justice systems for failing his client time and again and putting him in the position for this to happen. The grand jury launched an investigation that resulted in a 153-page report lambasting both the mental health and criminal justice systems. According to Finkelstein, the grand jury's recommendations provided the impetus for establishment of Broward County's mental health court. Wonder how many other jurisdictions in America could withstand such scrutiny? It should also be noted that Hasselbrack (2001) reports that the family of Finklestin's client received a $17 million award as the result of a civil suit against Florida's Department of Children and Families (Slate, 2003, p. 25–26) in Slate, R.N. (2003). From the jailhouse to Capitol Hill: Impacting mental health court legislation and defining what constitutes a mental health court. *Crime & Delinquency, 49*(1), p. 6–29.

are also adaptations of mental health courts outside the United States, such as in Canada (Boyle, 1998) and England and Wales (Mikhail et al., 2001).

Of 90 mental health courts in the United States that responded to an online survey, the Council of State Governments (2005a) reported that the majority of mental health courts were located in southern and western states, with over 40 percent of all of the nation's mental health courts contained within the four states of California, Florida, Ohio, and Washington. Specialized juvenile mental health courts have been developed (Arredondo et al., 2001) in Los Angeles, Santa Clara, and Ventura County, California; Escambia County, Florida; Hamilton, Huron, Otawwa, Seneca, and Summit counties in Ohio and King County, Washington that are specifically specializing in the mental health needs of juveniles (National Center for Mental Health and Juvenile Justice, 2005). The Council of State Governments (2005b) reports that the only mental health court that they are aware of that has programs focusing exclusively on females is the Behavioral Health Court in San Francisco, California.

Mental health courts are considered the most recent of the problem-solving or specialty courts (Grudzinskas, Clayfield, Roy-Bujnowski, Fisher, & Richardson, 2005). Mental health courts are aimed at problem-solving by minimizing punitive approaches and maximizing treatment options (Sublet, 2005; Tonry, 2006). Problem-solving courts, which incorporate the concept of therapeutic jurisprudence, such as mental health courts, have been embraced by national institutions such as the Conference of Chief Justices and the Conference of State Court Administrators (Gunther, 2005). Broward County's mental health court was founded on the principle of therapeutic jurisprudence and has been used as an example for a number of different jurisdictions considering implementation of their own mental health courts (Slate, 2000).

The aim of mental health courts is to protect society while applying the tenets of therapeutic jurisprudence and striving for linkages to dignified treatment with the goal of ending needless recycling of persons with mental illnesses through the criminal justice system. Mays and Thompson (1991) have referred to the courts as the gatekeepers of America's jails in their ability to directly influence jail populations. According to Stone (1997), individuals with inadequate community health placements and lack of insurance coverage can find their mental health deteriorating and may end up in jail. Since most jails, even those with diversion programs, do not have follow-up programs to oversee the therapeutic progress of offenders once they return to the community, the cycle continues (Steadman, Morris, & Dennis, 1995; Walsh & Bricourt, 1997). Mental health courts have emerged due to an inability to adequately treat persons with mental illnesses in correctional facilities, overcrowding in jails and prisons impacted by persons with mental illnesses and judicial dissatisfaction with high recidivism rates among this population (Acquaviva, 2006).

As discussed in Chapter 1, therapeutic jurisprudence principles avoid looking solely backward, finding fault, assessing blame, and imposing punishment with little, if any, consideration for the consequences of decisions rendered by the justice system. Instead, therapeutic jurisprudence, as practiced within mental health courts embraces the concept of looking forward and considering the ramifications of decisions long after a person's encounter and contact with the justice system has ended. One of the basic tenets of this mental health court philosophy is to "respond ... to crime by seeking to rehabilitate the offender and repair the harm suffered by the victim and community rather than by punishing the offender according to retributive or deterrent principles" (Lanni, 2005, p. 359).

Daicoff (2006) compares the traditional court process to that of mental health courts utilizing therapeutic jurisprudence. In the traditional system, adjudication is the primary focus, whereas with therapeutic jurisprudence the main concern is after adjudication and on alternative means to resolve disputes. The judge acts more as an arbiter in the traditional process and more as a coach with the use of therapeutic jurisprudence principles. Reflective of the past versus future focus, the traditional system is based on precedent, and under therapeutic jurisprudence principles, the emphasis is on planning. Participants and stakeholders are limited with the traditional process and exhaustive with the inclusiveness of the therapeutic jurisprudence approach. Lastly, the traditional system is formal, legalistic, and efficient, while the herapeutic jurisprudence approach is informal, common-sensical, and effective.[2]

---

2. This distinction between the formality of the traditional courtroom and the informality of the mental health court is reflected in the following examples, and is indicative of the need for continuing legal education. Howard Finkelstein, Chief Public Defender in Broward County Florida, indicated that fortunately one of the first cases that ultimately made it to the nation's first mental health court involved a gentleman that had just been released from the hospital. Upon release, the fellow stood on the steps of the hospital waiting for a stretch limousine to come pick him up and drive him to New York to be married to Joan Rivers. The limousine never materialized, and hospital attendants called the police. The subject was arrested, and, at the initial appearance, the judge did not appreciate the comportment of the man who had been waiting for Joan Rivers. Before the case eventually made it before the mental health court, the presiding judge charged the man with contempt of court and ordered him to spend 179 days in jail (Slate, 2000). This is quite a contrast to the less rigid atmosphere that can be found in most mental health courts. For example Judge Scott Anders of Vancouver, Washington's mental health court allows consumers appearing before

The goals of the mental health court include cooperation between the criminal justice and mental health systems, identification of the most effective and least restrictive treatment interventions, effective legal advocacy for the mentally ill, assessment of mental health service delivery and receipt of services, involvement of consumers and family members in the court process, and diversion to community mental health treatment programs (Cowart, 1997). In her Broward County mental health court, Judge Lerner-Wren (1997) reports that she practices therapeutic jurisprudence in an attempt to balance first and foremost public safety and then the treatment needs and constitutional rights of those appearing before the court. This concept is supported even by the prosecutor's office, which recognizes that public safety is maintained by the Court's ability to examine long-term treatment plans and keep defendants closely monitored and functioning in the community instead of revolving through the door of the criminal justice system (Raybon, 1997).[3] In other

---

his court to address him by his first name (S. Anders, personal communication, November 29, 2001). Obviously, there is a need for the education of most judges, and lawyers for that matter, regarding the signs and symptoms of mental illness and appropriate measures for processing persons with mental illnesses who encounter the criminal justice system. Vickers (2001) has been instrumental in getting mental illness awareness training mandated by the Florida Bar as part of continuing legal education credits (Slate, 2003, p. 26) in Slate, R.N. (2003). From the jailhouse to Capitol Hill: Impacting mental health court legislation and defining what constitutes a mental health court. *Crime & Delinquency, 49*(1), p. 6–29.

3. In a telephonic interview on June 29, 1998, Assistant State Attorney Lee Cohen in Broward County indicated the following: Traditionally, prosecutors are generally viewed as punitive in their orientation. However, we should punish when punishment is deserved, but when someone does not possess the mental capacity to form the intent to commit a criminal offense then they should not be punished. The goal is to ensure public safety and bring justice by prosecuting and/or restoring competency. Restoring competency with an aim toward prevention of future deviant acts and reoccurrences of mental aberrations can serve to bring justice. Assistant State Attorney Cohen also added that the Mental Health Court allows for more time and more information in rendering decisions and ensures more efficiency by having all the knowledge and resources managed within one courtroom. Prosecutors were much more inclined to make referrals to the mental health court, while the defense bar was reluctant to have their cases addressed in the mental health court arena Slate, 2003, p. 26) in Slate, R.N. (2003). From the jailhouse to Capitol Hill: Impacting mental health court legislation and defining what constitutes a mental health court. *Crime & Delinquency, 49*(1), p. 6–29.Similarly, Mark Kammerer with the Cook County State Attorney's Office in Chicago informed this writer, on September 26, 2006 at the 2nd Annual National Conference on Crisis Intervention Teams in Orlando, Florida, that after they implemented a mental health court within their jurisdiction that indeed it was almost like a role reversal with the legal participants (M. Kammerer, personal communication, September 26, 2006).

words, the aim of mental health court is to become part of the solution instead of remaining part of the problem, with the Court instituted to counter the recurring process that revolves persons with mental illnesses in and out of jails with much longer stays than those encountered by similarly situated non-mentally ill defendants (Finkelstein and Brawley (1997).

Judge Lerner-Wren describes in her own words the beginnings and the essence of the nation's first mental health court in Broward County, Florida. She places particular emphasis on the principle of therapeutic jurisprudence, giving persons with mental illnesses the opportunity to participate in the less rigid proceedings of the mental health court, and securing linkages to treatment while ensuring public safety.

Mental Health Courts:
A Treatment Oriented Approach to the Criminalization
of the Mentally Ill in the United States.

"Graciousness enhances, not weakens, the practice of Law; and decency and jurisprudence are not mutually exclusive."

(*The Miami Herald*,
on the passing of U.S. Court Justice Lewis Powell)

Criminal Courts in the United States have typically been concerned with Mental Illness and Mental Retardation only insofar as the mental disability of the defendant is raised to question competency or sanity. The focus of concern in these instances is on legal issues (i.e. restoration of competency and criminal responsibility) and not on clinical treatment and recovery.

In June, 1997, Broward County, Florida implemented the nation's first criminal court dedicated to addressing the complexities of the mentally ill in the criminal justice system. An extension in theory of drug courts and other specialty treatment oriented courts, this court-based diversionary strategy was the historic outgrowth of a number of converging perceptions. There was a perception in the community that the jail had become the largest de facto hospital, due to a severely under funded and highly fragmented community-based system of care. There was also a law enforcement perception that it was easier and quicker to arrest and book individuals that may be psychiatrically acting out than to have them evaluated at a local crisis center or hospital. The lack of a coordinated police friendly central crisis system was cited as contributing to the arrest of those in psychiatric crisis. FN1. Broward County Grand Jury Report, Spring 1995)

The concept for a specialized Mental Health Diversionary Court was conceived by Public Defender Howard Finkelstein, through the creation of a mental health criminal justice task force, assembled to seek solutions. The Task Force, a cross-section of mental health advocates, lawyers, judges, community treatment providers, social service administrators and family members met for years before settling on a course of action.

County Court Criminal Judge Ginger Lerner-Wren was selected to preside over this voluntary, part time criminal division based on her expertise in mental health disability law and community-based systems of care. It should be noted, while the Broward court model shares some values and goals of a drug court, its objectives and procedures are vastly different and highly individualized. It is important to recognize mental disability is not a crime although often the manifestations of psychiatric symptoms have led to the criminalization of this population. Consequently, real differences between the drug court and mental health court models exist. Jurisdictions must become educated on the differences, understand guiding principles and promote and protect substantive constitutional legal rights as traditional legal processes are transformed into therapeutic proceedings.

Strong charismatic judicial leadership is essential as different complex and independent systems, criminal justice, and mental health and substance abuse must come together in collaboration. A well stated shared vision and commitment must be developed and maintained. For Broward, the Judicial Construct of Therapeutic Jurisprudence was adopted as the philosophy of the court which addresses low level non-violent misdemeanor offenses.

The goals of Broward's Mental Health Court are to:

- Create effective interactions between the criminal justice and mental health systems.
- Ensure legal advocacy for the Mentally Ill Defendant
- Ensure that mentally ill defendants do not languish in jail because of their mental illnesses.

- Balance the rights of the defendant and the public safety by recommending the most appropriate, workable disposition using existing community-based resources.
- Increase access for the mentally ill defendant to community-based treatment and services and utilize the court to integrate and help ensure access to care (including housing, case management, substance abuse treatment, peer services, primary health care, etc.)
- Reduce the contact of the mentally ill defendant with the criminal justice system by creating a bridge between the systems.
- Monitor the delivery and adequacy of community treatment and services.
- Solicit participation from consumers and family members in the court process whenever possible.
- Promote recovery and the reduction of stigma surrounding the illnesses.

Guiding Principles:
- That the court process should be trauma informed, dignified, individualized, consumer-based and recovery oriented. Participants must be permitted to tell their stories.
- Public Safety is always paramount to treatment.
- Court participation should be voluntary, confidentiality protected respecting private patient medical records, and constitutional rights and legal rights should never be sacrificed for treatment.
- The Court environment is significant and unique. A Judge for example, should strive to be empathetic, compassionate and therapeutic when possible while clearly and continually restating participant goals and expectations. The Court should make efforts to honor personal treatment choice and create an environment of trust and dignity. Strength-based language should be used, and Procedural Due Process and giving voice to the court participant is extremely vital.

A Problem-solving Team Approach and a Community Collaborates

Broward's Mental Health Court was the model for 1999 Federal Legislation called the Criminal Reduction and Diversionary Court Legislation (FN2. National Public Law 106515). Since the trend of Mental Health Courts and other Court-based diversion strategies have emerged there is no consensus on one particular model. Many communities have adapted parts of Broward's Model or developed their own, while striving to adhere to overarching guiding principles and treatment objectives. Many communities have implemented juvenile mental health courts, felony mental health courts and integrated dockets for treatment oriented courts generally.

To date, the Department of Justice, Bureau of Justice Assistance, SAMHSA and other policy organizations continue to share information, research, evaluate and identify the growth of these specialty courts nationally. More formal education and cross training on Mental Health Disability Law, mental health and substance abuse treatment issues, evidence-based research and systems of care models need to continue to be provided to judges, lawyers, forensic clinicians, case managers and others who work in and support these courts.

Again, great care must be taken to study these court-based models and ensure every defendant's constitutional and other legal rights are protected. The complex balancing of these differing and various considerations must be understood. There are definite legal and clinical boundaries, as well as limitations of any Mental Health Court or court-based diversion strategies. Further, as community-based collaboration improves and strengthens, much care must be taken to sustain relationships, keep media relations strong and carefully manage risk. In 2003, The President's New Freedom Commission on Mental Health in its Final Report, "Achieving the Promise: Transforming Mental Health Care In America" recommended that every State create and develop a comprehensive and integrated State Forensic Plan which includes the array of pre-booking and post-booking diversion and re-entry strategies to help keep those more appropriate for community care— in the community, as well as improved Correctional Care for the incarcerated offender. More information on Mental Health Courts can be found through The Bureau of Justice Assistance, U.S. Department of Justice website.

—G. Lerner-Wren, personal communication, July 17, 2007

The Broward County Mental Health Court

The Broward County Mental Health Court was established in 1997 in the County Court Criminal Division via administrative order by Chief Circuit Judge Ross (Broward County Circuit Court, 1997). Upon implementation the

Court was charged with processing mentally ill misdemeanants, as long as they were not facing driving under the influence, domestic violence, or assault (unless their victim voluntarily consented for the case to be handled in mental health court) charges.

Two contractual employees were provided to help the judge in making assessments within the courtroom and in follow-up. One was the court clinician, a licensed clinical social worker, from the Florida Department of Children and Families, who offers clinical expertise to the Court in assessing treatment needs. The other was a court monitor from a local private mental health center who keeps the court informed of the treatment status and compliance of participants.

Formal referrals to the Court, as specified in the administrative order establishing the Court, could come from sources such as other judges, assistant district attorneys and defense attorneys, and the Court will decide if the accused meets the necessary criteria. Others, including family members, the police and jail personnel, can informally initiate referrals. As depicted in Figure 1, the diagram delineates the typical processing of cases that Judge Wren presides over in the Broward County Mental Health Court.

Broward County has also modified the probable cause affidavit required for all arrested individuals within the state of Florida so that officers can check off on a form whether they noticed any sign of mental illness during the arrest process to alert others involved in processing a subject. If a person is taken to jail, such notification is noted at booking so that proper handling will follow. Also, at booking, each arrestee's pertinent information is registered into a computer system and then cross referenced with mental health care providers in the area to establish any history of mental illness. In addition, Broward County has implemented mobile crisis stabilization units, specially trained clinicians in the transportation and treatment of the mentally ill. Before these units, the process for civilly committing individuals was often time consuming, keeping law enforcement officers busy for hours, away from their other duties. Thus, officers found it simpler and time efficient to take the mentally ill to jail, as opposed to becoming tied up by the commitment process. With mobile units, the police who meet a mentally disoriented subject on the street can merely call the unit, which responds to the chosen location and transports the subject to a suitable receiving facility, thereby freeing the police to return to their normal duties.[4] Persons with mental illnesses ap-

---

4. R. Slate witnessed the mobile crisis stabilization unit being summoned to the Judge's courtroom to remove a debilitated, jailed, individual for civil commitment processing during observation of the court in operation.

Figure 1

Arrest

→ Day 1 →

Magistrate Court (Referrals)

→ Day 1 →

Mental Health Court Staff Notified

Day 1 ↓

Second Hearing

After release from crisis stabilization
to make judicial determinations re:

Case Track

• Is subject willing to seek treatment?

• May determine competency

• Based on individual evaluation

• Are there issues of dangerousness?

• Does subject want to challenge charges by trial?

To Judicially Review Case

• Assess adequacy and relevancy of treatment

• Is subject compliant?

• Has subject gained stability by living in community?

• Are other treatment or social needs being met?

Disposition

• May impose pre-trial release conditions

• May dispose of case

• May sentence

• Additional statuses may follow

Initial Hearing

• May send to crisis stabilization unit for independent evaluation under civil commitment law

• May dispose of case

• May sentence

• May impose pretrial-release conditions

• May determine that the individual doesn't meet criteria for the mental health court

• May order competency evaluations if appropriate

Diagram modified from Slate, R.N. (2000). Courts for mentally ill offenders: Necessity or abdication of responsibility. In G.L. Mays & P.R. Gregware (Eds.) *Courts and Justice* (2d ed.) p. 442. Prospect Heights, IL: Waveland Press.

pearing before the Broward County Mental Health Court had increased access to mental health services (Boothroyd, Poythress, McGaha, & Petrila, 2003; Levin, 2006). Also, Petrila (2002) reports in an initial assessment in Broward County, Florida that mental health court clients perceive the court as fair and non-coercive, and mental health court clients were found to be able to access treatment services more effectively than misdemeanants processed through the traditional criminal court system. Also, Christy, Poythress, Boothroyd, Petrila, and Mehra (2005) found that participants in Broward County's Mental Health Court had significantly shorter stays in jail than those in a comparable group.

Mental Health Court Dynamics/Models

The Broward County Mental Health Court has set an example that other courts have striven to emulate. However, there is no single model of a mental health court that is suitable to all communities (Goldkamp & Irons-Guynn, 2000; Lurigio et al., 2001; Steadman et al., 2001; Watson, Hanrahan, Luchins, & Lurigio, 2001; Watson, Luchins, Hanrahan, Heyrman, & Lurigio, 2000). Each jurisdiction has to collaboratively assess available resources, personnel, and orientations to determine what is right for a particular area. Differences in mental health courts vary widely in terms of eligibility, plea agreements, supervision, incentives, sanctions for noncompliance, and completion standards. Some courts just handle misdemeanants, some just felonies, some exclude those charged with certain crimes, such as domestic violence, crimes against children, driving while impaired or violent felonies, and some courts insist on a guilty plea while others defer prosecution as long as the individual is compliant with program directives (Levin, 2006). Boothroyd, Mercado, Poythress, Christy, and Petrila (2005) indicate that while there is no single mental health court model a commonality among these courts is the diversion of persons with mental illnesses from the criminal justice system into treatment.

In general, the term 'mental health court' describes:

> A specialized docket for certain defendants with mental illnesses that substitutes a problem-solving model for traditional court processing. Participants are identified through specialized screening and assessments, and voluntarily participate in a judicially supervised treatment plan developed jointly by a team of court staff and mental health professionals. Incentives reward adherence to the treatment plan and other court conditions, non-adherence may be sanctioned,

and success or graduation is defined according to specific criteria (Council of State Governments, 2005c, p. 2).

Thompson, Osher, and Tomasini-Joshi (2007) identify a number of essential elements of a mental health court. According to them, planning and administration of a mental health court is guided by a broad range of stakeholders from the criminal justice, mental health, and substance abuse treatment systems. They also maintain that a target population should be identified based on public safety concerns and a community's treatment capabilities with consideration of the connection between a defendant's offense(s) and mental illness. There should also be timely identification of participants in the court's program and linkage to relevant services, with clearly delineated terms of participation and focus on both public safety and treatment concerns. Participants should be allowed to make informed choices, and it should be ensured that decisions are competently entered into. Confidentiality for consumers of mental health services should be assured, and information divulged should not be used against those individuals returned for criminal processing. The team of criminal justice and mental health professionals should be employed to monitor individuals and ensure compliance with court dictates, with evidence-based services engaged in the community when practicable. Lastly, data should be collected and assessment should occur to ensure sustainability and community support for the mental health court program (Thompson, et al., 2007).

Judge Angela Cowden presides over one of the nation's newest mental health courts in Polk County, Florida. She describes her court in the following terms:

Before October 2007, Polk County had no Mental Health Court (MHC). However, as of January 2008, Polk County has a viable MHC, with 28 contract participants and more referrals every week. Our program is a voluntary diversion of persons charged with misdemeanor criminal offenses, and who suffer from a mental or developmental illness. With the help of a dedicated team including a case coordinator, treatment providers, case managers, and the commitment of the State Attorney's Office, the Public Defender's Office, County Probation, Pre-trial services, the Clerk's Office and others from Court Administration, we have created a vision for our Court.

Our vision is, on an individual basis, to treat each person's needs, to re-connect the broken threads of help, treatment, trust and confidence that these people have lost through years of untreated mental illness. We expect responsibility and accountability for actions, but temper those expectations with the understanding that many issues need to be resolved before treatment can be effective. We are working to create a safety net for individuals who, through loss of resources, cannot access treatment, jobs, medications, and other support.

Each of us on the team believes that, if we are able to turn around even one life and make permanent changes for the future for just one person, we have done well for that person and for society as a whole. We truly expect more success than that, and believe that the future is bright for Polk County's Mental Health Court, as we look at expanding the Court to one day perhaps include Juvenile Mental Health and Felony cases as well (A. Cowden, personal communication, January 30, 2008).

According to Morabito (2007), "Failing to hold offenders with mental illness accountable for illegal behavior is beneficial to neither individuals nor communities" (p. 1586). Judge Cowden, who was formerly a prosecutor, addresses the shift from prosecutor to judge and the ability to some times have extended supervision over mental health court clients.

Transitioning from prosecutor to judge took a little time, but I had great training along the way and hope that in each role I have performed my duties to the best of my ability. As a judge, my role is as 'a neutral and detached magistrate', meaning I cannot advocate for one side or the other and must remain neutral until the case is concluded and I then make a decision based on the law as it applies to the case. In Mental Health Court that responsibility is modified to an extent to try to relate to the participants who come before me, to encourage their continued participation and compliance and to make the ultimate call if diversion is or is not appropriate, depending on the participant's willingness.

"Our prosecutor is involved, and aside from the fact that the State Attorney's Office at first was not keen on a diversion type of program, I believe they understand that, at this point, I can maintain jurisdiction of the participant longer than in some cases I could if they entered a plea and were placed on a type of probation. The charges remain open throughout the case until the person successfully completes a year of the diversion and only upon approval do the charges go away. This gives much incentive to complete the program or face going back to jail and receiving no help.

—(A. Cowden, personal communication, January 30,2008)

As Booker T. Washington once said, "Success is not measured so much by the position that one has attained in life as by the obstacles that one overcomes while trying to succeed."[5] First, Judge Stephanie Rhoades of Anchorage, Alaska, discussing "John" and "Violet," and then Probate Judge Mark Heath of Bennettsville, South Carolina, elaborates on "Bobby," "Latoya," "Dorothy" and "David" as they share examples of what they consider successful interventions that have occurred in their mental health programs some three thousand miles apart. Note the innovative therapeutic jurisprudence principles Judge Rhoades and Judge Heath embrace as they respond to those under their care, even providing house calls. This is certainly a different type of jurisprudence.

—S. Rhoades, personal communication, July 13, 2007

John's Story

John is a 52-year-old Caucasian male with a diagnosis of schizophrenia, undifferentiated type, cocaine dependence in full sustained remission, antisocial personality disorder, and also has several medical problems (diabetes, hypertension and congestive heart failure). John has an extensive criminal history dating back to the late 1970s—the crimes were mainly misdemeanor crimes, such as criminal trespass, minor drug related crimes, shoplifting, and malicious destruction of property. John's current charge was a felony, malicious destruction of property which was later reduced to a misdemeanor criminal mischief charge. John was at the bank where he was attempting to cash his weekly check from his payee and became angry with the teller who would not cash the check as it was post dated. John left the bank and smashed the bank window with a trash can sitting next to the bank door. The police were quickly dispatched to the scene and within ten minutes had located a suspect matching the description of John. When John was asked about what happened at the bank he informed the police officer he threw a trash can at the door because he was angry the teller did not cash his check and now he did not have money to buy cigarettes.

John was arrested at the scene—John was initially housed in general population in the Department of Corrections (DOC) until it came to the attention of the mental health staff that John was re-

5. Retrieved from the World Wide Web on August 22, 2007: See http://www.brainyquote. com/quotes/quotes/b/bookertwa107996.html.

ceiving services from the local mental health center and had a history of multiple psychiatric hospitalizations. John was assessed by the DOC psychiatrist and it was discovered that John had been homeless for much of the past year and had been off his psychiatric medications for several weeks. John was restarted on medications and the DOC began the discharge planning process, obtaining releases of information for the mental health provider to determine where John would be housed upon release from the DOC. John spent several weeks in jail as his case was a felony and he could not afford to bail out of jail; when the charge was reduced to a misdemeanor John was immediately referred to the mental health court. The mental health court was explained and John agreed to work with the specialty court. He was assigned a case coordinator who helped devise a release plan— due to John's health problems, history of homelessness, and difficulty caring for himself it was determined an assisted living facility would be an appropriate fit. The mental health court case coordinator worked with the treatment provider to secure funding for the Assisted Living Facility (ALF) and arrange for immediate placement. John was not keen about living in an ALF—the facility specialized in housing persons with mental health disorders—John wanted independence but agreed to try the ALF.

John got off to a rocky start. Upon release from jail he did not appear for his next court hearing—it was discovered he was seen at the psychiatric emergency room and admitted to the state psychiatric hospital for treatment. To complicate matters, John's health problems began to deteriorate and his risk for stroke increased. John was treated in the hospital and released back to the ALF where he did well for several months. John began to refuse to take his medical and mental health medication and refused to come to court. He began to have problems with his roommates which placed him at risk of eviction, his psychiatric symptoms increased, and his blood pressure and diabetes were out of control, resulting in psychiatric hospitalization where both psychiatric and medical needs were again cared for. After this hospitalization John seemed to get much better—he was started on new psychotropic medication with less side effects, lost weight and improved his health enough to discontinue a portion of his diabetes medication. He still needed close monitoring for his health problems and began to settle in at the ALF, where his medications were monitored and he took a more active role in caring for his health. John expressed wanting to have more money for a trip out of state but was unable to afford this on his limited income. He started working with a job coach and got a job cleaning in a warehouse and was able to save funds to make his trip out of state to visit family he had not seen in many years. After doing well for several more months, John was recommended for graduation from mental health court. John expressed his appreciation to the judge upon graduation for the support and encouragement received during participation. Upon graduation John's charges were dismissed.

We now here from John every couple of months; he comes in the court to say hello, still living in the ALF, works at his job in the warehouse, and visits relatives out of state every year. John had a history of 27 criminal convictions spanning over 20 years. Since his graduation three years ago, he has remained out of the criminal justice system. He is now housed, reengaged with his family, employed, and successfully managing his medical and mental health symptoms.

Violet's Story

Violet is a 22-year-old African American with a diagnosis of Bipolar Disorder, most recent episode manic, with psychotic features, a history of marijuana, cocaine, and amphetamine abuse and personality disorder. Violet is the youngest of seven siblings and grew up in the foster care system. Violet was physically and sexually abused by an older brother prior to foster care placement and does not have contact now with any of her siblings. She was placed in a foster care setting at the age of 14 with an affluent family who adopted her at age 16; the family is still very much involved with Violet. Violet had her first psychiatric hospitalization at the age of 17; after release from the hospital Violet spent two months in the youth mental health treatment facility out of state. She has two assault convictions which involved assault of her adoptive mother.

Violet has a poor history of medication compliance with her chief complaint that medications make her gain weight. As a result, Violet has had six psychiatric hospitalizations in a four year period; Violet voluntarily admitted herself at the last admission and left within three days against medical advice. Within 24 hours, Violet was in jail. Violet was charged with a misdemeanor theft charge. She entered a Wal-Mart store, loaded the cart until it was overflowing with snacks from the grocery store and ran from the store into the street causing several cars to swerve to miss hitting her. Police were dispatched and as the officers approached Violet, she began screaming that she did not take anything and threw herself on the road, blocking lanes of traffic. Violet was arrested and taken in to custody. Violet was not able to be arraigned in custody, appeared to be experiencing visual and auditory hallucinations, and making threats to kill herself, other inmates, and correctional staff. Substance use was suspected but Violet was uncooperative and a screening could not be conducted. The court requested a competency evaluation based on the client's erratic behavior—the evaluation included a review of previous hospitalizations which indicated the client would likely be restored to competency within a 14 day period.

Violet was transferred to the state psychiatric hospital for competency restoration and started on medications; Violet expressed the concern about weight gain and was started on newer medications that did not cause weight gain problems. Violet responded well to the medications and was found to be competent to proceed with her legal case—she was arraigned and chose to participate in the mental health court program. With assistance from the court case coordinator, Violet was connected to a case manager and therapist to work on immediate needs. Safe and sober housing, as well as recent suspected substance use were of immediate concern—Violet participated in a substance abuse assessment and was able to enter into a pre-treatment bed immediately upon discharge from jail. Violet was able to participate in pre-treatment activities for several weeks until a residential dual diagnosis bed opened through a Salvation Army program. Violet stayed in the residential program for 90 days—she found a sponsor while in treatment and continued with the aftercare portion of treatment for six months as an outpatient. Violet was referred to a specialized housing program for clients who cycled through institutions. This program was able to set her up with her own apartment and help with funds for furniture and other basic household items. The case manager from the housing program helped Violet with the social security application process and benefits were granted, helping to pay the 30% of the income for rent. Violet responded very well to the medication regimen she was prescribed, with very few side effects (and no weight gain). She began working with the state Division of Vocational Rehabilitation program and was able to secure grant funding to go to college and began courses. She obtained her drivers license, was able to purchase a car with help from her adoptive parents, completed community work service and paid all fines associated with the criminal charge. She began group and individual therapy to address trauma issues from childhood and successfully completed the group portion and continues with an individual monthly session. Violet was recommended for graduation and her case was dismissed. She has had no new criminal charges in two years (Stephanie Rhoades, District Court Judge, Mental Health Court, Anchorage Alaska, personal communication, July 13, 2007).

—M. Heath, *personal communication, June 21, 2007*

Bobby's Story

In January 2006 I first met Bobby face to face. His file showed that he had been in and out of institutions since 1990. His diagnosis was paranoid schizophrenia. Bobby had graduated from high school and spent one year in college. Upon completion of his first year, he had a personality change. He became unable to return to school or manage his daily affairs. After being released again from an institution, Bobby became non-compliant with treatment for outpatient counseling, so he was brought into court to explain himself to me. After talking with him, it was obvious that a charge for contempt of court meant nothing to him nor was he concerned about serving time in the local jail. I realized that the firm and strict approach was not working and began to talk with him about his personal life. I asked Bobby if he would return to counseling and advise the doctor if the medication was having side affects that were not tolerable. The next day, I saw his mother at the post office and told her how much I enjoyed talking with her son. She concurred that he had enjoyed it also. I began to call Bobby and spend some time just letting him know that someone cared about him and his life. Since this time, he has obtained a part-time job with the school system and has not had to be institutionalized again.

Latoya's Story

Latoya was a very efficient, productive, and a quiet secretary. She could outwork any two people that had the same job. She spoke only when spoken to, had work provided ahead of time and assignments were always ready when you asked for them. She worked so hard that at times I begged her to bring a book, needle point, or some other distraction rather than working all the time. A very professional "workaholic" would be a good description of her. On December 31st one year she left wishing me a Happy New Year. When she returned to work on January 2nd, she would not be quiet, did not want to stay in the office, and was unable to type any documents. She seemed very hyper and out of control. After referring her to the local mental health center, the examination showed there was nothing wrong with her. Upon this finding, I immediately called the local mental health office and asked for a second opinion. When she was reexamined, she was diagnosed as manic depressive. Her condition deteriorated to the point that she had to be physically removed from her job, restrained, and taken to the state hospital. After being out of work for several months, Latoya came back to work. She was provided with a letter concerning the mandatory condition that she seek mental health counseling as part of her return to work. After about nine months, I began to notice things were not quite right. She was again taken to the state hospital for several months. Upon her release, she advised me that she would be returning to work immediately. As a result of her failure to provide a letter from her doctor that she could return and threatening the upper management, she was fired. LaToya finally received the counseling and medications that she needed and has once again become a productive member of the work force.

Dorothy's Story

Dorothy, a 48-year-old African-American woman, was arrested in October 2004 for Assault and Battery of a High and Aggravated Nature. The family reported that Dorothy had quit taking her meds and her behavior had been becoming more and more erratic. She lit torches in the front yard of her rural home and would then dance and chant in an erratic manner. Her family was poorly educated, did not understand the dynamics of mental illness, and if anything, was embarrassed by her 'fool behavior.' Dorothy was interviewed at the local jail by the representative from our Mental Health Court, and it was obvious that severe mental illness was the primary cause for her erratic behavior. She explained to the mental health court worker that voices had led her to a certain building in the county and that

God was telling her she owned it. In her mind, the man that approached her—the legitimate owner of the property—was a serious threat, and thus she needed to attack him. She was confused by being arrested, as her reality was that he was in the wrong and she was in the right. Dorothy received 2 years probation, with the special condition that she also work 2 years with the local Mental Health Court program. She was diagnosed as having a form of schizophrenia and put on antipsychotic medications by the local psychiatrist. The improvement in her mental clarity was obvious within a few weeks—she became insightful to her illness, realized the importance of medication compliance, and confessed that she had had moments in the past wherein she would go off her meds and have to be hospitalized.

The weekly appointments gave her a chance to be educated as to her illness and help her family understand the importance of medication compliance (i.e., the client must take meds daily, not just when decompensating). Dorothy continues to have struggles—her medication co-pay is expensive, she has been denied disability status, and she has had difficulty finding a job because of background checks showing her arrest. However, she has not been re-arrested since this event, graduating from the program after 2 years of participation. Her family reports significant improvement overall and now are more closely connected to the local mental health center should problems arise that need addressing.

David's Story

David had been placed on probation for assaulting his neighbor. Upon his initial interview, his version of the offense was that he had been trying to sleep as he worked at night. The neighbor on several occasions continued to play his radio very loudly. After repeatedly asking the person to turn it down, he lost his composure and assaulted the neighbor. As we got into the interview, he disclosed that his wife had been having an affair and their marriage was already going sour after just a few years. When asked if he had ever thought about hurting himself or killing himself, he became visibly upset and left the office without permission. The next day after visiting him at his home, I explained to him that I thought he should go to the local mental health center and talk to them about depression. He agreed to go see them and after sev-

eral months on an antidepressant, he was able to return to a normal
way of life and salvage his marriage (Probate Judge Mark Heath, Bennettsville, South Carolina, personal communication, June 21, 2007).

Fields (2006) indicates that most mental health courts across the country
handle misdemeanants, but the Brooklyn Mental Health Court processes felons,
as does the mental health court in Chicago, which accepts persons with mental illnesses charged with non-violent and non-sex offender felonies (Murphy,
Friedman, & Andriukaitis, 2007). Fisler (2005) notes that defense attorneys
sometimes object to misdemeanants being processed in mental health courts
because defendants can be placed into treatment on a misdemeanor for a year
and then face potential jail sentences for a year for failures to comply with conditions of release. Public defenders are often resistant to diversion, particularly
for misdemeanors, because more extensive probation may expose one to longer
periods under control of the criminal justice system; defense attorneys may prefer opting for a 20-30-60-day sentence instead (Murphy et al., 2007). Thus,
some attorneys believe it is easier with less interference from authorities to serve
a short sentence as opposed to having to be compliant with longer term treatment conditions. Keele (2002) maintains that defense attorneys in the mental
health court setting must be willing to shed some of their traditional defense modes
and embrace among other things a holistic approach considering the consequences of their actions into the future beyond the current case at hand.

According to the Bazelon Center for Mental Health Law,

Mental Health Courts [are] becoming increasingly likely to accept
felony defendants but argue ... that misdemeanants are ill suited for
mental health courts because they should be diverted from the criminal justice system entirely [via] prebooking diversion programs....
Mental health courts should close their doors to people charged with
misdemeanors[,] as [s]ome ... jails will not accept misdemeanants
(primarily because of overcrowding) regardless of mental health status (Redlich, Steadman, Petrila, Monahan, & Griffin, 2005, p. 537).

While all courts under the Americans with Disabilities Act have a duty to accommodate persons with mental illnesses, specialized mental health courts
continue to be developed and more and more are filling that role. Bernstein and
Seltzer (2003) do not view mental health courts as a panacea and recommend
that they only be utilized when individuals are facing significant jail or prison
time, with particular focus on individual rights and provision of appropriate
levels of community mental health services.

While no single model may constitute the make-up of a mental health court, Goldkamp and Irons-Guynn (2000) identified the following commonalities in four of the earliest mental health courts in Fort Lauderdale, (Broward County) Florida; Seattle, Washington; Anchorage, Alaska[6]; and San Bernardino, California: A special docket comprised mainly of nonviolent mentally ill misdemeanants (exceptions were found in San Bernardino, which would allow felony cases, and in Fort Lauderdale, where the court would hear battery cases with voluntary consent from the victim).

- Mentally ill defendants with lengthy criminal histories who were suitable for processing were accepted in an attempt, with proper treatment interventions, to keep them from reprocessing through the criminal justice system.

6. Judge Stephanie Rhoades of the Anchorage, Alaska Mental Health Court in the following commentary expounds on the establishment of their court shortly after emergence of the nations' first mental health court in Broward County, Florida. In 1998 the Alaska Court System established a mental health court project—the Coordinated Resources Project (CRP)—in the Anchorage District Court to address the needs of mentally disabled misdemeanants. The court works to divert misdemeanor offenders with mental disabilities away from jail and into appropriate community treatment. The court focuses mainly on the therapeutic needs of the defendant. Mentally disabled defendants who adhere to treatment requirements cycle through jails and psychiatric hospitals far less than those who do not. The mental health court involves two designated judges, designated prosecutors and defense attorneys, the defendant and his/her community treatment provider(s) and two project case coordinators who assist the defendant in locating appropriate community treatment and services and provide hands-on monitoring of the defendant's treatment plan through regularly held status hearings. Participants receive assistance from the project in developing, coordinating, and monitoring an individualized treatment plan. The coordination and monitoring of community treatment plans is provided by the Alaska Department of Corrections' Jail Alternative Services (JAS) project case coordinator or the Alaska Alcohol Safety Action Program (AASAP) case coordinator. The case coordinators play a key role in assisting the therapeutic court participant with linkage to appropriate and needed community resources. Eligible participants for mental health court are Alaska Mental Health Trust Authority beneficiaries (persons with severe and persistent mental disorders, developmental disabilities, traumatic brain injuries, dementia, organic brain disorders, and alcoholism with psychosis). Participants who enter the therapeutic court present with unique problems, and the emphasis on developing an individualized plan is essential to a participant's long term success. Too often the mental health, substance abuse, and criminal justice service systems are fragmented. The case coordinators are skilled in identifying appropriate resources and act as boundary spanners to assist the participant in accessing existing services in the community (*S. Rhoades, personal communication, July 13, 2007*).

- Judges, with varying styles, who apply the principles of therapeutic jurisprudence in order to give voice to persons with mental illness who appear before the court.
- Memorandums of understanding (MOUs) are initiated between criminal justice and mental health agencies that serve to specify roles and responsibilities in a team approach for various entities and outline interagency agreements on supervision and monitoring of individuals coming before the court to facilitate compliance with court requirements.
- Key community players coming together collaboratively from the original planning stages to periodic meetings and continuing for evaluation after the court is in operation; these participants include the presiding judge and his/her staff, officials from both the defense and the prosecution, law enforcement executives to include detention managers, mental health clinicians and administrators connected to public and/or private community mental health treatment providers, mental health advocates to include persons with mental illness and family members, and sometimes probation officers.
- Initial assessment, with clinicians involved, as to any history or signs and symptoms of mental illness; if so, this typically results in transferring the person with mental illness voluntarily from jail to treatment as efficaciously as feasible.
- Available community linkages to support services and treatment, with multi-agency and system collaboration.

—(Goldkamp & Irons-Guynn, 2000)

Rogers (2005) adds that follow-up status assessments with incentives for compliance and sanctions for non-compliance with court dictates presided over by the court and treatment providers typically characterize the operation of mental health courts.

In addition to the courts studied by Goldkamp and Irons-Guynn, Griffin, Steadman, and Petrila (2002) examined four more mental health courts as well, in Santa Barbara, Indianapolis, and two more in Washington State. From their analysis they discovered three types of post-booking statuses among the eight mental health courts. Some jurisdictions withheld adjudication without a plea being entered, and, providing the court's treatment regimen was successfully completed, dismissal of charges would ultimately result; in other judicial districts, sentence imposition would be deferred, after entering a plea and/or adjudication, contingent on satisfying treatment stipulations by the court; and other judicial circuits convicted persons with mental illnesses and then placed them under probation supervision, sometimes via a deferred or suspended sentence.

Contrary to the standard practice in drug courts, Griffin et al. (2002) found that most of the courts they examined, excluding San Bernardino which heard felony cases, rarely utilized jail as punishment for not complying with treatment requirements imposed by the court, and charges were usually dismissed after successful adherence to treatment regimens. One jurisdiction allowed the retraction of guilty pleas, and another, after dismissal of charges, allowed for the possibility of expungement of arrest records following successful completion of treatment requirements.

In their analysis, Griffin et al. (2002) found court supervision of persons with mental illnesses came in three different formats via: community mental health treatment providers, probation officers or mental health court staff, or a combination of both mental health treatment professionals and probation officers on teams to monitor and aid in compliance. Watson et al. (2000) pointed out that state law may need to be examined to determine if individuals not convicted of a crime can legally be placed on probation or supervised release.

In addition to monitoring compliance to treatment protocols, status hearings allow probation officers and/or mental health professionals to apprise the court periodically of clients' progress (Lurigio & Swartz, 2000; Petrila, Poythress, McGaha, & Boothroyd, 2001). Probation officers and mental health court treatment professionals serve as boundary spanners linking persons with mental illnesses to essential treatment services and other vital needs such as housing, benefits, and vocational/employment options (McCampbell, 2001; Steadman et al., 2001).

Fifty-six percent of the 90 mental health courts responding to a survey indicated that they accept misdemeanor and felony cases on a case-by-case basis, while 34 percent of the courts reported accepting only misdemeanor cases, and 10 percent of the courts handled only felony cases (Council of State Governments, 2005a). Guilty pleas were required to be entered by participants in forty percent of the mental health courts that responded to the Council of State Governments (2005a) survey. A diagnosis of a serious and persistent mental illness or an Axis I disorder [see DSM IV] was required for acceptance into 60 percent of the mental health courts surveyed, eighty-eight percent of the respondent mental health courts indicated that a drug court is also in existence within their jurisdiction, and almost half of the mental health courts reported the presence of some type of police-based diversion program such as CIT within their community (Council of State Governments, 2005a).

There appear to be distinctive stages in the evolution and growth of mental health courts. Redlich et al. (2005) distinguished in their research between first generation and second generation mental health courts. They indicated that first generation mental health courts tend to be more misdemeanant focused, avoid convictions, and rely more so on mental health clinicians to supervise and monitor treatment compliance of mental health court participants in the community. Second generation mental health courts tend not to be primarily restricted to non-violent misdemeanors; they are more likely to employ a post-adjudicative format, utilizing supervision affiliated with the criminal justice system, such as probation officers, and, in an attempt to gain compliance, participants could have the sanction of jail imposed when necessary (Redlich at al., 2005). They also advise that based on the evolution of mental health courts thus far there may come a time in the development of third and fourth generation mental health courts where persons with mental illnesses accused of misdemeanors will no longer be processed by these courts.

Explanation and Results from Various Mental Health Court Programs

A number of studies have assessed the characteristics and results of implementation of mental health court programs across the country. "When outpatient treatment is mandated either through mental health courts or outpatient commitment statutes participating persons tend to do better than nontreatment control samples[;] some preliminary evidence supports the theory that initial mental health court comprehension is predictive of future success or failure in the court" (Redlich, 2005, p. 614) and is likely to lessen perceptions of coerciveness.

In a study of seven mental health courts, Steadman, Redlich, Griffin, Petrila, and Monahan (2005) found that when compared with others in the traditional criminal justice system mental health court clientele tend to be older, Caucasian, and women. Herinckx, Swart, Shane, Dolezal, and King (2005) found that graduation from the mental health court program was a critical factor in preventing individuals from recycling back into the criminal justice system, as graduates of the program in Clark County, Nevada were almost four times more likely not to recidivate as compared to those individuals who did not successfully complete the program. They also determined that participants one year after enrollment in the program were four times more likely to not be arrested compared to the year prior to their enrollment in the program, resulting in 54 percent of the participants not being arrested after one year in the program and a 62 percent reduction in probation violations over the same time period. Recidivism was also reportedly reduced via mental health courts in North Carolina (Hiday, Moore, Lamoureaux, & Magistris, 2005; Moore & Hiday, 2006), Oregon and Washington (Levin, 2006; Trupin & Richards, 2003).

In the North Carolina study researchers found that mental health court treatment programs not only decrease the number of re-arrests for participants but also tend to lessen the severity of any subsequent arrests. Those individuals who completed mental health court programs were even less likely to be re-arrested than participants who withdrew from the program (Moore & Hiday, 2006).

In Oregon fewer mental health court clients were arrested in the year after enrollment with the court, fewer inpatient and more outpatient treatment days were needed, and less crisis interventions were needed for this group than in the year before they became enrolled in the mental health court's service program. In Washington, both probation violations and re-arrests decreased after persons with mental illnesses completed a mental health court program (Levin, 2006). Also, Trupin and Richards (2003) in a study of mental health courts in Seattle, Washington determined in a nine month follow-up that those who opted to participate in the courts' programs were significantly less likely to be booked after entry into the program compared to bookings prior to beginning the program; participants had fewer bookings than those who opted not to engage in the courts' programs. When participants do not perceive their interactions with the court as coercive and view the mental health court process as procedurally fair they are more likely to be cooperative with court imposed terms and conditions (Poythress et al., 2002) and the more likely they are to be satisfied with the outcomes of their interaction (Miller, 1997).

Ridgeley et al. (2007) reports on a Brooklyn mental health court study that found that entry into the mental health court program resulted in improved psychosocial adaptations and significant decreases in abuse of substances and psychiatric hospitalizations. Over a four year span of time the Brooklyn mental health court has overseen 244 felons, and only 19 of these individuals have been returned to jail for violations of their court imposed conditions (Fields, 2006).

Cosden, Ellens, Schnell, and Yamini-Diouf (2005) examined the mental health court program in Santa Barbara, California, where individuals were placed in intensive case management in the form of assertive community treatment teams and were compared with those placed in less intensive case management environments through traditional court processes. They found that mental health court participants with intensive case management protocols in place reflected greater decreases in abuse of substances and engagement in illegal activity, and mental health court clients showed greater reductions in time spent in jail and improvements in performance than those assigned to traditional case management.

Ridgely et al. (2007) point out limitations of earlier studies and indicate that their study is to date the only evaluation to assess mental health court costs and to measure the influence fiscally of these courts on the social welfare, mental health, and criminal justice systems. Ridgely et al. (2007), in their two-year study of the Allegheny County Mental Health Court, discovered a "leveling off of mental health treatment costs and [a] dramatic drop in jail costs yielded a large and statistically significant cost savings at the end of [their] period of observation" (p. 20). They reported a total cost savings of $9,584.00 per mental health court participant (n = 66) over the two-year period of the evaluation for a total savings of over a half million dollars as a result of the implementation of the mental health court in Allegheny County. In their study of the Allegheny County, Pennsylvania mental health court they found that it costs less to divert persons with mental illnesses from the criminal justice system into treatment via mental health courts than it does to jail them. While initial savings may not be formidable, over time it was determined that the mental health court can result in governmental savings as recidivism and use of expensive treatments such as hospitalization decreases. Start-up costs may be a little more initially, but better results are evident over time as a therapeutic environment develops and takes hold. Thus, diverting persons with mental illnesses from jails saves money (Rivera, 2004).

Areas of Concern

Mental health courts are not without their critics. It has been discovered that mental health courts do increase access to treatment for persons who appear before them; however, ample treatment services need to be in place, and courts have little control over the caliber of the services dispensed (Boothroyd et al., 2005; Levin, 2006; Mason, 2005). This probably has more to do with inadequacies of mental health providers than with the mental health court (Boothroyd et al., 2005).

Mental health court judges can help negotiate and navigate treatment services, relying on what is available, and must learn to prioritize the services and are not really in a position to create new services (Haimowitz, 2002). Judge Stephanie Rhoades of the Alaska District Court in Anchorage describes her efforts at ascertaining mental health treatment and expresses her concerns about inadequacies in the availability of such treatment in the following discussion. Her concerns about services are representative of issues identified in the research literature.

The mental health court is reliant upon existing community resources to link a participant to for treatment. For example, a person with a mental health diagnosis is eligible for services at the community mental health center. A person with a developmental disability (DD) is typically eligible for DD services through the specialized facilities (ARC, ASSETS, or HOPE Community Resources). A person with a traumatic brain injury may be eligible for services at any of these agencies depending upon their individual circumstances, and also may benefit from ACCESS Alaska services which specialize in working with persons with brain injuries. Challenges arise in a person's unique situation at any one of these agencies. With Medicaid refinancing of previously grant-funded services, we see challenges with reduced services for clientele—previous case management, individual and group services are now more limited. Grants which previously assisted indigent clients now are not available. The DD waitlist is years long. Adults with FASD are extremely difficult to link to services as very limited services exist in the community.

There are a number of community gaps which contribute to the costly, unnecessary and repeated jail, hospital, and other institutional stays. The number one challenge the mental health court faces is being able to link participants to safe, sober, and affordable housing. Homelessness is very serious. In one Alaska Department of Corrections study: 35% of people with mental illnesses were released from jail to homelessness; too often mentally ill persons are indigent and can not afford housing, food, clothing and other basic necessities on release from jails/institutions. The mental health court does receive funds from the Alaska Mental Health Trust Authority to help with emergent housing, food, transportation and medical needs. Funds are limited and typically are a one time only expenditure for individual participants.

Another challenge area is ensuring that when a mentally ill person is released from jail or a psychiatric hospital that linkages to community mental health services are available. Mentally ill persons may run out of medications before they can see an outpatient psychiatric provider, resulting in erosion of mental stability. The mental health court has case coordinators that aid in setting expedited intake appointments so that a participant can access services and not run out of medication. There are special projects that attempt to address some of the problems, but even with more intensive services we continue to see a reduction in outreach services for beneficiaries.

A huge problem area exists with accessing services for those with co-occurring disorders. There are not enough treatment slots for people with co-occurring substance abuse and behaviorally challenging mental health disorders, including persons with developmental disabilities and traumatic brain injuries. Intake appointments for substance abuse assessments take 3 to 4 months, and treatment placement occurs several months after the initial assessment.

Special needs housing and treatment for the most behaviorally challenged individuals is extremely difficult to access. These are persons who frequent emergency systems (psychiatric emergency room, psychiatric hospital, jail, shelters). These are persons with significant behavior challenges, seriously mentally ill youth in transitions, and seriously mentally ill individuals convicted of sex offenses or certain violent crimes. The bottom line is that many Alaska Mental Health Trust Authority beneficiaries have chronic co-occurring mental health and substance use disorders that will require long-term treatment for both disorders in the community or they will predictably return to jail.

A continuum of services does exist within the department of corrections and in the outpatient behavioral health community. Over the years these programs/initiatives have resulted in increased collaboration between agencies, which helps beneficiaries, but the reality is there continues to be significant challenges if treatment and housing services do not exist. This continuum of services helps divert persons from the criminal justice system and provides a level of support to assist beneficiaries to remain in the community. Without adequate and appropriate treatment and housing services for beneficiaries, we will see the inevitable recycling of these individuals into institutions and continued high usage of expensive emergency services.

Substance Abuse Services

For mental health court participants who experience co-occurring mental health and substance abuse disorders, a substance abuse assessment is typically incorporated into the treatment plan and the recommendations from the assessment are followed. In Anchorage and around the state, there are limits to services available for dually diagnosed populations, especially if prior criminal history or behavioral issues interfere with recommended placement. A therapeutic court participant may receive substance abuse services in a residential or outpatient setting, with aftercare services provided through the substance abuse treatment program for a period of time (depending upon the treatment program and types of services offered). Specialized treatment services for special populations are available (ex. a person with a mental illness, developmental disability, traumatic brain injury, gender specific services, culturally appropriate services). Aftercare services may include skill training groups with an emphasis on relapse prevention for the special population. Clients are encouraged to attend self help twelve step programs during treatment and encouraged to continue attendance after treatment.

Continued Care Services

Many of the clients are linked to continued care services during their participation in the mental health court. Continued care is built in to the long-term plan for care after a participant has graduated or terminated from the therapeutic court program. Many court participants typically continue care with the local community mental health center and/or specialized treatment agency they are connected to during court participation.

Aftercare and/or continued care may include the following components for participants in the mental health court:
Crisis intervention and stabilization, psychological/psychiatric assessment, intensive case management, medication management, anger management, group, individualized and/or family therapy, parenting classes, individualized "wraparound" services, linkages to supportive, transitional, or independent housing, assistance with entitlements, protective payeeship, conservatorship, and guardianship, employment, training, and vocational services, transportation services and linkages to other support services.

—(S. Rhoades, personal communication, July 13, 2007)

The provision of treatment services to a participant in a mental health court program may result in a rationing of services when there is limited availability of treatment resources, whereby such treatment may delay or even prevent intervention for a person who is in need of mental health services and has not been arrested (Haimowitz, 2002). Likewise, some claim that scant resources are relegated to the priority population of mental health court defendants and diverted away from other needy persons with mental illnesses in the population (Clark, 2004; Goldkamp & Iron-Guynn, 2000; Steadman et al., 2001; Watson et al., 2001). However, Honberg (2002) reports that any diversion of funds from the criminal justice system can usually be absorbed with local resources already in existence. Furthermore, those most needing treatment would be those who because of their inappropriate behavior cannot avoid contact with the criminal justice system. Instead of begrudging those individuals treatment for their mental health problems, perhaps we should be pressuring our lawmakers and policymakers for sensible solutions and improving the availability of sufficient mental health treatment services.

Lurigio et al. (2001) maintain that a major problem for mental health courts is inadequate housing and co-occurring treatment resources.[7] Seltzer (2005) cautions that mental health courts are not a panacea in and of themselves because, without proper resources, beyond medication, in place to focus on housing and employment, they may function as a coercive force similar to outpatient commitment. Indeed, there is a question as to whether mental health courts are coercive (Goldkamp & Irons-Guynn, 2000; McCampbell, 2001). As one judge explains, individuals "agree to be coerced" (Levin, 2006, p. 36). Haimowitz (2002) concurs that concerns have been expressed about mental health courts being coercive and potentially widening the net of criminal justice control over the citizenry.

Some question whether a person who is mentally ill can make a rational or competent decision to voluntarily participate in treatment. However, Petrila et al. (2001), in their initial review of the mental health court in Broward County, discovered that the court used several diagnostic tools to determine an individual's competence and allowed the individual to choose whether or not to participate in the mental health court process. Also, Honberg (2002) found no evidence supporting the coerciveness of mental health courts and instead indicated "that judges are bending over backwards to protect the rights of and afford due process to individuals who come through [mental health] courts" (p. 36). Similarly, Rivera (2004) reported that when given the option nearly 95 percent of clients in one mental health court opted for treatment in the community. Since participants were allowed to choose, Rivera did not find the mental health court process coercive and indicated that those who opted for processing via the mental health court were more than twice as likely to receive treatment as offenders in counties without mental health courts. Griffin et al.

---

7. The Council of State Governments (2005c) estimates that three-fourths of offenders with mental illnesses are also experiencing a co-occurring substance abuse disorder; Peters and Osher (2003) address how co-occurring disorders should be considered in specialty courts such as mental health courts (see Peters, R.H. & Osher, F.C. (2003). Co-occurring disorders and specialty courts. Delmar, NY: The National GAINS Center).

(2002) caution that focusing on the coercive argument may lead to under-valuing the increased benefits of teamwork between mental health and criminal justice agencies.

Some maintain that mental health courts may result in longer sentences than those imposed through the traditional criminal justice system; however, mental health court proponents argue that stopping the vicious cycle of recidivism is the long range goal for this population (Petrila et al., 2001). Haimowitz (2002) does acknowledge that individuals may wind up under the court's scrutiny for longer periods of time than had they served a short custodial sentence and advocates deferring adjudication for an extensive period of time to give treatment an opportunity to work and avoid findings of guilt or guilty pleas. Reintegration into the community and lowered recidivism rates are more likely to be accomplished by those courts that do not accept guilty pleas which serve to hamper obtainment of housing and meaningful employment opportunities (Seltzer, 2005).

Some express concern that persons who are identified as mentally ill and processed through a specialized mental health court docket will be stigmatized (Clark, 2004); however, compliance with mental health court requirements, attaining suitable treatment, and possibly avoiding a criminal record in the future are less stigmatizing, more hopeful, and more benevolent than the heartless recycling of persons with mental illnesses through the system. The alternative to mental health court is imprisoning persons with mental illnesses for actions for which they are not to blame and giving them little to no treatment while their symptoms worsen, with no plans for community follow-up; this process guarantees failure via recidivism and is expensive for taxpayers.

The confidentiality of medical records of persons with mental illnesses who end up before mental health courts is another concern that is related to the issue of stigma (Goldkamp & Irons-Guynn, 2000). Competent individuals appearing before the court can sign waivers to allow release of mental health assessments and records to the court for consideration in determining the best way to proceed. Mental health court judges can also limit inquiries so that no Fifth Amendment rights regarding self incrimination are violated, by focusing on the mental health of persons before the court—not on elements of a potential crime. Family members of persons with mental illnesses are not bound by the doctor-patient privilege and can also prove to be a good source of information for the court and its officers. Also, mental health clinicians used by the court can facilitate the dispensing of information from one mental health provider to another. Additionally, via interagency computer networks, jailers can apprise mental health providers of those being booked into jail so that cross checks can be done to determine if they have received mental health treatment in the past, as is done in Broward County, Florida. Murphy et al. (2007) indicate that law enforcement officers as first responders are exempt from the Health Insurance Portability and Accountability Act (HIPAA) requirements and have an obligation to meet the mental and physical health care needs of individuals while in their custody.

Sometimes laws on privacy can be more restrictive than HIPAA dictates and may require modification to ease the sharing of information from one system to another. In similar fashion to the process used in Broward County, Florida's mental health court, Texas, via passage of a state law, is able to divert detainees with mental illnesses from the criminal justice system to treatment by cross referencing new detainees in databases connected with mental health centers across the state and identifying those in need of mental health treatment (Wolf, 2006). Likewise, via a data-link, which required a change in state law, anyone booked into the Cook County Jail in Chicago can be cross checked with the mental health client list for the state of Illinois to see if anyone being booked into jail has received mental health services in the past three years (Murphy et al., 2007).

Some critics of mental health courts argue that such courts actually result in increases in the criminalization of persons with mental illnesses— particularly those involved in minor types of offenses (Barr, 2001; Clark, 2004). However, Honberg (2002) argues that since minor offenders with mental illnesses usually have alarmingly high criminalization rates and mental health courts infrequently impose custody on participants there is no evidence of such increased criminalization, and, instead, mental health courts are actually set up to foster alternatives to the traditional criminal justice process.

Some mental health advocates argue that misdemeanants should be excluded from mental health court jurisdiction as a matter of course (Levin, 2006). According to the Bazelon Center for Mental Health Law,

> Mental Health Courts [are] becoming increasingly likely to accept felony defendants but argue … that misdemeanants are ill suited for mental health courts because they should be diverted from the criminal justice system entirely [via] prebooking diversion programs.… Mental health courts should close their doors to people charged with misdemeanors[,] as [s]ome … jails will not accept misdemeanants (primarily because of overcrowding) regardless of mental health status (Redlich et al., 2005, p. 537).

Of course, before mental health courts refuse to process persons with mental illnesses accused of misdemeanors linkages to ample community treatment services must be assured.

It appears that mental health courts are effective for the criminal justice system, but are they effective for the mental health system? Just as we saw the success of police diversion programs is contingent upon sufficient community treatment resources, much depends on the services available, not just compliance with medications (Levin, 2006).

Public Safety vs. Civil Liberties

Balancing public safety and civil liberties in the legal arena is a tenuous task at best. "Some have argued that the informality of the mental health court and the lack of adversarial process results in a diminution of individual rights that need to be preserved in the criminal courts" (Petrila 2002, p. 2). Hardin (1993), however, counters: "Far from respecting civil liberties, legal obstacles to treating the mentally ill limit or destroy the liberty of the person."

Traditional legal processes have a tendency to ignore therapeutic jurisprudence principles. As emphasized by Miller (1997, p. 1174), "The central thesis of the procedural justice approach … is that participants in formal decision making processes are often more concerned with the perceived fairness of the processes than with the results." Attorneys tend to concentrate on their clients' civil liberties and desires in the adversarial process (Miller, 1997), even if their clients' requests are irrational or not in their clients' best interests. Lawyers are not inclined to consider ramifications of their legal decisions and are prone to disregard the long-term outcomes of those decisions (Finkelman & Grisso, 1994). "Winning" the case at hand for many attorneys takes priority in the adversarial arena, even if their legal tactics ultimately bring about tragic results for their client and society (Pawel, 2001). As noted by Mills (1979) in his discussion of the legal process, "The exultation of winning dampens any moral feelings you have…. I'm not concerned with … the consequences of [my client] going free," (p. 247).

Winick (1997) contends that the criminal defense model is not conducive to addressing the mental health treatment needs of those who pass through the traditional court system, and this approach can actually be considered antitherapeutic. "Advocates for treatment courts assume that traditional legal process impedes access to treatment, and argue that breaking the cycle of arrest, release from jail, and re-arrest without community treatment warrants a more explicitly therapeutic approach by the courts." (Petrila, 2002, p. 2)

Funding from federal legislation has supported the implementation and continuing operation of mental health courts. Congress authorized $4 million to be dispensed by the U.S. Attorney General to provide funding under President Clinton (Public Law, 2000). Congress also appropriated $5 million to the Substance Abuse and Mental Health Services Agency (SAMHSA) to aid criminal justice diversion projects specifically for persons with mental illnesses (M. Thompson, personal communication, March 18, 2002). More recently SAMSHA had approximately three quarters of a million dollars available in 2007 to fund two diversion projects (SAMHSA, 2007). President Bush signed the Mentally Ill Offender Treatment and Crime Reduction Act (MIOTCRA) into law in 2004 which authorized federal grant monies for mental health court and other diversion projects, plus made funds availabale for treatment while incarcerated and re-entry into the community (Bossolo, 2004). In the first fiscal year of operation, the Bureau of Justice Assistance oversaw funding for thirty-seven mental health courts in twenty-nine different states for a total of $5.5 million in allocations (Sublet, 2005). The funding allocated for MIOTCRA for fiscal year 2008 by House and Senate subcommittees, awaiting approval by the full Congress, is $10 million (R. Honberg, personal communication, June 29, 2007).

Some have marveled at the appropriation of funds by Congress for the establishment of mental health courts without outcome data being available and have acknowledged the growing popularity of mental health courts (Griffin et al., 2002). The emergence and evolution of mental health courts prior to their establishment as an evidence-based practice has been significantly impacted by the continuing and growing frustration with the overcrowding of jails and prisons with persons with mental illnesses (Petrila, 2002; Wolff & Pogorzelski, 2005).

Of course, a concern with external funding sources is that they may dry up after an initially specified period of time. Therefore, it is important to have accurate data keeping mechanisms in place to monitor and report outcomes so that community leaders can clearly see the advantages of investing in worthy programs aimed at addressing the needless recycling of persons with mental illnesses through the criminal justice system. Indeed, there is a need for more valid outcome data so mental health courts can be established as an evidenced-based best practice which can attract more adequate funding (Council of State Governments, 2005c; Steadman, 2005).

Conclusion

Steadman (2003) suggests that it may take 18 months or longer from the initiation of a diversionary program such as a mental health court before positive returns can be realized. The initial outlay of resources and personnel costs of a mental health court may be higher than the current total expenditures for incarceration of persons with mental illnesses. Additionally, initially guaranteeing treatment services and access to antipsychotic medications may be more expensive than merely putting persons in jail and having them mentally decompensate. However, the long-range objective must be to prevent people from recycling through the system. We must vigilantly collect outcome data to show the advantages of mental health courts.

The influx of persons with mental illnesses into the criminal justice system has aided public mental health systems by shifting costs from these agencies to local and state correctional facilities (Seltzer, 2005). Sublet (2005) advocates increasing the number of mental health courts and contends that mental health courts can keep mental health providers accountable. Mental health court judges are uniquely positioned to sanction clients, law enforcement, and mental health providers when necessary to ensure compliance with the court's dictates (Wolff & Pogorzelski, 2005).

More and more judges are taking action against providers for not satisfactorily meeting court requests for the provision of adequate mental health treatment. For example, a judge in Denver, in an attempt to remove persons with mental illnesses languishing in jail cells, threatened to levy fines against or lock up the director of the state mental health institution unless treatment beds were provided (Pankratz, 2006). Likewise, in Florida, the director of the State Department of Children and Families (DCF) who was charged with the responsibility of tending to the mental health needs of the citizenry, when faced with a lack of resources, resigned from her position as the secretary of DCF. Her resignation was submitted and accepted amidst being held in contempt of court and fined $80,000 by a circuit judge for not meeting the statutory obligations of limiting jail stays and ensuring treatment outside the criminal justice system for persons with mental illnesses (Rushing, 2006).

The courts act as gatekeepers to treatment for the impoverished mentally ill, yet with managed care's emphasis on cost containment and branching out into the public arena as seen with Medicaid, the government has attempted to place guards at the gate to control expenses (Petrila, 1998). Pertila points out that courts can even hold managed care authorities in contempt of court for failure to comply with treatment orders.

According to San Bernadino, California Mental Health Court Judge Tara Reilly, the average cost per year of an individual housed in the county jail there is $12,000, while the average cost per year of housing a special needs person with mental illness in the jail is in the range of $32,000 to $35,000 a year (Reilly, Bush, & Honberg, 2007). Thus, it would behoove administrators and benefit taxpayers to explore more fiscally sound and effective alternatives to incarceration through such mechanisms as mental health courts. In a short period of time, mental health courts have enjoyed significant success in reducing recidivism rates of persons with mental illnesses who encounter the criminal justice system, and Acquaviva (2006) recommends that short-sighted policymakers should begin funding these model court projects indefinitely instead of relying on temporary grants.

Bruce Winick, considered one of the pioneers of the therapeutic jurisprudence movement, acknowledges that some alternatives, like assertive community treatment and police diversion programs, may indeed be better interventions than utilizing mental health courts, but he favors the use of mental health courts over the criminalization of persons with mental illnesses, realizing that the mental health system has a tendency to drop its problems on the courthouse doorsteps (Stefan & Winick, 2005). Haimowitz (2002) does not see mental health courts as the only answer but agrees that they can be part of the solution. Lurigio et al. (2001) contend that the implementation of an integrated, specialized mental health court is a step toward establishing "a unified, accountable, case management system for maintaining the mentally ill in the community" (p. 188). This certainly places some judges in an unfamiliar role as treatment planners and systems navigators in communities struggling with the provision of mental health services to the citizenry, and these are emerging roles that not all judges are willing to play (Petrila, 2002). While there is plenty of abdication of responsibility to go around, judges are clearly and legitimately positioned to ensure accountability in the treatment of persons with mental illnesses who encounter the criminal justice system.

> Active judicial involvement and the explicit use of judicial authority to motivate individuals to accept needed services and to monitor their compliance and progress characterize the Therapeutic Jurisprudence of the new problem solving courts. It is a hands-on approach with the judge, no longer merely a detached referee or umpire ruling on evidentiary and procedural issues between the competing parties and interests, but a choreographer, directing the dance of a 'holistic' resolution employing public health concepts to the amelioration of social and behavioral problems that cause individual suffering and deterioration of the quality of community life (Mason, 2005, p.4).

In consideration of the consequences of past shortsighted decisions rendered, Goldkamp and Irons-Guynn (2000) contend that the establishment of mental health courts operating on the principles of therapeutic jurisprudence will produce collaborative changes in the mental health and criminal justice systems that will link individuals to appropriate treatment and halt the recidivism of persons with mental illnesses through the criminal justice system. When that occurs mental health courts will have served their purpose and will no longer be necessary. Until that time, though, there are not enough mental health court judges that are sufficiently motivated and positioned to require all parties, including mental health providers, to be responsible and avert unnecessary suffering for persons with mental illnesses and society.

Change in bureaucracies is slow and arduous. History indicates that collaboration between the criminal justice and mental health systems has been difficult and infrequent. Sensitivity, awareness and political activation of judges will force collaborations and determine, to a large extent, the success of alternatives to imprisonment for the mentally ill offender. The next chapter examines the importance of discharge planning for persons with mental illnesses in both the diversion and re-entry processes.

References

Acquaviva, G. L. (2006). Mental health courts: No longer experimental. *Seton Hall Law Review* 36, pp. 971–1013.

Arredondo, D. E., Kumli, K., Soto, L., Colin, E., Ornellas, J. Davilla, Jr., R. J. et al. (2001). Juvenile mental health court: Rationale and protocols. *Juvenile and Family Court Journal* 52(4), pp. 1–19.

Barr, H. (2001). Mental health courts: An advocate's perspective. New York: Urban Justice Center. Retrieved August 10, 2003 from the World Wide Web: http://www.urbanjustice.org/publications/pdfs/mentalhealth/MentalHealthCourts.pdf.

Bernstein, R., & Seltzer, T. (2003). The role of mental health courts in system reform. *University of the District of Columbia Law Review* 7, pp. 143–162.

Boothroyd, R. A., Mercado, C. C., Poythress, N. G., Christy, A., & Petrila, J. (2005). Clinical outcomes of defendants in mental health court. *Psychiatric Services* 56(7), pp. 829–834.

Boothroyd R. A., Poythress N. G., McGaha A., & Petrila J. (2003). The Broward County mental health court: process, outcomes, and service utilization. *International Journal of Law and Psychiatry* 26(1), pp. 55–71.

Bossolo, L. (2004, November 4). Mentally ill offender treatment and crime reduction act becomes law. Washington, DC: American Psychological Association. Retrieved from the World Wide Web on July 30, 2007: http://www.apa.org/releases/S1194_law.html.

Boyle, T. (1998, January 22). Special court for mentally ill seen in March: Need recognized for 'awful long time,' judge says. *The Toronto Star*, p. B3.

Broward County Circuit Court (1997). Administrative Order: Creation of a Mental Health Court Subdivision within the County Criminal Court Division. Issued by D. Ross, Chief Judge, Seventeenth Judicial Circuit, Broward County, Florida.

Christy, A., Poythress, N. G., Boothroyd, R. A., Petrila, J., & Mehra, S. (2005). Evaluating the efficiency and community safety goals of the Broward County mental health court. *Behavioral Sciences & the Law* 23(2), pp. 227–243.

Clark, J. (2004). *Non-speciality first appearance court models for diverting persons with mental illness: Alternatives to mental health courts.* Delmar, New York: Technical Assistance and Policy Analysis Center for Jail Diversion.

Cosden, M., Ellens, J., Schnell, J., & Yamini-Diouf, Y. (2005). Efficacy of a Mental Health Treatment Court with assertive community treatment. *Behavioral Sciences and the Law* 23(2), pp. 199–214.

Council of State Governments (2005a). Mental health courts: A national snapshot. Bureau of Justice Assistance, Office of Justice Programs, Washington, DC: U.S. Department of Justice. Retrieved from the World Wide Web on June 27, 2007: http://www.ojp.usdoj.gov/BJA/pdf/MHC_National_Snapshot.pdf.

Council of State Governments (2005b, October). San Francisco behavioral health court to focus on women with mental illness. Retrieved from the World Wide Web on June 29, 2007: http://consensusproject.org/updates/announcements-and-events/Oct-2005/SFBHC-announcement.

Council of State Governments (2005c). A guide to mental health court design and implementation. New York: Council of State Governments.

Cowart, G. R. (1997). Mission statement. *Mental Health Court News* 1(1), p. 3.

Daicoff, S. (2006). Law as a healing profession: The "comprehensive law movement." *Pepperdine Dispute Resolution Law Journal* 6, pp. 1–61.

Denckla, D., & Berman, G. (2001). Rethinking the revolving door: A look at mental illness in the courts. New York: Center for Court Innovation/State Justice Institute. Retrieved August 10, 2003 from the World Wide Web: http://www.courtinnovation.org/pdf/mental_health.pdf.

Elwell, M. F. (1998). Broward county's mental health court: An emergency response to mentally ill petty offenders. Rockville, Maryland: National Institute of Corrections. National Institute of Justice.

Finkelstein, H., & Brawley, D. (1997). The mission of the mental health court is to address the unique needs of the mentally ill in our criminal justice system. *Mental Health Court News* 1(1), pp. 1–2.

Fields, G. (2006, August 21). In Brooklyn court, a route out of jail for the mentally ill. *Wall Street Journal*, p. A1.

Finkelman, D., & Grisso, T. (1994). Therapeutic jurisprudence: From idea to application. *New England Journal on Criminal and Civil Confinement* 20, pp. 243–257.

Fisler, C. (2005). Building trust and managing risk: A look at a felony mental health court. *Psychology, Public Policy and Law* 11, pp. 587–604.

Goldkamp, J. S., & Irons-Guynn, C. (2000). *Emerging judicial strategies for the mentally ill in the criminal caseload: Mental health courts in Fort Lauderdale, Seattle, San Bernardino, and Anchorage.* Washington, DC: U.S. Department of Justice, Office of Justice Programs, Bureau of Justice Assistance.

Griffin, P. A., Steadman, H. J., & Petrila, J. (2002). The use of criminal charges and sanctions in mental health courts. *Psychiatric Services* 53(10), pp. 1285–1289.

Grudzinskas, A. J., Clayfield, J. C., Roy-Bujnowski, K., Fisher, W. H., & Richardson, M. H. (2005). Integrating the criminal justice system into mental health service delivery: The Worcester diversion experience. *Behavioral Sciences and the Law* 23(2), pp. 277–293.

Gunther, J. B. (2005). Reflections on the challenging proliferation of mental health issues in the district court and the need for judicial education. *Maine Law Review* 57, pp. 541–552.

Haimowitz, S. (2002). Can mental health courts end the criminalization of persons with mental illness? *Psychiatric Services* 53(10), pp. 1226–1228.

Hardin, H. (1993, July 22). Uncivil liberties. *Vancouver Sun.* Retrieved October 22, 2007 from the World Wide Web: http://www.psychlaws.org/GeneralResources/Article1.htm.

Hasselbrack, A. M. (2001). Opting in to mental health courts. *Corrections Compendium* 26(10), pp. 4–25.

Herinckx, H. A., Swart, S. C., Shane, M. A., Dolezal, C. D., & King, S. (2005). Rearrest and Linkage to Mental Health Services Among Clients of the Clark County Mental Health Court Program.*Psychiatric Services* 56(7), pp. 853–857.

Hiday, V. A., Moore, M. E., Lamoureaux, M., & Magistris, J. D. (2005). North Carolina's mental health court. *Popular Government* 70(3), pp. 24–30.

Honberg, R. S. (2002, December). Mental health courts: An alternative to criminalization. Retrieved April 21, 2002 from the World Wide Web: http://www.chadd.org/webpage.cfm?cat_id'7&subcat_id'38.

Keele, C. E. (2002). Criminalization of the mentally ill: The challenging role of the defense attorney in the mental health court system. *University of Missouri-Kansas City School of Law*, 71, pp. 193–210.

Lamb, H. R., Weinberger, L. E., & Reston-Parham, C. (1996). Court intervention to address the mental health needs of mentally ill offenders. *Psychiatric Services* 47(3), pp. 275–281.

Lanni, A. (2005). The future of community justice. *Harvard Civil Rights-Civil Liberties Law Review* 40, pp. 359–405.

Lerner-Wren, G. (1997). Message from the judge. *Mental Health Court News* 1(1), p. 2.

Lerner, Wren, G., & Finkelstein, H. (1997). Florida county diverts offenders in nation's first specialty mental health court. *Mental Health Weekly* 7(33), p. 1, 6.

Levin, A. (2006). MH courts garner mostly favorable reviews. *Psychiatric News* 41(8), pp. 32–37.

Lurigio, A. J., & Swartz, J. A. (2000). Changing the contours of the criminal justice system to meet the needs of persons with serious mental illness. In J. Horney (Ed.). *Policies, processes, and decisions of the criminal justice system* (45–108). Washington, DC: U.S. Department of Justice, National Institute of Justice.

Lurigio, A. J., Watson, A., Luchins, D. J., & Hanrahan, P. (2001). Therapeutic jurisprudence in action: Specialized courts for the mentally ill. *Judicature* 84(4), pp. 184–189.

Mason, B. G. (2005, October). Mental health courts: The newest development in problem-solving courts and therapeutic jurisprudence. *The Nebraska Lawyer*, pp. 4–8.

Mays, G. L., & Thompson, J. A. (1997). The political and organizational context of American jails. In J. A. Thompson and G. L. Mays, eds., *American Jails: Public Policy Issues*, 3–21. Chicago: Nelson-Hall.

McCampbell, S. W. (2001). Mental health courts: What sheriffs need to know. *Sheriff*, 53(2), pp. 40–43.

McGaha, A., Boothroyd, R. A., Poythress, N.G., Petrila, J., & Ott, R.G. (2002). Lessons from the Broward County mental health court evaluation. *Evaluation and Program Planning* 25, pp. 125–135.

Mikhail, S., Akinkunmi, A., & Poythress, N. (2001). Mental health courts: A workable proposition? *Psychiatric Bulletin* 25, pp. 5–7.

Miller, R. D. (1997). Symposium on coercion: An interdisciplinary examination of coercion, exploitation, and the law: III. Coerced confinement and treatment: The continuum of coercion: Constitutional and clinical considerations in the treatment of mentally disordered persons. *Denver University Law Review* 74, pp. 1169–1214.

Mills, J. (1979). I have nothing to do with justice. In J.J. Bonsignore et al. (Eds.) *Before the Law: An Introduction to the Legal Process* (2nd ed.) pp. 239–252. Boston: Houghton Mifflin Company.

Moore, M. E., & Hiday, V. A. (2006). Mental health court outcomes: A comparison of re-arrest and re-arrest severity between mental health court and traditional court participants. *Law and Human Behavior* 30(6), pp. 659–674.

Morabito, M. S. (2007). Horizons of context: Understanding the police decision to arrest people with mental illness. *Psychiatric Services* 58(12), pp. 1582–1587.

Murphy, J., Friedman, F., & Andriukaitis, S. (2007, June 22). How NAMI members can contribute to building CIT in your community. San Diego, California: National Alliance on Mental Illness Annual Convention.

National Center for Mental Health and Juvenile Justice (2005). Juvenile mental health courts program descriptions: Processes and procedures. Delmar, New York: National Center for Mental Health and Juvenile Justice.

Osher, F., Steadman, H. J., & Barr, H. (2003). A best practice approach to community reentry from jails for inmates with co-occurring disorders: The APIC model. *Crime & Delinquency* 49(1), pp. 79–96.

Pankratz, H. (2006, December 5). State standoff on mentally ill. *The Denver Post.* Retrieved from the World Wide Web on June 29, 2007: http://www.denverpost.com/search/ci_4786248.

Pawel, M. A. (2001). Imprisoning the mentally ill: Does it matter? *Criminal Justice Ethics* 20(1), p. 2, 66.

Petrila, J. (2006, August 7). Future issues in forensic services. Annapolis, Maryland: National Association of State Mental Health Program Directors Annual Meeting.

Petrila, J. (2002, November). Policy brief: The effectiveness of the Broward mental health court: An evaluation. Louis de la Parte Florida Mental Health Institute, Tampa, Florida, University of South Florida.

Petrila, J. (1998). Courts as gatekeepers in managed care settings. *Health Affairs* 17(2), pp. 109–117.

Petrila, J., Poythress, N. G., McGaha, A., & Boothroyd, R. A. (2001). Preliminary observations from an evaluation of the Broward County mental health court. *Court Review* 37, pp. 14–22.

Poythress, N., Petrila, J., McGaha, A., & Boothroyd, R. (2002). Perceived coercion and procedural justice in the Broward mental health court. *International Journal of Law and Psychiatry* 25(5), pp. 517–533.

Public Law (2000). pp. 106–515, *America's Law Enforcement and Mental Health Project Act.*

Raybon, K. (1997). State attorney perspective. *Mental Health Court News* 1(1), pp. 2–3.

Redlich, A. D. (2005). Voluntary, but knowing and intelligent? Comprehension in mental health courts. *Psychology, Public Policy and Law* 11, pp. 605–621.

Redlich, A. D., Steadman, H. J., Petrila, J., Monahan, J., & Griffin, P. A. (2005). The second generation of mental health courts. *Psychology, Public Policy and Law* 11, pp. 527–538.

Reilly, T., Bush, S., & Honberg, R. (2007, June 23). Courts as catalysts: Innovative approaches to jail diversion and community re-entry. San Diego, California: National Alliance on Mental Illness Annual Convention.

Ridgely, M. S., Engberg, J., Greenberg, M. D., Turner, S., DeMartini, C., & Dembosky, J. W. (2007). Justice, treatment, and cost: An evaluation of the fiscal impact of Allegheny County mental health court. Council of State Governments. Santa Monica, California: the Rand Corporation. Retrieved from the World Wide Web on June 29, 2007: http://www.rand.org/pubs/technical_reports/2007/RAND_TR439.pdf.

Rivera, R. M. (2004). The mentally ill offender: A brighter tomorrow through the eyes of the mentally ill offender treatment and crime reduction act of 2004. *Cleveland State University Journal of Law and Health*, p. 19, 107–139.

Rogers, R. T. (2005, July 6). Mental health courts fad or future? Butler County, Ohio: Butler County Probate Court. Retrieved from the World Wide Web on July 5, 2007: http://216.239.51.104/search?q=cache:8nLTqA3AYPcJ:www.butlercountyprobatecourt.org/pdf/Mental%2520Health%2520Courts%2520-Illustrated.pdf+mental+health+courts+fad+or+future%3F+rogers&hl = en&ct=clnk&cd=1&gl=us.

Rushing, J. T. (2006, December 2). DCF Chief to leave in February: Hadi resigns day after $80,000 court fine. *The Florida Times Union.* Retrieved from the World Wide Web on June 29, 2007: http://www.jacksonville.com/tu-online/stories/120206/met_6587356.shtml.

SAMHSA (2007). Grant announcement: Targeted capacity expansion grants for jail diversion programs. Rockville, Maryland: Substance Abuse and Mental Health Services Agency. Retrieved from the World Wide Web on July 30, 2007: http://www.samhsa.gov/Grants/2007/SM_07_004.aspx.

Seltzer, T. (2005). Mental health courts: A misguided attempt to address the criminal justice system's unfair treatment of people with mental illnesses. *Psychology, Public Policy, and Law* 11, pp. 570–586.

Slate, R. N. (2000). Courts for mentally ill offenders: Necessity or abdication of responsibility. In G.L. Mays & P.R. Gregware (Eds.) *Courts and Justice* (2nd ed.) (432–450. Prospect Heights, IL: Waveland Press.

Steadman, H. J. (2007, June 21). Treatment not jails: New leadership and promising practices. San Diego, California: National Alliance on Mental Illness Annual Convention.

Steadman, H. J. (2005). A guide to collecting mental health court outcome data. New York: Council of State Governments.

Steadman, H. J. (2003, June 24). Technical Assistance and Policy Analysis Center for Jail Diversion Meeting. Bethesda, Maryland.

Steadman, H. J., Davidson, S., & Brown, C. (2001). Mental health courts: Their promise and unanswered questions. *Psychiatric Services* 52(4), pp. 457–458.

Steadman, H. J., Morris, S. M., & Dennis, D. L. (1995). The diversion of mentally ill persons from jails to community-based services: A profile of programs. *American Journal of Public Health* 85(12), pp. 1630–1635.

Steadman, H.J., Redlich, A.D., Griffin, P., Petrila, J., & Monahan, J. (2005). From referral to disposition: Case processing in seven mental health courts. *Behavioral Sciences & the Law* 23(2), pp. 215–226.

Stefan, S., & Winick, B.J. (2005). Foreword: A dialogue on mental health courts. *Psychology, Public Policy, and Law* 11, pp. 507–526.

Stone, T.H. (1997). Therapeutic implications of incarceration for persons with severe mental disorders: Searching for rational health policy. *American Journal of Criminal Law* 24, pp. 283–358.

Sublet, C. (2005). Has the cold mercy of custodial institutionalization been supplanted by the cold merciless steel of the jailhouse? *Kansas Journal of Law & Public Policy* 15, pp. 159–183.

Thompson, M., Osher, F., & Tomasini-Joshi, D. (2007). Improving responses to people with mental illnesses: The essential elements of a mental health court. Council of State Governments Justice Center: Criminal justice/Mental Health Consensus Project. Bureau of Justice Assistance. Retrieved from the World Wide Web on February 3, 2008: http://consensusproject.org/mhcp/essential.elements.pdf.

Tonry, M. (2006). Purposes and functions of sentencing. *Crime and Justice* 34, pp. 1–53.

Trupin, E., & Richards, H. (2003). Seattle's mental health courts: early indicators of effectiveness. *International Journal of Law and Psychiatry, 26*(1), 33–53.

Walsh, J., & Bricourt, J. (1997). Services for persons with mental illness in jail: Implications for family involvement. *Families in Society: The Journal of Contemporary Human Services* (Jul.-Aug.), pp. 420–428.

Watson, A., Hanrahan, P., Luchins, D., & Lurigio, A. (2001). Mental health courts and the complex issue of mentally ill offenders. *Psychiatric Services* 52(4), pp. 477–481.

Watson, A., Luchins, D., Hanrahan, P., Heyrman, M. J., & Lurigio, A. (2000). Mental health court: Promises and limitations. *The Journal of the American Academy of Psychiatry and the Law* 28, pp. 476–482.

Winick, B. J. (1997). The jurisprudence of therapeutic jurisprudence. *Psychology, Public Policy and Law* 3, pp. 184–206.

Wolf, S. (2006). Criminal law: Mentally impaired offenders and the criminal justice system. *Texas Bar Journal* 69, pp. 244–247.

Wolff, N., & Pogorzelski, W. (2005). Measuring the effectiveness of mental health courts: Challenges and recommendations. *Psychology, Public Policy, and Law* 11(4), pp. 539–569.

CHAPTER 6

DISCHARGE PLANNING: DIVERSION & RE-ENTRY

"America is the land of the second chance, and when the gates of the prison open, the path ahead should be a better life."

—President George W. Bush

In 1957 Jackson Toby expounded on his stakes in conformity theory (Williams & McShane, 2004). The basic premise of his theory is that individuals will conform to societal expectations when they have a reason for or stake in doing so. Of course, the stakes in conformity theory assumes rationality. The inability to meet basic human survival needs can be tough on anyone but particularly those released from jail or prison and especially for those persons released from such institutions who are struggling to maintain lucidity. Without proper linkages to services such as housing, vocational/employment opportunities and mental health treatment, we can only expect the continued recycling of persons with mental illnesses through the criminal justice system and needless suffering for these individuals and society. Without appropriate intervention, failure should be expected and will continue to abound.

This chapter examines the variability of discharge planning around the country and discusses a number of exemplary programs. The role of probation, parole, and Assertive Community Treatment (ACT) in ensuring adherence to treatment dictates is also discussed.

The purpose of the criminal justice system "is the protection of the order and security of society" (Kittrie, 1978, p.12). The motto "protect and serve" emblazoned on police cars is expected of criminal justice professionals empowered with the authority to take our freedoms away from us. The protect and serve credo is to be adhered to for all individuals in free society by criminal justice professionals, and this mantra does not cease to exist once an individual is brought under the supervision, custody and care of the criminal justice system. There also is a duty to protect and serve those under the criminal justice system's control, just as the free citizenry's interests are to be considered. For example, New York City's Department of Correction's mission statement as of the year 2000 indicates as follows:

> The Department of Correction provides custody, control and care of misdemeanants and felons sentenced to one year of incarceration or less; detainees awaiting trial or sentence; newly sentenced felons awaiting transportation to State correctional facilities; alleged parole violators awaiting revocation hearings; and State prisoners with court appearances in New York City. Professional care and services, including health and mental health care, opportunities for religious observance, educational instruction, vocational training and substance abuse counseling are provided (Giuliani, 2000, p. 37).

The word "care" is mentioned three times in the above statement, and mental health care is specifically referenced. These glowing words appear to portray an appropriate degree of sensitivity; however, the reality of how the New York City Department of Correction in practice was carrying out the "custody," "control," and "care," and offering "professional ... services" to persons with mental illnesses was horrific and inexcusable.

Four mornings a week, between 2 and 6 am, New York City Department of Correction's buses would drop off persons with mental illnesses, who had received psychiatric care while in jail, at Queens Plaza with a $1.50 in cash and a two-fare Metrocard (Barr, 2003a; Parish, 2007). Why between 2 and 6 a.m. for drop offs? The citizenry would be much less likely to become aware of such a practice. This practice ultimately led to what is known as the *Brad H.* lawsuit (Barr, 2003a). At the time the suit was filed, Brad H. was actually a 44-year-old homeless man with schizophrenia who had been treated 26 times in jail for mental illness but never received any linkage to treatment in the community or assistance with accessing Medicaid benefits, Social Security disability payments or shelter upon any of his releases back into the community (Saulny, 2003).

The *Brad H.* complaint addressed a practice in which at least 25,000 jail inmates a year were receiving mental health treatment in jail, but almost no one received discharge planning for release which literally set individuals up to fail and return to the criminal justice system (Barr, 2003a). As noted by Barr (2003a), mental health treatment in jails and prisons has been mandated by the U.S. Supreme Court in *Estelle v. Gamble*, 1976; however, discharge planning has largely been ignored by such institutions and the Brad H. attorneys pursued the Department of Correction on the prohibition against cruel and unusual punishment and a New York State law, entitled the Mental Hygiene Law that dictates that providers of inpatient mental health treatment services must provide discharge planning. Barr (2003a).

The assistance sought in the *Brad H.* class action suit asked for each of the following upon release from jail for persons with mental illnesses: an adequate supply of medication, at least a shelter with a bed, access to mental health services, and assurance of immediate benefits like Medicaid and food stamps without a 45-day waiting period (Bernstein, 2000). When one of the attorney's for Brad H. was queried about how much such a plan would cost the City, she replied that based on what they were currently doing, it should save them a fortune. "On January 8, 2003, the parties settled the case with an agreement that the City would provide people who have received mental health treatment or have taken medication for a mental health condition while in jail with discharge planning" (Parish, 2007, p. 6). The settlement went into effect in June of 2003 and compliance is to be monitored for an initial five years by attorneys for the plaintiffs and by two special court appointed monitors—Henry Dlugacz and Erik Roskes (Parish, 2007).

While litigation can be long, drawn out, costly, and protracted, sometimes that is what it takes to right injustices. Without intervention, the New York City system was clearly setting individuals up to fail and recycle through the criminal justice system at great costs in terms of needless human suffering for persons with mental illnesses and sometimes other members of society with whom the mentally ill interact, as well as causing a financial burden.

Of particular concern is the high level of recidivism that occurs for persons with mental illnesses and the financial costs associated with such recycling.

> Offenders with mental illnesses report extremely high rates of recidivism; … [a]ccording to [one] study, more than 70% of the mentally ill offenders who were released from the Lucas County Jail in Lucas County, Ohio, were re-arrested within a three-year period. A second study showed that 90% of the mentally ill inmates in the Los Angeles County Jail were repeat offenders, and nearly 10% of those mentally ill offenders had been incarcerated on ten or more instances (Rivera, 2004, p. 132).

In Broward County, Florida, Sheriff Jenne indicates that it costs his agency $80 a day to house a general population inmate and $130 a day to detain a person with mental illness; in Miami the costs of treating inmates with mental illnesses is $125 per day, while the cost for healthy inmates averages $18 a day (Miller & Fantz, 2005). By diverting inmates with mental illnesses from the jail to community treatment in Pinellas County, Florida, treatment costs $60 a day per individual diverted (Miller & Fantz, 2005).

Furthermore, AC Treatment programs, which are discussed later in more detail, cost less than incarceration at anywhere from $9,000 to $14,000 per participant per year and less than hospitalization (over a $100,000 a year) or group homes (over $30,000) a year (Edgar, 1999). The Thresholds program in Chicago utilizes a version of ACT and is a program aimed at linking persons with mental illnesses released from jails to treatment in the community to reduce re-arrests, re-incarcerations, and re-hospitalizations (Lurigio, Fallon, & Dincin, 2000). Thresholds' clients can enter the program from pretrial or postadjudication stages. Those entering the program from the pretrial may do so from referral while awaiting trial in the community or via referral while being supervised by pretrial services as they await trial. After adjudication, persons with mental illnesses are referred to Thresholds by judges or probation officers (Lurigio et al., 2000).

> In a study of the first 30 patients enrolled in the Thresholds Jail Project, the total number of jail days dropped from 2,741 in the previous year to 469 during the first year of enrollment. The total number of hospital days dropped from 2,153 to 321 for the group. Total savings in jail costs during the one-year study period was $157,000, and total savings in hospital costs was $917,000 (Lamberti, Weisman, & Faden, 2004, p. 1289).

Dincin (2002) compares costs associated with the first 30 persons with mental illnesses to enter the Thresholds program and complete two years of service to finances expended upon them two years prior to entering the Thresholds program. He reports that jail days were reduced by 82.5% (with at least $209,000 saved); psychiatric hospital days were reduced by 84.7% (with at least $1,154,000 saved); the total estimated savings per person enrolled in the Thresholds program over the two years is $18,873.

Definitions

The distinctions between diversion and re-entry and what constitutes discharge planning sometimes overlap and can be somewhat murky. Often times the terms diversion and re-entry are used interchangeably, and discharge planning can take place with both diversion and re-entry.

According to the Technical Assistance and Policy Analysis (TAPA) Center for jail diversion:

The term 'jail diversion' refers to programs that divert individuals with serious mental illnesses (and often co-occurring substance use disorders) away from jail and provide linkages to community-based treatment and support services. The individual thus avoids arrest or spends a significantly reduced time period in jail and/or lockups on the current charge or on violations of probation resulting from previous charges.

Key jail diversion program activities include:

- Defining a target group for diversion,
- Identifying individuals as early as possible in their processing by the justice system,
- Negotiating community-based treatment alternatives to incarceration, and
- Implementing linkages to comprehensive systems of care and appropriate community supervision consistent with the disposition of the criminal justice contact. (TAPA, 2007)

While all diversion programs engage in some form of identification and linkage, there is no definitive model for organizing a jail diversion program. Different jail diversion strategies are needed because local criminal justice systems vary so much in size, structural characteristics, levels of perceived need, resources available within the communities' mental health and substance abuse services network, and local politics and economics" (TAPA, 2007).

Although Travis (2005) focuses on state prisoners returning to society, he indicates re-entry applies to an offender's return to the community, regardless of whether supervision or conditional release is imposed, from any type of incarceration, including juvenile institutions, jails, and federal correctional facilities. Travis also notes that approximately 20 percent of the more than 630,000 prisoners who re-enter society each year do so unconditionally and indicates that one-third of prisons fail to link prisoners with mental illnesses with mental health treatment providers upon release into the community. In a National Institute of Corrections study, less than half of the responding corrections departments acknowledged partnering with community mental health providers to facilitate linkages to treatment for persons with mental illnesses returning to the community from prison.

'Discharge planning' refers to the practice whereby a provider of mental healthcare develops a plan for the continuation of a patient's treatment after the patient's discharge from the provider's care. It is universally recognized as an essential part of adequate mental health treatment.... Discharge planning includes assistance in obtaining continuing mental health treatment, public benefits, and housing upon release, depending on an individual's diagnosis, level of functioning, and need for social services (Parish, 2007, p. 6).

In other words, if a jail or prison has been providing mental health treatment to one in their custody, upon release, it would logically follow that there is a responsibility to ensure for the provision of care upon leaving the correctional institution's custody.

Extensive information on diversion and re-entry of persons with mental illnesses from the criminal justice system can be obtained from the GAINS Center (2007a). Also, a series of fact sheets are available from the GAINS Center (2007b) addressing matters pertaining to the diversion and re-entry of females with mental illnesses from the criminal justice system; information on persons with co-occurring disorders involved with the justice system can be ascertained from the GAINS Center (2007c).

Realizing that discharge planning can apply to both diversion and re-entry programs[1], the essential elements and examples of discharge planning will be discussed. Then, we will turn our attention to the benefits and specific examples of diversion and re-entry programs.

Discharge Planning

Although discharge planning has long been considered a necessary component of effective psychiatric treatment in the community, Steadman and Veysey (1997), in an analysis of jail services, found such planning for those who had been jailed to return to the community to be the least often provided mental health service offered by jails and, the larger the jail, the least likely discharge planning was to occur. For example, 17 of 21 jails in New Jersey participated in a study by Wolff, Plemmons, Veysey, and Brandli (2002); the researchers found that only three jails reported developing discharge plans for

---

1. Hands Across Long Island (HALI) (2007) is a grassroots mental health self-help organization that offers a number of forensic programs to assist persons with mental illnesses that have encounters with the criminal justice system; the programs include both pre-booking diversion and re-entry planning. HALI works with the local police to provide mobile outreach and potential diversion from the criminal justice system to persons with mental illnesses. Note this single program can serve both the functions of diversion and re-entry.

a majority of their inmates with mental illnesses reentering society, and only two of the jails indicated that on a regular basis they provided psychotropic medications to individuals as they transitioned back into society.

Haimowitz (2002) advocates for treatment protocols to address co-occurring disorders, the use of ACT, peer involvement, and the inclusion of housing and employment services to assist persons with mental illnesses who encounter the criminal justice system. Rivera (2004) recommends that multidisciplinary teams work with inmates with mental illnesses on discharge planning and linkages to treatment in the community. Sultan (2006) argues that re-entry efforts for persons with mental illnesses must begin on the first day of incarceration and starts with intake screening. She maintains that re-entry counselors are needed as transitional case managers in correctional facilities, as current processes, unfortunately, typically leave it up to the incarcerated individual to plan their own transition from custody to free society, perhaps with a limited supply of medication and often no assurances of linkages to treatment in the community. Fulwiler (2000) also contends that inmates with mental illnesses should be engaged in release planning early on during their incarceration. He also indicates that family members should be involved in the discharge planning process and indicates that the National Alliance on Mental Illness is a valuable resource in communities throughout the country for offering support and advice to consumers of mental health services returning from prison and their family members.

Dr. Joyce Burland, in fact, developed the National Alliance on Mental Illness Family-to-Family Education program, which is a 12-week peer education curriculum for families of persons with mental illnesses. This program empowers family members to seek supports, realize that they are not alone, and come to a better understanding of their loved ones' illnesses (NAMI, 2007). With the lack of mental health benefits available, many families serve as the primary caregiver for their mentally ill loved ones. Such education is essential for family member caregivers.

Bjorklund (2000) found that the earlier discharged state hospital patients were linked to peer support in the community the greater the chances that they would experience successful reintegration in the community. Likewise, providing restrictions could be relaxed to allow convicted felons to associate with each other, perhaps similar peer linkages with persons with mental illnesses who have had encounters with the criminal justice system could be facilitated.[2]

---

2. The National Alliance on Mental Illness (NAMI) also operates a peer-to-peer program, developed by Kathryn McNulty, that strives to enhance recovery and self-worth,

Two such programs are in operation in New York. Understanding the value of work in assisting with recovery and bringing about self-empowerment, the Howie T. Harp Center in New York City was founded in 1995 to prepare consumers of mental health services for human service field careers. Since that time the Center has trained more than 200 consumers and placed more than 150 in jobs; they also train forensic peer specialists who know what it is like to be incarcerated to work with others who currently find themselves entangled with the criminal justice system (Harper, 2002). Power (2006) also identifies the Howie T. Harp Center as a collaborative model for employment training and placement for consumers of mental health services. Hands Across Long Island (2007) is another re-entry program that provides peer support via "bridgers" who work with inmates two months prior to release and up to four months after release to facilitate successful re-entry.

To ensure continuity of care linkages must be established between jail personnel, and community treatment providers, and clinicians in the community should be instructed on how to track persons with mental illnesses who enter into the criminal justice system. Community treatment providers should make contact with their client's jail-based clinician, and such connections should serve to facilitate discharge planning which should link persons with mental illnesses to community treatment services prior to release into the community. Included in discharge planning should be the provision of housing, a month's supply of medication, expedited reinstatement of benefits, and the establishment of specialized probation and parole caseloads for supervision of persons with mental illnesses that have had encounters with the criminal justice system. For those inmates with mental illnesses released from court as opposed to the jail, offices should be set up in courthouses to allow these individuals to check for linkages to treatment and shelter in the community (Barr, 2003b).

Osher, Steadman, & Barr (2003) identify their assess, plan, identify, and co-ordinate (APIC) model as a best practice model created for discharge planning from jails. As they maintain, persons with mental illnesses who have brief contacts with jails require quick interventions that are somewhat different from individuals with extensive stays in jails and prisons. They reason that transition planning is bi-directional; thus, partnerships need to be established in the community with key stakeholders such as mental health providers and probation officers, even bringing them into the jail setting to assist with the APIC model.

---

while also serving to de-stigmatize mental illness and educate the general public Retrieved from the World Wide Web on August 2, 2007; for further information see http://www.nami.org/template.cfm?section=Peer-to-Peer.

They emphasize that once individuals' needs are assessed, plans for identifying necessary community treatment services after release and coordinating the plan to make sure services are delivered in the community must be undertaken.

Programs discussed below in Maryland and Massachusetts involve more than just traditional classification caseworkers in the treatment discharge process. Maryland's Community Criminal Justice Program (MCCJTP) has been featured by the National Institute of Justice; the MCCJTP is a multiagency partnership, initiated by the state, between mental health and criminal justice entities to screen for mental illness in jails, provide treatment and aftercare plans and linkages to treatment for persons with mental illnesses in jails, and the program now also includes provisions for services to persons with mental illnesses on probation or parole (Conly, 1999). The Hampden County Correctional Center in Massachusetts provides a model example of pre-release planning and community partnerships (Sultan, 2006). Clinicians engage in a dual practice within the community of Ludlow, Massachusetts and within the correctional facility; individualized re-entry plans are realized, and persons with mental illnesses are matched with treatment providers in the zip code that they will be returning to upon release (Sultan, 2006). As indicated by Sultan (2006), recidivism in the Hampden County Correctional Center is substantially lower than the national average.

Forensic transition teams (FTT), comprised of caseworkers and clinicians, have been established by the state department of mental health in Massachusetts to assist with discharge planning and linkages to community treatment for individuals with mental illnesses leaving prisons and jails; with prison releasees with mental illnesses more readily identifiable due to longer stints incarcerated, jails may want to consider ways to expedite evaluations and assessments to ensure adequate release planning. The FTT follows individuals selected for the program for three months after release, and after the first year of operation of the program, almost 60% of the program's participants were residing in the community and utilizing mental health services, while only ten percent were known to have been re-incarcerated and 20% had been hospitalized immediately after arrest (Hartwell & Orr, 1999). Hartwell (2004) also found that offenders with co-occurring disorders, as opposed to mental illness only, on average pose more of a challenge for FTT members upon release from correctional institutions and require more specialized interventions, such as a need for appropriate housing, to prevent potential re-contact with the criminal justice system.

In a study of 261 persons with mental illnesses discharged from jails and tracked for three years, it was determined that the obtainment of case management services while in jail was significantly positively related to procurement of community-based case management services after release; "recipients of community case management were significantly less likely than nonrecipients to be arrested for either any offense (60 percent versus 77 percent ...) or a violent offense (52 percent versus 71 percent)" (Ventura, Cassel, Jacoby, & Huang, 1998, p. 1333). This is a positive sign. Providing mental health case management services both within and outside jail will help ensure the treatment of persons with mental illnesses in the community and prevent them from recycling back into the criminal justice system.

In *Wakefield v. Thompson*, a federal appellate court considered an 8th Amendment claim at a California prison regarding whether the refusal to provide medication upon release to a mentally ill inmate constituted cruel and unusual punishment (Human Rights Watch, 2003). The court held that the state

> must provide an outgoing prisoner who is receiving and continues to require medication with a supply sufficient to ensure that he has that medication available during the period of time reasonably necessary to permit him to consult a doctor and obtain a new supply. A state's failure to provide medication sufficient to cover this transitional period amounts to an abdication of its responsibility to provide medical care to those, who by reason of incarceration are unable to provide for their own medical needs.... For all newly discharged offenders, the highest risk of recidivism is in the first six months after release from prison. Finding housing and employment, gaining access to public assistance, reuniting with friends and family, and other aspects of making the psychological and physical adjustment to a life outside of prison can present challenges to any former prisoner. Mentally ill offenders who do not receive adequate discharge planning or a continuity of treatment upon release are at a particular disadvantage during this crucial readjustment. According to the Council of State Governments: individuals with mental illnesses leaving prison without sufficient supplies of medication, connections to mental health and other support services, and housing are almost certain to decompensate, which in turn will likely result in behavior that constitutes a technical violation of release conditions or a new crime (Human Rights Watch, 2003).

Inmates with mental illnesses often struggle to meet basic survival needs such as food, shelter and job concerns. Navigating the bureaucratic maze to access government benefits and services can prove daunting for anyone but much more so for persons with mental illnesses who may be symptomatic when they are first released from prison into an uncertain future into society. Department of Correction (DOC) involvement in discharge planning varies from state to state.

In Nebraska, for example, inmates released into the community with mental illnesses are usually given a 14-day supply of medication and given names of community mental health providers, but no appointments are made for them. Released prisoners in Arkansas receive a one-week supply of psychotropic medicine and are urged to choose a private mental health provider upon release. Absent that, DOC personnel will try to make an appointment for them with a public provider, but there are no guarantees, as the availability of public services varies widely around the state. Virginia provides a 30 day supply of medication at release, and inmates with mental illnesses have a release plan devised in conjunction with mental health counselors. Also, the DOC makes an effort to make appointments for after-care for those released. However, there are not enough community resources, and some exit prison with no appointments established. North Carolina purportedly individualizes a treatment plan for persons with mental illnesses being released from prison and provides a 30-day supply of medication, as well as makes an appointment with a mental health provider for the release and provides the contact information for the provider to the inmate (Human Rights Watch, 2003).

Notice that an essential element missing from all of these discharge plans is a follow-up component. In other words, there is no single entity designated as being responsible for ensuring that individuals upon release from custody see mental health providers and engage in treatment. As will be discussed in the last chapter, failure to ensure such follow-up can lead to tragic consequences.

Most states, though not required by federal law to do so, strike prisoners from Medicaid rolls and require application for reinstatement of Medicaid benefits upon release. Supplemental Security Income (SSI) benefits are required to be terminated upon being incarcerated for a year or longer by federal law, and the law mandates that Social Security Disability Insurance (SSDI) benefits be suspended, but not terminated, at the point of incarceration. It generally takes a month and a half to three months to have benefits reinstated after release from custody, which is hardly conducive to continuity of care. Varying degrees of assistance are rendered by states to inmates in securing benefits upon release; some DOCs establish mechanisms to ensure that benefits are available upon release, with some DOCs assisting in completing applications for reinstatement of benefits (Human Rights Watch, 2003).

Of course, just because benefits are reinstated and even appointments with mental health providers are in place upon release, there is no assurance that each prisoner with mental illness will receive treatment upon release. Examples of several states' efforts regarding how soon benefits are restored for released inmates follow. The Maine DOC attempts to keep benefit eligibility in place for inmates; while prisoners do not enjoy benefit coverage while locked up, they do not have to apply for reinstatement of benefits upon release, as they are automatically eligible. In Virginia some prisoners prior to release are assisted by counselors in applying for benefits reinstatement, with some eligible for reinstatement of Medicaid on the day of release. However, not all prisoners get the paperwork completed and processed in time for discharge and so do not hit the streets with benefits in place. In North Carolina, although efforts are made to initiate benefit reinstatement applications prior to release, not all releasees are successful in doing so, and not all benefits offices will allow early applications for reinstatement. The DOC in Kansas does not assist prisoners with Medicaid benefits. Prisoners scheduled to be released are to meet with an SSDI services agent to determine their eligibility for benefits. Providing an inmate proves to be eligible for SSI, the DOC will then assist with that application process so hopefully benefits will be available upon release. However, due to being ineligible or due to time constraints, not all inmates have coverage upon release. For those without benefits who will be on parole after release from custody responsibility is then passed on to a parole officer to render assistance in the application process (Human Rights Watch, 2003).

Some states try to expedite the reinstatement of benefits for inmates being discharged into the community by assisting the inmates with the completion of necessary forms. The Connecticut DOC has been working with the Department of Social Services to devise a program to assist inmates in applying for dropped Medicaid or SSI while incarcerated. The DOC in Massachusetts has declared that all inmates with mental illnesses will have health care coverage at discharge from prison. However, the state agency that oversees Medicaid prohibits incarcerated individuals from making application. Even so, the DOC routinely assists inmates in their preparation for reinstatement of benefits before discharge with hopes of approval. With the two agencies working together collaboratively for a solution, DOC officials hope to see the policy modified (Human Rights Watch, 2003).

Sometimes assisting inmates with accessing benefits upon their release might not only require modifying policies but may also require changing state laws. In Tennessee the Department of Human Services, not the DOC, does all screening for benefits eligibility for inmates after release. Theoretically, individuals are to have an appointment with a mental health provider within two weeks of discharge. However, in reality, some individuals have waited as long as two months after release to get such an appointment, allowing ample time for an individual's mental status to decompensate. Suspicions are that providers are reluctant to give uninsured ex-prisoners appointments, as there is no certainty that payment will be received for services rendered (Human Rights Watch, 2003).

The majority of state SSI and Medicaid offices refuse to receive applications from incarcerated individuals who are asking for reinstatement of benefits upon release. Therefore, in a non-therapeutic jurisprudence way of looking at things, many correctional agencies across the country do not perceive this application process as their job, as it has to with inmates after they have left the physical custody of prison authorities. In Arkansas the DOC refers inmates to Community Mental Health Centers upon release that can assist them in making application for reinstatement of benefits, but no assistance with the process is allowed or offered while individuals are incarcerated—ensuring a gap in the receipt of benefits after release. The Department of Correctional Services' (DCOS) authorities in Nebraska indicated that they have no idea about how to get benefits reinstated upon an inmate's release, and the DCOS does nothing to assist inmates with the process (Human Rights Watch, 2003).

In a study of four states, Minnesota, New York, Pennsylvania, and Texas, the common elements of success in making sure that prisoners with mental illnesses have access to Medicaid for mental health treatment and Supplemental Security Income (SSI) and Social Security Disability Insurance (SSDI) for access to benefits upon leaving prison and returning to the community were identified. Commonalities among the states included: interagency involvement, whereby at least two different agencies would coordinate efforts to properly handle enrollments; new programs or agencies were established in each state and/or specialized caseloads were established for staff to focus on acquiring specific benefits; and identification of inmates ready for release and initial discharge planning occurred anywhere from one to three months prior to their anticipated release. Promising practices worth consideration in the four states were delineated and included clear specification of agency responsibilities; information sharing between agencies via technology; early release planning; and coverage of benefits for releasees up to 45 days after their release to ensure access to needed medication and food. Communication is key, even among county agencies, and clarifications regarding convoluted federal rules over eligibility requirements should be sought from the Social Security Administration (SSA) and the Centers for Medicare and Medicaid Services (CMS) (Council of State Governments, 2007a).

Diversion

Police-based diversion and mental health courts have been discussed in previous chapters. The segment of this chapter will focus on diverting persons with mental illnesses from the criminal justice system. However, as previously indicated, there is a blurring of the lines between diversion and re-entry.

Criminal justice diversion programs generally can be classified as either prebooking or postbooking. Prebooking implies that diversion occurs prior to arrest charges being entered by law enforcement, and postbooking indicates that diversion is transpiring after an individual has been booked into jail with charges entered against him or her (Steadman, Deane, Borum, & Morrissey, 2000). Previously discussed police-based diversion programs, such as CIT, would be illustrative of prebooking diversion, while mental health courts can be indicative of postbooking diversion. Some believe the combination of pre and post booking diversion programs can provide quite a tandem in terms of linking persons with mental illnesses to treatment in the community. For example, Kathryn Power (2006), the Director of the Substance Abuse and Mental Health Services Administration's (SAMHSA) Center for Mental Health Services (CMHS), touts Ohio's CIT and mental health courts as collaborative models of diversion. The Kent Center's court clinic program in place at the Kent County Courthouse in Rhode Island provides intervention pre or post adjudication and facilitates as an education and consultation consortium with the criminal justice community. A Kent Center clinician performs evaluations and referrals and acts as a liaison for linkages to appropriate community services for persons with mental illnesses appearing before the court (A. Stoltz, personal communication, October 10, 2007).

A 1994 survey of jails with a capacity for 50 or more detainees resulted in responses from 760 jails, and researchers determined that only 52 of those jails had formal diversion programs for persons with mental illnesses that were congruent with their research specifications (Steadman, Barbera, & Dennis, 1994). Thus, approximately seven percent of jails examined were determined to have a formal diversion program in place.

Both the Council of State Governments (2002) and the President's New Freedom Commission on Mental Health (2003) recommend support for implementing programs for diverting persons with mental illnesses from jails. In NAMI's Grading the States Report, the two highest scoring states, Connecticut and Ohio, were bolstered by their significant use of programs to divert persons with mental illnesses from jail (Daly, 2006).

Steadman et al. (1999) maintain that

> two core elements are necessary for diversion programs: aggressive linkage to an array of community services, especially those for co-occurring mental health and substance use disorders, and nontraditional case managers. … Major goals for mental health diversion programs include the avoidance or the reduction of jail time…, an overall reduction of recidivism rates, and continuing linkage of … detainees with comprehensive community-based services" (p. 1623).

As noted by Steadman, Morris, and Dennis (1995), jail diversion programs do not operate merely to let persons with mental illnesses out of jail; to be successful they must provide discharge planning, establish linkages to treatment in the community, and ensure follow-up. To ease reintegration into to the community, Seltzer (2005) maintains that guilty pleas for persons with mental illnesses should be avoided, as they serve as a hindrance to meaningful employment and to obtaining housing.

Munetz and Griffin (2006) have delineated a model for diversion of persons with serious mental illnesses from the criminal justice system and linkage to treatment in the community. Their model encompasses both pre and post booking diversion with five intercept points identified for intervention in the criminal justice process. The five points in sequential order are (1) police and emergency service providers; (2) after arrest at initial hearings (as seen for example in the statewide post booking diversion program in Connecticut); (3) after first appearance hearings via assessments in jail, by the court, or forensic evaluations and commitments; (4) discharge planning and linkage to appropriate treatment should be ensured for individuals re-entering the community from jails, prisons and hospitals; and (5) the utilization of community corrections, for example, probation officers, to assist in linking individuals to treatment in the community.

Examples of Diversion Programs

As noted by Clark (2004) there are two critical decision points after arrest: the pre-trial release decision and the decision as to whether or not to defer prosecution. Of course, flight and dangerousness are the two primary considerations involved in pre-trial release decisions. In a number of jurisdictions, pre-trial service agents advise judges on this decision and have the ability to supervise individuals in the community with court imposed conditions in place while awaiting further processing. Prosecutors in a number of jurisdictions may decide to defer prosecution, particularly with persons with mental illnesses charged with misdemeanors. Depending on the jurisdiction, sometimes these prosecutorial decisions must be approved by the court. This deferment can result in charges being reduced or even dismissed upon successful completion of treatment program requirements for a specified period of time. Sometimes screening and access to these deferred prosecution programs for persons with mental illnesses can take extensive periods of time, however, Clark (2004) notes that the process for pre-trial release and deferred prosecution can be streamlined and expedited and points to two exemplary jurisdictions that have done so: Hamilton County (Cincinnati), Ohio (pre-trial release) and the state of Connecticut (deferred prosecution). Clark (2004) goes on to identify one other model deferred prosecution jurisdiction in Jefferson County, Kentucky and nine other model pretrial release jurisdictions in Washington, DC; Winnebago County, Illinois; Montgomery County, Maryland; Wayne County, New York; Cuyahoga County, Ohio; Tulsa County, Oklahoma; Montgomery County, Pennsylvania; Shelby County, Tennessee; and Harris County, Texas.

In a study of three pre-booking (Memphis, Tennessee; Montgomery County, Pennsylvania; Multnomah County, Oregon) and three post-booking (Phoenix/Tucson, Arizona; Hartford, New Haven, and Bridgeport, Connecticut; and Lane County, Oregon) jail diversion programs, Steadman and Naples (2005) arrived at several conclusions regarding jail diversion. They noted that jail diversion resulted in less time spent in jail, with an average of two months more spent in society for persons with mental illnesses diverted from jail, and this was accomplished without increased risk of victimization to the citizenry. Steadman and Naples (2005) also reported that in terms of costs in their analysis, jail diversion results in lower costs for the criminal justice system and greater costs for the mental health system as individuals with mental illnesses are diverted to treatment. In the short run, at least, they acknowledge that the costs incurred by the mental health system as a result of jail diversion are typically higher than the savings realized by the criminal justice system. However, more extensive research is needed to access this over time, as substantial cost savings in both systems may be realized over time as individuals are linked to treatment and stabilized without as great a need for expensive treatment interventions as when initially returning to the community from jail.

The Montgomery County Emergency Service (MCES) in Pennsylvania, referred to above and discussed in Chapter 4, is engaged in both pre and post booking diversion efforts, includes a secure psychiatric facility, mobile crisis capability, and treatment referrals and works closely with prosecutors, public defenders, the courts, parole officers, and corrections officials to successfully divert individuals from the criminal justice system (MCES Quest, 2002). Draine and Solomon (1999) point out that the MCES program has been used as a model for a number of other jail diversion programs.[3] Also, diversion involves initial identification of a problem and then to what services one will be diverted.

The previously discussed tragedy that brought Linda Gregory, Alice Petree, and Sheriff Donald Eslinger together also led to establishment of a pre-booking mental health diversion program at the Seminole County jail in Florida. Jail detention deputies screen new admittees for signs and symptoms of mental illness and offer a voluntary six-month community treatment program in lieu of jail to those identified as in need of mental health treatment (Taylor, 2002).

Boccaccini, Christy, Poythress, and Kershaw (2005), in a study of individuals with mental illnesses diverted again through the same diversion program in Broward County and Hillsborough County, Florida, found that about 20% of those diverted over an 18 month period were re-diverted through the same program at least once. However, they report this finding is consistent with expected return rates for other means of accessing mental health treatment such as seen with involuntary examination and hospitalization.

The National Association of Counties identified five jail diversion programs in three states that are reflective of best practices for diverting persons with mental illnesses from jail: Butler, Clermont, and Hamilton counties in Ohio; Miami—Dade County, Florida; and Los Angeles County, California (Buchan, 2003). In Los Angeles, the organization was particularly impressed with the Mental Evaluation Teams (MET) geared towards pre-booking diversion and the Village Agency (Village Integrated Service Agency, Integrated Services for Homeless Mentally Ill) which aims to provide housing and services to persons with mental illnesses who are homeless and/or in risk of incarceration as well as providing these services to such persons re-entering the community from the criminal justice system. At the

---

3. For a discussion of the intricacies of the MCES jail diversion program see Draine, J., & Solomon, P. (1999). Describing and evaluating jail diversion services for persons with serious mental illness. Psychiatric Services, 50(1), p. 56–61.

time of Buchan's (2003) publication, 20 MET teams total were in operation serving Long Beach, Los Angeles, and Pasadena, pairing police with mental health clinicians when responding to calls regarding persons with mental illnesses in crises; based on the last fiscal year's available data, the diversion from the criminal justice system appears to be working, as of 7,121 calls for crisis intervention only 107 resulted in arrests by the METs. Buchan (2003) also reported impressive statistics regarding the Village Agency's efforts as well, examining data for 720 participants 12 months prior to their participation in the program and 12 months after their enlistment, he found a "77% increase in permanent housing[;] 65% reduction in the number of incarcerations[;] 80% decrease in the total number of days participants were incarcerated[;] 33% reduction in hospital admissions[;] and 250% increase in the number of participants employed full-time" (p. 7).

The TAPA Center on Jail Diversion in outlining a guide to forming community coalitions for jail diversion provide the examples of four model programs in Harris and Tarrant counties in Texas, Marion County, Indiana, and Albany County, New York (Cook & Ingoglia, 2003). The Center indicates that while taking in consideration the particular needs of a jurisdiction, the key elements to developing successful jail diversion programs include quickly initiated mental health screenings with accurate assessments and linkage to community mental health services; community base services that are comprehensive in nature to meet a variety of individual needs, with treatment plans focused on recovery and allowing for consumer choice; addressing mental as well as physical healthcare, with utilization of case management services; there should be assistance with obtaining housing and supported education, as well as provisions for integrated treatment of co-occurring disorders; and all of this it is recommended should take place within the least restrictive environment possible (Cook & Ingoglia, 2003).

The Bexar County Jail Diversion Program in San Antonio, Texas has been identified as a model program, and, in fact, its successes prompted the Texas legislature to enact legislation requiring all community mental health centers to devise state-approved jail diversion strategies (Bexar County Jail Diversion Program, 2006). This jail diversion program over a two and one-half year time span resulted in somewhere between $3.8 to $5.0 million in savings to the criminal justice system in Bexar County. The program is arranged in three phases: to initially screen persons with mental illnesses picked up by law enforcement and make alternative recommendations to magistrates prior to booking, to identify persons with mental illnesses who have been booked into the criminal justice system and make recommendations for alternative dispositions such as a mental health bond or relocation to a mental health facility, and to ensure that persons upon release from jail are provided linkages to mental health treatment.

The program also includes a Crisis Care Center that is open around the clock and provides a valuable resource for law enforcement as a one-stop receiving facility, providing psychiatric care, housing, and social work capabilities. Prior to the opening of the Crisis Care Center, it was not uncommon for law enforcement officers to wait up to 12 hours when bringing a person with mental illness in to be evaluated; now wait times on average for such screenings are a little over an hour. (Bexar County Jail Diversion Program, 2006).

An example of another partnership between mental health and criminal justice practitioners exists in Harris County, Texas. Community mental health personnel literally follow individuals into the jail system to provide continuity of care. CIT is in place, as well as an ACT team, and a mobile crisis outreach team that can come to and assist persons with mental illnesses released from jail into the community who have difficulty accessing community mental health treatment. Pretrial service personnel are at an individual's first appearance before the court to provide relevant clinical information, and individuals being booked into the jail are cross referenced with a mental health database system. In stages like those found in Bexar County, persons with mental illnesses are screened, identified, tracked, diverted when possible, and linked to treatment. Advance notification from the county jail and from the Texas state prison system is made to the Mental Health And Mental Retardation Authority upon the impending release of persons with mental illnesses from custody to assist in linking individuals to treatment in the community. Specialized psychiatric and intensive case management services for persons with mental illnesses on pretrial release, probation, and parole are available under the New START program in Texas (Harris County Mental Health And Mental Retardation Authority, 2005).

The Nathaniel Project is unique in that it is a two-year alternative to incarceration program established in New York City for persons with mental illnesses who have committed a felony (Barr, 2001). The program targets violent felons, especially when it is believed that the offense committed was the result of previous lack of access to appropriate treatment. Most referrals to the program come from defense attorneys, but referrals have also been made from mental health workers, judges and prosecutors. They refer to their program as "intrusive case management" (Barr, 2001, p. 44) due to the intensive scrutiny that participants receive, as clients can be physically seen up to seven days a week and are seen a minimum of three days a week in the initial phase of the program. Usually a client pleads guilty and is released to the custody of the program. If they successfully complete the program, participants will not be sentenced to incarceration; if they fail, they will receive extensive sentences in state prison.

> In a world with a mental health system comprehensive enough to meet the needs of everyone with a serious mental illness, and where incarceration was used sparingly, the Nathaniel Project would not be necessary. However, given that our mental health system is broken, and incarceration is being used as a solution to many social problems, we believe that the Nathaniel Project is a model that can be used to help some of the most disenfranchised mental health consumers leave the criminal justice system and build new lives (Barr, 2001, p. 44).

Examples of two public defenders that actually embrace the role of therapeutic jurisprudence can be found in Stephen Bush and Bob Dillinger. Stephen Bush (2002), a public defender in Memphis, Tennessee, discusses the involvement of the Memphis Police Department's CIT program, pre-trial services, and the Memphis Public Defenders Office in linking persons with mental illnesses from the criminal justice system to treatment in the community. He describes Conditional Orders of Release (CORE) that the courts have used in Memphis to release persons with mental illnesses represented by the public defender's office into the community while awaiting disposition of their case. The public defenders office actually gets involved in brokering services for treatment and linking individuals to those services via an employed "boundary spanner" funded from a state mental health grant (Bush, 2002). Conditional release can serve as a logical means to link individuals voluntarily to treatment, and such accepted treatment can prove advantageous to persons with mental illnesses in obtaining more favorable case dispositions with the prosecutor's office (Bush, 2002).

Bob Dillinger, the public defender for Pinellas and Pasco Counties in Florida, received a $1 million grant to divert persons with mental illnesses from jail (Tisch, 2005). Dillinger estimates that the diversion program has saved the jail almost $6 million, as housing a person with mental illness in the Pinellas County jail runs approximately $79 a night; however, the diversion program is able to locate treatment center beds that cost as little as $30 a night. In addition to the public defender's office, the diversion program is a collaborative effort with the sheriff's office, the prosecutor's office, the courts, and clinicians who assist in identifying persons with mental illnesses who qualify for diversion to treatment (Tisch, 2005).

In Miami, Judge Steve Leifman has established a mental health program that incorporates, pre-booking diversion via CIT and post-booking diversion whereby mentally ill misdemeanant defendants are identified within 24–48 hours after arrest, assessed by a jail psychiatrist and a determination is made with the court as to whether to divert for mental health treatment to an appropriate mental health facility. The court has in place an integrated comprehensive treatment program, equipped with a court case management specialist and access to adult living facilities and an ACT team to assist persons with mental illnesses diverted from jail. (Perez, Leifman, & Estrada, 2003).

If you have never visited a Clubhouse, you should see the sense of empowerment and de-stigmatization that occurs there. You can literally walk inside a certified Clubhouse and not be able to discern the persons with mental illnesses from the staff. A Clubhouse is a community of persons purposefully organized to provide support to persons living with mental illnesses. For a list of Clubhouses around the world, consult the International Center for Clubhouse Development (2005). Via Clubhouse participation, individuals are provided opportunities to regain friends, family, work, school, and needed services (Clubhouses, 2006). Clubhouse participation cannot be court ordered because participation in Clubhouses is voluntary; however, Clubhouses can be used as diversions from jail as long as involvement is not coerced (E. Steele, personal communiction, June 23, 2007).

Re-entry

President George W. Bush, in his 2004 State of the Union address, as he unveiled a $300 million proposal for offenders returning to the community, stated, "America is the land of the second chance, and when the gates of the prison open, the path ahead should be a better life" (Couturier, Maue, and McVey, 2005, p. 82). Far from a better life, many persons with mental illnesses leaving prisons enter the community only to decompensate and return to incarceration. Colgan (2006) reports that recidivism rates are high across the country for persons with mental illnesses released from prisons, with over half of state inmates reporting having had " 'three or more prior sentences to probation or incarceration' " (p. 307). According to Lovell, Gagliardi, & Peterson (2002), there have been few outcome studies that focus on the release and progress of persons with mental illnesses released from prison; one of the few studies undertaken suggests that the re-arrest rate for this population was 64 percent compared to 60 percent for persons without mental illnesses, while 48 percent of the persons with mental illnesses released from prison were hospitalized while out of prison and only one percent of individuals without mental illnesses required hospitalization after release from prison.

> The usual prejudices that hinder community treatment of the mentally ill may be more severe for mentally ill offenders who may be thought to pose a greater risk to public safety.... [C]ommunity agencies and practitioners sometimes assess mentally ill offenders' risk of violence and overestimate their professional liability risks. Thus, they may be reluctant to provide outpatient treatment for mentally ill offenders (Lovell et al., 2002, p. 1291).

Although not statistically significant, Lovell et al. (2002) found that individuals who went on to commit new felonies after release from prison were those who had generally been linked to mental health services for shorter periods of time (60 percent fewer hours of treatment during the first year of release or until accosted for commission of a felony) and later after their release (initial mental health system linkage was initiated approximately two months later for those who went on to commit felonies versus those who did not. They also indicate that their "finding that mentally ill offenders rarely commit serious violent offenses deserves special emphasis" (p. 1295).

They acknowledge that this determination

> may lead well-meaning advocates to argue for more extensive social services mainly on the grounds of public safety—that is, unless better services are provided, mentally ill offenders will put the rest of society at risk. A hidden danger of this reasoning is that it presumes that mentally ill offenders are high-risk consumers. This supposition may only reinforce public fear and, ironically, discourage efforts to reach out to mentally ill offenders and keep them engaged in community mental health and other social services. This report provides strong evidence that even mentally ill offenders who have been convicted of serious felonies resulting in prison sentences rarely commit serious violent crimes after release (Lovell et al., 2002, p. 1295).

It is likely that minor offenses will land an individual with mental illness in jail prior to perpetration of a felony, and, with most persons with mental illnesses not being able to make bail, jail can be a good place to begin treatment interventions.

> The vast majority of their offenses, such as public intoxication, trespassing, possession of drugs, and aggressive panhandling, are more a reflection of a marginal urban existence than a violation of the basic rights of other citizens. In the end, the principal victims of

mentally ill offenders are the mentally ill offenders themselves. This by itself is sufficient reason for committing more resources to supporting and treating mentally ill offenders while they are incarcerated and when they leave jails or prisons (Lovell et al., 2002, p. 1296).

Also, see Draine and Herman's (2007) discussion of the possible adaptability of the critical time intervention model, a nine month, three part process that has successfully been used in discharges from homeless shelters and psychiatric institutions, to prisons for re-entry of persons with mental illnesses into society.

Criminal justice authorities are growing tired of the recycling of persons with mental illnesses and the criminal justice system being a costly dumping ground. Wilson and Draine (2006) in a study of 50 prisoner re-entry programs for persons with mental illnesses nationally found that criminal justice authorities headed 37 of the initiatives for the programs. Provided this trend continues, Wilson and Draine (2006) maintain "the criminal justice system will become a primary funder of treatment services for offenders with mental illness who are returning to the community" (p. 875). This could be further indicative of the mental health system's reluctance to deal with this population.

Draine, Wolff, Jacoby, Hartwell, and Duclos (2005) offer a new model for consideration when persons with mental illnesses are re-entering the community from prison or extended stays in jail and indicate that there are barriers to release in the community that must be considered and addressed if persons with mental illnesses are to be successfully reintegrated into society. They contend that re-entry plans too often focus on the individual being released and available mental health treatment services without considering reservations that community residents and even community treatment providers may have about dealing with this population; they offer that their model provides a vantage point for initiating discussions within communities to reduce these barriers to re-entry. Also, Rotter, McQuistion, Broner, and Steinbacher (2005) indicate clinicians need to be aware of the inmate survival code and cultural resistance to sharing sensitive information with authorities, and they describe two programs (Sensitizing Providers to the Effects of Correctional Incarceration on Treatment and Risk Management [SPECTRM] and Re-entry After Prison/Jail [RAP]) in New York City aimed at closing the divide between inmates with mental illnesses re-entering society and clinicians.

Some jurisdictions have established ex-offender programs to try to ensure linkages to mental health treatment in the community. Housing is a primary concern of ex-offenders re-entering the community, and several programs focus on the housing needs of persons with mental illnesses re-entering the community from incarceration. Prorams with an emphasis on housing include The 6002 Program in Seattle, The Gaudenzia House in Philadelphia, Shelter-Plus in Maryland, and Criminal Justice Centers and psychiatric halfway houses in Connecticut. Some of the programs have been quite successful. For example, Joan Gillece, with the Maryland Mental Hygiene Administration, reports that before the Maryland program was established 80 percent of severely mentally ill persons released from jail were re-arrested within a year, but now, with housing in place, the recidivism rate has dropped dramatically to four percent for this population (Human Rights Watch, 2003).

A number of re-entry programs for persons with mental illnesses discharged from incarceration to the community rely on ACT teams or parole officers to monitor those released into the community, sometimes with parole officers actually assigned as members of ACT teams. Again, recalling the interchangeability of re-entry and diversion programs, diversion programs likewise often rely on probation officers and ACT teams for supervision, with probation officers sometimes as members of ACT teams.

Assertive Community Treatment

Lamberti et al. (2004) indicate that an emerging trend to prevent arrest and incarceration is the use of ACT, which they refer to as forensic assertive community treatment (FACT). They note that the effectiveness of diversion "is likely to depend on the availability of appropriate services in the community[, and] many diversion programs lack effective linkages to" treatment (p. 1285). ACT was initially developed to assist persons with severe mental illnesses to function in the community, while attempting to prevent homelessness and hospitalizations. ACT "engages high-risk individuals in care by using mobile services that are available around the clock and by performing active outreach. Engagement is further promoted through delivery of comprehensive services, including mental health and addiction treatment, transportation, financial services, and vocational support" (Lamberti et al., 2004, p. 1286).

> The ACT team's services include mental health and drug treatment, health education, nonpsychiatric medical care, case management, ongoing assessments, employment and housing assistance, family support and education, and client advocacy. Extensive and reliable

services are available 24 hours a day, 7 days a week, 365 days a year (Lurigio et al., 2000, p. 540).

Lamberti et al. (2004) in a seminal study examined 16 programs in nine states that utilized FACT in conjunction with persons with mental illnesses with entanglements with the criminal justice system; 13 of these FACT programs' main referral source was from the local jail; and 11 of these FACT models employed probation officers as members of the team. "Eight programs ... had a supervised residential component, with five providing residentially based addiction treatment" (Lamberti et al., 2004, p. 1285)[4]. While reductions in hospital utilization and extended stays in the community have been attributed to ACT, this treatment approach has not demonstrated convincing results in terms of lowering arrest and incarceration rates. Seventy percent of recent studies have indicated no effect by ACT, and 10 percent of studies have shown a worsening effect on arrest and incarceration rates. However, positive results of FACT teams have been uncoered (Lamberti et al., 2004). For example, of "the first 18 patients treated in the Arkansas Partnership Program, [s]eventeen patients had remained arrest free and without substance abuse while living in the community an average of 508 days. In a study comparing outcomes among 41 patients during the year before and after enrollment in Project Link, the "average number of days in jail per patient was significantly reduced (Lamberti et al., 2004, p. 1289). "Significant reductions were also noted in the number of arrests and hospitalizations, along with improved community functioning" (Lamberti et al., 2004, p. 1289). ACT ... appears to be effective in managing community-based care for people with severe mental illnesses" (p.168).

For persons with mental illnesses to be successfully diverted from jail access to treatment is necessary, and ACT provides for this linkage. Therefore, according to Lamberti et al. (2004), joining ACT with the jail diversion process should produce positive results. An example of such a joint approach is Project Link, utilizing ACT in a comprehensive approach to prevent arrest and in-

---

4. Of the 16 programs, eight of them were in California. The others were in Birmingham, Alabama—Birmingham Jail Diversion Project; Little Rock, Arkansas—Arkansas Partnership Direct; St. Petersburg, Florida—Suncoast Center Forensic FACT Team; Chicago, Illinois—Thresholds Jail Program; Portland, Maine—Project DOT (Divert Offenders to Treatment); Rochester, New York—Project Link; Hamilton, Ohio—Substance Abuse and Mental Illness Court Program; and Madison, Wisconsin—Community Treatment Alternatives (Lamberti et al., 2004).

carceration of persons with mental illnesses in Rochester, New York. Project Link is dissimilar from traditional ACT programs in several significant aspects.

> These differences include its requirement of a history of arrest for admission, its use of jail as the primary referral source, its close partnership with multiple criminal justice agencies to divert clients from further involvement with the criminal justice system, and its incorporation of residentially based addiction treatment. Research has suggested that this program may be effective at reducing rates of arrest, incarceration, and hospitalization as well as improving community adjustment (Lamberti, et al., 2004, p. 1286).

Lamberti et al. (2004) indicate that publications consistently tout the effectiveness of the adaptability of ACT to effectively reduce arrest and imprisonment rates for persons with mental illnesses, however, such research has lacked methodological rigor.

Project Link (1999) is comprised of five community service agencies in Monroe County, New York. Project Link is aimed at preventing recidivism and promoting community reintegration of persons with mental illnesses. Combining elements of ACT and intensive case management, Project Link has significantly decreased the number of persons with mental illnesses in jail and the number of hospitalizations. Enrollment into Project Link can come from a number of sources, police, public defender's office, or hospitals, with the most referrals coming from prisons and jails.

Project Link incorporates a mobile treatment team (taking mental health services to clients when necessary) and has treatment residences staffed around the clock. A preliminary assessment of the program revealed that as a result of Project Link's (1999) alternatives to incarceration "the average monthly jail costs for the entire group dropped from $30,908 to $7,235 or from $672 to $157 per consumer" (p. 1478–1479). Therapeutic leverage is used with those individuals who remain justice involved and have probation or parole officers, as their help is enlisted to reinforce treatment conditions. Lamberti (2007) considers the crucial components for stopping the criminal recidivism of persons with mental illnesses the use of this legal leverage combined with linkage to competent treatment services.

Consumer satisfaction with Project Link was 4.6 out of 5, seemingly indicating a lack of coercion. Project Link, unlike most studies involving ACT and intensive case management, resulted in a significant contribution to reducing incarceration among consumers of mental health services (Project Link, 1999). Lamberti et al. (2001) conclude, as did the Project Link (1999) article, that

Project Link may actually succeed in reducing jail and hospital recidivism by utilizing service integration. Project Link integrates and spans healthcare, social services and the criminal justice system. Project Link combines a mobile treatment team, a forensic psychiatrist, a dual diagnosis treatment residence, and culturally competent staff (Lamberti et al., 2001). Via integration, Project Link brings together three complimentary models of service delivery and literally "'makes a whole out of parts'" (Lamberti et al., 2001, p. 73), orchestrating seamless care for the patient.

The main difference in FACT and ACT is the extent to which emphasis is placed on the prevention of arrest and incarceration. With the FACT teams, a priority is focusing on mentally ill offenders by requiring a criminal history and relying upon a predominance of referrals from criminal justice agencies, and this is bolstered with the inclusion of probation officers on 69% of the FACT teams included in the study (Lamberti et al., 2004). Engaging probation officers in the process can allow for legal leverage to nudge individuals into treatment thereby avoiding costly and anti-therapeutic incarceration. While some concerns have been expressed that ACT was never to be coercive in nature and the use of probation officers may violate that principle (Solomon & Draine, 1995a), the role of the probation officer may be a little different working with this population compared with the traditional role of probation officers (see Roskes & Feldman, 2000; Slate, Feldman, Roskes, & Baerga, 2004; Slate, Roskes, Feldman, & Baerga, 2003). The emphasis should be on therapeutic outcomes and not so much overly zealous focus on revocations of probation. While more outcome data is needed, FACT is perceived as a promising model of prevention and care for persons with severe mental illnesses (Lamberti et al., 2004).

Florida has established a number of ACT teams across the state to enhance services to persons with mental illnesses, and some of those programs have a few members that may be involved in some way with the criminal justice system. However, the Suncoast Center for Community Mental Health in St. Petersburg represents Florida's only forensic ACT team designed to exclusively handle individuals charged with felonies, albeit nonviolent in nature. The FACT team makes periodic progress reports to the court to ensure that there is compliance with conditions of release (Kilroy & Wagner, 2004).

Although not cited by Lamberti et al. 2004, Conklin (2000) indicates that Detroit-Wayne County, Michigan, has a Mental Health-Corrections Outreach Intensive Treatment (M-COIT) program that is based on the ACT approach, incorporates a multidisciplinary team of clinicians, probation/parole officers and vocational officers, and is aimed at reintegrating parolees and offenders with severe mental illnesses who have maxed out their sentences back into the community. Another example of a program employing ACT principles, not included in the study by Lamberti et al. 2004, is the Connections Program, funded via a competitive grant from the California legislature, that was a partnership between the sheriff's office, the probation department, and clinicians in San Diego and found that participants in the program had significantly less arrests, convictions, and time served in jail than a comparison group of non-participants (see Burke & Keaton, 2004). However, as is often a concern with initiating programs via governmental grants, if there is not buy-in and financial support garnered in local jurisdictions when the state or federal funding cycle ceases, the program will also end, as was the case in San Diego for the Connections program.

Community Treatment Alternatives is a FACT program in Madison, Wisconsin, that has achieved significantly positive results in reducing recidivism and jail time among those they serve. All clients in this program have either been incarcerated or are facing charges that could lead to incarceration, and, significantly, 85% of those who complete their legal obligation to participate in the program stay in the program voluntarily afterwards. One might surmise that these individuals felt like they were valued and had input into critical treatment decisions—otherwise, why else would they stay on? (R. Honberg, personal communication, July 29, 2006).

It is maintained that persons with mental illnesses can be effectively managed by systems with single points of entry, such as ACT, whether those being supervised are encountered pretrial, after trial, or after release from custody. ACT appears to warrant credibility and should be further explored for managing persons with mental illnesses who encounter the criminal justice system (Lurigio et al., 2000).

Cuddeback, Morrissey, and Cusack (2008) recommend that standardized FACT eligibility guidelines should be developed. They also suggest a sufficient amount of FACT programs should be put in place to assist in jail diversion in metropolitan areas to serve at least 44 percent of persons with severe mental illnesses within a catchment area. The need for operation of FACT models in rural areas still requires assessment and evaluation.

Parole

As of 1997, Camp and Camp (1997) found no specialized programs for parolees with mental illnesses; it was determined in a survey of parole administrators that less than 25 percent of the respondents did not offer any specialized programs for individuals with mental illnesses under their supervision (Lurigio, 2001; Petersilia,

2003; Travis, 2005). In *Closs v. Weber* (2001), the 8th circuit upheld the decision that parole could legally be revoked as a result of a parolee agreeing to mental health treatment as a condition of release but refusing to accept the psychotropic medication prescribed for him. Today, several examples of parole supervision of persons with mental illnesses have been identified in the research literature.

Travis (2005) identifies one model program operated by the Georgia Department of Corrections called Transition and Aftercare for Probationers and Parolees (TAPP). In a partnership between corrections and the Georgia Department of Human Resources, Mental Health Division, case managers are assigned to prisoners being released into the community and to probationers, and the case managers can render assistance with mental health and medical care, as well as help with housing and job needs.

In addition to the Hampden County re-entry model previously discussed by Sultan, Travis, Solomon, and Waul (2001) also tout specialized programs for parolees in California as models worthy of consideration (Lurigio, 2001). Five parolee outpatient clinics serving over 9,000 parolees with mental illnesses have been established in Fresno, Los Angeles, Sacramento, San Diego, and San Francisco. These clinics are staffed by psychiatrists and psychologists and exclusively tend to the mental health needs of parolees; unfortunately, it is believed that half of the parolees in need of services are not served, as they live outside of one of these catchment areas. Travis et al. (2001) also cite California's Conditional Release Program, a community-based program for prisoners with mental illnesses who are moved from correctional facilities to state hospitals and ultimately as a condition of parole to outpatient psychiatric care in the community. Research indicates that parolees who do not participate in this specialized program are four times more likely to re-offend than those who do; similar results have been demonstrated with analogous programs in New York and Oregon (Travis et al., 2001).

Couturier et al. (2005) report on a tracking system to monitor inmates with mental illnesses being paroled and maxing out their sentences in Pennsylvania. They found that inmates with mental illnesses were more likely to max out their sentences as opposed to being paroled. With this realization, the Pennsylvania Department of Corrections has partnered with other agencies, to include the Pennsylvania Board of Probation and Parole and the Office of Mental Health, to establish re-entry protocols and begin planning meetings with interdisciplinary treatment teams at 12 and six-month intervals before the return of offenders with mental illnesses to the community. The discharge planning includes waivers for release of inmate information; contacts with mental health providers and law enforcement personnel (if the offender is considered dangerous) in the community where the inmate is to return; completion of the necessary paperwork to ensure continuity of benefits for obtaining mental health services in the community; if necessary, arrangements made for civil commitments upon release; and provision of a month's supply of psychotropic medication to facilitate adherence to the treatment regimen until care can be continued in the community (Couturier et al., 2005). They also discuss model corrections/mental health relationships in Pittsburgh and Philadelphia, as well as several specialized community living programs in Pennsylvania.

New York State mental health and parole authorities have been able to work out agreements for specially trained parole officers with specialized caseloads, with no more than 25 parolees, monitoring persons with mental illnesses who have returned to the community from the criminal justice system. New York City's Nathaniel Project, which accepts persons with mental illnesses charged with serious offenses is also noteworthy for its efforts to procure housing and obtain funding for housing for such individuals. Haimowitz (2004) also reports on innovative programs in Texas that partner with regional Social Security offices to enable inmates with mental illnesses to file for reinstatement of benefits and food stamps three months prior to discharge from prison are also worhty of consideration (Hamiowitz, 2004). In addition, Haimowitz (2004) believes that collaborations are extremely important to success and advocates the use of databases linked across justice and mental health systems, cross training of mental health and criminal justice personnel, and written memorandums of understanding, to include delineation of "who is responsible for what" (p. 374).[5] Haimowitz (2004) also cautions that we should be careful "to guard against mental health services' drifting toward social control functions" (p. 375).[6]

Probation

As of 1984, Solomon and Draine (1995b) indicate that they were not aware of any studies that specified how often probation and parole agencies utilized mental health services. Skeem amd Louden (2006) estimate that roughly 15 percent (at least 500,000 persons) of individuals on probation, supervised re-

---

5. See the discussion in the concluding chapter regarding the events leading up to the massacre at Virginia Tech and seeming lack of knowledge regarding responsibility for monitoring individuals referred by the court for treatment.

6. See similar concerns echoed by Steadman and Honberg in Chapter 4 on law enforcement follow-ups with persons with mental illnesses that they encounter in crises.

lease or parole have mental illnesses, and Lurigio and Swartz (2000) reveal that 15 percent of probation departments nationwide reported having specialized programs for probationers with mental illnesses. Slate et al. (2003) report 18 percent of the 19,731 individuals under federal probation officer or pretrial officer supervision (parole, supervised release, conditional release or probation) have a special condition of mental health treatment imposed upon them. A federal court has also upheld the imposition of mental health treatment as a legitimate condition for compliance with supervised release (see *USA v. Bull*, 2000, WL 754942 [11th Cir.]).

Generally, most probation officers are not properly skilled to deal with persons with mental illnesses in terms of community supervision (Veysey, 1994). Though they have been criticized for their isolationism and a lack of interagency cooperativeness, probation officers and departments are strategically positioned to operate in the spirit of therapeutic jurisprudence as positive change agents (Slate et al., 2003; 2004). Probation officers have been considered resource brokers or boundary spanners who can operate to identify community resources, such as in the areas of mental health, housing and vocational/employment possibilities, and then properly match those in need of services under their supervision to appropriate services (McCampbell, 2001; Steadman et al., 2001). Solomon and Draine (1995a) discussed the boundary spanning role performed by forensic case managers between criminal justice authorities and the community mental health system. They also discuss the conflicts that can emerge between case managers and probation officers, as there may be mixed loyalties, and they suggest that intensive case management may actually set clients up for re-incarceration, as under such scrutiny noncompliance with treatment dictates are more likely to be uncovered. According to Skeem and Louden (2006), persons with mental illnesses under community corrections control are twice as likely as persons without mental illnesses to have their community supervision revoked.

Rivera (2004) suggests that probation departments develop specialized mental health caseloads supervised by select officers. Some agencies have devised specialized programs to handle persons with mental illnesses under their supervision; for example, in Chicago a specialized program for probationers has been implemented (Lurigio & Swartz, 2000) and for those under federal supervision in the community in Baltimore, the Northern District of Illinois, the Western District of Texas, the Eastern District of Tennessee, and New Jersey (Slate et al., 2004). Probation officers have become members of ACT teams, for example, in Sacramento (Sheppard, Freitas, & Hurley, 2002).

Skeem and Petrila (2004) identify the establishment of specialized probation caseloads comprised of persons with mental illnesses as a promising strategy. The traditional role of probation officers as attuned to public safety remains and is combined with a therapeutic role, whereby the officer also focuses on the rehabilitation of the probationer. The balancing of this dual role of monitor and treater is addressed in the research literature by Roskes and Feldman (2000). With this added dimension, emphasis on problem solving and therapeutic approaches to what may have traditionally been more of a focus on revocation occurs when potential violations arise. Skeem and Petrila note that specialized caseloads for persons with mental illnesses emerged a little over 25 years ago and have accelerated in the past five years, and they do not anticipate this trend will slow down anytime soon. They do caution that those agencies with specialized caseloads should consider reduced caseloads, increased probation officer training for those with specialty caseloads, and not merely using probation officers to ratchet up surveillance of persons with mental illnesses in the community but instead to engage them as therapeutic agents.

Some probation agencies conduct specialized training for their officers supervising persons with mental illnesses. Skeem and Louden (2006) identified 137 probation agencies with at least one mental health caseload, and this was further narrowed down to 66 specialty agencies to be compared with 25 traditional agencies while trying to keep geographic location and population in mind for meaningful comparisons. They were able to specify five key elements that characterized a specialty model focusing on providing correctional supervision to persons with mental illnesses in the community. The five key elements most associated with specialty caseloads were (1) a caseload exclusively devoted to the specialized supervision of persons with mental illnesses; (2) considerably reduced caseloads for officers supervising persons with mental illnesses, thus caseloads approximately two-thirds less than traditional caseloads—45 persons supervised versus 135 persons; (3) extensive and continued specialized training for officers, typically with anywhere from 20 to 40 extra hours a year of training; (4) officers do more than monitor and refer persons with mental illnesses and are actively engaged with teams of treatment providers and assist individuals in accessing benefits and services such as housing and meaningful employment; and (5) officers operate as problem solvers, not just rule reminders, and involve the participation of offenders in their treatment plan (Skeem & Louden, 2006). While Skeem and Louden (2006) stated that the verdict is still out on whether specialty models lessen the probability of probationers' rearrest over the long term, they reported that two studies indicate that stakeholders believe specialty caseloads are more successful than traditional ways of handling probation caseloads; three studies found that specialty models are better at linking persons with mental illnesses to care in the community, enhancing their well-being, and lessening the chances of revocation of their probation.

In terms of parole, Skeem and Louden (2006) indicate that there are two studies that suggest specialty models have been successful in lessening the probability of persons with mental illnesses violating parole, at least in the short term. Skeem and Louden (2006) conclude by saying,

> The research reviewed here suggests that specialty caseloads improve [the] functioning [of persons with mental illnesses], enhance access to services, and reduce the risk of probation violation.... [E]xisting practices hold promise. Implementing these practices may prevent offenders with mental illness[es] from becoming more deeply entrenched in the criminal justice system, which would better realize the supervision goal of facilitating their re-entry to the community (p. 341).

Specialized training takes place in New York State for probation officers supervising persons with mental illnesses and co-occurring disorders. The goals there are multi-faceted and include an emphasis on public safety as the primary goal, as well as the promotion of recovery and reducing recidivism, all in the spirit of therapeutic jurisprudence (Massaro, 2003).

Some of the federal probation training of mental health specialists has been modeled after the Memphis CIT training. Training programs typically focus on identifying and augmenting resources and linking individuals to appropriate treatment. Federal probation officers need, for example, to be able to navigate and access multiple entities, such as the bureau of prisons, the courts, probation, law enforcement, the community mental health system, and patients/offenders. A number of probation officers serving as mental health specialists in the federal system have extensive educational credentials in mental health, some as licensed counselors, social workers and even psychologists (Slate et al., 2004).

Slate et al. (2004) recommend 40 hour annual training for those entrusted with supervision of persons with mental illnesses in the community and a caseload of no more than 35 to ensure optimum supervision and linkages to treatment. Training components should also address how the criminal justice system has become the de facto mental health system, de-escalation techniques, and the development of and adherence to memorandums of understanding (mous) between agencies.

Lastly, Skeem and Petrila (2004) maintain that Health Insurance Portability and Accountability Act (HIPAA) concerns can be allayed by the fact that court orders can satisfy HIPAA requirements, and probation conditions can be crafted in such a manner as to obtain consent in writing of the probationer for release of mental health records. Formal agreements (mous) can be entered into in advance between probation and various mental health and social service agencies with formal agreements hashed out for the sharing of information from one agency to the other; "[a]lternatively, in the prototypic specialty agency, the probation officer often becomes part of the treatment team, such that as a practical matter 'confidentiality ceases to exist' " (Skeem & Petrila, p. 15, 2004).

Conclusion

Whether it is called diversion or re-entry, discharge planning is essential to successful reintegration of persons with mental illnesses back into society from encounters with the criminal justice system. The keys to successful discharge of persons with mental illnesses from the criminal justice system are having access to sufficient services, ensuring linkages to treatment, and providing follow-up to ensure compliance with treatment protocols. Follow-up is necessary to ensure that discharge plans are carried out. Otherwise, the continual cycle of setting persons with mental illnesses up to fail will be repeated again and again.

With states under the burden of an enormous fiscal crisis, looking to cut corners wherever they can, programs for the mentally ill are especially vulnerable. Cutting funds to such programs for persons with mentall illnesses is short sighted because the cost of the mentally ill returning to prison is greater in the long run than the cost of providing them adequate transition counseling and treatment upon release. Without good discharge planning and post-release programs, seriously mentally ill prisoners are likely to cycle endlessly between prison and the community, their illnesses worsening, and chances increasing that they will end up in the high security units within the prison system. Successful release plans for the mentally ill include partnerships between departments of corrections and other state agencies, the availability of post-release treatment, early enrollment in Medicaid or another form of health care coverage, and pre-release counseling that begins well before a prisoner's release.

The proper funding of discharge planning and post-release programs is a crucial public policy issue. In an era in which the United States incarcerates hundreds of thousands of seriously mentally ill men and women in its prisons, it serves neither the mentally ill nor the broader community to shortchange the transitional programs that could serve to break these linkages between mental illness and imprisonment in 21st century America (Human Rights Watch,

2003). There is a desperate need for more adequate mental health services after arrest, better treatment availability for persons with mental illnesses after release into the community, individualized case management and outreach, the assurance of appropriate housing arrangements in the community, and assurance that the concerns of family members of the person with mental illness are addressed and supports are put in place to assist them in monitoring their loved one's condition (Lamb, Weinberger, & Gross, 2004).

In fact, Osher and Steadman (2007) in an examination of the adaptation of evidence-based practices to the criminal justice system for justice involved persons with mental illnesses suggest that research reinforces the need for supportive housing, ACT, and integrated treatment for co-occurring disorders as potentially successful interventions. Such practices employed with discharge planning at either the diversion or re-entry stage can prove instrumental in bringing about promising resolutions.

Another process touted by some as a means for persons with mental illnesses in crisis to avoid the criminal justice system is outpatient commitment. However, as we will see in the next chapter, the success of civil commitment depends largely on the availability of services as have the alternatives to the criminal justice system discussed in this chapter.

References

Barr, H. (2001). The Nathaniel Project: An alternative to incarceration for seriously mentally ill felony offenders. Community Mental Health Report 1(3), pp. 43–44.

Barr, H. (2003a). Transinstitutionalization in the courts: Brad H. v. City of New York, and the fight for discharge planning for people with psychiatric disabilities leaving Rikers Island. *Crime & Delinquency* 49(1), pp. 97–123.

Barr, H. (2003b, November 26). Prisons and jails: Hospitals of last resort. New York City: Soros Foundation. Retrieved from the World Wide Web on July 9, 2007: http://www.prisonpolicy.org/scans/MIReport.pdf.

Bernstein, N. (2000, July 13). Freed inmates must get care if mentally ill. New York Times. Retrieved from the World Wide Web on July 12, 2007: http://query.nytimes.com/gst/fullpage.html?sec=health&res=9E0DE1DC1F38F930A25754C0A9669C8B63.

Bexar County Jail Diversion (2006). Providing jail diversion for people with mental illness. Psychiatric Services 57(10), pp. 1521–1523.

Bjorklund, R. W. (2000). Linking discharged patients with peers in the community. *Psychiatric Services* 51(10), p. 1316.

Boccaccini, M. T., Christy, A., Poythress, N., & Kershaw, D. (2005). Rediversion in two postbooking jail diversion programs in Florida. *Psychiatric Services* 56(7), pp. 835–839.

Buchan, L. (2003, June). Ending the cycle of recidivism: Best practices for diverting mentally ill individuals from county jails. Washington, DC: National Association of Counties.

Burke, C., & Keaton, S. (2004, June). San Diego County's Connections Program Board of Corrections Final Report. San Diego, CA: San Diego Regional Association of Governments. Retrieved from the World Wide Web on July 9, 2007: http://www.sdsheriff.net/library/connections_grant_final. pdf.

Bush, S. C. (2002). Using conditional release as a strategy for effective linkage to community mental health services: The Memphis Public Defenders Office model. Community Mental Health Report 2(6), pp. 81–82, 94–95.

Camp, C., & Camp, G. (1997). The corrections yearbook. South Salem, NY: Criminal Justice Institute.

Clark, J. (2004). Non-speciality first appearance court models for diverting persons with mental illness: Alternatives to mental health courts. Delmar, New York: Technical Assistance and Policy Analysis Center for Jail Diversion.

Closs v. Weber. (2001, February 9). Mentally ill parolee must take medication. *Corrections Digest* 32(6), p. 3.

Clubhouses (2006). Clubhouses: Communities creating opportunities for people with mental illness. New York: International Center for Clubhouse Development. Retrieved from the World Wide Web on July 11, 2007: http://www.iccd.org/article.asp?articleID=3.

Colgan, B. A. (2006). Prison and detention: Teaching a prisoner to fish: Getting tough on crime by preparing prisoners to reenter society. *Seattle Journal for Social Justice* 5, pp. 293–328.

Conklin, C. (2000, April 26). M-COIT: An innovative cross-systems approach to assisting seriously mentally ill ex-offenders reintegrate and remain in the community. Presented at the 2000 GAINS Center National Conference, Miami, Florida.

Conly, C. (1999, April). Coordinating community services for mentally ill offenders: Maryland's community criminal justice treatment program. Washington, DC: U.S. Department of Justice, National Institute of Justice.

Cook, W. & Ingoglia, C. (2003, October). Jail diversion for people with mental illness: Developing supportive community coalitions. Delmar, New

York: TAPA Center for Jail Diversion, A Branch of the National GAINS Center, pp. 1–6.

Council of State Governments, Police Executive Research Forum, Pretrial Services Resource Center, Association of State Correctional Administrators, Bazelon Center for Mental Health Law, and the Center for Behavioral Health, Justice, and Public Policy (2002). Criminal Justice/Mental Health Consensus Project. New York: Council of State Governments.

Council of State Governments (2007a). Ensuring timely access to Medicaid and SSI/SSDI for people with mental illness releases from prison: Four state case studies. New York: Council of State Governments. Retrieved from the World Wide Web on July 12, 2007: www.reentrypolicy.org/reentry/Document_Viewer.aspx?DocumentID=998.

Couturier, L., Maue, F., & McVey, C. (2005). Releasing inmates with mental illness and co-occurring disorders into the community. *Corrections Today* 67(2), pp. 82–85.

Cuddeback, G. S., Morrissey, J. P., & Cusack, K. J. (2008). How many forensic assertive community treatment teams do we need? *Psychiatric Services,* 59(2), 205–208.

Daly, R. (2006). States get disappointing marks on mh report card. *Psychiatric News* 41(8), p. 8, 71.

Dincin, J. (2002, December 11). Personal Communication. Executive Director of the Thresholds Jail Program. Chicago, Illinois.

Draine, J., & Herman, D. B. (2007). Critical time intervention for reentry from prison for persons with mental illness. *Psychiatric Services* 58(12), pp. 1577–1581.

Draine, J., & Solomon, P. (1999). Describing and evaluating jail diversion services for persons with serious mental illness. *Psychiatric Services* 50(1), pp. 56–61.

Draine, J., Wolff, N., Jacoby, J. E., Hartwell, S., & Duclos, C. (2005). Understanding community re-entry of former prisoners with mental illness: A conceptual model to guide new research. Behavioral Sciences and the Law, p. 23, 689–707.

Edgar, E. (1999). The role of PACT in recovery. *NAMI Advocate* 21(1), pp. 14–15.

Fulwiler, C. (2000). Release planning for inmates with mental illness. *Correctional Health Care Report* 1(3), pp. 37–38, 48.

GAINS Center (2007a). Jail diversion; re-entry. Delmar, New York: The National GAINS Center. Retrieved from the World Wide Web on July 9, 2007: http://gainscenter.samhsa.gov/html/resources/publications.asp#jaildiv.

GAINS Center (2007b). Women's 8 part series. Delmar, New York: The National GAINS Center. Retrieved from the World Wide Web on July 9, 2007:http://gainscenter.samhsa.gov/html/resources/publications.asp#women.

GAINS Center (2007c). Co-occurring disorders. Delmar, New York: National GAINS Center. Retrieved from the World Wide Web on July 9, 2007: http://gainscenter.samhsa.gov/html/resources/publications.asp#disorders.

Giuliani, R. W. (2000). City of New York Fiscal 2000 Mayor's Management Report: Volume I—Agency Narratives. New York.

Haimowitz, S. (2004). Slowing the revolving door: Community reentry of offenders with mental illness. *Psychiatric Services* 55(4), pp. 373–375.

Haimowitz, S. (2002). Can mental health courts end the criminalization of persons with mental illness? *Psychiatric Services* 53(10), pp. 1226–1228.

Hands Across Long Island (2007). Forensic. Central Islip, New York. Retrieved from the World Wide Web on July 12, 2007: http://www.hali88.org/ forensic.htm.

Harper, T. (2002, October 28). Howie T. Harp Advocacy Center. Presented at the National GAINS Center Conference in San Francisco, California.

Harris County Mental Health And Mental Retardation Authority (2005). Jail detention and diversion plan. Houston, Texas. Retrieved form the World Wide Web on July 7, 2007: www.mhmraharris.org/LocalPlan/documents/8-HarrisCountyJailDiversionPlan2005.pdf.

Hartwell, S. W. (2004). Comparison of offenders with mental illness only and offenders with dual diagnoses. *Psychiatric Services* 55(2), pp. 145–150.

Hartwell, S. W., & Orr, K. (1999). The Massachusetts forensic transition program for mentally ill offenders re-entering the community. *Psychiatric Services* 50(9), pp. 1220–1222.

Hartwell, S. W., & Orr, K. (2000, November/December). Release planning: And the distinctions for mentally ill offenders returning to the community from jails versus prisons. *American Jails*, pp. 9–12.

Human Rights Watch (2003, October). Failure to provide discharge planning. New York: Human Rights Watch. Retrieved from the World Wide Web on July 12, 2007: http://www.hrw.org/reports/2003/usa1003/24.htm.

The International Center for Clubhouse Development (2005). ICCD International Clubhouse Directory. New York: The International Center for Clubhouse Development. Retrieved from the World Wide Web on July 11, 2007: http://www.iccd.org/ClubhouseDirectory.aspx.

Kilroy, R., & Wagner, L. (2004). The facts about a forensic F.A.C.T. Team. *NAMI Florida Sun* 6(6), p. 10.

Kittrie, N. N. (1978). The right to be different: Deviance and enforced treatment. 1–2 Baltimore: John Hopkins University Press.

Lamb, H. R., Weinberger, L. E., & Gross, B. H. (2004). Mentally ill persons in the criminal justice system: Some perspectives. *Psychiatric Quarterly* 75(2), pp. 107–126.

Lamberti, J. S. (2007). Understanding and preventing criminal recidivism among adults with psychotic disorders. *Psychiatric Services* 58(6), pp. 773–781.

Lamberti, J. S., Weisman, R., & Faden, D. I. (2004). Forensic assertive community treatment: Preventing incarceration of adults with severe mental illness. *Psychiatric Services* 55(11), pp. 1285–1293.

Lamberti, J. S., Weisman, R. L., Schwartzkopf, S. B., Price, N., Ashton, R. M., & Trompeter, J. (2001). The mentally ill in jails and prisons: Towards an integrated model of prevention. *Psychiatric Quarterly* 72(1), pp. 63–77.

Lovell, D., Gagliardi, G. J., & Peterson, P. D. (2002). Recidivism and use of services among persons with mental illness after release from prison. *Psychiatric Services* 53(10), pp. 1290–1296.

Lurigio, A. J. (2001). Effective services for parolees with mental illnesses. *Crime & Delinquency* 47(3), pp. 446–461.

Lurigio, A.J., Fallon, J.R., & Dincin, J. (2000). Helping the mentally ill in jails adjust to community life: A description of a postrelease ACT program and its clients. *International Journal of Offender Therapy and Comparative Criminology* 44(5), pp. 532–548.

Lurigio, A. J., & Swartz, J. A. (2000). Changing the contours of the criminal justice system to meet the needs of persons with serious mental illness. In J. Horney (Ed.). Policies, processes, and decisions of the criminal justice system (p.45–108). Washington, DC: U.S. Department of Justice, National Institute of Justice.

Massaro, J. (2003). Persons with serious mental illness and co-occurring substance disorders on probation or in ATI programs (draft). New York State Office of Mental Health, Division of Community Care Systems Management, Community Forensic Services.

McCampbell, S. W. (2001). Mental health courts: What sheriffs need to know. *Sheriff* 53(2), pp. 40–43.

MCES Quest (2002, December). Criminal justice diversion of the mentally ill, 2(2), 1–8. Montgomery County, Pennsylvania: Montgomery County Emergency Service, Inc.

Miller, C., & Fantz, A. (2005, September 11). A new kind of jail. *The Miami Herald*, p. 1B.

Munetz, M. R., & Griffin, P. A. (2006). Use of the sequential intercept models as an approach to decriminalization of people with serious mental illness. *Psychiatric Services* 57(4), pp. 544–549.

NAMI (2007). Family to family education program. Arlington, Virginia: National Alliance on Mental Illness. Retrieved from the World Wide Web on July 7, 2007: http://www.nami.org/Template.cfm?Section=Family-to-Family.

Osher, F. C., & Steadman, H. J. (2007). Adapting evidence-based practices for persons with mental illness involved in the criminal justice system. *Psychiatric Services* 58(11), pp. 1472–1478.

Osher, F., Steadman, H. J., & Barr, H. (2003). A best practice approach to community re-entry from jails for inmates with co-occurring disorders: The APIC model. *Crime & Delinquency* 49(1), pp. 79–96.

Parish, J. J. (2007, April 30). Testimony: Status of the implementation of the Brad H. Settlement. New York: City Council Hearing. Retrieved from the World Wide Web on July 11, 2007: www.urbanjustice.org/pdf/publications/BradHTestimony.pdf.

Perez, A., Leifman, S., & Estrada, A. (2003). Reversing the criminalization of mental illness. *Crime & Delinquency* 49(1), 62–78.

Petersilia, J. (2003). When prisoners come home: Parole and prisoner reentry. New York: Oxford University Press.

Petrila, J., Ridgely, M.S., & Borum, R. (2003). Debating outpatient commitment: Controversy, trends and empirical data. *Crime & Delinquency* 49(1), pp. 157–172.

Project Link (1999). Prevention of jail and hospital recidivism among persons with severe mental illness. *Psychiatric Services* 50(11), pp. 1477–1480.

Power, A.K. (2006, April 6). System transformation at the interface of the criminal justice and mental health systems. Boston, Massachusetts: National GAINS Center Conference.

President's New Freedom Commission on Mental Health (2003). *Achieving the Promise: Transforming Mental Health Care in America.* Final Report. DHHS Pub. No. SMA-03-3832. Rockville, MD.

Rivera, R. M. (2004). The mentally ill offender: A brighter tomorrow through the eyes of the mentally ill offender treatment and crime reduction act of 2004. *Cleveland State University Journal of Law and Health*, p. 19, 107–139.

Roskes, E., & Feldman, R. (2000). Treater or monitor? Collaboration between mental health providers and probation officers. *Correctional Mental Health Report*, p. 1, 69–70.

Rotter, M., McQuistion, H. L., Broner, N., & Steinbacher, M. (2005). The impact of the "incarceration culture" on reentry for adults with mental illness:

A training and group treatment model. *Psychiatric Services* 56(3), pp. 265–267.

Saulny, S. (2003, January 9). City agrees to help care for mentally ill inmates after release. The New York Times. Retrieved from the World Wide Web on July 11, 2007: http://query.nytimes.com/gst/fullpage.html?sec=health&res=9502EFD9103EF93AA35752C0A9659C8B63.

Seltzer, T. (2005). Mental health courts: A misguided attempt to address the criminal justice system's unfair treatment of people with mental illnesses. *Psychology, Public Policy, and Law*, p. 11, 570–586.

Skeem, J. L., & Louden, J. E. (2006). Toward evidence-based practice for probationers and parolees mandated to mental health treatment. *Psychiatric Services* 57(3), pp. 333–342.

Skeem, J., & Petrila, J. (2004). Problem-solving supervision: Specialty probation for individuals with mental illnesses. *Court Review*, p. 40, 8–15.

Sheppard, R., Freitas, F., & Hurley, K. (2002, October 28). Assertive community treatment and the mentally ill offender. Paper presented at the National GAINS Center Conference, San Francisco.

Slate, R. N., Feldman, R., Roskes, E., & Baerga, M. (2004). Training Federal Probation Officers as mental health specialists. *Federal Probation* 68(3), pp. 9–15.

Slate, R. N., Roskes, E., Feldman, R., & Baerga, M. (2003). Doing justice for mental illness and society: Federal probation and pretrial service officers as mental health specialists. *Federal Probation* 67(3), pp. 13–19.

Solomon, P., & Draine, J. (1995a). Jail recidivism in a forensic case management program. *Health & Social Work* 20(3), pp. 167–173.

Solomon, P., & Draine, J. (1995b). Issues in serving the forensic client. *Social Work* 40(1), pp. 25–33.

Steadman, H. J., Barbera, S. S., & Dennis, D. L. (1994). A national survey of jail diversion programs for mentally ill detainees. *Hospital and Community Psychiatry* 45(11), pp. 1109–1113.

Steadman, H. J., Deane, M. W., Borum, R., & Morrissey, J. P. (2000). Comparing outcomes of major models of police responses to mental health emergencies. *Psychiatric Services* 51(5), pp. 645–649.

Steadman, H. J., Morris, S. M., & Dennis, D. L. (1995). The diversion of mentally ill persons from jails to community-based services: A profile of programs. *American Journal of Public Health* 85(12), pp. 1630–1635.

Steadman, H. J., & Naples, M. (2005). Assessing the effectiveness of jail diversion programs for persons with serious mental illness and co-occurring substance use disorders. *Behavioral Sciences and the Law*, p. 23, 163–170.

Steadman, H. J., & Veysey, B. (1997, January). Providing services for jail inmates with mental disorders (Research in brief). Washington, DC: National Institute of Justice.

Steadman, H. J., Stainbrook, K. A., Griffin, P., Draine, J., Dupont, R., & Horey, C. (2001). A specialized crisis response site as a core element of police-based diversion programs. *Psychiatric Services* 52(2), pp. 219–222.

Steadman, H. J., Deane, M. W., Morrissey, J. P., Westcott, M., Salasin, S., & Shapiro, S. (1999). A SAMHSA research initiative assessing the effectiveness of jail diversion programs for mentally ill persons. *Psychiatric Services* 50(12), pp. 1620–1623.

Sultan, B. J. (2006). Policy perspective: The insanity of incarceration and the maddening reentry process: A call for change and justice for males with mental illness in United States prisons. *Georgetown Journal on Poverty Law & Policy* 13, pp. 357–382.

TAPA Center (2007). Definition: Jail diversion. Delmar, New York: National GAINS Center. Retrieved from the World Wide Web on July 9, 2007: http://gainscenter.samhsa.gov/html/tapa/jail%20diversion/definition.asp.

Taylor, G. (2002, January 27). Sheriff offers way out of jail. Orlando Sentinel. Retrieved from the World Wide Web on July 6, 2007: http://www.namiscc.org/News/2003/Newsletters/Spring/TAC-April25-2003.htm.

Tisch, C. (2005, February 21). Mentally ill in jail diverted to help. St. Petersburg Times. Retrieved form the World Wide Web on July 7, 2007: http://www.sptimes.com/2005/02/21/Northpinellas/Mentally_ill_in_jail_.shtm.

Travis, J. (2005). But they all come back: Facing the challenges of prisoner reentry. Washington, D.C.: The Urban Institute Press.

Travis, J., Solomon, A. L., & Waul, M. (2001). From prison to home: The dimensions and consequences of prisoner reentry. Washington, DC: Urban Institute, Justice Policy Center.

USA v. Bull (2000). Mental health treatment as probation condition upheld by eleventh circuit. Correctional Mental Health Report, (May/June 2001), p. 9.

Ventura, L. A., Cassel, C. A., Jacoby, J. E., & Huang, B. (1998). Case management and recidivism of mentally ill persons released from jail. *Psychiatric Services* 49(10), pp. 1330–1337.

Veysey, B. (1994). Challenges for the future. In Topics in community corrections (p.3–10). Longmont, CO: U.S. Department of Justice, National Institute of Corrections.

Williams, F .P., & McShane, M. D. (2004). *Criminological Theory*, 4th ed. Upper Saddle River, New Jersey: Prentice-Hall.

Wilson, A. B., & Draine, J. (2006). Collaborations between criminal justice and mental health systems for prisoner reentry. *Psychiatric Services* 57(6), pp. 875–878.

Wolff, N., Plemmons, D., Veysey, B., & Brandli, A. (2002). Release planning for inmates with mental illness compared with those who have other chronic illnesses. *Psychiatric Services* 53(11), pp. 1469–1471.

CHAPTER 7

OUTPATIENT COMMITMENT

"In a free society you have to take some risks. If you lock everybody up, or even if you lock up everybody you think might commit a crime, you'll be pretty safe, but you won't be free."

—Former United States Senator Sam Ervin

"[The prosecutor] tells me he'd like society to be protected from someone like me. I would have liked it if society had protected me from myself."

—Arthur Bremer[1]

"The opposition to involuntary committal and treatment betrays a profound misunderstanding of the principle of civil liberties. Medication can free victims from their illness—free them from the Bastille of their psychoses—and restore their dignity, their free will, and the meaningful exercise of their liberties."

—Herschel Hardin

With pedophiles we have seen the reliance upon the civil commitment process at the completion of the service of their criminal sentences so that they may be detained and not prey upon society (see *Kansas v. Hendricks*, 1997; *Seling v. Young*, 2001). However, some fear such an expansion of the civil commitment process will provide a slippery slope for the infringement upon the civil liberties of persons with mental illnesses. As stated by former United States

---

1. These were the words of Arthur Bremer to the judge in his case after being convicted in 1972 of the attempted murder of Governor George Wallace. Yet Bremer declined any mental health evaluation or treatment during his incarceration. He was sentenced to 53 years in prison and was released seventeen and a half years early in November of 2007, see Skipp, C. & Campo-Flores, A., (2007, November 19) The Gunman Walks Free, Newsweek, p. 31–32.

Senator Sam Ervin, "In a free society you have to take some risks. If you lock everybody up, or even if you lock up everybody you think might commit a crime, you'll be pretty safe, but you won't be free" (Neubauer, 1992, p. 21).

Outpatient commitment is a civil procedure offered by some proponents as a more economical and less intrusive means than the criminal justice system for handling persons with mental illnesses who are decompensating. Outpatient commitment is dependent upon the quality and extent of mental health services available in a particular area, thereby creating a wide range of variability in its use. The use of outpatient commitment is a controversial and divisive issue, and there is no consensus on its effectiveness that is not contingent upon the availability of mental health treatment services in a specific jurisdiction.

Involuntary outpatient commitment[2] is considered to be "[t]he most debated mechanism for mandating community treatment" (Petrila, Ridgely, & Borum, 2003, p.158) for persons with mental illnesses. Some consider outpatient commitment as a potential mechanism to lessen recidivism and violence with some persons with mental illnesses (Petrila et al., 2003). The stated purpose of outpatient commitment is to try "to prevent relapse, hospital readmission, homelessness, and incarceration" (Swartz, Swanson, Kim, & Petrila, 2006, p. 43). However, when outpatient commitment has been used it has often been used as a backend procedure, not in the way it has been touted as a front-end procedure. Petrila et al. (2003) report that outpatient commitment has mainly been used as an outlet for discharges from inpatient care instead of being utilized as a mechanism for persons in the community to ascertain treatment. In other words, when used, it has largely been used as a means of re-acclimating persons with mental illnesses being released from the hospital and returning to society; we will discuss its lack of use shortly.

Outpatient commitment orders are an attempt to require individuals with mental illnesses as a condition of remaining in society to take psychotropic medications and follow treatment regimens (Allen & Smith, 2001). "Outpatient commitment involves a court order mandating a person to follow a treatment plan or risk sanctions for noncompliance, such as potential involuntary hospitalization and treatment" (Torrey & Zdanowicz, 2001, p. 337). Civil commitment dockets are similar to mental health court dockets, with

---

2. Involuntary outpatient commitment is also known as assisted outpatient treatment (Geller & Stanley, 2005b). Typically individuals who view outpatient commitment favorably refer to it as assisted outpatient treatment or assisted treatment and those opposed to it call it involuntary outpatient commitment.

civil commitment dockets being overseen by probate judges in most states and with the distinction that mental health courts involve persons with mental illnesses who are facing criminal charges while civil commitments do not involve the criminal court process (Rogers, 2005). Outpatient commitment involves the civil court process whereby a judge mandates that a patient adhere to a specified treatment regimen or face potential sanctions such as forcible transport to treatment by the police (Wagner, Swartz, Swanson, & Burns, 2003).

The ultimate penalty for not following involuntary outpatient commitment strictures is not criminal in nature but is instead a civil sanction-forced hospitalization. According to Appelbaum (2005), "[T]he law's only 'teeth' should patients fail to comply with a judicial order for outpatient treatment [is] to permit them to be picked up and detained for up to 72 hours to determine whether they me[e]t inpatient commitment criteria" (p. 791), as individuals cannot be forcibly medicated unless determined to be incapacitated. Upon an outpatient commitment patient failing to comply with treatment dictates most outpatient commitment statutes allow the presiding clinician to ask the police to bring the non-compliant patient to an outpatient facility where efforts will be undertaken to encourage the patient to comply with the treatment regimen or be evaluated for inpatient hospitalization; commissions for treatment can be followed by conditional release (Swartz et al., 2006). Conditional release is the earliest type of outpatient commitment, having emerged at the beginning of the twentieth century with the primary purpose of reintegrating persons back into society (Cornwell, 2003).

Outpatient commitment treatment plans may compel an individual to engage "in full-day treatment programs, undergo urine and blood tests, frequently attend meetings of addiction self-help groups, enter psychotherapy with a particular therapist, or reside in a supervised living situation" (Allen & Smith, 2001, p. 342). In a number of states persons may have treatment orders extended and be ordered into treatment regimens without clear guidelines as to when the order ceases to exist. Persons who are considered dangerous are usually placed in inpatient hospitalization, not in outpatient commitment, nor would persons who are currently incompetent typically be protected by outpatient commitment (Allen & Smith, 2001). Instead, outpatient commitment aims "to override the expressed wishes of a legally competent person who is thought to have some potential to become dangerous or gravely disabled in the future" (Allen & Smith, 2001, p.342).

Generally in the research literature, three types of outpatient commitment are discussed. These three types are conditional release from the hospital (whereby individuals can be returned to hospital care if they are non-compliant with treatment protocols or otherwise deteriorate), outpatient commitment as an alternative to hospitalization (considered less restrictive than hospitalization), and preventive outpatient commitment which can involve forced medication in the community utilizing a lesser standard than that necessary for involuntary hospitalization (with the goal of intervening to stop deterioration to the point that civil commitment criteria are met and becomes necessary, thereby thwarting the necessity for involuntary hospitalization) (see O'Connor, 2002; Saks, 2003; Schopp, 2003).

Currently, forty-two states and the District of Columbia have some form of civil involuntary outpatient commitment authorized by statute (Appelbaum, 2005; Honig & Stefan, 2005; Swartz et al., 2006). In what has been described as a growing trend, states such as New Mexico and Virginia, prior to the Virginia Tech shooting incident, have recently rejected expansive involuntary outpatient treatment statutes (U.S. Psychiatric Rehabilitation Association, 2007). While the Senate failed to bring New Mexico's version of Kendra's Law to a vote, Albuquerque became the first city in the nation to enact a local ordinance embracing Kendra's Law, only to have the ordinance struck down by a district court judge for conflicts with state law and exceeding the city's authority (Ludwick, 2006).

The most well known and researched of these outpatient commitment statutes is Kendra's Law.[3] Petitioners, with a supporting affidavit from a doctor, initiate court proceedings for outpatient commitment under Kendra's Law

---

3. Kendra's Law is more formally known as the N.Y. Mental Hygiene Law 9.60(C)-(D) (2004). Under this law, a court may order an individual into assisted outpatient treatment under the following circumstances. The statutorily-defined eligibility criteria for Assisted Outpatient Treatment (AOT) are: (1) be eighteen years of age or older; (2) suffer from a mental illness; (3) be unlikely to survive safely in the community without supervision, based on a clinical determination; (4) have a history of non-adherence with treatment that has (a) been a significant factor in his or her being in a hospital, prison or jail at least twice within the last thirty-six months; or (b) resulted in one or more acts, attempts or threats of serious violent behavior toward self or others within the last forty-eight months; (5) be unlikely to voluntarily participate in treatment; (6) be, in view of his or her treatment history and current behavior, in need of AOT in order to prevent a relapse or deterioration which would be likely to result in: (a) a substantial risk of physical harm to the individual as manifested by threats of or attempts at suicide or serious bodily harm or conduct demonstrating that the individual is dangerous to himself or herself, or (b) a substantial risk of physical harm to other persons as manifested by homicidal or other violent behavior by which others are placed in reasonable fear of serious physical harm; (7) be likely to benefit from AOT; and (8) if the consumer has a health care proxy, any directions in it will be taken into account by the court in determining the written treatment plan. Nothing, however, precludes

(Perlin, 2003). Petitioners can include "parents, spouses, persons with whom the subject resides, children, siblings, a qualified treating psychiatrist, or a probation or parole officer charged with supervising the individual" (Perlin, 2003, p. 195). The doctor is to establish in the affidavit that he or she has seen the patient in the last ten days and deems that the patient is in need of outpatient commitment, or, if an examination of the patient has not been possible, the doctor is to state why he or she believes outpatient commitment is necessary. The doctor submitting the affidavit is required to testify at a hearing before the patient/respondent who is given notice and is authorized to have legal counsel present. The treatment plan provided by the doctor must demonstrate that the recommended intervention is the least restrictive alternative under the circumstances. The court may also order an involuntary examination of the patient/respondent at this stage. Upon satisfaction that the least restrictive alternative for intervention is in place and clear and convincing evidence outpatient commitment is needed, the court may direct the patient to initially be placed in outpatient commitment status for up to six months (Perlin, 2003).

Tragedy and Outpatient Commitment

As we have seen throughout this book, tragedy often drives policy, and this proves to be no exception with outpatient commitment. As we will discuss, tragedy led to the implementation of Kendra's Law in New York that resulted from the horrific killing of Kendra Webdale by being pushed in front of a subway train by a man with schizophrenia (Campbell, 2002; Huggins, 2004; Watnik, 2001). Watnik (2001) also points out that in addition to the tragic death of Kendra Webdale, other horrific events, including the shooting by police of a person with mental illness swinging a sword on a passenger train and the pushing by a person with untreated schizophrenia of Edgar Rivera in front of a subway train that resulted in the severing of both of Rivera's legs, provided the impetus for the passage of Kendra's Law in New York.

Tragedy also led to court-ordered outpatient commitment reform in Florida. Alan Singletary, a man with schizophrenia wounded two deputies and shot and killed Seminole County Deputy Sheriff Gene Gregory before Singletary was shot and killed himself by law enforcement during a 13-hour standoff. Singletary's sister, Alice Petree, and Deputy Sheriff Gregory's widow, Linda

---

a person with a health care proxy from being eligible for AOT (see New York Mental Hygiene Law 9.60(C)-(D) (2004).

Gregory, joined forces with Seminole County Sheriff Donald Eslinger and the Florida Sheriffs' Association to push the change in the law through the legislature (TAC, 2005).[4]

Laura's Law, which establishes outpatient treatment in California, is named after Laura Wilcox who, along with two other individuals, was shot and killed by a man with mental illness in Nevada County, California (Moller, 2006). Tragedy led to a failed initiative to invoke a Kendra's Law in New Mexico, as a person with mental illness was charged with killing two law enforcement officers and two other individuals (Jadrnak, 2006).

Outpatient Commitment Even When Authorized by Statute Is Typically Not Used

Many states seldom use their outpatient commitment statutes (Appelbaum, 2005; Honig & Stefan, 2005), and Honig and Stefan (2005) conclude after their review of research studies that there is little evidence to support the effectiveness of outpatient commitment. Over half (23) of the states with some form of outpatient commitment laws seldom compel treatment (O'Connor, 2002). The National Stigma Clearinghouse (2007) maintains that "[o]f the 42 states that have laws permitting court-ordered treatment of psychiatric outpatients, only one, New York, actively uses its coercion statute (Kendra's Law)" (p. 1). In fact, "[a]s of June 2000, forty-five of the sixty-two counties in New York had not used Kendra's Law. As of September 2002, three years after the law went into effect, twenty-one counties still had not issued a single court order. Another twenty-three counties have issued orders in less than five cases.... The law cannot be effective if it is not used" (O'Connor, 2002, p. 363).

Perhaps outpatient commitment doesn't deserve all the attention it has received. Monahan, et al. (2005) in a study of five sites that used leverage to attempt to get persons with mental illnesses to comply with treatment in the community identified four types of leverage: housing, criminal justice sanctions, outpatient commitment, and money (money handlers or representative payees). They discovered that an extensive amount of research and focus has re-

---

4. Linda Gregory and Alice Petree also provide quite a powerful tandem as crisis intervention team trainers for law enforcement officers as well, as they join together to share their compelling story.

volved around outpatient commitment and similar judicial directives, yet this is the most seldom used form of leverage (used with12 to 20 percent of patients). They found that the provision of housing was the most frequently used form of leverage to try to obtain compliance with treatment protocols (used with 23 to 40 percent of patients), and, with the exception of one site, the second most utilized form of leverage was the threat of involvement with the criminal justice system if individuals did not adhere to treatment (used with 15 to 30 percent of all patients, with between 38 to 49 percent of the patients in the study having been charged with a crime). Also, they noted that the leading case on outpatient commitment, *In re K.L.*, 806 NE 2d 480 (Court of Appeals of New York 2004) upheld outpatient commitment because very little coercion was determined to be involved in the process.

Fritz (2006), indicates "California passed a forced-treatment law in 2003 after Dr. Torrey's group pushed for it but has yet to use it on anyone. Researchers say only about eight to ten states frequently use their laws" (p. A1). "In Michigan, Dr. Torrey's group enlisted the aid of the parents of 24-year-old Kevin Heisinger, a college student beaten to death in 2000 at a Kalamazoo bus station by a Vietnam veteran with a history of schizophrenia. A year later a proposed 'Kevin's Law' was unveiled" (Fritz, 2006, p. A1). "In Florida, the group teamed with the Seminole County sheriff after a plumber who was diagnosed as mentally ill wounded two deputies in 1998 and shot another to death. They quickly won the lobbying clout of the Florida Sheriff's Association" (Fritz, 2006, p. A1); "Ultimately, California in 2003 passed 'Laura's Law.' But the nations' largest state allocated no money and forbade counties from shifting resources from other mental-health programs. The law has yet to be used. In 2004, California voters approved a 1% tax on people with incomes of at least 1$ million to be used for mental-health programs, and Dr. Torrey's group wants to see some of that go for Laura's Law" (Fritz, 2006, p. A1). "Michigan and Florida experienced similar battles. Their laws didn't go into effect until last year" (Fritz, 2006, p. A1). Even though the law went into effect in Florida in January of 2005, in three years of existence, only seventy-one out-patient commitment orders have been issued—with a lack of treatment resources in the community identified as one of several contributing factors to such poor utilization of the statute (Petrila & Christy, 2008). Likewise, in Michigan the law has been used sparingly as well (Fritz, 2006). Esposito, Westhead, and Berko (2008) acknowledge roughly half of the outpatient commitment orders in Florida have been issued in Seminole County with a sheriff who has been an advocate for the process. While they concede this option has been used sparingly, they maintain when it has been utilized it has led to reduced hospitalization, incarceration, and costs.

Outpatient Commitment as an Alternative to Criminal Justice System Involvement

Traditional, restrictive civil commitment processes, such as the Lanterman-Petris-Short Act in California, enacted with the intention of protecting civil liberties, actually, according to Karasch (2003), ironically end up depriving individuals of their freedom, as, due to restricted access to treatment, some individuals with mental illnesses find themselves incarcerated for minor offenses within the criminal justice system. Criminalizing a person with mental illness ensures a criminal record that can be accessed and used to cue criminal justice officials in to the behavior of a person with mental illness (Lamb & Weinberger, 2005). Such criminalization of a person with mental illness is doubly stigmatizing, as the individual's status is damaged because of the mental illness as well as the criminal record.

Outpatient commitment, though civil in nature, has been touted as a means to divert persons with mental illnesses from the criminal justice system and link them to treatment in the community. Zdanowicz (2001) notes that mental health providers, with constrained budgets, may be content to have the criminal justice system assume the responsibility for handling the mentally ill in their facilities. She encourages sheriffs to champion the cause for changes in commitment laws, making it easier to get a person with mental illness into treatment. In fact, the National Sheriffs' Association supports statutes that allow courts to order involuntary outpatient treatment in the community (Faust, 2003). As noted by Faust (2003), something is terribly wrong with the process when the only means to acquire involuntary treatment for some families is to have their loved one with mental illness arrested. One shouldn't have to commit a crime to get help. Faust(2003) contends, "It is time to shift the responsibility of caring for the mentally ill back to the professionals who are trained to do so rather than waiting until only law enforcement and corrections can respond" (p. 7).

Zdanowicz (2001) argues such a mechanism for increased access to treatment has been found to reduce hospital admissions, violence, and is believed likely to reduce jail admissions. Indeed, advocates promote outpatient commitment as a more suitable option than incarceration, forced hospitalization, or homelessness (Allen & Smith, 2001). Early studies identify positive benefits of outpatient commitment to include "reductions in arrests and the frequency and length of hospitalizations, as well as improvements in treatment compliance for patients discharged from psychiatric care" (Cornwell, 2003, p. 226). However, due to methodological flaws in these early studies, nothing conclusive can be said about the benefits of outpatient commitment (Cornwell, 2003).

The mental health and criminal justice systems are inextricably linked and, as noted by Petrila et al. (2003) what occurs in the mental health system affects what occurs in the criminal justice system and vice versa. Lamb and Weinberger (1998) contend as opportunities for civil commitment decrease involvement with the criminal justice system increases. Dvoskin and Steadman (1994) acknowledge that the better mental health providers can successfully treat persons with mental illnesses the more likely jail admissions will be reduced and positive results will occur for persons with mental illnesses and the criminal justice system.

Persons who have been court ordered to outpatient commitment have been found to be likely to have had encounters with the criminal justice system and to perceive their experiences across multiple systems as coercive and reported little satisfaction with treatment received (Swartz et al., 2006). Torrey and Zdanowicz (2001) do not view outpatient commitment as a panacea; however, they argue that it is a commonsensical and compassionate approach in a world without outpatient commitment that is plagued with increasing homelessness, suicide, violence, and incarceration among persons with mental illnesses.

Questions of Coerciveness, Stigmatization, and Infringements on Freedom

Questions of coerciveness, stigmatization, and infringements on civil liberties surround outpatient commitment. Critics of outpatient commitment view it as unlawful, and inherently anti-therapeutic (Cornwell, 2003). Some contend that outpatient commitment "appears to violate the constitutional rights to travel, to privacy, to personal dignity, to freedom from restraint and bodily integrity, to freedom of association, and to the free communication of ideas" (Allen & Smith, 2001, p. 343).[5] Petrila (2002) notes that there has been considerable debate about whether legal rights are sufficiently protected in civil commitment proceedings. Outpatient commitment is believed to be a mis-

---

5. Hoge & Grottole (2000) analyze the 1987 American Psychiatric Association's Task Force on Involuntary Outpatient Commitment report, which endorses mandatory outpatient commitment, and conclude that the supported standard is violative of individual liberties and does not exclusively require imminent danger to one's self or another for commitment to transpire. (See Hoge, M.A., & Grottole, E. (2000). The case against outpatient commitment. *The Journal of the American Academy of Psychiatry and the Law, 28*(2), p. 165–170).

guided policy because it is perceived as anti-therapeutic due to its coerciveness and stigmatizing potential (Cornwell, 2003). As a result of the potential coerciveness and effectiveness of outpatient commitment, it remains controversial and of interest (Appelbaum, 2001; Petrila et al., 2003; Torrey & Zdanowicz, 2001; Wagner et al., 2003).

Some opponents of outpatient commitment argue that outpatient commitment is stigmatizing, but Torrey and Zdanowicz (2001) counter that the greatest cause of stigma for persons with mental illnesses is their violent outbursts, and outpatient commitment provides a mechanism for reducing such violent episodes. Generally, Cornwell (2003) agrees that persons with mental illnesses, as long as compliant with medication and treatment regimens, are no more violent than persons without mental illnesses. However, he is concerned about that small percentage who are not compliant that can lead to an association between mental illness and violence, and he believes outpatient commitment can allow for intervention to prevent decompensation that can serve to thwart the violence that leads to worsening stigma for persons with mental illnesses (Cornwell, 2003).

Several anti-therapeutic aspects to Kendra's Law that serve to blur the association between criminal and civil mental health disability law have been identified. By utilizing specific prison and parole agents with supposed mental health expertise, by bringing more persons with mental illnesses under the umbrella of the public mental health system,[6] and by falsely promulgating a causal linkage between dangerousness and mental illnesses, the public's view and stigmatization of persons with mental illnesses may be even further distorted (Perlin, 2003).

Winick (2003), one of the founders of therapeutic jurisprudence, advocates use of police-based diversion programs and mental health courts as more therapeutic alternatives to coercive outpatient commitment. While Winick (2003) acknowledges that more research is needed regarding what therapeutic impact preventive outpatient commitment has, he cautions that:

> it is a model that relies on coercion rather than voluntary choice, [and] there is reason to question whether it will produce more favorable treatment outcomes than its alternatives. To the extent that preventive outpatient commitment involves court-ordered intrusive

---

6. Saks (2003) concurs that outpatient commitment serves to widen the net of those coerced, but it allows many to avoid forced hospitalization and remain in the community, thwarting recidivism and possibly ensuring voluntary compliance with future outpatient commitment(s).

psychotropic medication, it raises serious constitutional concerns. The two older models of outpatient commitment, conditional release and least restrictive alternative outpatient treatment, both promote liberty and, if properly applied ... can have significant therapeutic value (p. 134–135).

On the contrary, preventive outpatient commitment, particularly when forced medication is involved restricts liberty and can bring about anti-therapeutic results. Deception can prove to be coercive when there are implications that medication is required, and this in turn can undermine trust and interfere with treatment goals (Winick, 2003).

The coercive nature of outpatient commitment statutes whereby patients mistakenly perceive the false implications that they will be forced to take medications if they are noncompliant " 'devalues the individuals being served, and undermines the physician-patient relationship.... A strategy that relies on patient misinformation to foster its success violates ethics principles, the integrity of the physician-patient relationship, and the notion of informed consent' " (Perlin, 2003, p. 183).

The most controversial component of today's outpatient commitment statutes, including Kendra's Law, is the connection between commitment and forced medication. This forced drugging is viewed as a core element of outpatient commitment; outpatient commitment, if it is not already, will become the equivalent of forcing medication (Perlin, 2003).

The court's order may also require the patient to self-administer psychotropic drugs or accept the administration of such drugs by authorized personnel as part of an assisted outpatient treatment program, but may not order treatment that has not been recommended by the examining physician and included in the written treatment plan (Perlin, 2003, p.194).

Perlin (2003) notes that such treatment regimens may be instituted to span an entire year.

According to Perlin (2003), some courts to keep outpatients compliant with medication regimens have utilized criminal contempt of court citations, but higher courts have not always upheld such tactics. This option is not available under Kendra's Law, as only a doctor can find someone in need of involuntary hospitalization, and an individual can be transported and held for up to 72 hours to assess whether involuntary treatment is needed (Perlin, 2003). The statute explicitly stipulates, "that an order of assisted outpatient treatment shall not be grounds for involuntary civil commitment" (Perlin, 2003, p. 196).

"However, at its core, outpatient commitment requires a person, on pain of entering police custody and undergoing rehospitalization, to comply with the treatment decisions of another person, undermining the fundamental right of a competent, nondangerous person to determine the course of his or her treatment" (Allen & Smith, 2001, p. 343).[7]

"The Bazelon Center opposes involuntary inpatient civil commitment except in response to an emergency, and then only when based on a standard of imminent danger of physical harm to self or others and when there is no less restrictive alternative."[8] The Bazelon Center is particularly concerned about the coercive nature of the involuntary commitment process and the potential for infringement upon individual rights. As such, the Bazelon Center also opposes involuntary outpatient commitment as well unless premised on the imminent danger standard cited above (Bazelon Center, 2000).

Indicative of crisis driving policy, Kendra's Law has been referred to as "'a knee-jerk response to a political and media-driven problem'" (Campbell, 2002, p. 202). Campbell (2002) continues on to note that:

> People with mental illness are often skeptical of the system to begin with, and when the state starts invoking its police power to take away their liberties, they are less likely to seek treatment voluntarily in a community mental health setting. In places like the District of Columbia, where U.S. Marshals will arrest individuals who do not comply with their outpatient commitment programs and civilly commit them as inpatients, the mentally ill live in fear of being confined in the district mental hospital.... 'There is a kind of terror'

---

7. Patch & Arrigo (1999) report that the police do not believe that it is a proper utilization of their role and assets to involve them in the involuntary hospitalization process; however, they note that law enforcement personnel are more effective than they might think in ensuring successful civil commitments when compared to attempts by others. (See Patch, P.C., & Arrigo, B.A. (1999). Police officer attitudes and use of discretion in situations involving the mentally ill: The need to narrow the focus. *International Journal of Law and Psychiatry, 22*(1), p. 23–35.

8. Levine (2007) describes the difficulty in applying the restrictive imminent danger standard in the civil commitment process under Florida's former statute: "'It's not against the law to think you're Napoleon. It's only a problem if you [perceive yourself as] Napoleon and you go to war.'" Unless a person is considered an imminent danger to him or herself, he or she cannot be held under such a restrictive statute. (see Levine, A. 2007. Institutional madness: As South Florida's mental health system spirals out of control, troubled minds are meeting tragic, preventable ends. Retrieved from the World Wide Web on June 28, 2007: http://artlevine.blogspot.com/articles/Institutional%20Madness.htm).

among the mentally ill, who often do not understand the law well enough to realize that seeking mental health treatment does not automatically mean involuntary inpatient commitment or the forced administration of drugs. Thus, the punitive threat of statutes like Kendra's Law hang over the heads of the mentally ill and coerce them into submitting to a treatment plan that they may not believe is in their best interest.[9] ... Aside from forcibly medicating the mentally ill, what else is being done to better their lives? In particular, what is being done to help the most vulnerable and desperately ill individuals (p. 203)?[10]

Swartz, Wagner, Swanson, Hiday, and Burns (2002) maintain that perceptions of coercion by individuals in outpatient commitment arrangements are increased the more case managers actively attend to non-compliance issues. Furthermore, they found the longer that an individual was subjected to outpatient commitment the more likely they were to perceive their experience as coercive. They also reported that feelings of being coerced were more likely to be expressed by African-Americans, single individuals who were not cohabitating, those with substance abuse problems, those with anosognosia (lack of insight), and those with more severe symptoms.

Those who feel they have been treated fairly, given voice and not coerced in the outpatient commitment process are more likely to reflect better qualities of life and may potentially be more apt to comply with treatment regimens in the long term (Watson & Angell, 2007). Whether hospitalization is

---

9. Similarly, Cornwell (2003) reports on a North Carolina study where most of the participants felt coerced to take psychotropic medication erroneously believing that if they did not it would be forcibly administered. However, Cornwell (2003) does not necessarily mean that outpatient commitment is anti-therapeutic because even those involuntarily hospitalized believe their treatment has helped them and are satisfied, and, at discharge, those who have been medicated against their will report that they believe the decision to do so was the right one.

10. Campbell (2002) indicates that under New York Governor George Pataki funding for supportive housing for persons with mental illnesses was not replenished, and Pataki's administration commenced to closing down hospitals resulting in persons such as Andrew Goldstein being forced into the streets homeless and psychotic. Campbell (2002) contends that anywhere from 33 percent to 50 percent of homeless persons are mentally ill. "However, Kendra's Law fails to address the greater problem of the homeless mentally ill[;] [i]f we are to seriously address the issue of violence among the mentally ill, it is necessary to do more than simply drug them and put them back on the streets without any resources and support to help them get well (Campbell, 2002, p. 204).

voluntary or forced, if patients perceive they had a voice in the matter they are significantly less likely to view the process as coercive (Cornwell, 2003). O'Connor (2002) concurs that persons are more amenable to participating in a program when they perceive that they have a voice and are treated as equal partners. Although Kendra's Law has been challenged for its coercive nature (Flug, 2003), Cornwell (2003) maintains the two exemplary models for giving a voice to patients in developing their treatment plans are found in New York (Kendra's Law) and South Dakota. However, there is concern that Kendra's Law may be too easy to utilize over use of involuntary civil commitment. Also, under Kendra's Law, treatment orders can be enacted with the outpatient in absentia, certainly a far cry from therapeutically giving voice to someone in their treatment options (Perlin, 2003).

Perlin (2003) does believe that there are therapeutic components associated with Kendra's Law. He believes that positive aspects include that publicity about the law may actually entice more persons with mental illnesses to seek treatment, and utilization of a judicial process with representation by legal counsel can ensure procedural protections, due process, and fairness.[11] However, Perlin (2003) concludes though Kendra's Law has some therapeutic aspects, "it is the wrong answer to a difficult and intractable problem" (p.208).

Both the extremes of deinstitutionalization and involuntary hospitalization have proven to be miserable failures, and, with such a backdrop, outpatient commitment has been touted as a panacea. Outpatient commitment should be utilized in a limited role when patients can competently choose between outpatient commitment with involuntary medication or involuntary hospitalization, with the hope such choice would bind them to the treatment should future need arise (Saks, 2003).

Proponents of outpatient commitment are adamant in their responses to critics. Zdanowicz (2003–2004, p. 1) asks, " 'what is the impact of coerced care compared to no care at all?' The consequences of non-treatment are all too well documented: relapse symptoms, re-hospitalization, homelessness, arrests, victimization, suicide, and episodes of violence. But what is the impact of coerced care?" She maintains that research indicates that coerced treatment does not have an adverse impact on persons with mental illnesses in the majority of instances. In fact, she contends that it is actually beneficial. According to Torrey and Zdanowicz (2001), in retrospect those forced

---

11. Also, as evinced in a North Carolina study, use of outpatient commitment may lead to a reduction in the victimization of persons with mental illnesses (Perlin, 2003).

to take medications believe it was in their best interest to do so, with almost three-fourths of persons with mental illnesses in that situation saying so afterwards. Gardner et al. (1999) found that the majority of patients who initially believed that they did not require hospitalization modified their assessment after hospital discharge and indicated that they had actually been in need of hospital care.

> However, perceptions of coercion were stable from admission to follow-up, and patients' attitudes toward hospitalization did not become more positive. Coerced patients did not appear to be grateful for the experience of hospitalization, even if they later concluded that they had needed it (Gardner et al., 1999, 1385).

Geller and Stanley (2005a) maintain that ideally clinicians would indeed prefer to engage voluntary and willing patients with mental illnesses in treatment; however that is not always reality. They maintain that evaluative research measures should also consider risk management and quality of life outcomes, not just utilization of services. Torrey and Zdanowicz (2001) indicate that treating willing patients is not always possible and contend that outpatient commitment is necessary because they maintain that anywhere from 40 to 50 percent of persons with severe and persistent mental illnesses may lack insight into their illnesses. In other words, they don't realize that they are ill. "This loss is seen in some neurological disorders, such as Alzheimer's disease, and in some individuals who have had cerebrovascular accidents (strokes). In the most extreme form of such loss, a person who has suffered a stroke may lack awareness that his or her leg is paralyzed, despite obvious evidence to the contrary" (Torrey & Zdanowicz, 2001, p. 337).

Saks (2003) believes coercion and infringement on freedom come with outpatient commitment but much less so than with involuntary hospitalization. Pandya (2007), currently the President of the National Alliance on Mental Illness, maintains that outpatient commitment obligates the mental health provider to treat the patient, minimizes coercion, and that being hospitalized is certainly more of an infringement on one's liberties than being allowed to exist in the community (see also Perlin, 2003). Furthermore, Pandya (2007) adds that the reality is that doctors are much more willing to release an individual into the community if there is some legal mechanism in place to assist in ensuring compliance with treatment plans.[12] Past president of the American Psy-

---

12. According to Geller and Stanley (2005b), "As judges are understandably hesitant to find individuals to be an imminent danger to themselves or others and then order their re-

chiatric Association, Sharfstein (2005) advised that "[w]e must balance individual rights and freedoms with policies aimed at caring coercion" (p. 3); he
indicated that he views both mental health courts and mandatory outpatient
treatment as examples of how caring coercion can bring about positive results.

Outpatient commitment "standards typically require a documented history
of violence or prior inpatient hospitalization to justify commitment," and,
under such circumstances, forced medication for outpatients would likely be
constitutional (Cornwell, 2003, p. 224). Of course, just because something is
legal does not necessarily indicate that it constitutes sound policy (Appelbaum,
2005). Some opponents view outpatient commitment as an infringement on
civil liberties; however, Torrey and Zdanowicz (2001) state that persons with
medical illnesses are routinely hospitalized against their will in this country so
as not to contaminate others, and, in that situation, as with persons with mental illnesses, they contend that "medically needed treatment should be provided in the best interest of both the individual and society" (p. 340). According
to Torrey and Zdanowicz (2001):

> This point was best expressed by Herschel Hardin, a former member
> of the board of directors of the British Columbia Civil Liberties As-
> sociation. He wrote, 'The opposition to involuntary committal and
> treatment betrays a profound misunderstanding of the principle of
> civil liberties. Medication can free victims from their illness—free
> them from the Bastille of their psychoses—and restore their dignity,
> their free will, and the meaningful exercise of their liberties' (p.
> 340); (see Hardin, 1993).

Straticzuk (2000) reasons that some persons' mental illnesses interfere with
their capacity to enable themselves to get better. Their refusal to take measures to recover is not out of some romantic notion of freedom of choice, but
it is due to the fact that their very ability to rationally consider their situation
is impaired (Straticzuk (2000). When such a situation arises where one cannot
engage in a rational uncontroversial decision to take measures toward recovery, then it is our societal duty to intervene and do so for them (Straticzuk,
2000). Treffert (1973) maintains, "In our zeal to protect basic, human freedoms ... we have created a legal climate in which mentally ill patients, and
sometimes the people around them, are dying with their rights on" (p. 1041).

---

lease to the community at the same hearing, an effective outpatient commitment statute
must include a non-danger based eligibility standard, or at least a dangerous standard more
broadly defined than the inpatient standard" (p. 128).

The prospects for outpatient commitment to be effective are similar to the prognosis for the success of mental health courts, as everything revolves around the availability of services. Any chance for positive outcomes from outpatient commitment only occurs when court orders are accompanied with intensive mental health services, as a court order by itself, without adequate services, is not sufficient to ensure positive results (Perlin, 2003; see Ridgely, Borum, & Petrila, 2001). Also, many of those opposed to outpatient commitment argue that less coercive means must be exhausted and shown totally ineffective before resorting to such a compulsory mechanism as outpatient commitment (Appelbaum, 2001). Some of those less intrusive means for consideration are discussed below.

Advance Directives

A possible avenue to avoid outpatient commitment and ascertain "voluntary" treatment in the community or via hospitalization without involving the courts is an advance directive.[13] An individual voluntarily declares in a psychiatric advance directive their treatment desires for some future time when he or she may be incapacitated (Hiday, 2003). An advance directive is similar to a living will "do not resuscitate" clause but obviously with different options.

> In an advance directive, a competent person with mental illness makes a "Ulysses contract" in which she or he specifies desired and/or undesired treatment, or specifies a proxy to make treatment decisions. Just as Ulysses contracted with his crew to keep him tied to the mast no matter what he said about releasing him when the Sirens tempted him to his death, a patient with severe mental illness contracts to have treatment no matter what she or he says about not wanting or needing it when illness causes deterioration accompanied by thinking and behavior common only to the deteriorated condition. By the stated wishes of the competent persons with mental illness, coercion occurs in his or her deteriorated condition when

---

13. The Bazelon Center for Mental Health Law has information and forms available on their website for creating Advance Directives for psychiatric care should the need arise. Bazelon Center. (2007). Forms for creating an advance psychiatric directive. Washington, DC: Bazelon Center for Mental Health Law. Retrieved from the World Wide Web on July 6, 2007: http://www.bazelon.org/issues/advancedirectives/templates.htm.

she or he does not think [treatment] is needed and resists it (Hiday, 2003, p.24).

Psychiatric advance directives typically come in two varieties: instructional or designation of a health care proxy (Srebnik & La Fond, 1999). Instructional directives are to be specified when a person is rational and simply instruct a mental health provider in what is to be done should one decompensate to the point that they are unable to make rational decisions, and designation of a health proxy is analogous to establishing a durable power of attorney to identify in advance someone you designate to make mental health treatment decisions for you if you become irrational (Srebnik & La Fond, 1999).

Advance directives and health proxies, when properly established by competent individuals, can also serve to help ensure that future mental health treatment is voluntarily entered into (Winick, 2003). Patient and civil rights proponents advocate psychiatric advance directives especially for persons who have been forced into treatment in the past to possibly allow them some control over any future involvement with the civil commitment process (Hiday, 2003). However, a concern is that when totally rational one may enter into an advance directive, but upon becoming irrational may revoke the advance directive. Thus, this becomes a murky area, as decisions will have to be made as to whether the person is rational enough to then undo the legal mechanism that he or she had put in place earlier.

Torrey and Zdanowicz (2001) caution, "Advance directives will not help those who are unable to recognize that they will need assistance with treatment in the future[;] for at least a third of patients, assertive case management is not effective, which suggests that additional assisted interventions are needed" (p. 339). Unfortunately, the utility of advance directives is largely unknown, as they are not often utilized (Hiday, 2003).

Representative Payees

The concept of a representative payee allows an individual to designate an individual to receive any benefit payments on their behalf and help them manage his or her money, and this process contributes to a reduction in homelessness and hospitalization (Torrey & Zdanowicz, 2001). While there is reportedly no research that demonstrates its ability to enhance treatment compliance, "[t]he U.S. Third Circuit Court of Appeals ruled that a man with epilepsy was not entitled to SSDI unless he complied with his prescribed antiseizure medication regimen. Thus a legal precedent has been set for use of this mechanism to enforce compliance (Torrey & Zdanowicz, 2001, p. 339).

Conditional Release

In a number of states patients discharged from involuntary hospital stays can be released into the community on the condition that they be compliant with a specified treatment regimen to include taking prescribed medication. Conditional release is used extensively in New Hampshire and has been successful in ensuring medication compliance and reducing violence among participants (Torrey & Zdanowicz, 2001).

Conservatorship or Guardianship

A court appointed individual acts as a surrogate to make decisions for a person that has been deemed legally incompetent in a conservatorship or guardianship arrangement. This is a legal mechanism that has been used extensively with persons with mental retardation but it can also be used with persons with mental illnesses. This process has proven very influential in ensuring treatment compliance (Torrey & Zdanowicz, 2001).

Violence Emphasized

Karasch (2003) indicates that the public demonstrates more concern about persons with mental illnesses who are dangerous and is apathetic towards the non-violent mentally ill as is evidenced by the paucity of resources allocated to the mental health system. "Advocates for involuntary treatment[, such as Torrey and Zdanowicz,[14]] have focused on public fears about mental illness and violence, which likely increases the stigma felt by people who have been

---

14. It should be noted that Fuller Torrey's sister has schizophrenia, Jonathan Stanley, an attorney with TAC, has bipolar disorder (Fritz, 2006), and Mary Zdanowicz, Executive Director of the TAC, has a sister and a brother with schizophrenia (see Zdanowicz, M.T. (2007). Biography of Mary T. Zdanowicz, Executive Director of the Treatment Advocacy Center, Arlington, Virginia. Retrieved from the World Wide Web on July 5, 2007: http://www.psych-laws.org/PressRoom/Bio2.htm).

diagnosed as having mental illnesses" (Allen & Smith, 2001, p. 342). Appelbaum (2001) contends that the fear of violence from persons with mental illnesses is likely the primary reason for the impetus to implement outpatient commitment laws; however, he views it as a weak justification for such statutes, as most persons with mental illnesses are not violent.

Furthermore, Appelbaum (2001) maintains that even if an individual met outpatient commitment requirements there is no clear and conclusive evidence that outpatient commitment would prevent any of these types of acts. In similar fashion to Walker's (2006) admonition about crisis driving policy, Appelbaum (2001) states that "here, as in most circumstances, a handful of highly visible cases constitute a dubious basis for social policy" (p. 347).

Outpatient Commitment Is Ineffective

Although research had demonstrated the general ineffectiveness of involuntary outpatient commitment, "New York passed Kendra's Law as an emotional response to a tragedy caused by an individual with mental illness" (O'Connor, 2002, p. 313). Pollack, McFarland, Mahler, and Kovas (2005) found involuntary outpatient commitment of low intensity and for a short duration to result in better treatment compliance for program participants but found no meaningful effect on arrests or subsequent psychiatric hospitalizations.

Swartz, Swanson, and Monahan (2003) found that most persons exposed to outpatient commitment did not feel it was beneficial because they did not feel they needed to continue it, or it had not made them more compliant with treatment. Thus, the majority of persons view outpatient commitment as ineffective, show little appreciation for its value, and are ambivalent towards it at best (Swartz et al., 2003).

Steadman et al. (2001), while acknowledging methodological problems, in an examination of Bellevue Hospital's involuntary outpatient commitment program in New York City found no significant differences as a result of involuntary outpatient commitment in terms of arrests, re-hospitalizations, or total days of hospitalization. The researchers also noted that at the time of their assessment research, with the exception of one study, the empirical evidence has provided little credibility for the effectiveness of involuntary outpatient commitment.

Maloy (1992) indicates, in what is referred to as the MacArthur study, that there is no conclusive evidence that outpatient commitment is effective in addressing treatment compliance and argues an emphasis on the provision of services would likely go further toward ending the recycling of patients through the system. Allen and Smith (2001) concur that there is a lack of evidence regarding the effectiveness of outpatient commitment, and they argue it may actually push persons with mental illnesses away from turning to mental health treatment providers for help.

Outpatient Commitment Is Effective

McKinney (2006) acknowledges faults with outpatient commitment but argues "it is at least one possible solution for mentally ill individuals who have a history of non-compliance and re-hospitalization" (p. 46). There are concerns that outpatient commitment patients may receive preferential treatment services over others in need of mental health treatment, but this could be because this group is where the greatest need resides (Wagner et al., 2003). Torrey and Zdanowicz (2001) concede this preferential treatment may be true assuming there is a limited amount of funds. Yet, Torrey and Zdanowicz (2001) and their colleague Jon Stanley (J. Stanley, personal communication, June 23, 2007) contend outpatient commitment should actually lower expenses by resulting in fewer costly hospitalizations and less incarcerations thereby benefiting all patients.[15] In essence, Torrey and Zdanowicz (2001) suggest that those opposed to outpatient commitment are implying that persons who voluntarily seek treatment services are more deserving than those who lack insight into their illnesses and avoid treatment.

Again, as with mental health courts, the key to the effectiveness of outpatient commitment revolves around the availability of intensive treatment services for a prolonged period of time. There are those that contend that recent research supports the notion that treatment outcomes for persons with mental illnesses can be enhanced via outpatient commitment by extensive periods of exposure to intensive treatment services (Swanson et al., 1997, 2000, 2001; Wagner et al., 2003). Of course, the problem is that many locales do not enjoy such expansive mental health treatment services.

Legally forcing individuals into outpatient commitment in and of itself will not enhance treatment services that are overextended and under funded. Coercion without adequate services is likely to ultimately fail, no matter how po-

---

15. However, Ridgely et al. (2001), in a review of the two generations of studies on outpatient commitment, note that no studies have been undertaken to assess the cost-effectiveness of outpatient commitment.

litically expedient it seems at the time. Successful outpatient commitment is largely a function of case managers and their ability to access and leverage resources including inpatient hospitalization and may have little to do with the wording of statutes as to whether compliance is obtained (Swanson et al., 1997). Of course, if there were sufficient resources in place to begin with it is possible that the need for such outpatient schemes would be minimal. Swartz, et al. (1999) concluded that "Outpatient commitment can work to reduce hospital readmissions and total hospital days when court orders are sustained and combined with intensive treatment" (p. 1968).

According to Leone (2000), there have been two generations of studies examining outpatient commitment. While indicating positive effects overall of outpatient commitment, the first set of studies had critical methodological problems. Two studies comprise the second set of studies which were more methodologically sound. One of these studies demonstrated that when enhanced services were available and received for extended periods of time, as in the North Carolina study where services were received for six months or more (see Swanson et al. 2000; Swartz et al. 2001), court directives were successful in lessening hospital admissions and violence. Although improved services were present in the other second generation study, no significant effects were realized with outpatient commitment (Leone, 2000). Policy Research Associates, in a study conducted at New York City's Bellevue Hospital, found that "in terms of re-hospitalizations, days spent in the hospital, arrests, quality of life or symptomatology measures, and treatment continuance …'there is no indication that, overall, the court order for outpatient commitment produces better outcomes for clients or the community than enhanced services'" (Cornwell, 2003, p. 227).

The North Carolina study did show that subjects with extended outpatient commitment, a 180 days or more, coupled with receipt of intensive outpatient treatment

> had fewer hospital admissions and fewer days in the hospital, were more likely to adhere to community treatment, and were less likely to be violent or to be victimized. Extended outpatient commitment was also associated with fewer arrests of participants with a combined history of multiple re-hospitalizations and previous arrests. (Swartz et al., 2001, p. 325).

At the time Leifman (2001), a Miami judge, writes endorsing outpatient commitment, 41 states permit some form of assisted outpatient commitment. He maintains that "[t]he most comprehensive study [to date] demonstrated that long-term assisted outpatient treatment reduced the risk of arrest by 74 percent, the probability of violence by 50 percent and hospital admissions by 72 percent." Cornwell (2003) maintains that it was not just the court ordered treatment that rendered the positive results but the combination of the availability of extensive and intensive outpatient services.

Pataki and Carpinello (2005) report in their final analysis of Kendra's Law, which led to the renewal of the law, that " [t]hree years prior to assisted outpatient treatment (AOT), 23% of AOT recipients had at least one incarceration. While in AOT, only 3% of recipients experienced an incarceration, a decrease of 87%. Over the same time comparison, the incidence of arrest, psychiatric hospitalization, and homelessness declined 83%, 77%, and 74% respectively" (p. 17). "There has been an 89% increase in use of case management services among AOT recipients" (p. 21). A "44% decline in the incidence of harmful behaviors (e.g. suicide threats, self harm, ... harm to others," (p. 21) alcohol abuse, drug abuse, etc) was also reported (Pataki, & Carpinello, 2005).

Unlike many other states, New York pumped substantial funding into case management and intensive treatment services upon the passage of their involuntary outpatient treatment legislation (Kendra's Law), with rates of participation in services increasing dramatically; "[h]armful behaviors dropped by 44 percent, including a 47 percent decrease in physical harm to others. Arrest, incarceration, psychiatric hospitalization, and homelessness all dropped by between 74 percent and 87 percent. It seems clear that, as a group, patients did better with assisted outpatient treatment than they had previously" (Appelbaum, 2005, p. 792).

Both the North Carolina and New York outpatient commitment processes share a commonality that serves to make them effective. Both programs have a sufficient amount of intensive and prolonged mental health treatment resources.

The Legal Foundation for Outpatient Commitment

With the implementation of Kendra's Law in New York particular emphasis has been placed on the preventive commitment aspect, and Kendra's law has successfully withstood due process and equal protection challenges in the courts (O'Connor, 2002). Kendra's Law has withstood constitutional challenges, most importantly in New York's highest court In the matter of *K.L.*, *1 NY3d 362 (2004)*. However, Appelbaum (2005) again cautions that just because something is constitutional does not indicate that it is automatically representative of sound policy.

Geller and Stanley (2005b) conduct a review of both U.S. Supreme Court cases (*O'Connor v. Donaldson, 422 U.S. 563 [1975]; Foucha v. Louisiana, 504 U.S. 71 [1992]; Addington v. Texas, 441 U.S. 418 [1979]*) and decisions rendered by the highest courts in three state systems (*In re Detention of LaBelle, 728 P.2d 138 [Washington, 1986]; State of Wisconsin v. Dennis H., 647 N.W.2d 851 [Wisconsin, 2002]; In re K.L., 806 N.E.2d 480 [New York, 2004]* and conclude that outpatient commitments based on less than imminent dangerousness standards are constitutional.

Decades prior to the tightening of commitment standards in the 1960s "essentially anyone who was adjudged suffering from a mental illness could be involuntarily placed in treatment, often with no more than two physicians signing a certificate. This lax standard resulted in many commitments deemed, in retrospect, to be arbitrary, discriminatory, and clinically unnecessary" (Geller & Stanley, 2005b, p. 129). Reacting to these abuses, almost every state revised their mental health laws to require that court-ordered treatment for persons with mental illnesses was restricted to those who typically posed an imminent or immediate danger to themselves or others. Since that time a number of states have modified their involuntary treatment laws to include other factors besides dangerousness, such as, "a deteriorating condition, need for treatment, inability to make informed treatment decisions, likelihood of becoming dangerous absent treatment, and the capability of independent functioning" (Geller & Stanley, 2005b, p. 130), with a finding of each of these factors allowing for intervention without a finding of imminent dangerousness.

In other words, dangerousness as the sole legitimate standard for intervention and involuntary treatment with persons with mental illnesses has subsided. More and more the standard for dangerousness is expanding, as are other rationales for intervention. The state via its police power is empowered to protect the citizenry from the potential dangerousness of persons with mental illnesses and, under its parens patriae (parent of the country) role, is authorized to intervene and care for those unable due to their mental status to look out for themselves (Geller & Stanley, 2005b).

The Washington Supreme Court determined that outpatient commitment criteria conditioned "on whether a person with mental illness 'manifests severe deterioration in routine functioning evidenced by repeated and escalating loss of cognitive or volitional control over his or her actions and is not receiving such care as is essential for his health or safety'" is constitutional (Geller & Stanley, 2005b, p. 134). The "court approved the continued hospitalization of one of the petitioners because, although his 'condition was in the process of stabilizing,' he was likely to be medication non-compliant and consequently deteriorate if released" (Geller & Stanley, 2005b, p. 134).

In Wisconsin, if individuals are incapable of rendering rational treatment decisions for themselves, and there is likelihood such persons will suffer as a result of their inability to make such decisions, such individuals may be placed in outpatient commitment (Geller & Stanley, 2005b). Such individuals "are clearly dangerous to themselves because their incapacity to make informed medication or treatment decisions makes them more vulnerable to severely harmful deterioration than those who are competent to make such decisions. The state has a strong interest in providing care and treatment before that incapacity results in a loss of ability to function" (Geller & Stanley, 2005b, p. 135–136).

> These alternative historical predicates tailor the law to the state's use of its *parens patriae* power to aid those consistently incapable of maintaining needed treatment in the community and the invocation of its police powers in the instance of an individual who has previously been dangerous as a result of non-compliance with treatment, particularly prescribed medications (Geller & Stanley, 2005b, p.136–137). While the law does not include specific enforcement provisions, non-compliance is a factor in a physician's consideration of an evaluation for involuntary hospitalization (Geller & Stanley, 2005b, p.136–137).

As stated in *In re Urcuyo*, "The court recognized the substantial interest that a government has in providing treatment to those incapacitated by severe psychiatric disorders, pronouncing, 'Kendra's Law provides the means by which society does not have to sit idly by and watch the cycle of decompensation, dangerousness and hospitalization continually repeat itself'" (Geller & Stanley, 2005b, p. 137). Geller and Stanley (2005b) conclude, "the abrogation of the opportunity for treatment is a much greater impediment to autonomy and self determination than is the denial of treatment in the name of sustaining the faux liberty of a psychotic state" (p. 138).

Honig and Stefan (2005) counter that the evaluation of involuntary commitment precedent by Geller and Stanley at the U.S. Supreme Court level is not exhaustive and does not reflect the Court's recent tenor in such cases as *Kansas v. Crane*, 534 U.S. 497 (2002) which necessitates that "dangerousness" be an essential component for imposing involuntary civil commitment. Honig and Stefan (2005) do concede "that a person can be involuntarily confined in most states without being imminently dangerousness" (p. 139). However, Honig and Stefan caution that the legal analysis engaged in by Geller and Stanley does not properly consider or negate complex issues surrounding rights to refuse treatment and forced medication.

The case of *Wyatt v. Stickney, 325 F. Supp. 781, 785* (M.D. Ala 1971) led to the deinstitutionalization of hospitals in Alabama and extended basic human rights to persons with mental illnesses. Prior to this decision, involuntary commitment was a first resort, and today it is a last resort. Via the Mental Health Liaison Program in Montgomery County, Alabama, whereby, in addition to the initial assessment for outpatient commitment performed by the receiving hospital, a mental health counselor evaluates the individual being referred, makes recommendations to the court and assists with linkages to treatment (McKinney, 2006).

McKinney (2006) reviews several cases from Alabama that expound on what it takes to be considered a substantial harm to self or others. In one case a female had locked herself in her room refusing sustenance and communication with her family, resulting in extensive malnourishment and weight loss; the court held that if a person was determined to be mentally ill and that her illness is resulting in such neglect that it poses a clear and present threat of significant harm to her well being then outpatient commitment can be authorized as long as she is not rational enough to make informed decisions about her care.

In another case in Alabama, McKinney (2006) discusses a woman who when not medication compliant had a history of starting fires and four months prior to her recommitment procedure actually struck another patient with a tray. "The Court held that: 'If a patient is no longer dangerous only because she is on medication or in a structured environment, then clearly whether she will take her medication or be in a structured environment after release should be considered prior to release'" (McKinney, 2006, p.40). In this case "the Court considered an act which had occurred four months earlier—a recent, overt act. In addition, the Court viewed the patient's history as a predictor of future behavior" (McKinney, 2006, p.40–41). McKinney (2006) asserts, "A patient's history and diagnosis, along with current behavior and professional recommendations should all be taken into consideration. When making decisions regarding a person's liberty, the court needs as much information as possible" (p. 46).

"Commitment on account of dangerousness to others serves the police power, while commitment for dangerousness to self partakes of the *parens patriae* notion that the state is the ultimate guardian of those of its citizens who are incapable of caring for their own interests. Valid exercise of the *parens patriae* power presumes an incapability to manage one's affairs that approximates, if it is not identical with, legal incompetence to act (McKinney, 2006, p. 40).

In yet another case out of Alabama, McKinney (2006) informs us " 'in the case of dangerousness to others, the threat of harm comprehends the positive infliction of injury, ordinarily physical injury, but possibly emotional injury as well. In the case of dangerousness to self, both the threat of physical injury and discernible physical neglect may warrant a finding of dangerousness' " (p. 40–41).

Asking for Help and Not Receiving It

In the days leading up to Julio Perez pushing Edgar Rivera in front of an oncoming subway train, Perez expressed desires to be hospitalized, his recommended hospitalization by caseworkers was passed over by psychiatrists, and his attempts to re-continue his medication were thwarted by a canceled Medicaid card. On the very day of the tragic incident, Perez, an Army veteran, to no avail, even made a last ditch effort to seek help at the emergency room of a Veteran's Administration Hospital. Some five hours later, Rivera would be pushed into the path of the oncoming train (Bernstein, 1999). Even when there is treatment initially, the ability to get the patient to continue treatment can be difficult. Appelbaum (2001) indicates "even Russell Weston, who shot and killed two capitol police officers, was "lost to follow-up [treatment] after his discharge from a Montana state hospital" (p. 25).

Andrew Goldstein had repeatedly asked for treatment and support services, and the State neglected to respond to his cries for help (Flug, 2003; Appelbaum, 2001). In fact, "[h]e signed himself in voluntarily for all 13 of his hospitalizations" (Winerip, 1999, p. 44). "Goldstein had begged for help; he had voluntarily checked himself into psychiatric hospitals and asked to be given psychotropic drugs" (Campbell, 2002, p. 204). Campbell (2002) argues that merely coercing Andrew Goldstein to take his medication via an outpatient commitment law without adequate assistance, monitoring, and intensive mental health treatment services in place would not have prevented Kendra Webdale's death. Some people require around the clock supervision.

Michael Winerip's story of Andrew Goldstein is revealed in the following excerpts from his investigative report. On November 20, 1998, a month and a half before pushing Kendra Webdale to her death, Andrew Goldstein entered the emergency room at Jamaica Hospital in Queens requesting hospitalization. He reported he was hearing voices, his brain had been removed and he had been inhabited by people. Goldstein was unable to explain why his brain had been removed, but he said the voices were warning him that something would happen; he was unable to cope. He had a history of psychosis when off his medication (Winerip, 1999).

> At various times, he has told psychiatrists that he was turning purple, that he had shrunk six to eight inches, that he had lost his neck, had developed an oversize penis because of contaminated food and that a homosexual man named Larry was stealing his excrement from the toilet 'through interpolation' then eating it with a knife and fork. The voices seemed so real, so relentless, that on Nov. 24 a psychiatrist wrote, 'He requested eyeglasses so that he will find the people talking to him' (Winerip, 1999, p. 43–44).

He was hospitalized from November 24 to December 15 at North General before pushing Kendra Webdale (Winerip, 1999). Under the intense financial pressure of managed care to discharge psychiatric patients within three weeks Goldstein, though records reflect he was considered two weeks into his stay to be "disorganized, thought-disordered ... talking to himself ... very delusional," was set at that time for discharge the following week (Winerip, 1999, p. 45). Goldstein was released with a seven days' supply of medication and a piece of paper informing him to seek counseling at Bleuler Psychotherapy Center (Winerip, 1999). As Winerip (1999) says, "This was like a bad joke—that a man so sick, with his history, would be sent into the community with so little support" (p. 45). However, as had been the case in the past, missed appointments occurred, as did his ceasing to take his medication. It occurred in late December; Goldstein did not show for two appointments at the clinic (Winerip, 1999).

> He stopped taking his medication. If he had had an intensive-case manager or a group-home counselor, or both, it would have been their job to find him and see what was wrong. At Bleuler, it wasn't anyone's job. Instead, on Dec. 26, a Bleuler worker mailed a form letter requesting that Goldstein phone the clinic by Jan. 6, 1999, or else his case would be closed. On Jan. 3, 1999, at 5:06 P.M., the N train pulled into the station at 23rd Street and Broadway. Kendra Webdale was a vivacious 32-year-old who had come to the city three years before from upstate and was working as a receptionist with dreams of landing a big job in the music industry. To Andrew Goldstein, she was another stranger. He never saw her face. As he later wrote in his confession: "I felt a sensation, like something was entering me.... I got the urge to push, shove or sidekick. As the train was

coming, the feeling disappeared and came back.... I pushed the woman who had blond hair (Winerip, 1999, p. 45).

In October of 2006, after several attempts at justice, Andrew Goldstein entered into a plea bargain that would send him to prison for 23 years to be followed by five years of supervised release (Editorial, 2006).

The Need for Services

While court mandates may serve as leverage to push some toward treatment, without access to intensive services such court orders will prove ineffective. What is needed is the designation of intensive services and supervision for these persons with mental illnesses at greatest risk, with those at risk of violence and contact with the criminal justice system in need of constant case management. After a review of two generations of empirical evidence, the two most important aspects of court-mandated mental health care for decreasing recidivism and disruptive behaviors by persons with mental illnesses are elevated services and intensified supervision (Borum, 1999).

The "use of outpatient commitment is not a substitute for intensive treatment; it requires a substantial commitment of treatment resources to be effective" (Swartz, et al., 1999, p. 1968). In an evidence-based assessment of existing research, Ridgely et al. (2001) observed that merely making a statutory modification in criteria for involuntary outpatient commitment without substantial investment in the treatment services' infrastructure is futile. Court orders to outpatient commitment are relatively ineffective unless linkages to intensive mental health treatment services are available and assured (Perlin, 2003; Swartz et al., 2001). To have any plausible chance at success, involuntary outpatient commitment "statutes must require access to treatment to have the desired effect" (Petrila et al., 2003, p.165). Of course, involuntary outpatient commitment laws such as Kendra's Law do not guarantee that adequate mental health services will be available (Flug, 2003). Thus, just as we saw with mental health courts, it all comes down to what services are available.

Most communities do not adequately fund their community mental health services, and many locales do not provide adequate mental health treatment for their citizens with mental illnesses even though they are inundated with clients (McKinney, 2006; Petrila et al., 2003). In fact, "[t]he Bazelon Center for Mental Health Law estimates that spending by the 50 states on treatment for the seriously mentally ill is a third less today than it was in the 1950's (once numbers are adjusted for inflation and population growth) (Winerip, p. 46, 1999). Torrey and Zdanowicz (2001) acknowledge that public mental health treatment resources are inadequate in almost every state (see NAMI Grading the States Report, 2006), but they contend that persons with mental illnesses remain at risk and are potential victims. "They live on the streets and eat out of garbage cans. They are periodically jailed. Some are a clear danger to themselves or others. We believe that the public should not have to wait for services to improve while vulnerable persons and the public are at risk" (Torrey & Zdanowicz, 2001, p.339).

"New Mexico ranks last in the nation in per capita spending for people with behavioral health needs ($28.80).… You can't mandate treatment for people society thinks need it when the treatment doesn't exist. Involuntary outpatient commitment or treatment is based on the false premise that society can predict who may become a danger in the future" (Couch & Finlayson, 2007).

In Florida newspaper editorials advocating for the legislative endorsement of assisted outpatient commitment or what a Fort Myers newspaper called "court-ordered medication," the *Lakeland Ledger* acknowledged that mental health treatment resources are scarce, and the *Orlando Sentinel* boasted that the implementation of outpatient commitment would not create additional costs as such treatment would only take place in areas where services were available (Treatment Advocacy Center, 2003). What is needed is the ready availability of intensive community-based services and empowerment, participation, and self-determination of consumers of mental health services in their treatment regimens as opposed to coercion (Honig & Stefan, 2005).

While Lamb and Weinberger (2005) believe that outpatient commitment, intensive case management, and assertive community treatment,[16] even with treatment compliance conceivably monitored by probation officers can work for some persons with mental illnesses to keep them out of jails and prisons, they also decry a need for an increase in the number of psychiatric inpatient beds to provide a needed alternative to incarceration. Just because criminal justice diversion programs such as police-based diversion programs or mental health courts are established, this does not mean that there will be suffi-

---

16. Dvoskin and Steadman (1994) report on three projects that identify assertive community treatment or intensive case management as an aid in decreasing harmful behaviors, arrests and time incarcerated for persons with mental illnesses; while the data is lacking to make a conclusive statement about outpatient commitment's efficacy, when coupled with assertive community treatment it is more likely to result in allowing individuals with mental illnesses to peacefully reside in society (Cornwell, 2003).

cient resources available in the mental health system to provide for those singled out by such programs for diversion and linkage to treatment. Furthermore, with only so many resources to go around, others who have not come to the attention of criminal justice authorities may have their treatment delayed or do without, potentially resulting in them decompensating. Recently, in Texas, increased funding for the mental health system was attained in the legislature based on the reasoning that this would lessen the number of persons with mental illnesses incarcerated and could thwart the need to construct a prison (Lamb & Weinberger, 2005).

Conclusion

Some argue that outpatient commitment is coercive and offers a quick fix for a system that is fragmented and lacks resources to deliver needed services (Sirica, 2000). Kendra's Law in hindsight was a desperate effort to fix a problem. Campbell (2002) states:

> Kendra's Law is a failure not only because it is overbroad and fails to achieve its stated goals of providing the mentally ill with much-needed treatment, but because it ultimately places the nonviolent mentally ill in a position in which they must submit to the will of the State for fear of losing fundamental constitutional liberties. Unless Kendra's Law is reformed to address the due process concerns inherent in forcing the mentally ill to receive treatment, it will remain a prime example of how good intentions can easily become not only bad policy, but oppressive law (p. 205).

Outpatient commitment advocates maintain "that high-quality services cannot overcome the lack of" insight many individuals have into their illnesses (Sirica, 2000, p. 10). "[A]s outpatient commitment and other forms of coercion become more common, the policies must be tied to increasing resources for mental health services as well as making sure that the people who are subject to these actions believe that they have been treated fairly and with concern for their well-being" (Sirica, 2000, p. 10).

As can be seen from the National Alliance on Mental Illness (NAMI) position that follows on outpatient commitment, the need for services is acknowledged, as is lack of insight. Also, the gravely disabled who can't meet basic survival needs are considered, and an expansion of the dangerousness standard to include past history is allowed. Concerns are also expressed that such interventions should be a last resort. Involuntary commitment and court ordered treatment is addressed in the National Alliance on Mental Illness (2007) policy platform. NAMI contends that the availability of adequate comprehensive mental health services in the community will diminish the need for involuntary outpatient commitment. However, NAMI recognizes that when that goal is not realized and some persons with mental illnesses lack insight into their illnesses, as a last resort, in the best interests of individuals, involuntary inpatient and outpatient commitment and court-ordered treatment should be utilized. NAMI also supports broader standards for outpatient commitment to include the gravely disabled who are unable to provide for their basic needs and believes that dangerousness standards should go beyond the imminent criterion to allow for consideration of a prior history of violence on the part of individuals, which would prohibit needless deterioration of persons to the point where they are on the verge of dangerousness before intervention could occur (see NAMI, 2007).

> Whether outpatient commitment is adopted matters not just to those interested in public mental health, but to those in the criminal justice system as well. If outpatient commitment succeeds in the policy goals it espouses, then that should be of great interest to those in the criminal justice system who share the goals of reducing risk and obtaining treatment for individuals with serious mental illnesses. If outpatient commitment does not reach its goals then that should be of interest as well (Petrila et al., 2003, p. 169).

Realizing the scarcity of mental health funding, the controversy surrounding the possible coerciveness of outpatient commitment, and the potential for outpatient commitment to be a substitute for investment in community treatment resources, Petrila et al (2003) maintain that criminal justice professionals would do well to lobby for additional funds for mental health services as this would have a direct impact on criminal justice employees. As we have previously addressed and will again discuss in the next chapter, the criminal justice system is leading the way in obtaining funding for innovative programs concerning the interface of the mental health and criminal justice systems; there needs to be more influence from criminologists and research in this area reflected in the criminal justice literature.

The philosopher John Rawls (1971) in his book *Theory of Justice* delineates his "veil of ignorance" concept. The idea is that someone engaged in trying to design the optimal social contract would not know where he or she stood in society (Jedicke, 1997). They would not know "their class position or social status, their natural talents, abilities, intelligence or strength, and what their plan for a good life" (Jedicke, 1997) might be in designing such a contract, nor would they know their disabilities. This perspective should be used in considering the matter of outpatient commitment.

Not knowing their status as social actors with or without a disabilities, individuals might likely choose for themselves use of such a mechanism as outpatient commitment so that they might channel their energy and comport themselves accordingly. However, being able to determine what is right for others and forcing such a process on to them, until all other alternative measures have been adequately funded and tried, becomes more problematic. It is easier to choose what is appropriate for one's self than it is to choose what is right for others while trying to balance public safety and civil liberties. This, of course, still leaves room for involuntary civil commitment procedures for those who may lack insight into their illnesses that are assessed to be an imminent danger to themselves or others, and it allows for choice on the part of persons with mental illnesses through utilization of such measures as advance directives.

The problem, as pointed out by Winerip (1999), is that we have a mental health system driven by money, not by the well-being of individuals. A review of Andrew Goldstein's 3,500 page psychiatric file revealed "his repeated pleas for services that had no vacancies. There was no room at the inn.... [t]he time is long overdue to establish a social contract for the mentally ill" (Winerip, p. 70, 1999) in America. Regardless of the process chosen for intervention, the solution is the provision of sufficient mental health treatment services. The responsibility for providing sufficient mental health treatment resources lies squarely with the legislature. In the absence of such resources and mental health services, more and more persons with mental illnesses are winding up in jails, the focus of the next chapter.

References

Allen, M., & Smith, V. F. (2001). Opening Pandora's Box: The practical and legal dangers of involuntary outpatient commitment. *Psychiatric Services* 52(3), pp. 342–346.

Appelbaum, P. S. (2005). Assessing Kendra's Law: Five years of outpatient commitment in New York. *Psychiatric Services* 56(7), pp. 791–792.

Appelbaum, P. S. (2001). Thinking carefully about outpatient commitment. *Psychiatric Services* 52(3), pp. 347–350.

Bazelon Center for Mental Health Law (2000, April). Position statement on involuntary commitment. Washington, DC: Bazelon Center for Mental

Health Law. Retrieved from the World Wide Web on July 3, 2007: http://www. bazelon.org/issues/commitment/positionstatement.html.

Bernstein, N. (1999, June 28). Frightening echo in tales of two in subway attacks. *New York Times.* Retrieved from the World Wide Web on July 4, 2007: http://query.nytimes.com/gst/fullpage.html?sec=health&res= 9D07E0D6103AF93BA15755C0A96F958260.

Borum, R. (1999). Increasing court jurisdiction & supervision over misdemeanor offenders with mental illness. Department of Mental Health Law & Policy, Louis de la Parte Florida Mental Health Institute, University of South Florida, Tampa, Florida.

Campbell, K. M. (2002). Blurring the lines of the danger zone: The impact of Kendra's Law on the rights of the nonviolent mentally ill. *Notre Dame Journal of Law, Ethics & Public Policy* 16, pp. 173–205.

Cornwell, J. K. (2003). Preventive outpatient commitment for persons with serious mental illness: Exposing the myths surrounding preventive outpatient commitment for individuals with chronic mental illness. *Psychology, Public Policy and Law* 9, pp. 209–232.

Couch, S., & Finlayson, G. (2007, February 22). Investment in mental health pays off. *The Albuquerque Journal.* Retrieved from the World Wide Web on July 4, 2007: http://www.abqjournal.com/opinion/guest_columns/ 540223opinion02-22-07.htm.

Dvoskin, J. A., & Steadman, H.J . (1994). Reducing the risk of living with mental illness: Managing violence in the community. *Hospital and Community Psychiatry* 45, pp. 679–684.

Editorial (2006). Imperfect justice. *New York Post.* Retrieved from the World Wide Web on July 5, 2007: http://www.nypost.com/seven/10152006/ postopinion/editorials/imperfect_justice_editorials_.htm.

Esposito, R., Westhead, V., & Berko, J. (2008). Florida's outpatient commitment law: Effective but underused. *Psychiatric Services* 59, p. 328.

Faust, T. N. (2003). Shift the responsibility of untreated mental illness out of the criminal justice system, Sheriff 65(2), pp. 6–7.

Flug, M. (2003). No commitment: Kendra's Law makes no promise of adequate mental health treatment. *Georgetown Journal on Poverty Law & Policy* 10, pp. 105–129.

Fritz, M. (2006, February 1). Strong medicine: A doctor's fight: More forced care for the mentally ill. *The Wall Street Journal* p. A1.

Gardner, W., Lidz, C. W., Hoge, S. K., Monahan, J., Eisenberg, M. M., Bennett, N. S., et al. (1999). Patients' revisions of their beliefs about the need for hospitalization. *American Journal of Psychiatry* 156, pp. 1385–1391.

Geller, J. L., & Stanley, J. (2005a). Outpatient commitment debate: Response. *New England Journal on Criminal and Civil Confinement* 31, pp. 123–126.

Geller, J. L., & Stanley, J. (2005b). Outpatient commitment debate: Settling the doubts about the constitutionality of outpatient commitment. *New England Journal on Criminal and Civil Confinement* 31, pp. 127–138.

Hardin, H. (1993, July 22) Uncivil liberties. *Vancouver Sun* p. A15

Hiday, V. A. (2003). Preventive outpatient commitment for persons with serious mental illness: Outpatient commitment: The state of empirical research on its outcomes. *Psychology, Public Policy and Law* 9, pp. 8–25.

Honig, J., & Stefan, S. (2005). Outpatient commitment debate: New research continues to challenge need for outpatient commitment. *New England Journal on Criminal and Civil Confinement* 31, pp. 109–122.

Huggins, E. S. (2004). Assisted outpatient treatment: An unconstitutional invasion of protected rights or a necessary government safeguard? *Journal of Legislation* 30, pp. 305–325.

In re K. L., 1 NY3d 362 (2004).

In re Urcuyo, 714 N.Y.S.2d 862, (Sup. Ct. 2000).

Jadrnak, J. (2006, February 7). Not everyone backs Kendra's Law. *Albuquerque Journal*. Retrieved from the World Wide Web on July 4, 2007: http://www.nyaprs.org/pages/View_ENews.cfm?ENewsID=5217.

Jedicke, P. (1997, November 12). Notes on John Rawls. Retrieved from the World Wide Web on July 22, 2007: http://infotech.fanshawec.on.ca/faculty/jedicke/rawls.htm.

Kansas v. Hendricks, 521 U.S. 346 (1997).

Karasch, M. (2003). Where involuntary commitment, civil liberties, and the right to mental health care collide: An overview of California's mental illness system. *Hastings Law Journal* 54, pp. 493–523.

Lamb, H. R., & Weinberger, L. E. (1998). Persons with severe mental illness in jails and prisons: A review. *Psychiatric Services* 49(4), pp. 483–492.

Lamb, H. R., & Weinberger, L. E. (2005). The shift of psychiatric inpatient care from hospitals to jails and prisons. *The Journal of the American Academy of Psychiatry and the Law* 33(4), pp. 529–534.

Leifman, S. (2001, August 16). Mentally ill and in jail. *Washington Post*. Retrieved from the World Wide Web on July 2, 2007: http://www.psychlaws.org/GeneralResources/article50.htm.

Leone, T. (2000, December). Misdemeanor offenders with mental illness in Florida. Policy Brief. Louis de la Parte Florida Mental Health Institute. University of South Florida, Tampa, Florida.

Ludwick, J. (2006, October 19). Judge strikes down Albuquerque's Kendra's Law. *The Albuquerque Journal.* Retrieved from the World Wide Web on July 4, 2007: http://www.nyaprs.org/pages/View_ENews.cfm?ENewsID=6187.

Maloy, K. A. (1992). *Critiquing the empirical evidence: Does involuntary outpatient commitment work?* Washington, DC, Mental Health Policy Resource Center.

McKinney, Jr., R. (2006). Involuntary commitment: A delicate balance. *The Quinnipiac Probate Law Journal* 20, pp. 36–46.

Moller, D. (2006, March 2). Second try for Laura's law. TheUnion.com. Retrieved from the World Wide Web on July 3, 2007: http://www.the-union.com/apps/pbcs.dll/article?AID=/20060302/NEWS/103020136&template=printart.

Monahan, J., Redlich, A. D., Swanson, J., Robbins, P.C., Appelbaum, P. S., Petrila, J., et al. (2005). Use of leverage to improve adherence to psychiatric treatment in the community. *Psychiatric Services* 56(1), pp. 37–44.

NAMI (2006). *Grading the States: A Report on America's Health Care System for Serious Mental Illness.* The National Alliance on Mental Illness. Arlington, Virginia.

NAMI (2007). Public Policy Legal Issues. Arlington, Virginia: National Alliance on Mental Illness. Retrieved from the World Wide Web on August 9, 2007: http://www.nami.org/Template.cfm?Section=NAMI_Policy_Platform&Template=/ContentManagement/ContentDisplay.cfm&ContentID =38253.

National Stigma Clearinghouse (2007). Kendra's Law updates (2006—Current): A continuing experiment in compulsory psychiatric treatment. Retrieved from the World Wide Web on July 4, 2007: http://community-2.webtv.net/stigmanet/KENDRASLAWUPDATES/index. html.

Neubauer, D. W. (1992). *America's courts and the criminal justice system, 4th ed.* Pacific Grove, CA: Brooks/Cole.

New York Mental Hygiene Law 9.60(C)–(D) (2004).

O'Connor, E. (2002). Is Kendra's Law a keeper? How Kendra's Law erodes fundamental rights of the mentally ill. *Journal of Law and Policy* 11, pp. 313–367.

Pandya, A. (2007). Outpatient civil commitment: a family perspective. National Alliance on Mental Illness. A Consumer Journal for Mental Health Advocacy. New York City Voices. Retrieved from the World Wide Web on July 2, 2007: http://www.nycvoices.org/article_67.php.

Pataki, G. E., & Carpinello, S. E. (2005). Kendra's Law: Final report on the status of assisted outpatient treatment. New York: New York State Office of Mental Health.

Perlin, M. L. (2003). Preventive outpatient commitment for persons with serious mental illness: Therapeutic jurisprudence and outpatient commitment law: Kendra's Law as a case study, *Psychology, Public Policy and Law* 9, pp. 183–208.

Petrila, J., & Christy, A. (2008). Florida's outpatient commitment law: A lesson in failed reform? *Psychiatric Services* 59(1), pp. 21–23.

Petrila, J. (2002, November). The effectiveness of the Broward mental health court: An evaluation. Policy Brief. Louis de la Parte Florida Mental Health Institute. University of South Florida, Tampa, Florida.

Petrila, J., Ridgely, M. S., & Borum, R. (2003). Debating outpatient commitment: Controversy, trends and empirical data. *Crime & Delinquency* 49(1), pp. 157–172.

Pollack, D. A., McFarland, B. H., Mahler, J. M., & Kovas, A. E. (2005). Outcomes of patients in a low-intensity, short duration involuntary outpatient commitment program. *Psychiatric Services* 56(7), pp. 863–866.

Rawls, J. (1971). A theory of justice. Cambridge, Massachusetts: Harvard University Press.

Ridgely, M. S., Borum, R., & Petrila, J. (2001). *The effectiveness of involuntary outpatient treatment: Empirical evidence and the experience of eight states.* Santa Monica, California: RAND Institute for Civil Justice.

Rogers, R. T. (2005, July 6). Mental health courts fad or future? Arlington, Virginia: Treatment Advocacy Center ENEWS. Retrieved from the World Wide Web on August 6, 2005: www.psychlaws.org.

Saks, E. R. (2003). Preventive outpatient commitment for persons with serious mental illness: Involuntary outpatient commitment. *Psychology, Public Policy and Law* 9, pp. 94–104.

Schopp, R. F. (2003). Preventive outpatient commitment for persons with serious mental illness: Outpatient civil commitment: A dangerous charade or a component of a comprehensive institution of civil commitment. *Psychology, Public Policy and Law* 9, pp. 33–69.

Seling v. Young, 531 U.S. 250 (2001).

Sharfstein, S. (2005, September 2). Individual rights must be balanced with 'caring coercion.' *Psychiatric News* 40(17), p. 3.

Sirica, C. (2000, July 11). Outpatient commitment in mental health. Washington, DC: National Health Policy Forum: George Washington University. Issue Brief No. 757. pp. 1–12.

Srebnik, D. S., & La Fond, J. Q. (1999). Advance directives for mental health treatment. *Psychiatric Services* 50, pp. 919–925.

Steadman, H. J., Gounis, K., Dennis, D., Hopper, K., Roche, B., Swartz, M., et al. (2001). Assessing the New York City involuntary outpatient commitment pilot program. *Psychiatric Services* 52(3), pp. 330–336.

Straticzuk, A. (2000, October 2). Thoughts on assisted treatment. Personal communication from adjunct professor of Philosophy. Daytona Beach Community College, Daytona Beach, Florida.

Swanson, J. W., Borum, R. Swartz, M. S., Hiday, V. A., Wagner, H. R., & Burns, B. J. (2001). Can involuntary outpatient commitment reduce arrests among persons with severe mental illness? *Criminal Justice and Behavior* 28(2), pp. 156–189.

Swanson, J. W., Swartz, M. S., Borum, R., Hiday, V. A., Wagner, H. R., & Burns, B. J. (2000). Involuntary out-patient commitment and reduction of violent behaviour in persons with severe mental illness. *British Journal of Psychiatry* 176, pp. 324–331.

Swanson, J. W., Swartz, M. S., George, L. K., Burns, B. J., Hiday, V. A., Borum, R., et al. (1997). Interpreting the effectiveness of involuntary outpatient commitment: A conceptual model. *Journal of the American Academy of Psychiatry and Law* 25(1), pp. 5–16.

Swartz, M. S., Swanson, J. W., Hiday, V. A., Wagner, H. R., Burns, B. J., & Borum, R. (2001). A randomized controlled trial of outpatient commitment in North Carolina. *Psychiatric Services* 52(3), pp. 325–329.

Swartz, M. S., Swanson, J. W., Kim, M., & Petrila, J. (2006). Use of outpatient commitment or related civil court treatment orders in five U.S. communities. *Psychiatric Services* 57(3), pp. 343–349.

Swartz, M. S., Swanson, J. W., & Monahan, J. (2003). Preventive outpatient commitment for persons with serious mental illness: Endorsement of personal benefit of outpatient commitment among persons with severe mental illness. *Psychology, Public Policy and Law* 9, pp. 70–90.

Swartz, M. S., Swanson, J. W., Wagner, H. R., Burns, B. J., Hiday, V. A., & Borum, R. (1999). Can involuntary outpatient commitment reduce hospital recidivism? Findings from a randomized trial with severely mentally ill individuals. *American Journal of Psychiatry* 156(12), pp. 1968–1975.

Swartz, M. S., Wagner, H. R., Swanson, J. W., Hiday, V. A., & Burns, B. J. (2002). The perceived coerciveness of involuntary outpatient commitment: Findings from an experimental study. *Journal of the American Academy of Psychiatry and Law* 30(2), pp. 207–217.

TAC (2005). TAC announces advocacy award winners: Efforts of unlikely team result in new treatment law in Florida. *Catalyst, the newsletter of the Treatment Advocacy Center*. Arlington, Virginia: The Treatment Advocacy Center.

Torrey, E .F,. & Zdanowicz, M. (2001). Outpatient commitment: What, why, and for whom. *Psychiatric Services* 52(3), pp. 337–341.

Treatment Advocacy Center (2003, April 18). NAMI SCC website. Treatment Advocacy Center, Arlington. Virginia. Retrieved from the World Wide Web on July 2, 2007: http://www.namiscc.org/News/2003/Newsletters/Spring/TAC-April18-2003.htm.

Treffert, D. A. (1973). Letter: "Dying with their rights on." *American Journal of Psychiatry* 130, p. 1041.

U.S. Psychiatric Rehabilitation Association (2007, April 10). New Mexico's rejection of involuntary outpatient treatment a growing national trend; USPRA reaffirms its opposition to IOC. Retrieved from the World Wide Web on July 4, 2007: http://www.gmhcn.org/files/Articles/USPRAReaffirmsItsOppositiontoIOC.html.

Wagner, H. R., Swartz, M. S., Swanson, J. W., & Burns, B. J. (2003). Preventive outpatient commitment for persons with serious mental illness: Does involuntary outpatient commitment lead to more intensive treatment? *Psychology, Public Policy and Law* 9, pp. 145–157.

Walker, S. (2006). *Sense and non-sense about crime and drugs: A policy guide, (6th ed)*. Belmont, California: Thomson Wadsworth.

Watnik, I. L. (2001). A constitutional analysis of Kendra's Law: New York's solution for treatment of the chronically ill. *University of Pennsylvania Law Review* 149, pp. 1181– 1228.

Watson, A. C., & Angell, B. (2007). Applying procedural justice theory to law enforcement's response to persons with mental illness. *Psychiatric Services* 58(6), pp. 787–793.

Winerip, M. (1999, May 23). Bedlam on the streets. *The New York Times Magazine* 56, pp. 42–49; 70, 65–66.

Winick, B. J. (2003). Preventive outpatient commitment for persons with serious mental illness: Outpatient commitment: A therapeutic jurisprudence analysis. *Psychology, Public Policy and Law* 9, pp. 107–135.

Zdanowicz, M. (2001, May/June). A sheriff's role in arresting the mental illness crisis. *Sheriff* 62, pp. 38–40.

Zdanowicz, M. (Winter 2003–Spring 2004). Coerced care vs. no care. *Catalyst: The Newsletter of The Treatment Advocacy Center*, Arlington, Virginia.

CHAPTER 8

JAIL PROCESSING OF PERSONS WITH MENTAL ILLNESSES

"Jail is not the proper place for those who suffer from a mental illness"

—Montana Sheriff Chuck O'Reilly[1]

Police are often called the first line of defense against social disorder. If that assertion is true then jails are the second line of defense. Jails do not have the option of refusing admission to those detained by police. Jails are often the community resource of last resort. When other control structures, such as family, school, church, mental health services, welfare, and medical care, are inadequate or ineffective, jails are often relied upon to provide a number of services when behavioral problems arise. In communities where there are inadequate or limited in-patient mental health facilities, jails are needed to provide security for, and in some cases, treatment services to the mentally ill.

Ms. Lynn Hill (2006), a member of the National Alliance on Mental Illness, describes below problems her son encountered.

> My son is one of those with severe mental illness who is not receiving the care and treatment that he desperately needs because of lack of availability of treatment programs and waiting lists.... .In July, my son was found by a Marion County Sheriff's deputy walking up I-75 shirtless and shoeless, with bleeding feet. He was taken to a psychiatric center in Ocala for a psychiatric evaluation and was hospitalized there for 5 weeks. Part of the reason for his prolonged hospitalization was difficulty in achieving stabilization, however there

---

1. O'Reilly, C. (1995). The mentally ill should not be jailed. In W. Barbour, (Ed.), *Mental illness: Opposing viewpoints* (pp. 213–217). San Diego, CA: Greenhaven Press.

were no treatment programs or secure facilities that had openings for which he met the criteria and he was discharged to a psychiatric Assisted Living Facility (A.L.F). He missed a court date for a misdemeanor charge in Hillsborough County due to circumstances related to his psychiatric instability. In June he had called for a taxi to a job interview at 2:00 a.m. at a Tampa radio station that was nonexistent and for which he was unable to pay. The FACT (Florida Assertive Community Treatment) team contacted the Public Defender's Office in Hillsborough County and arrangements were made to take Michael to court to get the issue resolved.

Unfortunately, before this took place, my son deteriorated to a crisis state which required intervention from crisis intervention trained officers from the Pinellas County Sheriff's Department. The officers were very skilled in their interaction with my son, but because of the outstanding warrant from Hillsborough County, he was taken to jail, to await pick-up by a Hillsborough County deputy. My son was in the Pinellas County Jail for five days, when he was finally picked up and taken to jail in Hillsborough County, which is where he currently waits. He has currently been in jail a total of 16 days for the misdemeanor charge of inability to pay the $80.00 cab fare and failure to appear for his court date, and at what cost to taxpayers? According to recent statistics citing high numbers of those incarcerated with mental illness, my son's story is sadly just one of thousands, many of whom are much worse. The state is putting money into recovery programs, when people with severe mental illness are suffering and sometimes dying (suicide, etc.) for lack of adequate crisis stabilization, treatment programs, and secured housing where they can get the care that is desperately needed for critical stabilization....

> Lynn Hill, National Alliance on Mental Illness (NAMI) Pinellas,
> Member of Board of Directors, Palm Harbor

Jails hold an array of inmates for a wide variety of reasons (Applegate, Davis, Otto, Surette, & McCarthy, 2003). Jail facilities may range from a simple holding cell or lock-up in a small town or precinct to large complexes with medical and psychiatric treatment facilities. The training and qualifications of jail staff also varies from jurisdiction to jurisdiction. Since jails are funded by local tax revenues they are affected by local culture and politics. Historically, local officials viewed jails as a necessary evil and provided only the most basic needs to inmates in order to enhance the deterrent impact of the jail facility. In the last three decades the federal government became actively involved in administration of jails and rights of jail inmates. Supreme Court decisions in *Wyatt v. Stickney* (1972), *Estelle v. Gamble* (1976), *Deshaney v. Winnebago County Department of Social Services* (1989), and *Washington v. Harper* (1990) reflect attempts to balance community protection and the constitutional rights of the mentally disordered offender (Sun, 2005).

Often due to the transitory, short-term disruptive stays with less time for intervention, and lack of thorough classification schemas, inmates in jail have been found to exhibit greater symptoms of mental disorders than prison inmates. Inmates with mental illnesses and substance abuse problems create the greatest challenges for jail staff. Many inmates with mental illnesses also abuse drugs. As previously noted, this phenomena is termed "co-morbidity" or co-occurring disorders. Such inmates are more likely to commit suicide, harm themselves, and be involved in a physical altercation with a staff member or another inmate (James & Glaze, 2006). Once a detainee is labeled an inmate other potential service providers tend to absolve themselves of responsibility leaving the jail as the primary medical provider (Hench, 2007).

Mental Health Screening

The American Psychiatric Association (APA) has recommended that all correctional facilities provide at minimum mental health screening, referral and short-term treatment and discharge and prerelease planning. Most short term treatment is in the form of medication. All jails are now required by law to conduct mental health screenings at booking. These screenings can be very short but are useful in assessing whether an inmate needs immediate attention. The screenings are dependent upon the inmates' honesty and willingness to report previous treatment, use of psychotropic medicines, and thoughts about suicide (Seiter, 2005). Most assessments use The Diagnostic and Statistical Manual of Mental Disorders IV (DSM-IV) compiled by APA to measure clinical and personality disorders, aggressive behavior, substance abuse, and social functioning (Sun, 2005). Inmates that report they have experienced a mental health problem in the previous 12 months are given further evaluation to determine the need for a full psychiatric assessment. Psychiatric assessments are usually done by a certified psychiatrist. With increases in the number of mentally ill jail inmates the costs of assessments now comprise a larger portion of a jail's budget than in previous decades.

While there is no recent comprehensive survey of mental health services offered by jails across the United States, a 1997 survey indicated that of jails surveyed 835 provide some form of mental health screening (Morris, Steadman, & Veysey, 1997). A more recent survey in Texas indicated that while most jails offer psychiatric assessments 37% did not offer psychiatric assessments, and larger jails are more likely to offer assessments than smaller jails (Fabelo, 2000). Another important factor affecting the processing of the mentally ill offender is the variability and predictability of the initial screening. Such screens/assessments may contain anywhere from one to two questions to a complete psychiatric profile. One study found that 63% of inmates who were found with acute mental symptoms through independently administered tests were missed by routine staff screenings and were untreated at the time of the independent evaluation (Ford, Trestman, Osher, Scott, Steadman, & Robbins, 2007).

While many jails share mental health information with local mental health agencies they are just beginning to share information with other jails. Most jails in Texas house less than 50 inmates, are located in rural areas, don't have on-site health professionals, and do not keep mental health records in a computerized format (Fabelo, 2000). Shared databases that protect the confidentiality of mentally ill offenders need to be developed to fulfill the "discharge and prerelease programming" recommendations by the APA.

There are over 10 million adults booked into jails every year, and over 700,000 have active symptoms of mental illness (Mauer, 2002). Harris County jail has the largest capacity in the State of Texas (n=9,113) and is one of the largest jails in the United States. In 2006, 128,518 inmates were processed by the Harris County (Houston, Texas) jail. Using national estimates that at least 21% of jail inmates have a recent history of mental illness (James & Glaze, 2006), it is estimated that approximately 25,000 mentally ill offenders were processed by the Harris County jail alone in 2006.

The Los Angeles County Twin Towers is the largest jail in the United States and the largest single provider of mental health services in the United States. It holds an estimated 3,300 seriously mentally ill inmates on any given night (Sacramento Bee, 1999). It covers over 10 acres, 1.5 million square feet and can house approximately 4,000 male and female inmates. The two towers consist of a medical services building and the Los Angeles County Medical Center Jail Ward. Maximum security inmates and a large portion of the county's mental health inmates are housed in towers. The Medical Services Building provides inpatient housing for inmates with various levels of acute medical and mental health needs. Inmates requiring extended levels of health care service are transported to the Los Angeles County Medical Center (Twin Towers Correctional Facility, 2007). Overcrowding is an issue at the Twin Towers.

As discussed in Chapter 3, in the mid-1950s there were over half a million people in state mental hospitals in the U.S. In 1999, there were fewer than 60,000 people in state mental hospitals while jails housed more than 300,000 people with mental illnesses (National Association of State Mental Health Program Directors Research Institute, 2000). The arrest and jailing of inmates with serious mental health problems can have long term effects. Jail environments are stressful and can aggravate the mental health of even the most stable inmate. Of the approximately 15% of individuals in jails that have a major depressive disorder, 75% have a co-occurring substance abuse disorder (Walsh & Holt, 1999; Steadman et al., 1999). Individuals suffering from schizophrenia or bipolar disorder can be traumatized by the arrest, booking and detention process.

Jail Suicide

The rate of jail suicide is nine times that of the general population. The typical victim is a white single male, in his twenties, arrested for public intoxication, has no significant history of prior arrests, and dies within three hours of incarceration by hanging (Hayes, 1989). Previous studies indicate that mental health screening is critical to identifying and preventing suicide among at risk detainees. Some inmates will deny having thoughts of suicide. While most jails have screening policies in place there has been no comprehensive study to assess the policy implementation and effectiveness. The ability to screen inmates before placement in cells is critical to preventing suicide and is a significant challenge for jail booking officers during peak periods (Sun, 2005). Hayes (2000) identified several "signs" that booking officers should look for in determining whether an arrestee might be at risk for suicide: change in appetite, lethargy, expression of strong guilt over the offense, severe agitation or aggressiveness, noticeable mood or behavior changes, speaking unrealistically about getting out of jail, having increased difficulty in relating to others, preoccupation with the past, packing belongings or giving away belongings even though they are not to be released in the near future.

While at one time isolation was the preferred protocol in response to suicide ideation (thoughts of suicide), Hayes (2000) and others have argued against isolation, especially during the first 48 hours, which tends to increase suicide attempts. Suicide is a private phenomena and being in a room with others can serve as a deterrent. Instead it is recommended that treatment and security staff work together to keep the inmate in general population when and where possible. If an inmate is placed in isolation it is critical to keep them under constant supervision. This is most difficult because of the manpower necessary to conduct such supervision, and in the case of using cameras to monitor inmates in isolation, it is not uncommon for correctional officers to become bored and to become distracted. Since it takes less than a matter of minutes to complete suicide it is very difficult to constantly monitor inmates in isolation (Hayes, 2000; Hayes & Rowan, 1988; Couturier & Maue, 2000).

Most suicides occur when staff-to-inmate ratios are at their lowest, midnight to six a.m. Administrators can either add additional staff during this time or place other inmates in isolation cells with inmates to deter suicides during this time. Considering the unpredictability of human nature, the pairing of inmates in isolation cells is a difficult yet important tool in preventing suicides. There have been documented cases where the paired inmates were involved in deadly altercations. Beyond psychological screening, the training of staff to understand and assess psychological function is critical to preventing suicide and violence in the stressful jail environment (Hayes, 2000; Hayes & Rowan 1988; Couturier & Maue, 2000).

Jails suffer from "revolving door" inmate populations that are not absorbed (or absorbable) into the mainstream of everyday life. Limited sources of funding inhibit the jail, as an institution, to effectively intervene in the lives of offenders. Often times, mentally ill offenders that are jailed lose their eligibility for housing, medical, and employment benefits increasing the odds they will become homeless and re-enter the criminal justice system (Hench, 2007). Jails throughout the nation are struggling with this issue. Below is an example of the problems in Louisiana.

Mentally Ill Inmates Housed in Parish Prisons Part II
Oct. 23, 2007 05:14 PM CDT

There are not enough mental health beds across the state. So instead, patients are filling up emergency rooms and jails and desperately roaming the streets. What can be done to address the problem? *WAFB's Caroline Moses* takes a look.

Louisiana got a D– for our care of the mentally ill. Post-Katrina and Rita, the problem has grown, but its roots are much deeper. State Senator Tom Schedler of Mandeville says, "The institutions of the 21st century are now our hospital emergency rooms and hospitals and jails, in lieu of outpatient clinics and the old model institutions." Senator Schedler says state emergency rooms and jails are packed with mentally ill patients who do not belong there. Patients like O'Neil Lloyde Howes, who has been deemed mentally incompetent. He sits in a Tangipahoa jail cell for threatening a judge. The senator says, "In many cases, it's something as simple as a pill a day that could make these people function."

Instead, people like Howes are costing taxpayers' money. Senator Scheddler says, "If you put the true cost of incarcerating people at $40,000 or $50,000 a year and the cost of getting the streets with these problems, I would venture to say the numbers would be staggering." The excuse has been there's just not enough money to treat and reimburse the mentally ill. However, Schedler says it would actually be cheaper to address their illness head-on, rather than let patients end up in an improper facility. "But until we get insurance companies to recognize that and treat it as such and reimbursing, you're going to have this problem continually. If you and I have this problem tomorrow morning and more than likely, our insurance policies are not going to cover us," he says.

So, how can we deal with the problem until they do? "Have community volunteers trained to be able to recognize and assist in treating mental health patients," Schedler suggests. That's exactly what the Baton Rouge Police Department is working toward. Sergeant Don Kelly says, "We come into contact with them 24 hours a day, 7 days a week, and often times lack capacity to get them treatment they need." So, volunteer patrol officers will go through something called crisis intervention training to gain that capacity. He says, "In order to be able to identify people who are in mental health crisis and be able to take the appropriate steps working hand-in-hand with mental health professionals in [the] community to get those people quick help."

The Baton Rouge Police Department is just one component of many needed to appropriately treat mental illness. Schedler says, "Bottom line is everybody's got to be pulling the train in the same direction and unfortunately, that just hasn't been the case." It would take the police, mental health providers, emergency rooms, hospitals and the greater medical community to coordinate this effort.

Reporter: *Caroline Moses, WAFB ;*
Retrieved on October 24, 2007 from (NEWS
http://www.wafb.com/global/story.
asp?s=7227002&ClientType=Printable)

While there is a history of public opinion supportive of the notion that jails should be [bad] environments that discourage and deter offenders, there is some evidence that there is a change in public attitudes toward jails suggesting treatment services for inmates with mental health and substance abuse problems (Applegate et al., 2003). The ability of jails to satisfy both punitive and treatment expectations is perhaps their greatest challenge.

James and Glaze (2006) estimated that over 50% of all jail inmates have a mental health problem as evidenced by a recent history or symptom of mental health problems within the 12 months prior to their intake classification.[2] Others provide more conservative estimates of less than 20% (Council of State Governments, 2007; Ditton, 1999). In 1999, the U.S. Surgeon General declared untreated mental illness as the silent epidemic of our time (U. S. Department of Health and Human Services, 1999). Of course, one way to determine the prevalence of mental illness in a jail population is to count the number of individuals in custody who are taking psychotropic medication. For example, 19 percent of those housed in the Polk County Jail in Florida were prescribed psychotropic medication in March of 2008 (D. Zimmerman, personal communication, April 18, 2008). However, most mentally ill offenders do not receive treatment while they are in jail (Steadman, Deane, Morrissey, Westcott, Salasin, & Shapiro, 1999). Individuals with untreated mental illness are more likely to experience behavioral problems, interact with police, and go to jail (Cuellar, Snowden, & Ewing, 2007; Osher, Steadman, & Barr, 2003; Solomon & Draine, 1995; Teplin, 1984; Walsh & Bricourt, 1997).

In Florida, jails have become the largest public institution to provide psychiatric services. There are approximately five times as many mentally ill offenders in Florida jails than in Florida's psychiatric hospitals (Perez, Leifman, & Estrada, 2003). There are more offenders in jail and prisons with mental illnesses than in all state mental hospitals in the U.S. combined (Sigurdson, 2000).

While a number of untreated mentally ill are stuck in the revolving door between the street and the jail others are stuck in the revolving door between the jail and the state hospital. In one Florida case, a mentally ill inmate who was unfit to stand trial waited months in jail without treatment before transfer to a state mental hospital. In the state mental hospital he took medications and eventually convinced doctors he was competent. At that point he was returned to the county jail, where he legally refused treatment. Without medi-

---

2. It should be noted that methodological problems with this study are discussed in Chapter 3.

cine, the inmate's condition worsened until the court found him incompetent again and in need of placement in the state's mental hospital. With limited availability at the state mental hospital, the inmate remains in jail custody (Christian, 2005). At the time there were approximately 300 inmates in Florida waiting placement in a state mental hospital. Similar situations exist across the United States (Tisch & VanSickle, 2006). Christian (2005) refers to this process of being transferred back and forth between jail and the state mental hospital trying to ascertain competency as "riding the bus" (see also Toch, 1982).

One of the factors exacerbating the care of the mentally ill offender is that they are not transferred to state treatment facilities in a timely manner. In Florida, county jails are allowed to detain a mentally ill offender up to 15 days by law before transfer to state treatment facilities. The Florida Department of Children and Families (FDCF), which runs the state hospitals, in 2006 faced possible legal action for not transferring mentally ill jail inmates to state facilities. Judges in Miami (Dade County), at the time, even considered legal remedies to require FDCF to comply with the law or face contempt charges. The absurdity is that FDCF had an $8 billion budget surplus at the time (Goodnough, 2006). As discussed in Chapter 5, a Pinellas County judge even held the Director of FDCF in contempt of court, which resulted in her resignation. Attention by the media and state judges produced responses by Governor Jeb Bush and state legislators to provide additional funds to FDCF to reduce time mentally ill offenders spend in jail prior to transfer to a state treatment facility.

In a press release on May 9, 2007, the FDCF announced that the waitlist of mentally ill offenders in jail awaiting transfer had been reduced to zero under the leadership of newly elected Governor Crist and Secretary Butterworth. Using $16.6 million in state appropriated funds, 251 new forensic treatment beds were added. An additional $4.6 million was provided by the Florida legislature to improve diversion efforts and enhance community and in- jail mental health services (Florida Department of Children and Family Services, 2007). The tragedy is the needless harm to individuals, families, jail staff, and communities.

As discussed in Chapter 3, some of the blame for the lack of mental hospital beds can be placed on effects of the deinstitutionalization movement in the 1970s and 80s that cut funding for state mental hospitals and failed to adequately fund community mental health initiatives. The "after-shocks" of this policy have been exacerbated by a number of factors including what Downes (in Garland, 2001) called a "macho penal economy." According to Downes, control policy has been driven by a macho economy that has at its base a philosophy that values dominance and holds human weaknesses in contempt. This Darwinian, survival-of-the fittest approach to social order is reflected in trends during the recent

U.S. economic boom where incarceration populations set record highs and mental health institution populations set record lows (Ditton, 1999; Fabelo, 2000).

The fiscal and social benefits of incarcerating the mentally ill (especially non violent misdemeanor offenders) pale in comparison, at least in the short term, to the costs of not treating the mentally ill. As evidenced in Applegate et al. (2003), the informed public is beginning to view treatment and punishment from a new perspective.

In *Wyatt v. Stickney* (1972), an Alabama district court recognized the right of the mentally ill to receive treatment. This decision recognized the deplorable conditions in state mental hospitals and led eventually to the creation of alternatives to institutionalization. Today, the mentally ill are once again finding themselves lost in large, impersonal, ineffective, self-perpetuating, custodial environments. The difference is that most mental illness is treated in penal institutions. While jails were not designed to handle the large numbers of mentally ill offenders they are making adjustments to this demographic change in their populations by remodeling hospital and custodial facilities, modifying staff training and connecting with various community agencies to provide a more effective continuum of care.

New Diversion Initiatives

The CIT (Crisis Intervention Team) model discussed in Chapter 4 has been used to effectively handle individuals experiencing a mental health crisis. The CIT model was first developed in Memphis, Tennessee. The CIT model is currently used in multiple jurisdictions. Uniformed police officers receive specialized training to screen arrests and divert individuals in crisis to county mental health facilities. Program evaluation results show significant reductions in the number of inappropriate arrests and reductions in police violence and injuries. CIT has also been used in correctional settings effectively. The CIT model can reduce injuries among officers and inmates. Deputy Sheriff Michael Zabarsky of the Ventura County Jail, stated in a personal communication to Joyce Wilde, CIT Program Administrator, of the Ventura County Sheriff's Office, CA (2007, May 1):

> I learned during the training that the effects of a drug-induced psychosis are the same as a mental psychosis, and the main way to tell the difference is to wait three days and see if they detoxify. The main point I want to make is that your training changed the way I handled this event. It made me a better peace officer ... I firmly believe that

the CIT training enabled me to do several things: 1) Quickly access the situation and determine what needed to be done in order to have a good conclusion. 2) Recognize the symptoms of the psychosis and use the various CIT techniques provided in the training to "mentally control" the subject, not just physically control him. 3) Have the confidence to "step in" and direct resources. 4) Project confidence and expertise in a subject matter no one else present was trained for or able to understand. 5) Assure that no escalation of force was necessary to end this situation; I was able to keep my fellow officers from being over-bearing and applying too much force despite the fierce resistance. 6) Resolve the situation without compromising officer safety.

Jailing persons with mental illnesses costs more than twice as much as having mental health supports in place within the community (Greenberg, 2001). And, figures from the Polk County Jail, which has a special needs unit staffed by personnel with spcialized training, in Bartow, Florida, reveal that housing a person with mental illness in jail is more than twice as costly as housing a person without mental illness in jail, $99.61compared to $40.53 a day (J. Rice, personal communication, August 10, 2007). According to the Office of National Drug Policy, for every dollar invested in treatment, research has determined that four to seven dollars are saved in terms of the costs of crime and criminal justice (Treating Mental Illness Makes Sense, 2008).

CIT also has the potential of reducing fiscal costs associated with jail confinement. In the Miami-Dade jail, post-arrest diversion has saved over $200,000 in confinement costs (estimated at $100 a day for mentally ill offenders) and over $100,000 in psychiatric evaluation costs (Perez et al., 2003). The long term effects of reduced substance abuse, improved mental health functioning and employability are expected but not yet determined.

Special 'psych' jails planned: Leaders in Broward and Miami-Dade are designing what could be among the first county jails ever to be built for mentally ill inmates.

By Carol Marbin Miller and Ashley Fantz (2005)

Crammed four strong, men at the Miami-Dade Jail stare out of plexiglass cells that are the size of a bathroom. The cells are lighted 24 hours a day for security. They shiver in the chilly, Clorox-stung air, wearing jail-issue robes—patterned after X-ray vests—that barely cover their nude bodies. On the ninth floor—a mental hospital with bars—mattresses, bed sheets and underwear can be suicide tools.

The men sleep on metal bunks, are given food through a bolted slot and are let out of their cells twice a week to be sprayed with a hose attached to a concrete wall. "It's really unbelievable, a gulag," said Judge Steven Leifman, associate administrative judge of the Miami-Dade County Court who runs the county's mental health project. But South Florida, long a bellwether for the nation's social ills, now is poised to become a trend-setter for what many consider a significant social service reform: leaders in both Miami-Dade and Broward are designing what could be among the first county jails ever to be built specifically for inmates with chronic and severe mental illness.

For decades, Miami has warehoused some 1,200 mentally ill inmates at its jail each day. Broward's jail dispensed psychiatric drugs to an average of 1,211 inmates each day last year, nearly one-fifth the jail's population. The jails are, in essence, the state's largest asylums. Ordinarily a jail tour depresses Leifman. But now he has a reason to be optimistic. With a $22 million bond Miami-Dade voters approved last November, Leifman and other officials hope to outfit an existing state mental hospital with 50 short term residential beds and 100 jail beds for inmates with a diagnosed mental illness. Leifman's plan is to divert the vast majority of the nonviolent inmates back to the community as soon as they are healthy enough. Broward Sheriff Ken Jenne has pitched his proposal to about a dozen court, county and social service officials. In its very early stages, the project may call for a new building or one that can be retrofitted. It's likely the facility will be near the North Broward Detention Center in Pompano Beach.

'MORAL OBLIGATION'

"In 30 years of public office, the mentally ill in Broward have been ignored by the state and federal government and they've suffered tremendously," said Jenne. "You feel like you have a moral obligation to do something." It costs his Sheriff's Office $80 a day to house a regular inmate; $130 to house an inmate with mental illness. Assistant County Administrator Pete Corwin said the commissioners have discussed the project numerous times with Jenne over the past six months. Corwin said one of the possible designs include three towers which could hold as many as 1,400 beds. It will cost about $50 million to build and $100 per-inmate per-day to maintain, said Corwin. Structurally, Corwin commented, "We're trying to get natural light into the building so it's a softer feel than a jail. But you're still in jail; it's a secure facility."

While most national jail and mental health experts view the plans favorably, some worry the new psychiatric jails could exacerbate a trend toward providing meaningful psychiatric care only when people become sick enough to draw the attention of police. A 2004 Miami-Dade grand jury report said nine percent of Floridians suffer from some type of mental illness—three times the national average. Perhaps one-half to two-thirds of homeless people in the state have a chronic psychiatric disorder. And as community mental health spending failed to keep pace with the problem, police and corrections programs were forced to become social service agencies. Though he praises Jenne's good intentions, Broward Public Defender Howard Finkelstein said he fears the proposed jail may cement the practice of "criminalizing" people with mental illness.

MOST NOT DANGEROUS

The majority of inmates with mental illness are more annoying than dangerous, having been jailed for such crimes as vagrancy and public drunkenness. Most have become "frequent fliers" through the jail system, repeatedly flunking out of underfunded community programs. "It appears we are throwing in the towel," said Finkelstein. "It is easier and cheaper to lock 'em up than it is to treat them humanely and appropriately by housing them, and providing them treatment and shelter." Jenne responds, "The truth is that this is a population already incarcerated. We're not creating a new situation. There are people who don't want to live in the real world and face that. "Look, the mentally ill break the law sometimes and they need to be in jail," he continued.

Nationwide, numerous studies show county jails and state prisons house three times as many people with chronic mental illness as do state psychiatric hospitals. The costs of treating such inmates are staggering: In Broward, taxpayers pay $125 per-day for each inmate receiving mental health care, compared with $78 for inmates in the general population. Miami taxpayers also pay $125 per-inmate each day, significantly more than the $18 daily cost for healthy inmates. A program in Pinellas County, on the Gulf Coast, that diverts inmates with mental illness out of the jail and into community treatment costs, in contrast, half that amount, or $60 per day, said Pinellas Public Defender Bob Dillinger.

Mark Moening, who was diagnosed in 1986 with bipolar disorder, has been jailed a half-dozen times since, including stints in both Miami and Fort Lauderdale, mostly for misdemeanors, such as speeding. "I got cars that can do a buck-fifty. You don't want me driving when I'm manic," he said.

LITTLE PRAISE
Though Moening, 49, has been mostly stable for a decade or more, he offers little praise for Broward's public mental health system, from which he still receives care. "I know how bad it is," he says. But the community mental health system, he added, is still a vast improvement over jail. Moening, of Plantation, was in the psychiatric unit of the Broward jail for five days last year on a probation violation charge. "There's nothing that goes on there, other than lining up for meds. "You cannot expect the people who are locking you up behind bars to be the same compassionate people you need for your recovery," said Moening, who serves on Broward's Alcohol, Drug Abuse and Mental Health Planning Council. Leifman's proposal, which is attracting national attention, was designed to change that.

This month, the seven-story South Florida Evaluation and Treatment Center, about two blocks from the main jail on 17th Street and 17th Ave., is being studied as a suitable home for what could be the first one-stop-shop for jail inmates who are more ill than criminal.

"This is the future," said Leifman." This has never been proposed before anywhere in the country.

Henry Steadman is keeping a close eye on Miami-Dade and Broward's plans. He is the director of the National Gains Center, a 10-year-old federally funded think tank that specializes in the national crisis of jailing people with mental illness. He believes staffing is crucial.

"Will officers volunteer or get assigned to that post?" he said. "Are they going to feel, 'I'm being stuck with this job' rather than 'I want this job.'?"

Mental health advocates have warned both plans could have unintended consequences.

Miami Public Defender Bennett Brummer commended Leifman for "seeking the humane, rather than the punitive, approach" to treating mental illness. He also expressed concerns that plans such as Leifman's and Jenne's could further erode efforts to treat mental illness in the community.

"Although we find considerable merit in his proposal for a Mental Health Diversion Facility, we do so with caution," Brummer said. "As currently drafted, the initiative could unwittingly convey the impression that the best, if not the only, way to get needed psychiatric help is to be arrested."

Partnership for Active Community Engagement (PACE) is a "collaborative project involving the chief judge, the sheriff, the probation department, the mental health center, the public health department, and the local community justice services department" in Boulder, Colorado (Consensus Project Newsletter, 2007). PACE uses a multi-disciplinary team to provide an alternative for mentally ill offenders convicted of misdemeanors or felonies. Of the 467 inmates evaluated as potential participants 182 were admitted to the PACE program between July 2000 and March 2003. Prior to their entry in the PACE program 48 percent of the participants had arrests for misdemeanors and 52 percent had arrests for felonies. It is estimated that participation in the PACE program reduces the time spent by mentally ill offenders in jail by between 73 and 90 percent. At a cost of $61.50 per day of detention, savings were estimated at $615,492. Also participants' abilities to obtain and retain employment and achieve a stable housing situation increased dramatically. Estimates indicate that substance use among participants was reduced from 98 percent to 34 percent (Consensus Project Newsletter, 2007).

Previously discussed in Chapter 6, San Antonio Bexar County received an award from the American Psychiatric Association for its jail diversion program for offenders with mental illness. The Bexar County Jail Diversion Program has been successful in

> integrating health care, law enforcement, and the judicial system to transform the way mental health services are delivered to offenders with mental illnesses with low-level offenses. In doing so, the program has reduced the recidivism of persons with mental illness by providing access to appropriate treatment. Giving persons with mental illness the opportunity to stay out of jail has enhanced public safety by freeing up jail beds for violent offenders and has provided humane and confidential care for persons with serious mental illness who are involved in the criminal justice system. [3]

Jails across the country are making efforts to improve their treatment of offenders with mental illnesses. In a national effort to help local, state, and federal policymakers and criminal justice and mental health professionals with responses to people with mental illnesses who come into contact with the criminal justice

---

3. Retrieved on October 24, 2007 from http://psychservices.psychiatryonline.org/cgi/content/full/57/10/1521.

system The Criminal Justice/Mental Health Consensus Project, coordinated by the Council of State Governments Justice Center, has articulated a number of policy statements to guide improvements in the various components of the criminal justice system. Policy statement # 13 states: "Ensure that the mechanisms are in place to provide for screening and identification of mental illness, crisis intervention and short-term treatment, and discharge planning for defendants with mental illnesses who are held in jail pending the adjudication of their cases." Recommendations for implementation of this policy include:

a. Screen all detainees for mental illness upon arrival at the facility.
b. Work with mental health service providers, pretrial service providers, and other partners to identify individuals in jail who may be eligible for diversion from the criminal justice system. Facilitate the release of information to assist in the identification of need.
c. Ensure that the capability exists to provide immediate crisis intervention and short term treatment.
d. Facilitate a detainee's continued use of a medication prescribed prior to his or her admission into the jail.
e. Suspend (as opposed to terminate) Medicaid benefits upon the detainee's admission to the facility to ensure swift restoration of the health coverage upon the detainee's release.
f. Commence discharge planning at the time of booking and continue the process throughout the period of detention.[4]

According to Fabelo (2000), jails are faced with three key mental health issues:

1) Inadequate data collection, storage and reporting procedures make it almost impossible to know how many mentally ill offenders are in county jails. The absence of such information makes the formulation of policies difficult at best.
2) Data regarding the mental health (past and current) of a jailed offender results in duplication of services and slows response times to individuals experiencing a mental health crisis, endangering staff, other inmates, and the individual.
3) The presence and quality of mental health services is unclear. Development of standards of treatment and audits of the service providers remains to be established across jurisdictions.

---

4. Retrieved on October 24, 2007 from http://consensusproject.org/the_report/toc/ch-III/ps13-intake-detention.

Conclusion

Most jails are local, county or city, operations. They are influenced by local politics, funding allocations, available tax revenues, and the quality of staff that operate jails. Only a few of the innovations being implemented in jails across the country are referenced in this chapter.

Jails have not traditionally been viewed as playing a critical role in the treatment of the mentally ill. Jail management is changing. The Council of State Governments has provided recommendations for the training of correctional staff involved in the care of the mentally ill inmate. These recommendations are discussed in Chapter 9.

As a society we have become dependent upon the criminal justice system to provide solutions to many of the woes of modern life that it was not designed to handle or equipped to do. The use of jails for the seriously mentally ill is inappropriate under current funding, architectural, and operational constraints. Our overdependence on the criminal justice system is an issue that affects many facets of life in America. The management of mental illness must be a community responsibility. The failure to attend to shortfalls in funding of community mental health initiatives will continue to haunt those lives that intersect with the jail: offenders, families, and the legal community, and affect the quality of life for all.

References

Applegate, B., Davis, R., Otto, C., Surette, R., & McCarthy, B. (2003). The multifunction of jail: Policy makers' views of the goals of local incarceration. *Criminal Justice Policy Review* 14(2), pp. 155–170.

Christian, J. (2005). Riding the Bus: Barriers to Prison Visitation and Family Management Strategies. *Journal of Contemporary Criminal Justice* 21, pp. 31–48

Consensus Project Newsletter (2007). *PACE Program Description.* Retrieved June 5, 2007, from http://consensusproject.org/programs/one?program_id=237.

Council of State Governments (2007). Corrections. *Criminal Justice/Mental Health Consensus Project*, New York. Retrieved from the World Wide Web October 21, 2007: http://consensusproject.org/issue-areas/corrections/.

Cuellar, A. E., Snowden, L. M., & Ewing, T. (2007). Criminal records of persons served in the public mental health system. *Psychiatric Services* 58(1), pp. 114–120.

Couturier, L., & Maue, F. (2000), "Suicide prevention in a large statewide department of corrections: A full-court press to save lives" *Jail Suicide/Mental Health Update* 9(4), pp. 1–8.

Deshaney V. Winnebago County Social Services Department, 489 U.S. 189 (1989).

Ditton, P. M. (1999). *Mental health and treatment of inmates and probationers: Special report.* Washington, DC: U.S. Department of Justice, Bureau of Justice Statistics.

Downes, D. (2001). The macho penal economy: Mass incarceration in the United States—a European perspective. In David Garland (Ed.) Mass Imprisonment: Social Causes and Consequences (pp. 51–69). Thousand Oaks, CA: Sage.

Estelle v. Gamble, 429 U.S. 97 (1976).

Fabelo, T. (2000). Mentally ill offenders and county jails: Survey results and policy issues. Criminal Justice Policy Council. Austin, Tx.

Florida Department of Children and Family Services (2007, May 9). Forensic Mental Health Waitlist Drops to Zero Under Leadership of Governor Crist, Secretary Butterworth. Retrieved on October 25, 2007 from http://www.dcf.state.fl.us/news/prforensicupdate.shtml.

Ford, J., Trestman, R., Osher, F., Scott, J. E., Steadman, H. J., & Robbins, P. C. (2007). Mental Health Screens for Corrections. Washington, D.C.: National Institute of Justice/U.S. Department of Justice.

Goodnough, A. (November 15, 2006). Officials Clash over Mentally Ill in Florida Jails. New York Times. Retrieved on October 24, 2007 from http://www.nytimes.com/2006/11/15/us/15inmates.html?pagewanted=print.

Greenberg, S. F. (2001). Police response to people with mental illness. In M. Reuland, C.S. Brito, & L. Carroll (Eds.), *Solving crime and disorder problems: Current issues, police strategies and organizational tactics* (pp. 43–58) Washington, DC: Police Executive Research Forum.

Hill, L. (2006) Mentally ill left to wait in jails. Retrieved October 25, 2007, from http://www.itsyourtimes.com/?q=node/1800.

Hayes, L. (2000), Suicide risk despite denial (or when actions speak louder than words). *Jail Suicide/Mental Health Update* 10(1), pp. 1–6.

Hayes, L., & Rowan, J. (1988), *National Study of Jail Suicides: 7 Years Later.* Alexandria, VA: National Center on Institutions and Alternatives.

Hench, D. (2007, February 26). Mentally ill care in jails still flawed; report says. *Portland Press Herald*, p. B1.

James, D., & Glaze, L. (2006). Mental Health Problems of Prison and Jail Inmates. Bureau of Justice Statistics, U.S. Department of Justice, Washington, DC.

Mauer, M. (2002). Mentally Ill Offenders in the Criminal Justice System: An analysis and Prescription. Washington, DC: The Sentencing Project.

Mentally Ill Inmates Housed in Parish Prisons Part II (Oct 23, 2007). Retrieved on October 24, 2007, from http://www.wafb.com/global/story.asp?s=7227002&ClientType=Printable.

Miller, C. M., & Fantz, A. (2005, September 11). Special 'psych' jails planned. Retrieved from the World Wide Web on October 29, 2007: http://www.prisonpotpourri.com/PRISON_NEWS/Mental%20cases/Herald_com%20%2009-11-2005%20%20Special%20'psych'%20jails%20planned.html.

Morris, S. M., Steadman, H. J., & Veysey, B. M. (1997) Mental health services in US jails: a survey of innovative practices. *Criminal Justice Behavior* 24, pp. 3–19.

National Association of State Mental Health Program Directors Research Institute (2000). Closing and reorganizing state psychiatric hospitals: 2000. Retrieved March 1, 2001 www.rdmc.org/nri/SH_RPT.pdf.

Osher, F., Steadman, H. J., & Barr, H. (2003). A best practice approach to community reentry from jails for inmates with co-occurring disorders: The APIC model. *Crime & Delinquency* 49(1), pp. 79–96.

Perez, A., Leifman, S., & Estrada, A. (2003). Reversing the Criminalization of Mental Illness. Crime & Delinquency 49(1), pp. 62–78.

Sacramento Bee (March 17, 1999). Treatment, Not Jail: A Plan to Rebuild Community mental health.

Seiter, R. (2005). *Corrections: An introduction.* Upper Saddle River, New Jersey: Pearson/Prentice Hall.

Sigurdson, C. (2000). The mad, the bad, and the abandoned: The mentally ill in prisons and jails. *Corrections Today* 62(7), pp. 70–78.

Solomon, P., & Draine, J. (1995). Issues in serving the forensic client." *Social Work* 40(1), pp. 25–33.

Steadman, H. J. Deane, M. W. Morrissey, J. P., Westcott, M. L. Salasin, S., & Shapiro, S. (1999). A SAMHSA research initiative assessing the effectiveness of jail diversion programs for mentally ill person. *Psychiatric Services* 50(12), pp. 1620–1623.

Sun, K. (2005). Mentally Disordered Offenders in Corrections. In Rosalyn Muraskin, (Ed.) *New Correctional Issues.* Pearson/Prentice Hall Upper Saddle River, New Jersey

Teplin, L. A. (1984). Criminalizing mental disorder: The comparative arrest rate of the mentally ill. *American Psychologist* 39, pp. 794–803.

Tisch, C., & Vansickle, A. (2006). Mentally Ill Left to Wait In Jails: Hundreds of Inmates Wait Months for A Bed in a State Hospital. County Officials Blame

DCF. St. Petersburg Times. Retrieved On October 24, 2007 from http://www.Sptimes.Com/2006/09/20/News_Pf/Tampabay/Mentally_Ill_Left_To_.Shtml.

Toch, H. (1982). The disturbed and disruptive inmate: Where does the bus stop? *Journal of Psychiatry and Law* 10, pp. 227–249.

Treating Mental Illness Makes Sense (2008). Mental Health Association in North Carolina, Cape Fear Chapter. Retrieved from the World Wide Web on January 30, 2008: http://www.capefearhealthyminds.org/library.cgi?article=1115919700.

Twin Towers Correctional Facility (2007). Los Angeles County Sheriff's Office. Retrieved from the World Wide Web on October 21, 2007: http://www.lasd.org/divisions/custody/twintowers/index.html.

U.S. Department of Health and Human Services (1999). *Mental Health: A report of the Surgeon General* (DHHS Publication No. 0167-024-01653-5).

Walsh, J., & Bricourt, J. (1997). Services for persons with mental illness in jail: Implications for family involvement. *Families in Society: The Journal of Contemporary Human Services* (Jul.-Aug.), pp. 420–428.

Walsh, J., & Holt, D. (1999). Jail diversion for people with psychiatric disabilities: The sheriffs' perspective. *Psychiatric Rehabilitation Journal* 23(2), pp. 153–160.

Washington v. Harper, 494 U.S. 210 (1990).

Wyatt v. Stickney (M.D. Ala. 1972) 324 F. Supp. 781.

CHAPTER 9

DEALING WITH MENTAL ILLNESS IN THE PRISON POPULATION

It is deplorable and outrageous that this (TX) state's prisons appear to have become a repository for a great number of its mentally ill citizens. Persons who, with psychiatric care, could fit well into society, are instead locked away, to become wards of the state's penal system. Then, in a tragically ironic twist, they may be confined in conditions that nurture, rather than abate, their psychoses.

—Judge William Wayne Justice in *Ruiz v. Johnson*,
37 F. Supp. 2nd 855 S.D. Texas, 1999

As discussed in Chapter 3, approximately a half million people were treated in state mental hospitals in the 1950s. However, due to a number of reasons, including deinstitutionalization, restriction of civil commitment criteria, ease of police placement of persons with mental illnesses in jail, lack of adequate community mental health services and long term care beds, between 1960 and 2000, while the number of mental hospital patients steadily declined (see Figure 1), the number of mentally ill housed in jails and prisons rose to over 400,000 (National Alliance on Mental Illness, 2004). This trend is aggravated by the fact that inmates with severe mental disorders spend more time in prison and jails. The stigma of mental illness, the paucity of effective prison mental health treatment, and the inability of community mental health services to provide adequate post-release supervision and care have a combined effect of prolonging the incarceration experience. Prolonged periods of institutionalization in correctional settings tend to sustain abnormal and maladaptive behaviors rendering treatment and adjudication virtually indefinite (Teplin, 1994).

**Figure 1: Institutionalization in the United States
(per 100,000 adults)**

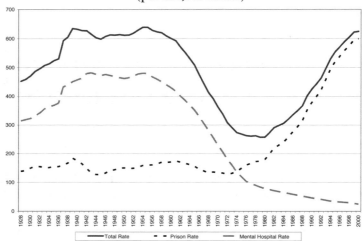

© Reprinted with permission. Bernard Harcourt, *From the Asylum to the Prison: Rethinking the In-carceration Revolution* 84 Texas L. Rev. 1–1755 (2006).

Problems with Treating the Mentally Ill in Prison

The management of prison populations requires different resources and different management strategies than those used 30 years ago. There are over 2.2 million inmates in U.S. prisons on any given day. Every year, 13.5 million people spend time in jail or prison. Ninety-five percent of them eventually return to life in our communities (Gibbons & Katzenbach, 2006).

According to data collected in 1999 in Table 1 (Bazelon Center, 2002), there are substantial differences between offenders with mental illnesses and other inmates. In most every category, inmates with mental illnesses in jails, prisons and on probation are more likely to have unstable employment and housing, a history of substance abuse, and more often to report deficits in social skills and adjustment (Bazelon Center, 2002).

In 2005, there were approximately 775,000 inmates in U.S. prisons with a mental health problem as measured by either treatment by a mental health professional or by the exhibition of symptoms as specified in the DSM-IV. The DSM-IV is the official manual of the American Psychiatric Association and is used in the diagnosis and classification of mental disorders. Fifty-six percent of state prisoners, forty-five percent of federal prisoners and sixty-four per-

Table 1
Characteristics of Offenders with Mental Illnesses
Compared with total population

UNSTABLE EMPLOYMENT AND HOUSING				
	Probation	Jail	State Prison	Federal Prison
unemployed in month before arrest	—	**47.1%** vs. 33.4%	**38.8%** vs. 30.4%	**37.7%** vs. 27.5%
homeless in year before arrest	—	**30.3%** vs. 17.3%	**20.1%** vs. 8.8%	**18.6%** vs. 3.2%
homeless at time of arrest	—	**6.9%** vs. 2.9%	**3.9%** vs. 1.2%	**3.9%** vs. 0.3%

DEFICITS IN SOCIAL SKILLS AND ADJUSTMENT				
	Probation	Jail	State Prison	Federal Prison
been abused physically or sexually	**38.8%** vs. 12.1%	**36.5%** vs. 12.5%	**36.9%** vs. 15.2%	**34.1%** vs. 7.6%
family member incarcerated	**40.3%** vs. 34.0%	**5.15%** vs. 45.1%	**41.5%** vs. 38.5%	**51.5%** vs. 45.1%
live in a **foster home**	**15.9%** vs. 6.5%	—	**26.1%** vs. 12.2%	**18.6%** vs. 5.8%
alcohol-abusing parent or guardian	**32.4%** vs. 19.2%	**29.3%** vs. 21.9%	**30.6%** vs. 22.2%	**24.6%** vs. 16.0%

SUBSTANCE ABUSE				
	Probation	Jail	State Prison	Federal Prison
history of **alcohol dependence**	**34.8%** vs. 22.1%	**37.9%** vs. 24.3%	**34.4%** vs. 22.4%	**23.9%** vs. 15.6%
used alcohol or drugs **at time of offense**	**49.0%** vs. 46.4%	**64.5%** vs. 56.5%	**58.7%** vs. 51.2%	**46.5%** vs. 33.0%
a **heavy drinker**	**45.7%** vs. 33.7%	**52.9%** vs. 38.0%	**48.8%** vs. 39.5%	**43.9%** vs. 29.2%
lost a job because of drinking	**19.4%** vs. 5.3%	**18.0%** vs. 10.3%	**16.7%** vs. 9.0%	**8.7%** vs. 4.7%
job or school trouble because of drinking	**25.2%** vs. 10.5%	—	**24.0%** vs. 13.8%	**15.4%** vs. 7.1%
been arrested or held at police station because of drinking	**45.7%** vs. 41.1%	**41.5%** vs. 30.7%	**35.2%** vs. 28.3%	**30.7%** vs. 18.3%

© Reprinted with permission from Bazelon Center for Mental Health Law (2002). Fact sheets for advocates: People with serious mental illnesses in the criminal justice system.

cent of jail inmates reported having a mental health problem in the 12 months prior to their interview (James & Glaze, 2006).[1]

In essence, every prison today is a quasi mental health institution. Not only are the numbers of mentally ill in prison increasing but there is an increase in the severity of the mental illnesses. Prisoners with the most severe mental disorders are least able to understand and abide by strict prison rules of behavior. Correctional psychiatry tends to focus on psychotic mental disorders such as bipolar disorder, major depression, and schizophrenia. Inmates with diagnosed psychoses suffer from a major break with reality. Such inmates may be delusional, hallucinate, or unable to communicate. Such disorders can be managed by medication—the most common form of treatment in prisons (Human Rights Watch, 2003).

Approximately 15 percent of state prison and 24 percent of jail inmates report psychotic episodes defined as being delusional, such as false beliefs that other people were controlling their brains or thoughts, could read their minds, and were spying on them, or reported seeing or hearing things others did not see or hear (hallucinations). This compares with 3.1 percent of persons in the U.S. population that suffer from a psychotic disorder (James & Glaze, 2006). In 2000, there were 70,000 prisoners in the United States that were actively psychotic (National Alliance on Mental Illness, 2004). In prisons, those that are weak or slow become targets for predators. Anti-psychotic medication can slow physical reaction times of inmates being treated making them susceptible to victimization. Like on the "outside," inmates shy away from prisoners with acute mental illnesses further exacerbating their stigmatization, isolation and contact with reality. Mentally ill inmates are seen by many inmates as pathetic and disruptive. While many mentally ill prisoners cope well with appropriate medication, treatment and supervision, the psychotic inmate is the most unpredictable and can be the most difficult to manage in the correctional setting. Victor Hassine, a prisoner in Pennsylvania, writing on his prison experiences contends that the increases in mentally ill offenders have "destroyed the stability of the prison system" (Hassine, 1996, p. 29).

While the symptoms of many mentally ill prisoners are subtle and are not easily detected by correctional staff, the seriously mentally ill inmate is easily detected: "they rub feces on themselves, stick pencils in their penises, bite chunks of flesh from their bodies, slash themselves, ..." (Human Rights Watch, 2003) and, in the case of Timothy Souders that follows, create the most challenges for security and treatment staff.

---

1. As noted in Chapter 3, there are methodological concerns regarding this study.

The Case of Timothy Souders

Timothy Souders had been diagnosed with anxiety and manic de-pressive disorders and had been treated on several occasions at a mental hospital. "After one hospital stay, he was caught shoplifting two paintball guns. He grabbed a pocket knife, threatened employ-ees, and then begged a cop to shoot him. Instead, he was stunned with a Taser." He pleaded guilty to resisting arrest and assault. He was sentenced to three to five years at the Southern Michigan Correc-tional Center. Following an episode where he "was running around outside in January with his clothes off, thinking he was a knight fighting dragons, an investigation concluded he needed urgent psy-chiatric care. As a result Souders was chained down, hands, feet and waist, up to 17 hours at a time. By prison rules, all of it was recorded on a 24-hour surveillance camera and by the guards themselves. The tape records a rapid descent: he started out apparently healthy, but in four days Souders could barely walk. In the shower, he fell over. The guards brought him back in a wheelchair, but then chained him down again. On Aug. 6th, he was released from restraints and fell for the last time. Souders had died of dehydration and only the surveil-lance camera took notice" (*60 Minutes*, February 11, 2007).

Correctional mental health staff are limited in the resources they have to deal with inmates that have personality disorders such as severe obsessive-com-pulsive disorder and severe generalized anxiety disorders. Such personality dis-orders can aggravate an inmate's ability to be compliant. The most common personality disorder is anti-social personality disorder (ASPD). Individuals with this disorder present a disregard for the rights of others, are aggressive, and impulsive. While there is some question by critics regarding the reliabil-ity of ASPD diagnoses, the ability to diagnosis the difference between the "bad" and the "mad" remains a challenge and is critical to maintaining ethical treat-ment and punishment (Human Rights Watch, 2003).

The Case of Richard Street

On Thanksgiving 2004, a notoriously incompetent inmate named Richard A. Street hanged himself in a segregation unit at the 800-in-mate, maximum-security state prison in Walpole. His death marked the start of a rash of 12 suicides in Massachusetts prisons in 26 months, compared with five in the nearly six years before. A look at

Street's prison experience might explain this phenomenon, which is unfortunate but not uncommon in modern prisons.

Street, 53, was described as a wretched man who had indiscriminately shot two people one night in Boston in 1980 and then went on to exhaust the patience and resources of the Massachusetts prison system. Suffering from schizoaffective disorder and calling himself "Jesus Christ, Future King of the Vampires," he would rant, self-mutilate, and perform naked pirouettes around a basketball in the prison yard.

Recently the state Department of Correction commissioned a report on suicide prevention in Massachusetts prisons and has promised to put its recommendations into practice. Street's chilling case starkly illustrates the need for changes ... In a six-week period, Street, a thin man with a bushy, reddish-brown beard and long dark hair, was twice found hanging in his cell. He repeatedly gouged his skin, swallowed a 1 1/2-inch piece of metal, and was taken to a local emergency room six times. He smeared feces in his hair and complained that solitary confinement was making him hurt himself.

Photographs show a handcuffed Street displaying a gruesome array of scabbed and mottled wounds on his legs and arms. Nonetheless, his records suggest a skepticism, common on the part of overworked prison clinicians, of Street's pathology. After he had been found "unresponsive" and with gauze tied around his neck, a clinician wrote that Street "is not depressed ... nor at risk of harm due to mental illness." He had been known to "feign unconsciousness," the record noted.[2]

In 2003, Human Rights Watch released a report declaring U.S. prisons were ill-equipped to deal with the increasing numbers of mentally ill offenders (Human Rights Watch, 2003). Only 60 percent of state and federal prisoners with mental illnesses receive any mental health treatment (Ditton 1999). About 10 percent of state inmates receive psychotropic medications and approximately 13 percent receive some form of mental health therapy or counseling. Less than 2 percent were housed in a 24-hour mental health unit (Beck & Maruschak, 2001).

While concerted efforts are made to structure and control prison life, they are difficult places to be for both the "kept" and the "keepers." Prisons are stress-

---

2. This report by Mary Beth Pfeifer for *The New York Times* was released March 1, 2007, after obtaining and reviewing prison records for Richard Street.

ful environments for inmates who are not mentally ill to navigate; for those with mental illnesses, prisons can be toxic and brutal environments. They are noisy, often overcrowded, filled with individuals competing for status and limited resources. They lack privacy and offer few opportunities for personal growth.

Mentally ill offenders can suffer from a variety of debilitating symptoms including delusions, hallucinations, and uncontrollable mood swings. Inmates with mental health problems are more likely to be charged with physical or verbal assault on a correctional officer or another inmate (James & Glaze, 2006) and for not following the orders of correctional officers (Adams, 1986). Twenty-one percent of federal prisoners with mental illnesses are involved in at least one fight compared to nine percent of prisoners without a diagnosed mental illness. Thirty-six percent of state prisoners with mental illnesses are involved in fights compared to 25 percent without a diagnosed mental illness. Sixty-two percent and 41 percent of state prisoners and federal prisoners with mental illnesses are formally charged with breaking prison rules, compared to 52 percent and 33 percent of inmates without mental illnesses respectively (Ditton, 1999).

Many mentally ill inmates serve their maximum sentence because their mental illness is not considered as a factor in disciplinary proceedings. However, Krelstein (2002) indicates that perhaps there could be a role for mental health clinicians to play as advocates when considering the potential dismissal of institutional charges against persons influenced by their mental illnesses. In 1999, Ditton reported that inmates with mental illnesses serve approximately 15 months longer sentences than other state prisoners based upon time of admission and expected date of release. In 2006, James and Glaze reported that inmates with mental illnesses serve 5 months longer sentences than other state prisoners. This could be linked to the severity of the illness. It may be that this disparity in time served is lessening between those with and without mental illnesses, but further investigation is needed to validate this possible trend.

Correctional Officers: On the Front Line

Correctional officers play a critical role in the maintenance of order in prison settings. Their job requires them to be in a constant state of vigilance. Inmates are not as stupid as some may think and are quite skilled in the art of manipulation and deception. It can be quite difficult to determine if an inmate, like at times a child, is acting out for attention or in fact in need of mental health care.

Correctional officers often spend years with some inmates. They get to know their moods and behaviors. They are responsible for making decisions to call in mental health professionals, when to remove someone from their cell, when to recommend placing them in protective custody, or when to ignore their behavior. The Washington State Department of Corrections has implemented a mobile consultation team to work with prison staff to address specific issues related to the management of mentally ill offenders (Adams & Toch, 2002).

According to the National Institute of Corrections (2001), the training of correctional staff on how to respond to offenders with mental illnesses is severely lacking. Only seven states reported providing correctional officers with more than four hours of training on dealing with mental illness issues in correctional settings. According to Doug Dretke, Director of the Correctional Management Institute, the Texas Department of Corrections has recently required 20 hours of specialized training for all correctional officers and increased the emphasis in pre-service training on mental illness issues (D. Dretke, personal communication, May 1, 2007).

Prisons are highly structured environments. In most states, prison operations are highly proscribed by department and institutional policy. Current prison design and operational protocols have yet to be sufficiently modified to deal with the plethora of challenges mentally ill inmates create.

The Human Rights Watch (2003) reported such a case when an inmate at Phillips Correctional Institution in Georgia warned staff he might snap and attack his cellmate. The guards responded by giving him a new cellmate. When the guards observed continued signs of aggression, instead of isolating the mentally ill prisoner, they brought him another cellmate. In the night, the inmate snapped and stomped his cellmate to death and shoved a pencil through his eye. This particular case illustrates the need to better manage mentally ill inmates. The liability to the agency and risk to inmates and staff will remain as long as protocols and lack of resources remain an issue for correctional executives.

As discussed in Chapter 8, the Council of State Governments, in the Criminal Justice/Mental Health Consensus Project[3], has provided a number of recommendations for each component of the criminal justice system. Policy Statement # 30 recommends to "Train corrections staff to recognize symptoms of mental illness and to respond appropriately to people with mental illness" (Council of State Governments, 2007). Specific recommendations for implementation of this policy include:

---

3. See http://consensusproject.org/downloads/Chapter_VI.pdf.

a. Provide basic training regarding mental health issues to all corrections staff who come into contact with detainees or inmates with mental illness.
b. Incorporate competency-based training in mental health issues in existing academy (pre-service) training programs and in-service programs for corrections staff.
c. Provide advanced training to corrections staff assigned to work specifically with inmates with mental illness.
d. Provide parole board members with training in order to inform them about issues regarding the release of people with mental illness from prison.
e. Provide training for parole officers to improve their ability to supervise parolees with mental illness.

Mental Health Treatment in Prisons

"Legally convicted prisoners are entitled to psychological or psychiatric care for serious mental or emotional illness. 'There is no underlying distinction between the right to medical care for physical ills and its psychological or psychiatric counterpart'" (Krelstein, 2002, p. 489). Generally, the mental health treatment of inmates should be on par with persons with mental illnesses in the community. "The 3 essential elements required to establish a constitutionally adequate correctional mental health system are sufficient program space and supplies, enough trained and/or experienced mental health staff to identify mental illness and provide treatment, and inmate access to these resources within a reasonable time" (Metzner, 2007).

The physical and social environments of most prisons run counter to the promotion of coping skills appropriate to life on the "outside." The goal of most correctional health systems is to stabilize the patient and to facilitate the maintenance of the mentally ill inmate in "general population," minimizing the need for limited and specialized services. The care of the mentally ill in prison is a difficult task at best. In many ways prisons have become the new asylums. Studies have indicated that inmates that receive mental health care can adjust to life in prison or jail (Stone 1997; Satel, 2003).

While prisons today provide a variety of resources to accommodate mentally ill offenders, including psychiatric hospital beds, separate intermediate care housing, therapy, medication, and targeted programming, in many states the waiting list for special services is long. The failure to respond in a timely and appropriate manner to mentally ill offenders presenting unacceptable behaviors effects virtually every facet of correctional life (Gibbons & Katzenbach, 2006). In 2000, the Bureau of Justice Statistics surveyed state correctional facilities to determine the types of mental health treatment offered in state correctional facilities. Table 2 describes the variance in mental health services offered to inmates by states. A total of 1,558 state correctional facilities were identified. Most correctional facilities screen inmates at intake, approximately 62 percent conduct psychiatric assessments, approximately 50 percent provide 24 hour mental health care, and almost 70 percent provide therapy/counseling and distribute psychotropic medications. Over a hundred correctional facilities report providing no services (Beck & Maruschak, 2001).

Perhaps the most significant issue confronting correctional executives is the lack of skilled mental health professionals willing to work in prisons. While protocols and facilities may exist to provide for the care of the mentally ill inmate, it is the professional correctional mental health provider that determines the quality and effectiveness of care inmates receive. The Commission on Safety and Abuse in American's Prisons reported in 2006 that inadequate staffing, high turnover, and burnout haunt many correctional mental health providers and inmates either receiving treatment or considering treatment. Human Rights Watch (2003) contends that serious mentally ill inmates often receive no treatment, are accused of malingering, and/or are treated as disciplinary problems.

The assessment of the prison systems' offerings of mental health services is an on-going and evolving process. Issues most commonly found in correctional mental health systems include understaffing, poor screening and tracking of mentally ill prisoners, misdiagnoses, and concerns related to proper medication and adequate access to specialized care for seriously ill prisoners. At this time, litigation has been the primary force behind reforms in correctional mental health services.

Prison executives dealing with strapped budgets have not taken advantage of the potential benefits of treating the mentally ill in prison. Many states have been or are either under orders by the United States Supreme Court (USCC) to substantially increase the quantity and quality of mental health services to inmates. The effects of cases like *Ruiz vs. Estelle* and *Wyatt vs. Stickney* were instrumental in forcing states to reallocate resources to care for the mentally ill offender. In the shadows of USSC mandated oversight of correctional operations, correctional executives are beginning to see mental health treatment as a useful proactive management tool.

Most of the jails and prisons in the U.S. were not designed to meet the needs of the increasing numbers of mentally ill inmates. While no prison system intentionally sets out to harm mentally ill prisoners, the existence of substandard

Table 2: Mental Health Screening and Treatment in State Correctional Facilities, June 30, 2000

Region and State	Total *	Number of facilities, by types of policy							
		Screen inmate at intakes	Conduct psychiatric assessment	Provide 24-hour mental health care	Provide therapy/ counseling	Distribute psychotropic medications	Help released inmates obtain services	No services provided	No date reported
Total	1,558	1,055	990	776	1,073	1,115	1,006	125	39
Northeast	233	154	163	152	173	178	167	5	3
Connecticut	20	17	17	13	18	16	16	0	0
Maine	8	6	5	3	7	7	6	0	0
Massachusetts	25	20	17	15	21	20	20	0	2
New Hampshire	8	4	5	4	7	7	7	0	0
New Jersey	43	27	24	14	23	30	25	3	0
New York	69	31	52	66	53	43	40	0	0
Pennsylvania	44	36	29	32	29	40	39	2	0
Rhode Island	7	7	7	0	7	7	7	0	0
Vermont	9	6	7	5	8	8	7	0	1
Midwest	301	190	167	140	207	210	196	25	1
Illinois	48	30	30	32	31	31	34	4	0
Indiana	25	17	14	14	15	13	13	4	0
Iowa	30	11	12	12	10	21	23	2	1
Kansas	11	9	8	9	9	10	11	0	0
Michigan	70	39	43	35	40	31	32	10	0
Minnesota	9	1	1	1	8	9	8	0	0
Missouri	28	27	0	0	27	27	27	1	0
Nebraska	9	2	2	0	9	9	0	0	0
North Dakota	3	2	2	1	2	2	2	1	0

Table 2: Mental Health Screening and Treatment in State Correctional Facilities, June 30, 2000 *continued*

Region and State	Total *	Screen inmate at intakes	Conduct psychiatric assessment	Provide 24-hour mental health care	Provide therapy/ counseling	Distribute psychotropic medications	Help released inmates obtain services	No services provided	No date reported
Ohio	34	34	34	26	33	32	29	0	0
South Dakota	4	2	3	1	3	4	3	0	0
Wisconsin	30	16	18	9	20	21	14	3	0
South	730	527	497	338	514	535	471	59	17
Alabama	35	16	21	13	21	26	11	3	1
Arkansas	15	12	12	12	12	12	12	3	0
Delaware	9	8	8	2	8	8	5	0	1
District of Columbia	6	2	2	3	2	3	4	2	0
Florida	106	98	90	1	88	88	85	8	0
Georgia	83	54	45	38	41	47	48	6	2
Kentucky	25	15	12	8	13	12	14	1	0
Louisiana	17	12	11	11	10	11	11	0	5
Maryland	26	12	14	13	18	18	22	2	0
Mississippi	28	12	11	5	8	9	2	9	1
North Carolina	80	49	55	31	68	73	61	0	2
Oklahoma	52	37	30	25	33	37	20	4	3
South Carolina	34	19	18	17	21	22	20	5	0
Tennessee	15	14	14	15	15	15	14	0	0
Texas	127	117	114	111	114	118	109	2	0
Virginia	61	44	34	31	34	30	29	14	0
West Virginia	11	6	6	2	8	6	4	0	0

Table 2: Mental Health Screening and Treatment in State Correctional Facilities, June 30, 2000 *continued*

Region and State	Total*	Number of facilities, by types of policy							
		Screen inmate at intakes	Conduct psychiatric assessment	Provide 24-hour mental health care	Provide therapy/ counseling	Distribute psychotropic medications	Help released inmates obtain services	No services provided	No date reported
West	294	184	163	146	179	192	172	36	18
Alaska	24	16	10	6	12	19	18	1	1
Arizona	16	15	13	13	14	14	12	0	1
California	86	50	35	28	41	36	38	13	12
Colorado	47	16	30	32	34	38	35	0	3
Hawaii	10	10	9	9	10	9	1	0	0
Idaho	13	7	5	6	5	10	7	1	0
Montana	8	6	5	4	6	6	4	0	1
Nevada	20	11	10	7	10	9	9	7	0
New Mexico	10	10	10	8	10	9	8	0	0
Oregon	13	13	10	7	9	12	11	0	0
Utah	8	6	5	4	5	6	7	0	0
Washington	30	17	15	17	17	17	15	13	0
Wyoming	9	7	6	5	6	7	7	1	0

*Includes 1,295 state-operated facilities, 22 facilities under joint state and local authority, 3 facilities operated by the District of Columbia, and 238 private facilities with more than 50% of their inmates held for state authorities.

Sources: Allen J. Beck and Laura M. Maruschak, *Mental Health Treatment in State Prison, 2000*, Bureau of Justice Statistics Special Report (Washington, D.C.: U.S. Department of Justice , July 2001), p. 5.

care limits the ability of mentally ill inmates to develop appropriate functioning behaviors. The delivery of care to the mentally ill offender is affected by a variety of factors including an effective screening and classification system, the availability of treatment, the quality of treatment, the orientation of the custodial and support staff, the design of the institution, and access to medication. Results from the 2003 Human Watch report indicate that while medication is readily available what is needed are the resources and commitment to determine what medication is needed and the staff necessary to monitor its distribution and effect.

Seventy percent of state prisons report that they conduct a psychological exam/screen of inmates (Beck & Maruschak, 2001). This means that thirty percent of inmates are not screened for mental illnesses. This equates to approximately 375,000 state inmates not screened for mental illnesses. Of those inmates, 23–39 percent (86,250–146,250) suffer from significant psychiatric disability. While it remains unclear how many of these inmates would benefit from psychiatric treatment, 15–20 percent will require some form of psychiatric intervention during their incarceration (Metzner et al., 1998). Applying these estimates to the 2004 inmate population data, (15%) 224,494 to (20%) 299,326 inmates would require some form of psychiatric intervention during their incarceration.

The quality of psychiatric intervention has a direct impact on prison environments, the safety of officers, staff, and inmates. Since almost all prisoners are eventually released, prison psychiatric intervention strategies have far reaching effects on families of inmates and members of local communities. According to Judge William Wayne Justice,

> it is deplorable and outrageous that this (TX) state's prisons appear to have become a repository for a great number of its mentally ill citizens. Persons who, with psychiatric care, could fit well into society, are instead locked away, to become wards of the state's penal system. Then, in a tragically ironic twist, they may be confined in conditions that nurture, rather than abate, their psychoses.
>
> —*Ruiz v. Johnson*, 37 F. Supp.2nd 855 S.D. Texas, 1999

Segregation/Super Max

Prisons throughout the United States have struggled to deal with the baddest of the bad and maddest of the mad. Inmates in crisis, who are persistent management problems, or may pose a danger to themselves, are often segregated from the general population. In recent years, prisons have designed high-tech, high-security facilities to deal with the worst inmates. These facilities have a variety of designations to include: high security, administrative segregation (ad seg), supermax, protective custody, and isolation. In 1999, there were over 20,000 inmates housed in supermax facilities. Haney (2003) and others have argued that lockdown for up to 23 hours a day in such isolation cells/units can produce or aggravate mental health problems. In fact, in *Madrid v. Gomez* (1995), dealing with California's Pelican Bay Security Housing Unit (SHU), it was determined that mentally ill prisoners and those with conditions making them susceptible to mental ilness should be banned from placement in the SHU due to its deleterious effects.

A national survey of wardens (Mears & Castro 2006) indicates unanimous support for supermax type facilities claiming they increase safety, order, and control and are useful in incapacitating violent and disruptive inmates. In reporting on the negative unintended consequences wardens acknowledged that supermax confinement diminishes mental health and increases suicide attempts. Furthermore, they reported that the mentally ill and nuisance inmates that are placed in such isolation receive little to no appropriate treatment or services.

Due to the anti-therapeutic milieu permeating incarceration in general, much less solitary confinement, the need for residential care has emerged for persons with mental illnesses who require a therapeutic environment separate from the general population. As a result, more and more correctional facilities are going to special needs housing units to provide for such things as residential treatment and supportive living units for anywhere from 30 to 50 inmates per housing unit (Metzner, 2007).

Rising Costs of Incarcerating the Mentally Ill

Public support for punishment has remained high despite studies demonstrating the long-term fiscal, ethical, and legal benefits of treating inmates (Cullen, 2006). While millions of dollars have been spent to build new prisons to satiate the public's desire to incarcerate and punish, spending on the treatment of mentally ill offenders is severely lacking. The number of offenders with mental illnesses sentenced to correctional facilities and the costs of treating them has increased dramatically in the last ten years. Izumi, Schiller and Hayward (1996) estimated ten years ago that California alone was spending between $1–2 billion a year arresting, housing and treating mentally ill inmates. The imprisonment of the mentally ill in the United States costs approximately $9 **billion** a year (National Alliance on Mental Illness, 2004). The burden on state and federal correctional facilities is at least a partial product of Medicare and Medicaid regulations limiting payment to clinicians for assertive community treatments (ACT). Investment in such as ACT strategies would allow community treatment teams to make home visits, administer medication, and provide in-home care, reducing re-hospitalization [and imprisonization] by up to 80 percent (Satel, 2003).

Conclusion

Inmates with mental illnesses are more likely to have been homeless, unemployed, under the influence of drugs or alcohol, living in foster care or an institution, physically or sexually abused while growing up, and/or exposed to a parent who abused alcohol (Ditton, 1999). The federal government has continued to decrease funding of community mental health care, shifting the burden of care to state and local governments. As a result, there are fewer inpatient facilities for the mentally ill. Lack of inpatient beds forces the mentally ill to seek services from hospital emergency rooms. Fellner (2003) contends that only the wealthy have access to mental health services in the community and that many prisoners could have avoided expensive incarceration had publicly funded treatment been available.

The success of correctional intervention in the new millennium is contingent upon the ability of wardens and their staffs to manage the mentally ill. The performance of correctional mental health systems is being scrutinized by court systems and a proliferation of prison "watchdog" groups like the Humans Rights Watch, The National Prison Project of the ACLU, the Vera Institute, and the Commission on the Safety and Abuse in America's Prisons. Taking care of the mentally ill offender enhances the order and functioning of the prison environment, reduces officer and inmate assaults, and increases the chance of successful re-entry. Until state and federal governments expand funding of mental health hospitals and community mental health treatment initiatives, prisons will be forced to do more with limited resources.

References

Adams, K. (1986). The disciplinary experiences of mentally disordered inmates. *Criminal Justice and Behavior* 13(3), pp. 297–316.

Adams, K., & Toch, H. (2002). *Acting Out.* APA Books: Washington, D.C.

Bazelon Center for Mental Health Law (2002). Facts sheets for advocates: People with serious mental illnesses in the criminal justice system. Retrieved on October 31, 2007 from: 200http://www.bazelon.org/issues/criminalization/factsheets.

Beck, A., & Maruschak, L. (2001). Mental health treatment in state prisons, 2000, NCJ-188215.

Bureau of Justice Statistics Special Report (1999). Mental Health Treatment of Inmates and Probationers. Washington, DC: Department of Justice.

The Commission on Safety and Abuse in American's Prisons (2006). Confronting Confinement. New York: Vera Institute.

Council of State Governments (2007). *Criminal Justice/Mental Health Consensus Project,* New York. Retrieved from the World Wide Web October 21, 2007: http://consensusproject.org/issue-areas/corrections.

Cullen, F. (2006). It's time to reaffirm rehabilitation. *Crime and Public Policy, 5(4),* 665–672.

Ditton, P. (1999). Mental Health Treatment of inmates and probationers. Bureau of Justice Statistics, NCJ-174463.

Fellner, J. (October, 2003). United States: Mentally ill mistreated in prison. Retrieved December 11, 2006 from http://hrw.org/english/docs/2003/10/22/usdom6472.htm.

Gibbons, J., & Katzenbach, N. (2006). *Confronting Confinement: A report of the Commission on Safety and Absue in American's Prisons.* Vera Institute of Justice: New York, N.Y.

Haney, C. (2003). Mental health issues in long-term solitary and "supermax" confinement. *Crime and Delinquency* 49, pp. 124–156.

Harcourt, B. E. (2007, January 15). The mentally ill, behind bars. *The New York Times.* Retrieved from the World Wide Web on October 31, 2007: http://www.law.uchicago.edu/news/harcourt-mentally-ill-prisoners/index.html.

Hassine, V. (1996). *Life without parole: Living in prison today.* Los Angeles: Roxbury.

Human Rights Watch (2003). *Ill equipped: U.S. prisons and offenders with mental illness.* New York, NY.

Izumi, L. T., Schiller, M., & Hayward, S. (1996). *Corrections, criminal Justice, and the mentally Ill: Some observations about costs in California: Mental health briefing.* San Francisco, Pacific Research Institute.

James, D., & Glaze, L. (2006). *Mental health problems of prison and jail inmates.* Bureau of Justice Statistics: Special Report, NCJ 213600, Washington, D.C.

Krelstein, M. S. (2002). The role of mental health in the inmate disciplinary process: A national survey. *The Journal of the American Academy of Psychiatry and the Law* 30, pp. 488–496.

Lamb, R., Weinberger, L., & Gross, B. (2003). Mentally ill persons in the criminal justice system: Some perspectives. *Psychiatric Quarterly, 75(2)*, 107–126.

Madrid v. Gomez, 889 F. Supp. 1146 (N.D. Cal. 1995).

Mears, D., & Castro, J. (2006). Warden's views on the wisdom of supermax facilities. *Crime and Delinquency* 52(3), pp. 398–431.

Metzner, J. L. (2007, September 1). Evolving issues in correctional psychiatry. *Psychiatric Times, 24*, 10. Retrieved from the World Wide Web on November 5, 2007: http://www.psychiatrictimes.com/showArticle.jhtml?articleID=201802883.

Metzner, J., Cohen, F., Grossman, L. S., & Wettstein, R. M. (1998). Treatment in jails and prisons, in Robert M. Wittstein, ed. *Treatment of Offenders with Mental Disorders in Jails and Prisons*, pp. 230–233.

Miller, R., & Metzner, J. (1994). Psychiatric stigma in correctional facilities, *Bulletin of the American Academy of Psychiatric Law* 22, pp. 621–626.

National Alliance on Mental Illness (2004, March). Spending money in all the wrong places: Jails and prisons. Arlington, Virginia: Retrieved from the World Wide Web on October 31, 2007: http://www.nami.org/Template.cfm?Section=Fact_Sheets&Template=/ContentManagement/ContentDisplay.cfm&ContentID=14593.

National Association of State Mental Health Program Directors Research Institute (2000). Closing and reorganizing state psychiatric hospitals: 2000. Retrieved March 1, 2001 from www.rdmc.org/nri/SH_RPT.pdf.

National Commission on Correctional Health Care (1992). Mental health services in correctional settings. Retrieved on October 30, 2007 from http://www.ncchc.org/resources/statements/mentalhealth.html.

National Institute of Corrections (2001). Provision of Mental Health Care in Prisons.

Pfeifer, M. B. (2007, March 1). Prison: A wasteland for mentally ill. The New York Times. Retrieved on October 30, 2007 from http://www.boston.com/news/globe/editorial_opinion/oped/articles/2007/03/01/prison_a_wasteland_for_mentally_ill?mode=PF.

Ruiz v. Johnson, 37 F. Supp.2nd 855 S.D. Texas, 1999.

Satel, S. (2003). Out of the asylum, into the cell. *The New York Times*, November 1, 2003, Section A; Column 1, New York.

Sixty Minutes (2007 , February 11). The death of Timothy Souder. (Retrieved on October 30, 2007, from: http://www.cbsnews.com/stories/2007/02/08/60minutes/main2448074.shtml.

Stone, T.H. (1997) Therapeutic implications of incarceration for persons with severe mental disorders: searching for rational health policy. *American Journal of Criminal Law* 24, pp. 283–358.

Teplin, L. (1994). Psychiatric and substance abuse disorders among male urban jail detainees, *American Journal of Public Health* 84, pp. 290–292.

Teplin, L. (1984). Criminalizing mental disorder: The comparative arrest rate of the mentally ill. *American Psychologist* 39, pp. 794–803.

Wyatt v. Stickney. 325 F. Supp 781(M.D. Ala.1971).

CHAPTER 10

PSYCHOLOGICAL PROFILES OF CRIMINAL JUSTICE PRACTITIONERS: HOW EXPERIENCES AND ATTITUDES SHAPE THE TREATMENT OF THOSE WITH MENTAL ILLNESSES

By Anand Pandya, M.D., Richard Lamb, M.D. and Suzanne Vogel-Scibilia, M.D.

"[S]he became the unsuspecting victim of a sick man and an equally sick system."

—Kim Webdale[1]

Introduction

Although deinstitutionalization provides the most important recent historical context for understanding the treatment of individuals with mental illnesses within the criminal justice system, a longer historical view shows us that prior to the establishment of a medical model for mental illness, the sys-

---

1. Kim Webdale referring in congressional testimony to her sister Kendra's death at the hands of Andrew Goldstein and the sick system that had ignored Goldstein's need for treatment, in Webdale, K. (2000, September, 21). *Testimony before the Subcommittee on Crime of the Committee on the Judiciary, U.S. House of Representatives.* Retrieved January 27, 2008 from the World Wide Web: http://commdocs.house.gov/committees/judiciary/hju67345.000/hju67345_0f.htm.

tem of criminal incarceration routinely overlapped with the system of care for those with mental illnesses. For example, the infamous *Asylum de Bicêtre* in Paris, where the Marquis de Sade was incarcerated, functioned simultaneously as a prison and a place for treatment of mental illness (Zilboorg, 1941). Thus, when Philippe Pinel removes the shackles from individuals suffering from mental illnesses in that asylum in 1793, an act that is often seen as a turning point for the whole field of psychiatry (Zilboorg, 1941), he was practicing what we would now call correctional psychiatry.

The long history of psychiatric treatment within the correctional setting would seem to offer a simple solution to the problems laid out in the earlier chapters, yet punishment rather than treatment remains the norm. With so many individuals with mental illnesses in the criminal justice system, why aren't more mental health practitioners working with this population? And what are the attitudes of uniformed criminal justice practitioners towards those with mental illnesses? This chapter answers both of these questions by providing two profiles: first an exploration of mental health providers and then an exploration of uniformed criminal justice practitioners.

A comprehensive review of all the factors that contribute to the limitations of correctional mental health systems is beyond the scope of a single chapter. It would need to cover the cultural and political forces that drive the correctional system towards retribution and away from investment in rehabilitation as well as the complexities of healthcare finance (a system that is in crisis in civil as well as correctional systems). Arguably these larger cultural and economic forces play a bigger role in the limitations of correctional mental health care than the factors that we consider here, all of which are on the level of individuals and internal psychological processes. Nonetheless, by attempting to put a human face on both mental health providers and uniformed criminal justice practitioners, we hope to open the door to a more complex analysis that a system-level theory alone cannot provide.

Attitudes towards Mentally Ill Offenders and the Criminal Justice System among Mental Health Providers: Biases and the Challenges of Developing a Committed Workforce

Mr. R. was a 27 year old unmarried man with a diagnosis of schizophrenic disorder, paranoid type. As a child and adolescent, he had no friends. He had all failing grades in his sophomore year of high school and, at this point, dropped out of school and continued living with his parents. He worked briefly at several fast food restaurants but was unable to do these jobs and was fired each time. At age 18, he was caught in a grocery store trying to steal some aluminum foil to be used to protect himself from "the x-rays." When approached by a store employee, he assaulted the employee, was arrested and taken to jail. He was seen by the jail psychiatrist who gave him a diagnosis of schizophrenic disorder, paranoid type. Anti-psychotic medications were prescribed but Mr. R did not believe he was ill and refused to take them. The jail psychiatrist wanted him hospitalized, but the County hospital admitting psychiatrist said he had no beds available and, in any case, Mr. R already had a place to stay, namely jail. Finally, Mr. R began to take medications, went into partial remission and was released by the judge to the family with a recommendation for psychiatric outpatient treatment.

Mr. R's parents took him to a community mental health clinic where the intake team concluded, "This person's non-adherence to psychiatric medications along with his history of violence could make him a problem in management beyond the capabilities of this clinic. Perhaps if we had outpatient commitment in this state, it would be different, though, even so, most of our staff would be reluctant to try." Mr. R was not accepted for treatment. After several weeks, Mr. R, who still did not believe he was ill, stopped taking his medications, again became psychotic and went to a supermarket where he stole some candy and was arrested for petty theft. In jail, he began to take medications, was released after a month with a sentence of time served and was again not accepted for treatment by the outpatient clinic. Over the next few years, this behavior was repeated a number of times. Finally, he was charged with petty theft with priors and assault and sentenced to a year in jail. Four months after Mr. R was released, he committed a similar offense and appeared in court. The judge felt he had no alternative but to send Mr. R to state prison. Criminalization was now confirmed.

Clearly, most mental health treatment facilities are not structured to successfully treat persons like Mr. R. and, as described in this chapter, community mental health staff are often reluctant to try. The reaction of many mental health professionals to the treatment of offenders with severe mental illnesses is important to note. That reaction generally is to avoid doing it. Before the National Alliance on Mental Illness (NAMI) began, persons with severe mental illnesses had the lowest priority in the mental health system; this was especially true in community mental health. This has changed, largely as a result of the advocacy of NAMI (Lamb, 1998), and persons with severe mental illnesses now have a very high priority, especially if they do not require psychiatric inpatient treatment, are adherent to psychiatric medications and are not violent. But a serious problem remains—those most in need are still avoided. Mental health professionals are disinclined to attempt to treat persons with severe mental illnesses, including severely mentally ill offenders, who may require expensive resources such as acute and long-term hospitalization, who have a history of being non-adherent to treatment, including medications, and who have a history of and/or pose a threat of violence. Lacking treatment, very large numbers of such persons commit a variety of minor, and sometimes major offenses as a result of their illnesses and thus find their way into our jails and prisons (Lamb & Weinberger, 2005).

Professionals in the mental health system are generally very selective in whom they choose to treat. They can do that because those most difficult to treat and most expensive to treat can simply be left in the criminal justice system. This is rationalized in a variety of ways—"they are just drug abusers," "they are really criminals," "if we only had more community treatment they could and would be treated successfully in the community." However, involuntary forms of community treatment, which is what many of these persons need, are not what many mental health professionals have in mind when they advocate community treatment.

A system of community treatment that relies solely on voluntary compliance may not provide adequate structure for many persons with severe mental illnesses (Belcher, 1988). Also needed for many severely mentally ill offenders are such mechanisms as outpatient commitment, court-monitored treatment, treatment as a condition of probation or parole, and psychiatric conservatorship (Lamb & Weinberger, 2005; Torrey, 1997; Swanson, Swartz, George, et al, 1997; Gerbasi, Bonnie, & Binder, 2000; Segal & Burgess, 2006).

Assertive Case Management

It is important to recognize that persons with severe mental disorders who are discharged from psychiatric hospitals or correctional institutions experience multiple problems that often cannot be adequately treated in traditional community-based facilities (Lamb & Weinberger, 1998). Thus placement in the community often results in repeated rehospitalization or reincarceration. Assertive case management, often involuntary, and as part of a comprehensive treatment program of psychiatric medication, supportive housing, and vocational rehabilitation, can reduce this cycle (Wilson, Tien, & Eaves, 1995).

The great majority of persons with severe mental illnesses need the basic elements of case management, which starts with the premise that each person has a designated professional with overall responsibility for his or her care (Dvoskin & Steadman, 1994). The case manager formulates an individualized treatment and rehabilitation plan with the participation of the mentally ill person and often the supervision of the court. There is an emphasis on patients' abilities to handle transition from incarceration to the community. As care progresses, the case manager monitors the mentally ill person to determine if he or she is receiving and complying with treatment, has an appropriate living situation, has adequate funds, and has access to vocational rehabilitation.

An assertive case management program deals with patients on a frequent and long-term basis, using a hands-on approach that may necessitate meeting with clients "on their own turf" or even seeing patients daily (Wilson, Tien, & Eaves, 1995). This form of contact and familiarity with clients helps the case manager and client anticipate and prevent significant decompensation.

It must be recognized, however, that before assertive case management can be practiced with persons with severe mental illnesses, including mentally ill offenders, mental health agencies in the community must be able to provide the degree of structure and limit setting needed by many of these persons. For instance, staff should insist that patients' days be structured through meaningful, therapeutic activities such as work, day treatment, and various forms of social therapy.

Staff needs to feel safe if their treatment is to be effective. Toward that end, mental health administrators need to take measures to ensure the safety of staff, such as metal detectors, adequate numbers of security personnel and readily available ways to summon them. When highly structured 24-hour care is required, it is important to have easy access to it.

The role of family members is an important aspect in the care of mentally ill offenders (Lamb, Weinberger, & Gross, 2004). Often overlooked are family members' needs for guidance and support. Families should be instructed in ways to help stabilize their relative. They should also be involved in support programs to help them during crises and in self-help programs so they can benefit from the experience of other families in similar situations.

Some Problem Attitudes
of Mental Health Professionals

Unfortunately, mental health professionals may be reluctant to treat mentally ill offenders, especially when there is a history of violence. If this barrier is to be overcome, mental health professionals must do a realistic assessment of the potential for violence, have adequate security, and take advantage of the important advances that have been made in recent years in the management of the violent behavior of severely mentally ill persons (Harris & Rice, 1997). Behavior therapy, antipsychotic medications, and adequately structured community housing are but a few examples.

A significant increase in mental health services for severely mentally ill persons, from outpatient treatment and assertive case management, both voluntary and involuntary, to highly structured 24-hour care, would no doubt result in far fewer mentally ill persons committing criminal offenses. However, the criminal justice system must not be viewed by mental health professionals as an appropriate substitute for the mental health system. The criminal justice system has been set up to reduce crime and to punish offenders. It is only with considerable difficulty that effective treatment can be practiced there. To the extent possible, treatment should take place in the mental health system rather than the criminal justice system.

Moreover, an enormous stigma is attached to people who have been categorized as both a person with mental illness and as an offender, and it is thus extremely difficult to place them in community mental health treatment and housing. Mental health providers may feel that such persons may re-offend and that they may be violent. These providers may also believe, often rightly so, that their facility, be it case management unit, clinic, day hospital or 24-hour residential treatment program, does not allow them to provide sufficient structure. Moreover, they may not want to provide the amount of structure that may be necessary.

Clearly, many persons with severe mental illnesses who commit criminal offenses present formidable challenges to treatment because of their treatment resistance, poor adherence with antipsychotic medications, potential dangerousness, high rate of substance abuse, and need for structure (Lamb, Weinberger, & Gross, 1999). To a large extent, the public mental health system has given up on them and allowed them to become the responsibility of the criminal justice system.

Using Authority Comfortably

A clear conception of the clinical uses and therapeutic value of authority appears to be a cornerstone of successful community treatment for severely mentally ill offenders (Lamb, Weinberger, & Gross, 1999). There is a need for treatment staff that are comfortable using authority and setting limits. When treatment is effective, the staff are not ambivalent about the use of authority. They are comfortable with insisting consistently and reasonably that any imposed conditions of probation or parole be followed, with monitoring patients' adherence to prescribed psychoactive medications, and with monitoring patients to detect the use of alcohol or illegal drugs. Staff do not have problems in insisting that patients live in appropriately structured and supportive residential settings as a condition for remaining in the community. They are willing to promptly rehospitalize patients at times of crises. If persons are on probation or parole, treatment staff are willing to recommend revocation of their community status and to return them to the responsible criminal justice agency with the opinion that community treatment is no longer appropriate.

On the other hand, staff ambivalence about using authority appears to be a major barrier to treatment. While there is certainly far more to treatment than setting limits and conducting surveillance, mental health professionals who complain that "I didn't go into this field to become a cop" may feel ambivalent about enforcing the conditions of this type of treatment or may have a need to always be the "good guy" with their patients. Under these circumstances, treatment will probably not go well.

It is crucial to tailor mental health services to meet the needs of mentally ill offenders and not treat them as if they were all compliant and cooperative, and in need of a minimum of controls. The lives of a large proportion are characterized by chaos, anxiety, sadness, and deprivation as they try to survive in a world for which they are ill prepared. They cry out for treatment and for structure, and it is the obligation of the mental health system to provide it. If effective and appropriate interventions are provided, these individuals may not only improve psychiatrically but may also engage in considerably less criminal behavior. For this to happen, there needs to be considerable change in the attitudes and biases of many mental health professionals.

A Psychological Profile of Law Enforcement: Increased Risk for Alcoholism and Post Traumatic Stress Disorder

Robert is a 26-year-old part-time patrolman for two local police forces who works about 55 hours a week. Because of his part-time status for both jobs, he carries no health insurance. The shifts are different between the two jobs so he also works irregular hours. One job involving 30 hours a week is in an urban area with a large number of violent crimes and drug offenses. The other job is with a suburban police department that is spread out over a large area that has frequent traffic accidents. During the suburban police shifts he often works alone at night. Robert has had a history of depression and anxiety since childhood when his parents went through a bitter divorce. He has taken antidepressant medication off and on for many years, but self discontinued it when he lost his parents' health insurance after his college graduation. He confides to a female co-worker that he is not sleeping and having nightmares involving visions of traffic fatalities and gunshot victims he has seen during his work. He feels anxious before and after work, often going out to bars to drink "a few" after his shifts. In addition to his sleep being disturbed, he feels his mood is more irritable. Lately, he finds himself getting angry at motorists who run out of gas or victims of domestic violence who are afraid to press charges. He reflects on being "burnt out" and "soured" towards the work he used to enjoy. He is unable to pursue his fitness work-outs or date socially because of his erratic and heavy job schedule. He would like to pursue a master's degree in social work but worries that this job has "ruined" him for work with the public. He does not believe he has depression— "It's the stress of this work—I've been fine for years". He is hesitant to present for treatment because he fears it will effect his plans to advance in the department. He swears his co-worker to secrecy and offers to take her out for a drink after work.

Although the problems and solutions listed so far in this chapter are an important factor in the psychiatric care of mentally ill offenders, the attitudes of law enforcement and criminal justice practitioners provides a much larger piece of the puzzle. This is an inevitable consequence of the fact that mental health treatment is not the main purpose of the criminal justice system and although the needs are great, anyone accused of a crime in this country will spend a lot more time with police officers, correctional officers, parole officers, probation officers and officers of the court than with mental health providers.

Some of the attitudes of practitioners within the criminal justice system are logical inverses of attitudes listed above for mental health practitioners. Just as mental health providers do not go into their field to be police officers, police officers do not go into their field to be mental health providers.

Tthe nature of criminal justice work is inherently more dangerous than most mental health work, and exposure to these hazards has psychological consequences that will further affect the treatment of mentally ill offenders. Elevated rates of stress-related psychiatric symptoms including Post-Traumatic Stress Disorder (PTSD), depression, anxiety and suicide have caused alarm within the law enforcement community (Collins & Gibbs, 1997). PTSD is a psychiatric illness defined as "the development of characteristic (anxiety and mood) symptoms following exposure to extreme traumatic stress involving direct personal experience of an event that involves actual or threatened death or serious injury, or other threat to one's physical integrity; or witnessing an event that involves death, injury or a threat to the physical integrity of another person." (American Psychiatric Association, 2000).

Post traumatic stress disorder is common within the first-responder occupations. In one study of suburban US police officers, over 13% met diagnostic criteria for PTSD (Robinson, Sigman & Wilson, 1997). Statistical regression analysis of this data showed that the best predictor of PTSD symptoms was exposure to death risk or life-threatening harm. Of officers who responded that they had PTSD symptoms, 63% stated that critical incident debriefing would be beneficial after stressful duty-related events (Robinson et al., 1997).

The diagnosis of PTSD requires symptoms in three separate categories: re-experiencing, numbing/avoiding and hyper-vigilance (American Psychiatric Association, 2000). Although re-experiencing and hyper-vigilance symptoms such as having nightmares, flashbacks, feeling anxious and jumpy are part of the popular conception of this disorder, according to some studies, the numbing and avoiding symptoms appear to be the most important in making the diagnosis (North et al., 2005). Although there are many possible numbing and avoiding symptoms, they all share in common that they lead an individual who has had a trauma to avoid thoughts and feelings that they associate with the trauma. When considering the response of criminal justice practitioners to mentally ill offenders, it is fruitful to consider the effects of these numbing and avoiding symptoms. Encountering an individual with mental illness exposes a police officer to the ill individual's emotional world that may contain much paranoia and anxiety. Criminal justice practitioners who are trying to avoid re-experiencing the thoughts and feelings of past traumatic events may have a particularly hard time being empathic to such mentally ill offenders. Furthermore, this numbing and avoiding is not experienced as a symptom of a disease by most individuals with PTSD. Most traumatized criminal justice practitioners may not notice that they are less empathic in such settings and if they did notice, they would probably believe that they are just "tuning out" a lot of distractions that would interfere with doing their job properly.

A related psychological phenomenon that may also impair criminal justice practitioners' capacities to provide sensitive treatment to those with mental illnesses is the symptom of dissociation. Dissociation is defined as "a disruption in the usually integrated functions of consciousness, memory, identity or perception of the environment" (American Psychiatric Association, 2000). Dissociative symptoms include amnesia as well as feelings that one's environment is unreal or that one is outside of his/her own body and observing personal actions from a distance (American Psychiatric Association, 2000). Carlier et al. (1996) found over ten years ago that the presence of PTSD or partial PTSD symptoms predicted dissociative symptoms in law enforcement personnel. Thus, criminal justice personnel who are grappling with past traumas are likely to also be coping with dissociative symptoms that further impair their performance when interacting with mentally ill offenders.

Although there is no way to make the criminal justice system completely safe from traumatic experiences, there are factors that can increase or decrease the risk of developing PTSD when exposed to such traumas. Notably, many factors that correlate with mental health effects are organizational issues such as work demands that impact one's home life, lack of control over workload, excessive work load, lack of ability to consult or communicate within the profession, and inadequate professional support. 1206 county police officers were given the General Health Questionnaire (GHQ) to assess levels of psychological strain. The upper 40th percentile reporting the highest levels of stress ranked both personal and occupational stressors higher than those who reported lower stress levels. This suggests that individuals who experience high stress tend to perceive all types of stressors as having a greater magnitude. The study further demonstrated an association between gender and ill psychological health—women are more likely to score higher on negative health questions in the GHQ (Collins & Gibbs, 2003).

In another study of 103 police personnel (Violanti & Arons, 1993), police organizational issues that created stress increased subjective psychological distress in the respondents by a factor of 6.3 times more than inherent police work stress. Since occupational culture is a significant factor in the development of psychiatric symptoms, changes in police management policies could reduce stress and psychiatric illnesses (see Slate, Johnson, & Colbert, 2007).

Police work stress and health research have produced few comprehensive national studies. One recent country-wide study of Norwegian police officers' physical and mental health as compared to Norwegian physicians and members of the general population provides insight into the relationship of both mental and physical health. Police, compared to another high risk group, physicians, showed more subjective health complaints and depersonalization (Berg, Hem, Lau & Eckeberg, 2006). The frequency of job pressure and lack of support were associated with both mental health and physical problems. Females showed more anxiety than males, and males showed more depression than females (Berg et al., 2006). Another study of 655 urban police officers showed no significant gender differences in PTSD symptoms, but did clearly replicate previous findings of greater PTSD symptoms in Hispanic-American police officers as compared to European-American and African-American colleagues (Pole et al., 2001).

Law enforcement duty especially in the United States creates long and erratic work hours often with fluctuating shift schedules and unit understaffing (Vila, 2006). Regular sleep patterns are often compromised. Little is known about how law enforcement incidents producing significant exposure to stress change an individual's sleep further. One study documented an increase in nightmares with critical incident exposure, yet routine work stress caused more changes in sleep quality (Neylan et al., 2002).

A similar dearth of information involves the impact of occupational work stress on aging criminal justice workers. One study on police officers over the age of 50 found two statistically significant associated risk factors for perceived increased work stress—exposure to actual risk and inappropriate coping behaviors such as chemical use or problematic gambling (Gershon, Lin & Li, 2002). In this study, perceived work stress was associated with a large number of symptoms such as chronic back pain, alcohol abuse, inappropriate aggressive behavior, PTSD symptoms, other physical health complaints, anxiety and depression.

Given this broad range of occupational risks that can affect interactions with mentally ill offenders, it becomes important to identify any protective factors or risk factors that influence who will develop these disorders. Clinicians have long sought to delineate both risk and resilience features for PTSD. Researchers in a San Francisco Veteran's Center have proposed a conceptual model for the development of PTSD symptoms which found multiple individual differences that increased one's risk of PTSD. Four of the strongest variables are greater distress at the time of the trauma, greater dissociation at the time of the trauma, greater routine work environment stress and lower levels of social supports (Marmar, 2006). Individual characteristics such as alexithymia, a lack of ability to verbalize feelings, are also associated with an increased risk of developing PTSD (McCaslin et al., 2006).

Recent literature has focused on law enforcement personnel suicide as an inevitable consequence of untreated depression and/or PTSD. Some research has documented a two to three times higher suicide rate for police over that of the general population (Slovenko, 1999; Mohandie & Hatcher, 1999). Recent work using stricter methodological techniques has found an incidence of suicide slightly lower than or equal to the general population (Berg, Hem Lau, Loeb & Ekeberg, 2003; Marzuk, Nock, Leon, Portera & Tardiff, 2002; Hem, Berg & Ekeberg, 2001). These lower rates need to be interpreted within the context of psychological screening, monitoring and fitness for duty evaluations inherent in police officer selection. The fact that these safeguards do not more substantially reduce the rate of suicide speaks to the combined effect of stress and ready access to weapons. In fact, most police suicides occur by use of firearms, a logical outcome in a population with easy access to guns and with individuals who are familiar and comfortable with firearm use (Heiman, 1977; Heiman 1975). Excessive alcohol use, a risk factor for suicides even in the general population, has been found to be common among law enforcement personnel (Davey, Obst & Sheehan, 2000; Richmond, Wodak, Kehoe & Heather, 1998; Violanti, Marshall & Howe 1985; Richmond, Kehoe, Hailstone, Wodak & Uebel-Yan, 1999). The risk of alcoholism, the risk of suicide and the risk of PTSD are all closely interwoven. Violanti (2004) has demonstrated that exposure to work events and symptoms of PTSD significantly increases the amount of alcohol used and the rates of suicidal thoughts among a group of 934 police officers, though older officers had lower rates suggesting better and more varied coping skills. Traumatic work exposure increases the risk of PTSD symptoms. These PTSD symptoms then increase the risk of suicidal thoughts and alcohol use. Factoring in the impact of PTSD and increased alcohol use causes a ten-fold increase in suicidal ideation (Violanti, 2004). Of course, as important as this pathway is, alcoholism and trauma are not the only predictive factors for suicide in the criminal justice field. As with the general population, a broad variety of stress increases the risk of suicide. Serious suicidal ideation has been associated with subjective health complaints, separated or divorced marital status, anxiety or depression (Berg et al., 2003). However, because these other complaints are seen at increased rates in individuals with trauma and alcoholism, it is difficult to sort out cause and effect.

Biological Effects

PTSD is known to cause a variety of biological changes that have been observed in criminal justice providers with this disorder. These include higher cortisol levels which are needed in periods of increased body stress, smaller brain volumes in one area, the hippocampus, associated with emotional regulation (Lindauer, Olff, van Meijel, Carlier & Gersons, 2006; Lindauer, Vlieger, Jalink, Olff, Carlier, Majoie, den Heeten & Gersons, 2004) and less brain activation in another brain area, the medial frontal gyrus, that is involved in logic, abstract thought and decision making (Lindauer, Booij, Habraken, Uylings, Olff, Carlier, den Heeten, van Eck-Smit & Gersons, 2004). These biologically based brain changes in law enforcement personnel suggest that psychiatric assessment and intervention for severe or persistent symptoms should be considered. Recent scrutiny has centered on the importance of having at-risk individuals seek appropriate help to lessen symptoms and disability despite reluctance within the profession to seek professional care.

Law enforcement personnel have often been described as being hesitant to seek help for psychological symptoms. 3,272 Norwegian police officers were assessed for frequency of help-seeking behavior compared to similar individuals in the general population. While help-seeking is generally unaffected by age, gender differences have been noted. Female police personnel were more likely than their male counterparts to contact health professionals of any kind. In the area of mental health care seeking, less than 10% of those reporting anxiety, depression or serious suicidal ideation had contacted a psychologist or psychiatrist. Using medication to cope with stress presented the strongest association with seeking help from a medical provider (Berg et al., 2006).

Peer Interventions May Help Criminal Justice Practitioners Overcome Their Attitude towards Mental Health Treatment

The logical next step for law enforcement personnel and administrators is to address the significant risk factors for work-related psychological distress with a comprehensive management plan. Traditional approaches to addressing work-related stress have often included fitness-for-duty assessments and reassignments that can produce significant stigma. Such consequences may produce substantial barriers to acknowledging psychological stress at the worksite and may even deter individuals from seeking counseling or psychiatric evaluations using their paid health insurance for fear that information about their condition may become available to their employers. Psychiatric treatments can be effective for reducing the symptoms of PTSD, depression, and other disorders associated with trauma, and many individual uniformed officers who have received such help have had full recovery of functioning both at work and at home. Some individuals do not respond to medication and some individuals will remain unable to function under the stress of frontline work but a larger barrier in many institutions may be a workplace culture that is unwilling to completely reassess the functional capacity of criminal justice practitioners who have recovered. Ongoing distrust by colleagues and employers that such recovery is possible can have long-lasting effects on the careers of those who seek help.

After 26 suicides occurred within the New York City Police Department (NYPD) over a two year period in 1994 and 1995, a non-departmental officer assistance program utilizing peer support counselors targeted police personnel who were reluctant to present for traditional forms of psychological support. These counselors were experienced officers from diverse backgrounds with the NYPD who received structured training in providing peer-based support (Dowling, Genet & Moynihan, 2005; Dowling, Moynihan, Genet & Lewis, 2006). The program, Police Organization Providing Peer Assistance (POPPA), stressed confidentiality and maintained a 24 hour telephone service where any officer could call in to discuss either personal or occupation-related concerns. The next day, or even the same day if needed, a trained peer specialist would have a personal session with the caller. Approximately three fourths of calls resulted in a face-to-face follow-up. This program was put to the test after the terror attacks on September 11, 2001. POPPA staff provided some of the most comprehensive data from ground zero law enforcement workers by doing surveys within their previously developed support and assistance framework. 28,232 of approximately 39,000 possible NYPD officers participated in the POPPA interviews (Dowling, Moynihan, Genet & Lewis, 2006). Despite these interviews occurring 15–27 months after the events of 9-11, over 34% related at least one current behavioral symptom such as hypervigilance or social isolation/withdrawal in response to the attacks. Greater than half described at least one emotional reaction such as sadness, irritability or anxiety. More than 43% reported one physical complaint such as headaches, insomnia or fatigue—while 24% endorsed a cognitive symptom such as impaired concentration or intrusive thoughts of the attacks. In total, over 68% of NYPD police personnel admitted at least one stress complaint related to the terrorist attack including 28% who had three or more. Besides documenting the marked residual stress reactions, POPPA also proved its effectiveness in providing the peer-supported contacts necessary to acquire the data needed to complete such a comprehensive study (Dowling, Moynihan, Genet & Lewis, 2006). Utilizing similar models of peer support and assistance in other programs would be a viable start in addressing psychological stress reactions and in ameliorating co-morbid psychiatric illness more comprehensively for law enforcement personnel.

9-11 Opens Old Wounds

Mr. S has worked for the NYC Sheriff's Office since before the 9-11 attacks and was involved in that disaster response. Although he was nowhere near the World Trade Center on the day of the attacks, he knows several individuals who died. His own motivation for entering law enforcement stems from another tragedy over a decade earlier when a lone gunman went on a shooting spree in a fast food restaurant in his neighborhood. Mr. S remembers hearing those gunshots from a few doors away. Mr. S was a teenager at that time and remembered the fear when he heard the gunshots from a few doors down and later thinking that he could have easily been one of those victims. That experience motivated him to enter a career that involved protecting his community. As a member of the Sheriff's Office, he is called upon to remove mentally ill individuals who have court orders requiring transportation to an emergency department for evaluation. This responsibility became a function of the Sheriff's Office after the New York Police Department refused to be involved in such transportations in the 1990s. Mr. S frequently ruminates about 9-11 and the people he knows who died in that tragedy. While other officers who were involved spend less time thinking and talking about 9-11, Mr. S gets more worked up when he talks about 9-11 and resents those who he feels "forgot their fallen brothers." Mr. S has learned that discussing this is a good way to get into an unproductive argument so he generally keeps to himself, preferring not to talk about anything rather than having "stupid conversations about stuff that doesn't matter." Mr. S does not discuss the shooting from his childhood although he was in greater danger during that attack than during 9-11. Mr. S's family has noticed that the righteous anger that Mr. S expresses around 9-11 resembles the strong feelings Mr. S had after the shooting when he dedicated his life to defending the community, but they had long ago learned not to talk with Mr. S about the shooting.

Recently, Mr. S and his partner were called upon for a removal of Mr. D, a mentally ill man. Mr. D answered the door holding a cat. When he was informed by Mr. S that he would need to go with them to the hospital, Mr. D asked to put some food out for the cat, first. Mr. S accompanied Mr. D to the kitchen where the cat jumped out of Mr. D's hands onto a counter where a gun was sitting. Between the sudden movement of the cat and the realization that there was a gun in the room, Mr. S was startled and instantly tried to regain control of the situation. He suddenly grabbed Mr. D and pulled him out of the kitchen. Mr. D who was unstable on his feet as a side effect of his medication ended up stumbling across the living room trying to regain his balance. Mr. S's partner may have momentarily wondered whether Mr. S was overreacting but without knowing anything about what dangerous history this mentally ill man has, he quickly moved to help his partner, handcuffing Mr. D and hustling him quickly out of the apartment. Mr. S was convinced that Mr. D was "high on something" based on the way that he stumbled off balance, so he was far too preoccupied with this potentially dangerous situation to worry about closing the apartment door as they left. Later Mr. D filed a complaint about this violation of normal procedure but the report filed by Mr. S and his partner seem to suggest that Mr. D was sufficiently uncooperative and erratic to explain some of the deviation from standard practice. However, Mr. S's supervisors remain concerned about his capacity to handle the responsibilities of the job.

Conclusion

Most criminal justice practitioners, do not, of course, have PTSD. But more subtle problems such as the situation between Mr. S and Mr. D may occur without a full psychiatric diagnosis. Because of the tremendous stigma against getting mental health treatment, peer interventions such as POPPA may be a more effective way to handle such cases. However, even interventions such as POPPA require a tremendous culture change among criminal justice practitioners. The more fundamental problem remains that mental health professionals who are better equipped to handle interactions with the mentally ill are not involved in a large fraction of situations where criminal justice practitioners, ill-suited to take their place, must intervene. The psychological profile of criminal justice practitioners combined with their inadequate training about mental illness, make bad outcomes inevitable when the mentally ill are abandoned by the system of psychiatric care. Thus, along with a change in the culture of criminal justice practitioners, there must be a change in the culture of mental health practitioners.

References

American Psychiatric Association (2000). *Diagnostic and Statistical Manual of Mental Disorders: DSM-IV Text Revision*. Washington, D.C: Author.

Belcher, J. R. (1988). Are jails replacing the mental health system for the homeless mentally ill? *Community Mental Health Journal* 24, pp. 185–195.

Berg, A. M., Hem, E., Lau, B., & Ekeberg, O. (2006). An exploration of job stress and health in the Norwegian police service: a cross sectional study. *Journal of Occupational Medicine and Toxicology* 1, pp. 1–26.

Berg, A. M., Hem, E., Lau, B., Loeb, M., & Ekeberg, O. (2003). Suicidal Ideation and Attempts in Norwegian Police. *Suicide and Life Threatening Behavior* 33(3), pp. 302–312.

Collins, P. A., & Gibbs, A. C. (2003). Stress in police officers: a study of the origins, prevalence and severity of stress-related symptoms within a county police force. *Occupational Medicine* 53, pp. 256–264.

Carlier, I. V., Lamberts, R. D., Fouwels, A. J., & Gersons, B. P. (1996). PTSD in relation to dissociation in traumatized police officers. *American Journal of Psychiatry* 153(10), pp. 1325–1328.

Davey, J. D., Obst, P. L., & Sheehan, M. C. (2000). The use of AUDIT as a screening tool in the police workplace. *Drug and Alcohol Review* 19, pp. 49–54.

Dowling, F. G., Genet, B., & Moynihan, G. (2005). A confidential peer-based assistance program for police officers. *Psychiatric Services* 56 (7), pp. 870–871.

Dowling, F. G., Moynihan, G., Genet, B., & Lewis, J. (2006). A peer-based assistance program for Officers with the New York City Police Department: report of the effects of September 11, 2001. *American Journal of Psychiatry* 163, pp. 151–153.

Dvoskin, J. A., & Steadman, H. J. (1994). Using intensive case management to reduce violence by mentally ill persons in the community. *Hospital and Community Psychiatry* 45, pp. 679–684.

Gerbasi, J. B., Bonnie, R. J., & Binder, R. L. (2000). Resource document on mandatory outpatient treatment. *Journal of the American Academy of Psychiatry and the Law* 28, pp. 127–44.

Gershon, R. R., Lin, S., & Li, X. (2002). Work stress in aging police officers. *Journal of Occupational and Environmental Medicine* 44 (2), pp. 160–167.

Harris, G. T., & Rice, M. E. (1997). Risk appraisal and management of violent behavior. *Psychiatric Services* 48, pp. 1168–1176.

Hem, E., Berg, A. M., & Ekeberg, O. (2001) Suicide in Police—a critical review. *Suicide and Life Threatening Behavior, 31(2)*, 224.

Heiman, M. F. (1977). Suicide among police. *American Journal of Psychiatry* 134, pp. 1286–1290.

Heiman, M. F. (1975). The police suicide. *Journal of Police Science and Administration* 3, pp. 267–273.

Lamb, H. R. (1998). Deinstitutionalization at the beginning of the New Millennium. *Harvard Review of Psychiatry* 6, pp. 1–9.

Lamb, H. R., & Weinberger, L. E. (1998). Persons with severe mental illness in jails and prisons: a review. *Psychiatric Services* 49, pp. 483–492.

Lamb, H. R., & Weinberger, L. E. (2005). The shift of psychiatric inpatient care from hospitals to jails and prisons. *Journal of the American Academy of Psychiatry and the Law* 33(4), pp. 529–534.

Lamb, H. R., Weinberger, L. E., & Gross, B. H. (1999). Community treatment of severely mentally ill offenders under the jurisdiction of the criminal justice system: a review. *Psychiatric Services* 50, pp. 907–913.

Lamb, H. R., Weinberger, L. E., & Gross, B. H. (2004). Mentally ill persons in the criminal justice system: some perspectives. *Psychiatric Quarterly* 75, pp. 107–122.

Lindauer, R. J. L., Booij, J., Habraken, J. B. A., Uylings, H. B. M., Olff, M., Carlier, I. V. E., den Heeten, G. J., van Eck-Smit, B. L. F., & Gersons, B. P. R. (2004). Cerebral blood flow changes during script-driven imagery in police officers with posttraumatic stress disorder. *Biological Psychiatry* 56(11), pp. 853–861.

Lindauer, R. J. L., Olff, M., van Meijel, E. P. M., Carlier, I. V. E., & Gersons, B.P.R. (2006). Cortisol, Learning, Memory, and Attention in Relation to

Smaller Hippocampal Volume in Police Officers with Posttraumatic Stress Disorder. *Biological Psychiatry* 59(2), pp. 171–177.

Lindauer, R. J. L., Vlieger, E. J., Jalink, M., Olff, M., Carlier, I. V. E., Majoie, C. B. L. M., den Heeten G. J., & Gersons, B. P. R. (2004). Smaller hippocampal volume in Dutch police officers with posttraumatic stress disorder. *Biological Psychiatry* 56(5), pp. 356–363.

Marmar, C. R., McCaslin, S. E., Metzler, T. J., Best, S., Weiss, D. S., Fagan, J., Liberman, A., Pole, N., Otte, C., Yehuda, R., Mohr, D., & Neylan, T. (2006). Predictors of Posttraumatic Stress in Police and Other First Responders. *Annals of the New York Academy of Science* 1071, pp. 1–18.

Marzuk, P. M., Nock, M. K., Leon, A. C., Portera, L., & Tardiff, K. (2002). Suicide Among New York police Officers, 1977–1996. *American Journal of Psychiatry* 159(12), pp. 2069–2071.

McCaslin, S. E., Metzler, T. J., Best, S. R., Liberman, A., Weiss, D. S., Fagan, J., & Marmar, C.R. (2006). Alexithymia and PTSD symptoms in urban police officers: cross-sectional and prospective findings. *Journal of Traumatic Stress* 19(3), pp. 361–373.

Mohandie, K.,and Hatcher, C. (1999). Suicide and violence risk in law enforcement: Practical guidelines for risk assessment, prevention and intervention. *Behavioral Sciences and the Law, 17,* 357–376.

Neylan, T. C., Metzler, T. J., Best, S. R., Weiss, D. S., Fagan, J. A., Liberman, A., Rodgers, C., Vedantham, K., Brunet, A., Lipsey, T. L., & Marmar, C. R. (2002). Critical incident exposure and sleep quality in police officers. *Psychosomatic Medicine* 64(2), pp. 345–352.

North, C. S., Pfefferbaum, B., Narayanan, P., Theilman, S., McCoy G., Dumont, C., Kawasaki, A., Ryosho, N., & Spitznagel, E. L. (2005). Comparison of post-disaster psychiatric disorders after terrorist bombings in Nairobi and Oklahoma City. *British Journal of Psychiatry* 186, pp. 487–493.

Pole, N., Best, S. R., Weiss, D. S., Metzler, T., Liberman, A. M., Fagan, J., & Marmar, C. R. (2001). Effects on gender and ethnicity on duty-related post-traumatic stress syndrome among urban police officers. *Journal of Nervous and Mental Disorders* 189(7), pp. 442–448.

Richmond, R. L., Wodak, A., Kehoe, L., & Heather, N. (1998). How Healthy are Police? A survey of lifestyle factors. *Addiction* 93, pp. 1729–1737.

Richmond, R. L., Kehoe, L., Hailstone, S., Wodak, A., & Uebel-Yan, M. (1999) Quantitative and qualitative evaluations to change excessive drinking, smoking and stress in the police force. *Addiction* 94, pp. 1509–1521.

Robinson, H. M., Sigman, M. R., & Wilson, J. P. (1997). Duty-related stressors and PTSD symptoms in suburban police officers; *Psychological Reports* 81(3 Pt 1), pp. 835–845.

Segal, S. P., & Burgess, P. M. (2006). Conditional release: a less restrictive alternative to hospitalization? *Psychiatric Services* 57, pp. 1600–1606.

Slate, R. N., Johnson, W. W., & Colbert, S. (2007). Police stress: A structural model. *Journal of Police and Criminal Psychology* 22, pp. 102–112.

Slovenko, R. (1999). Police Suicide. *Medicine and the Law* 18, pp. 149–151.

Swanson, J. W., Swartz, M. S., George, L. K., Burns, B. J., Hiday, V. A., Borum, R., et al. (1997). Interpreting the effectiveness of involuntary outpatient commitment: a conceptual model. *Journal of the American Academy of Psychiatry and the Law* 25, pp. 5–16.

Torrey, E. (1997). *Out of the Shadows: Confronting America's Mental Illness Crisis*. New York: Wiley.

Vila, B. (2006) Impact of long work hours on police officers and the communities they serve. *American Journal of Indian Medicine* 49(11), pp. 972–80.

Violanti, J. M., (2004). Predictors of police suicide. *Suicide and Life Threatening Behavior* 34 (3), pp. 277–83.

Violanti, J. M., & Arons, F. (1993). Sources of police stressors, job attitudes, and psychological distress. *Psychological Reports* 72(3 Pt 1), pp. 899–904.

Violanti, J. M., Marshall, J. R., & Howe, B. (1985). Stress, coping and alcohol use: the police connection. *Journal of Police Science and Administration* 13, pp. 106–110.

Wilson, D., Tien, G., & Eaves, D. (1995). Increasing the community tenure of mentally disordered offenders: an assertive case management program. *International Journal of Law and Psychiatry* 18, pp. 61–69.

Zilboorg, G. (1941). *A History of Medical Psychology*. New York: W. W. Norton & Co.

CHAPTER 11

THE INTERSECTION OF MENTAL ILLNESS AND CRIMINAL LAW

By Ronald S. Honberg, J.D.

'[T]he execution of an insane person simply offends humanity'... ; it 'provides no example to others,' ... ; ... 'it is uncharitable to dispatch an offender into another world, when he is not of a capacity to fit himself for it,' ... ; 'madness is its own punishment,' ... ; 'and ... executing an insane person serves no retributive purpose.'

—Justice Anthony Kennedy, in *Panetti v. Quarterman*
127 S. Ct. 2842, (2007), citing Justice Thurgood Marshall

Introduction

Throughout history, legislators and jurists have struggled to develop workable formulations for fairly considering the impact of mental illness on the behavior of criminal defendants. As far back as the ancient Roman times, there is evidence that the Roman legal codes recognized that some individuals could not be held accountable for criminal acts because they were "lunatics" (Collins, Hinkelbein, & Schorgl, 2007).

In modern times, the struggle to understand mental illness and its impact on behavior and to develop workable standards for evaluating mental illness in criminal cases has continued. Highly publicized cases involving defendants with mental illnesses such as John Hinckley and Andrea Yates have sparked public debates about whether these illnesses should be recognized as an "excuse" in criminal trials and, if so, under what circumstances.

This chapter identifies several important points in the criminal process during which mental illness frequently arises as a factor and explains how the law has evolved or is evolving in these areas. As we begin this discussion, several clarifications are necessary.

First, there are actually several legal terms in the criminal law that address the possible existence of mental illness or mental incapacity. Before the impact of mental illness on a person's alleged criminal misconduct is ever considered, the question of mental capacity may arise in the context of determining whether a person is "competent" to be interrogated or "competent" to stand trial. And, competency issues may arise at other points in the process as well. For example, competency issues have become increasingly important in the ongoing debate about the application of the death penalty to people with mental illnesses.

Second, the term "competency" in the criminal law context is not the same as the term "insanity." As will be explained subsequently, different definitions and legal considerations apply to these terms.

Finally, it is important to recognize that mental illness or even severe mental illness does not automatically equate with "insanity" or "competence" in criminal cases. In fact, as will be discussed throughout this chapter, many defendants with long and well-documented histories of severe mental illness are nevertheless found to be "sane" or "competent" in criminal cases—some are even sentenced to death.

Legal Competence in Criminal Cases

As stated above, competency issues may arise at a number of points in the criminal justice process. For example, questions may arise about whether a person with schizophrenia who confesses to a crime is sufficiently competent to waive his or her right to counsel or to fully understand and respond to questions during interrogation. Subsequently, concerns may arise about whether a criminal defendant with a mental or cognitive impairment is competent to stand trial. And, competency issues may arise even after conviction and sentencing, particularly in capital cases where defendants have been sentenced to death. This section will focus on the important concerns that arise in the determination of whether a defendant is competent to stand trial. The questions surrounding post-conviction competency, particularly competence to be executed, are discussed in the latter part of this chapter.

Competency to Stand Trial

The due process clause of the 5th and 14th Amendments of the U.S. Constitution have been interpreted as requiring that a criminal defendant must be sufficiently competent to understand the criminal process and the nature of the charges he or she is facing and be able to participate meaningfully in his or her own defense (*Drope v. Missouri, 1975*). The antecedents of this important doctrine are rooted in the British Common Law. The noted British jurist William Blackstone stated in his Commentaries that individuals known to be "mentally defective" should neither be allowed to plead or stand trial in criminal cases (Blackstone, 1768). While there is evidence that this doctrine was adopted into modern American law, the first formal articulation of the test for determining competency was set forth by the U.S. Supreme Court in *Dusky v. U.S.* (1960).

In *Dusky*, the Court reversed the conviction of a criminal defendant on the ground that the trial court record was insufficient to find that the defendant was competent to stand trial. In a terse, two paragraph opinion, the Court stated that the test for determining competency must be "whether (the defendant) has sufficient present ability to consult with his lawyer with a reasonable degree of rational understanding—and whether he has a rational as well as factual understanding of the proceedings against him" (*Dusky v. U.S*, 1960).

Significantly, the Court recognized that intellectual capacity to understand the nature of criminal proceedings was not enough—the inquiry into competency must also take into consideration the subjective perceptions of the defendant about the charges and the nature and purpose of the criminal process. In subsequent years, jurists and mental health professionals have struggled to develop workable methods for accurately evaluating and adjudicating competency in criminal cases.

Who Is Responsible for Raising Issues of Competency to Stand Trial?

Questions concerning the competency of criminal defendants to stand trial may be raised by defense attorneys, prosecutors, or trial court judges. One might assume that defense attorneys are best positioned to raise concerns about competency. However, as a practical matter, defense attorneys vary significantly in their understanding of mental illness. This problem is further compounded because some defendants may refuse to allow their attorneys to raise issues concerning mental illness, even when the symptoms are obvious.

Prosecutors may sometimes possess information that raises concerns about competency, such as the report of an arresting officer or a mental health professional who has evaluated or treated the defendant in the jail setting. But, mounting pressures on prosecutors to convict criminals may mitigate against these individuals raising competency concerns even when they should.

Thus, the U.S. Supreme Court has held on several occasions that ultimate responsibility for determining competency is vested with trial court judges whenever reasonable doubts arise (*Pate v. Robinson*, 1966). And, this responsibility includes ordering a competency evaluation if the demeanor or behavior of the defendant before the judge suggests that reasonable concerns about competency exist.

What Is the Standard for Determining Competency to Stand Trial?

As stated above, the Supreme Court in *Dusky* held that to be found competent, criminal defendants must have the present ability to consult with their attorney and participate meaningfully in their own defense. Does this merely require that defendants have the requisite intelligence to generally understand the criminal justice process or rather that they rationally understand the nature of the charges filed against them and how the criminal process relates to their particular circumstances?

The language of the Court's opinion in *Dusky* might seem to suggest the latter. However, state legislatures and courts have generally set a very low threshold for finding criminal defendants competent to stand trial. If a person has a rudimentary understanding of the nature of the charges that have been filed, the purpose of standing trial, the respective roles of defense counsel, prosecutor and judges, and the potential consequences of conviction, many courts will find that individual competent to stand trial. Even if the defendant's beliefs are colored by delusional thinking, this may not be enough to meet the threshold of being found incompetent to stand trial.

Consider the case of Scott Panetti, a man with schizophrenia. Panetti, who had an extensive history of severe mental illness with 14 hospitalizations in the 6 years preceding his crime, was tried for the capital murder of his parents-in-law in 1992. Despite testimony that he was highly delusional and unable to rationally consult with his attorney, he was found competent to stand trial. At trial, Panetti represented himself, dressed in a cowboy outfit, and attempted to subpoena Jesus Christ, John F. Kennedy and Anne Bancroft. He frequently spoke in a rambling, incoherent manner, asking irrational questions and citing biblical passages that had no apparent relevance to his case. Nevertheless, the trial proceeded, he was convicted, and sentenced to death (Blumenthal, 2004).

The difficulty of determining whether a defendant with a mental illness is competent to stand trial is compounded by the nature of these illnesses and the difficulty of accurately assessing an individual's state of mind at a given point of time. The symptoms of mental illnesses such as schizophrenia fluctuate in severity over time. An individual may be quite lucid and rational at one particular moment and delusional and irrational at another. Moreover, unlike mental retardation, severe mental illnesses do not necessarily result in impaired intelligence. Thus, an individual with schizophrenia may be perfectly capable of intellectually understanding the trial process and the nature of charges filed against him, yet believe, as Scott Panetti apparently did, that the real reason he was being tried was because the state was working in legion with the devil to stifle his preaching of the gospel. The complex questions concerning how to fairly evaluate competence in criminal cases has been the subject of much debate and little consensus among leading experts.

The American Bar Association (ABA) has recommended that an evaluation of a defendant's competence should touch on five areas. First, does the defendant have a fundamental understanding of the criminal justice process? Second, does the defendant have the ability to work with his or her defense attorney, without "paranoid distrust?" Third, does the defendant have the ability to recall and relate factual information relevant to his or her case? Fourth, is the defendant capable of testifying in his or her own personal defense? Finally, the ABA suggests that the threshold for finding a defendant competent should be higher in cases involving more serious charges and more complicated circumstances (American Bar Association, 1986).

What Happens When a Defendant Is Found Incompetent to Stand Trial?

Typically, if a trial judge finds that there is reasonable doubt about whether a defendant is competent to stand trial, the defendant will receive a more comprehensive mental health assessment, generally in a hospital setting. If it is found, based on this more comprehensive assessment, that the defendant is not competent to stand trial, the defendant will receive a period of mental health treatment with the goal of restoring competence to stand trial. Although the distinctions may be subtle, it is important to recognize that the goals of this treatment are not rehabilitation and recovery, but rather restoration of competency to stand trial. Thus, as soon as those responsible for providing treatment are satisfied that the defendant has regained competency, he or she will likely be transferred from the hospital back to jail with no guarantee of further psychiatric treatment.

In a 1972 case called *Jackson v. Indiana*, the U.S. Supreme Court held that defendants may not be indefinitely retained on the basis of being determined incompetent to stand trial. This particular case involved an individual with mental retardation and total deafness who had been detained on the basis of incompetence for a number of years after having been caught stealing a twenty-five cent candy bar from a convenience store (*Jackson v. Indiana*, 1972). In *Jackson*, the Court held that if, after a "reasonable" period of time, a defendant's competency to stand trial has not been restored, the state must either civilly commit that defendant to a treatment facility or release him.

Since the Supreme Court in *Jackson* did not define what constitutes a "reasonable" period of time, states and the federal government have interpreted this standard quite liberally. Consider the case of Russell Weston, a man who killed two U.S. Capital police officers in 1998 while in a highly delusional state. After being apprehended, Weston was found not competent to stand trial and sent to a federal forensic treatment facility in North Carolina. Today, nine years later, he remains in this facility, having yet to be restored to competence.

The Insanity Defense

It has long been recognized in both the British Common Law and American law that individuals who lack capacity to formulate criminal intent will not be held criminally responsible for their actions. The determination however of what constitutes lack of criminal responsibility, or "legal insanity", has long been a matter of controversy (Gutheil, 1999).

It is important to distinguish insanity or criminal non-responsibility from competency as discussed in the previous section. Whereas the determination of whether someone is competent to stand trial is limited to evaluating a defendant's present state of mind, the determination of criminal responsibility or sanity/insanity considers the defendant's state of mind at the time of the crime. As a practical matter, this is very difficult to do, particularly if a significant period of time has passed, as is often the case, from the time of the crime to the trial itself. Thus, the sanity evaluation requires delving into all aspects of the defendant's life, including his or her social history and relationships with family and friends.

Historical Background

In Great Britain, insanity was recognized as a valid defense as early as the 14th century (Reisner & Slobogin, 1990). In 1843, a decision was issued in the seminal McNaughton case that established a standard for insanity that is still followed either strictly or in modified form in a number of American jurisdictions. Daniel McNaughton was acquitted on charges of murdering the private secretary of the British Prime Minister, Robert Peel. The so-called "McNaughton standard" places the burden on the defense to prove that the defendant, at the time of his or her crime, "was laboring under such a defect of reason, from disease of the mind, as not to know the nature and quality of the act he was doing or, if he did know it, that he did not know what he was doing was wrong" (McNaughton, 1843, p.718).

The McNaughton decision immediately provoked criticism from those who felt that it was wrong to acquit an individual who had clearly committed the crime with which he was charged. Others, who supported the principle of recognizing diminished or non-responsibility as a criminal defense, criticized the decision because they felt that a standard that simply distinguishes the ability to understand the difference between good and bad or right and wrong did not accurately reflect the impact that mental illnesses might have on judgment and the ability to control one's own impulses (American Bar Association, 1986, pp. 331–332).

The McNaughton test focuses on a person's cognitive state at the time of the crime. However, severe mental illnesses, such as schizophrenia, have an impact on more than cognitive processes. In fact, a person suffering from schizophrenia may possess a superior I.Q. (consider John Forbes Nash, the Princeton mathematician and Nobel laureate chronicled in the book and movie *A Beautiful Mind*), but experience delusions and hallucinations so powerful that they overwhelm reason and rationality. How can these symptoms be reconciled with the approach to criminal insanity set forth in the McNaughton case?

In 1871, the New Hampshire Supreme Court established a far broader rule, known as the "product" test. Under this test, a person would not be held criminally accountable for an act that was the "product of mental disease" (*State v. Jones*, 1871). This is the broadest standard for insanity recognized by a U.S. Court to date. A similar form of this rule was adopted in 1954 by the U.S. Court of Appeals for the District of Columbia in a case called *Durham v. U.S.*, 1954. The so-called "Durham rule", stating that a defendant is not criminally responsible if his unlawful act "was the product of mental disease or defect" was ultimately rejected by state and federal courts as too broad. Under this test, anyone who could prove that his or her crime was connected in some way to a psychiatric diagnosis would be absolved of criminal responsibility.

Between 1884 and 1900, approximately one-third of the states adopted an additional prong to the McNaughton test. This so-called "irresistible impulse" rule focused beyond the defendant's *cognitive* state to his or her *volitional* state in stipulating that individuals who cannot control their actions should not be held criminally responsible for them (ABA Standards, 1986). The irresistible impulse criterion has been referred to by some in the legal arena as the "policeman at the elbow" test, meaning that persons in such a state would not be able to comport themselves within the bounds of the law even if they knew a police officer were at their side (del Carmen, 1991).

In 1955, the American Law Institute (ALI) developed yet another rule for insanity as part of the Model Penal Code. This rule states that a defendant is not criminally responsible for his or her act if, as a result of mental disease or defect, s(he) did not possess "substantial capacity either to appreciate the criminality of his conduct or to conform his conduct to the requirements of the law" (America Law Institute Model Penal Code, 1985). This test, which has become known as the "ALI standard" proved popular in a number of American jurisdictions—between 1955 and 1975, it was adopted as the standard for determining insanity in more than half the American states.

The "Hinckley" Backlash

In June, 1982, a Federal District Court in Washington, D.C. found John Hinckley not guilty by reason of insanity for the attempted assassination of President Ronald Reagan (*United States v. Hinckley*, 1981). The verdict engendered strong negative reactions from the public and led to a reexamination of the insanity defense in a number of states and by the U.S. Congress.

In the months and years following the *Hinckley* verdict, no less than 10 states changed their criteria for determining insanity from the ALI standard to the more restrictive McNaughton standard or a modified form of the McNaughton standard (Steadman, et.al., 1993). Additionally, in 1984, the U.S. Congress passed the *Insanity Defense Reform Act (IDRA)* which established the first federal standards for use in insanity defense cases. The IDRA adopted a standard for determining insanity in federal cases similar to McNaughton (18 U.S.C.A. § 20(a) Supp 1986).

By 1990, McNaughton had once again become the predominant standard for evaluating insanity. Twenty-five states, the District of Columbia and the federal courts recognized a form of the McNaughton test whereas twenty states incorporated the ALI test in their criminal statutes (Bard, 2005). This retreat from a more expansive definition of insanity prior to the Hinckley case has continued through today. Currently, Kansas has abolished the insanity defense, as have Idaho and Montana, but these latter two states allow for guilty but insane verdicts (Brakel, 2007; FindLaw, 2007); the insanity defense in other states such as Utah is so restrictive that it might as well be nonexistent (Thomson, 2004).

What Happens to People Who Are Found Criminally Non-responsible?

In most states, individuals found not guilty by reason of insanity are automatically committed to secure psychiatric facilities for evaluation. Following a statutorily defined period of evaluation, a hearing is held in which it is determined whether the individual meets the criteria for involuntary civil commitment. Criteria for involuntary civil commitment vary from state to state, but typically include (a) a diagnosis of a mental illness, (b) a finding that a person is dangerous to self or others, and/or (c) a determination that an individual is gravely disabled and unable to live safely in the community.

The few studies that have been done on the subject suggest that individuals found not guilty by reason of insanity generally are removed from society in secure psychiatric treatment facilities for as long or longer than if they had been convicted of the crime charged. An eight (8) state study comparing insanity acquittees with individuals convicted of comparable crimes revealed that lengths of confinement of insanity acquittees (albeit in psychiatric hospitals rather than prisons) are longer, on average, than lengths of incarceration of individuals convicted of comparable crimes (Silver, Cirincione & Steadman, 1994).

Informing Juries about the Consequences of Insanity Verdicts

Many states and several federal circuits either permit judges not to inform juries about the consequences of insanity verdicts or prohibit judges from doing so (Ellias, 1995). The rationale behind this is that informing juries about the potential consequences of their verdicts may prejudice their deliberations. Juries should base their decisions solely on the evidence that is presented to them (ABA, 1986).

However, concerns also exist about the potentially prejudicial aspects of not informing juries in insanity cases. If a juror believes that a finding of "not guilty by reason of insanity" may result in the person's release, that juror may be more likely to erroneously reject the insanity defense and convict the defendant, feeling that the interests of society are better served by removing the defendant from the community. This may particularly be true in cases involving violent crimes.

A panel of experts convened by the American Bar Association, having considered the evidence and other factors in support and against informing juries, recommended that courts should instruct juries "as to the dispositional consequences of a verdict of not guilty by reason of mental non-responsibility (insanity)" (ABA, 1986, p. 378).

In 1994, the U.S. Supreme Court addressed this issue directly. Upon being questioned by a Tupelo, Mississippi, police officer, Terry Lee Shannon walked away from the officer, took out a pistol, and shot himself in the chest. He was charged with unlawful possession of a firearm. At trial, he asserted an insanity defense. The jury rejected this defense and found him guilty. As he had three previous criminal convictions, he was sentenced to serve 15 years in a federal prison without the possibility of parole (*United States v. Shannon*, 1993). Shannon appealed his conviction, asserting that the judge's failure to instruct the jury that he would be involuntarily committed if the jury returned a verdict of not guilty by reason of insanity had a prejudicial impact on the jury's deliberations. The Supreme Court affirmed his conviction, holding that under the Insanity Defense Reform Act of 1984, a Federal Court is not required to instruct a jury as to the consequences of an insanity verdict (*Shannon v. U.S.*, 1994).

"Guilty but Mentally Ill"

A number of states have adopted "guilty but mentally ill" (GBMI) legislation as an alternative to "not guilty by reason of insanity." It should be noted that these jurisdictions have not eliminated the insanity defense. Rather, they have adopted GBMI as an additional option in cases in which the psychiatric status of the defendant is at issue.

As a practical matter, a verdict of "guilty but mentally ill" does not differ significantly from a verdict of "guilty." Despite inclusion of the term "mentally ill," this verdict neither guarantees mental health treatment for the defendant nor does it mitigate the severity of the punishment. In fact, at least one researcher has suggested that the average GBMI defendant receives a longer sentence than the average guilty defendant (Keilitz, 1987). This is perhaps not surprising when one considers the pervasive stigma associated with serious mental illness and continuing perceptions that individuals with these illnesses are more violent and less capable of being rehabilitated.

The Right of Prisoners to Mental Health Treatment

Sadly, people with serious mental illnesses are disproportionately represented in the criminal justice system. As discussed in Chapter 3, America's jails and prisons are now the largest psychiatric wards in the nation—16%, or approximately 350,000 individuals with serious mental illnesses are housed in America's jails and prisons on any given day, as compared to approximately 70,000 patients with serious mental illnesses in hospitals. On any given day, Rikers Island in New York City, the Cook County (Chicago) jail and the Los Angeles County jail hold more people with serious mental illnesses than any hospital in the U.S (Torrey, 1999). Most of these individuals, particularly those incarcerated in jails, have not committed violent crimes but rather non-violent misdemeanors or felonies such as trespassing, public nuisance, or petty thefts that are a direct consequence of their untreated mental illnesses (Torrey, 1999). These individuals are frequently in desperate need of psychiatric medications and mental health care.

Most jails and prisons have neither the resources nor the expertise to provide quality mental health treatment. Prisons or large urban jails may have a psychiatrist on call or a psychiatric nurse on staff, but these individuals are frequently overwhelmed by the numbers of people they have to serve as well as the poor conditions in which to serve them (Earley, 2006). Moreover, the costs of providing mental health treatment to inmates are borne entirely by counties (which typically operate jails) and states (which operate prisons) because under federal law, Medicaid (the largest payer of public mental health services) may not be used to pay for healthcare services in correctional facilities (42 USC Sect. 1905).

Eighth Amendment Rights

Inmates in jails and prisons do have a limited legal right to treatment however. This right is grounded in the Eighth Amendment of the U.S. Constitution, which prohibits the imposition of cruel and unusual punishment. In *Estelle v. Gamble* (1976), the U.S. Supreme Court first held that prisoners have an Eighth Amendment right to treatment and subsequent cases made it clear that this right extends to treatment for mental illnesses as well as physical illnesses (*Bowring v. Godwin*, 1977). However, this right is quite narrow. Proof of negligent treatment is not enough to establish a violation of the right to treatment. Rather, individuals seeking to assert their right to treatment must show first that they have a serious medical need and second that correctional officials were aware of this need and were "deliberatively indifferent" to addressing it (*Estelle v. Gamble*, 1976).

Serious Medical Need—Courts have varied in what they regard as "serious medical need" sufficient to trigger an eighth amendment right to treatment. However, there is growing consensus that serious mental illnesses, such as schizophrenia, bipolar disorder and major depression, meet the test of "serious medical need" because of their profound impact, particularly when untreated, on the ability of individuals to function (Cohen, 1998).

Deliberate Indifference—To establish deliberate indifference on the part of prison officials, it must be proven that prison officials were aware of an inmate's serious medical need but placed that inmate at serious risk by consciously disregarding that need. The burden is on the inmate to prove that the disregard of his or her medical need was wanton or willful. It is not enough to prove that prison officials should have known of this need (*Farmer v. Brennan*, 1994).

Minimally Adequate Treatment

Having established that prisoners with serious mental illnesses have an Eighth Amendment right to treatment, the next question that must be addressed is what constitutes minimally adequate "treatment" for these individuals. Does "treatment" in this context merely mean the amelioration of acute psychiatric distress or does it require long term treatment with a more rehabilitative, recovery-based purpose?

The fundamental components of a mental health treatment plan for inmates were set forth in a famous lawsuit in Texas, *Ruiz v. Estelle* (1980). The case was brought by a class of inmates incarcerated in Texas correctional facilities. In their lawsuit, these inmates raised allegations about overcrowding, staff brutality, inhumane conditions of confinement and grossly inadequate medical care in these facilities. With regard to mental health care, the lawsuit cited overall lack of treatment, the administration of inappropriately high dosages of psychotropic medications to control inmates with serious mental disorders, and placement of the most symptomatic, psychotic inmates in a substandard, overcrowded facility under extremely harsh conditions and little treatment.

In *Ruiz v. Estelle*, Judge William Wayne Justice held that correctional mental health treatment for inmates with serious mental illness must minimally include the following:

> First, there must be a systematic program for screening and evaluating inmates in order to identify those who require mental health treatment.... Second, treatment must entail more than segregation and close supervision of the inmate patients. Third, treatment re-

quires the participation of trained mental health professionals, who must be employed in sufficient numbers to identify and treat in an individualized manner those treatable inmates suffering from serious mental disorders.... Fourth, accurate, complete, and confidential records of the mental health treatment process must be maintained. Fifth, prescription and administration of behavior-altering medications in dangerous amounts, by dangerous methods, or without appropriate supervision and periodic evaluation, is an unacceptable method of treatment. Sixth, a basic program for the identification, treatment, and supervision of inmates with suicidal tendencies is a necessary component of any mental health treatment program (p. 1339).

Although this important decision was issued in 1980, its list of the essential components of minimally adequate correctional mental health frequently serves as the framework for evaluation today. Additionally, two other components have emerged in case law—those being *access to mental health services* and *the existence of adequate facilities and equipment to meet prisoners' mental health treatment needs.* (emphasis added) (Cohen, 1998).

Discharge Planning and Re-entry

Decisions in cases such as *Ruiz* and many others focus primarily on mental health treatment during periods of incarceration. Discharge planning and linkages with services are crucial to the successful re-entry of individuals with serious mental illnesses into the community. Unfortunately, most of these individuals are discharged without adequate planning to address their needs for treatment, supervision, benefits and housing (Haimowitz, 2004). Without adequate discharge planning and linkages to services, individuals with serious mental illnesses released from jails and prisons are likely to recidivate. For example, a New York study showed that 64 percent of discharged offenders with mental illnesses were rearrested within 18 months and a Ohio study showed similar results (Federa, 1991; Jacoby & Kozie-Peak, 1997).

The Eighth Amendment

At least one Court has held that the Eighth amendment right to treatment extends to discharge planning and linkage to services for individuals with mental illnesses released from jails and prisons. In *Wakefield v. Thompson* (1999), the Court of Appeals for the 9th Federal Circuit held that a valid Eighth Amendment claim was raised by an individual who was denied a two week supply of transitional medication upon his release from prison. Significantly, the Court stated that the state's obligation to provide medical care to prisoners does not end immediately at the time they leave the prison and return to the community. This is particularly true for prisoners who are unable to immediately provide for their own medical needs, such as people with mental illnesses who frequently must wait weeks or even months for appointments in the community. The Court stated:

> ... the state must provide an outgoing prisoner who is receiving ... medication with a supply sufficient to ensure that he has that medication available during the period of time reasonably necessary to permit him to consult a doctor and obtain a new supply. A state's failure to provide medication sufficient to cover this transitional period amounts to an abdication of its responsibility to provide medical care to those, who by reason of incarceration, are unable to provide for their own medical needs (*Wakefield v. Thompson*, 1999, p.1164).

Notwithstanding this decision, the likelihood that a Court will recognize the existence of an expansive Eighth Amendment right to discharge planning and follow-up services is uncertain at best, given the consistently limited reading of this right given by courts. The circumstances in *Wakefield* were unusual, in that the guard refused to provide Wakefield with a supply of medication even though he had been ordered to do so by the prison doctor, an example of "deliberate indifference" if ever there was one.

State and Local Statutes

As discussed in Chapter 6, state statutes may provide an alternative basis for asserting the legal rights of inmates to discharge planning and services. In 1999, the *New York Times* reported that inmates with mental illnesses were commonly released from New York City jails in the early morning hours with a subway token and no post-discharge arrangements in place (Winerip, 1999). A class action lawsuit was subsequently filed asserting that this was a violation of a State law requiring discharge planning and coordination between the jail system and the mental health system. The state court issued an injunction barring the City from continuing to violate the law by failing to implement discharge planning and treatment. After two unsuccessful appeals by the City, a settlement was reached whereby the City agreed to create a discharge planning program that would follow inmates with mental illness into the community (Barr, 2003; *Brad H. v. City of New York* [2000]; Hausman, 2003).

Notwithstanding the decisions in the *Wakefield* and *Brad H.* cases, it is unlikely that the glaring lack of adequate and appropriate discharge planning services for individuals with mental illnesses re-entering communities will be remedied through litigation. More promising is the growing consensus among policymakers, correctional and mental health professionals, and advocates that discharge planning and re-entry services make good sense and save public resources in the long run. For example, the Criminal Justice/Mental Health Consensus Project, an unprecedented collaboration among a variety of key stakeholders organized by the Council of State Governments, recommended a series of steps and best practices that states and communities can take to reduce the unnecessary incarceration of people with serious mental illnesses and to minimize recidivism among these individuals (Council of State Governments, 2002). Following up on the recommendations of the Consensus Project, a number of states, such as New York, Pennsylvania, Ohio and Texas, have taken steps to help people with mental illnesses successfully reintegrate into communities (Haimowitz, 2004). While far more must be done, there is growing understanding at federal state and local levels that effective community re-entry services lead to good outcomes, enhanced public safety, and long-term cost savings.

The Rights of Prisoners to Refuse Treatment

Just as prisoners have a limited right to treatment, they also have a right to refuse treatment. This right has been recognized at all levels of the criminal justice process, from the pre-trial stage to the post-conviction stage. The right to refuse treatment is grounded in the Due Process Clause of the 5th and 14th Amendments of the U.S. Constitution, based on the fundamental right of individuals to make autonomous medical decisions. The right to refuse treatment has been a source of considerable controversy and disagreement in the mental health field, with those who believe privacy and bodily integrity to be sacrosanct clashing with those who believe that involuntary medication is sometimes necessary to protect the well being of those who may at times be unable to make informed choices about treatment. Questions have arisen about the right to refuse treatment in the pre-trial context (particularly in cases where competency is at issue) and for those who are in prison after conviction. These two scenarios must be considered separately, because different legal issues are at stake.

The Right to Refuse Treatment in the Pre-trial Context

In August, 1999, Russell Weston, a man with a history of schizophrenia, burst into the U.S. Capitol and opened fire, killing two Capitol police officers and wounding several bystanders (Weil, 1998). In the days following the tragedy, it became known that Mr. Weston had a history of serious mental illness and had been committed to a state psychiatric hospital in Montana two years before the tragedy at the Capitol. After 53 days, he was discharged from the hospital with no follow-up care except for a brief supply of medication, a bus ticket to return to his family's farm in rural Illinois, and a referral to a local mental health center. No effort was ever made to inform his family about his severe mental illness and need for treatment. When he went to the mental health center, he was reportedly "bizarre and paranoid" but left after being informed that he was not legally obligated to participate in treatment. After several years with no treatment, Mr. Weston's schizophrenia spiraled out of control, culminating in his trip to Washington and deadly actions at the Capitol (Hull, 2001).

After recovering from physical injuries received when he was shot by police defending the Capitol, Mr. Weston was determined to be incompetent to stand trial and was transferred to a federal prison hospital in Butner, North Carolina, for the purpose of receiving treatment to restore his competency to stand trial. Mr. Weston refused to take antipsychotic medications, and a hearing was held to determine whether he should be medicated against his will (Honberg, 2000).

In the general treatment context, the competing interests implicated when a state seeks to override an individual's refusal to take medications concerns the individual's right to determine what shall be done with his or her own body on the one hand versus the state's obligation to protect the public interest (known as "police power") or to help those who are unable to help themselves (known as "parens patriae") on the other. In the pre-trial context, these competing interests may be different. The interests of the individual refusing medication may relate more to trial strategy than protecting autonomy—for example, an individual who is planning to assert an insanity defense may feel that his or her chances to succeed hinge upon remaining overtly psychotic or symptomatic. And, a state's interests may be less in helping an individual through treatment than in reducing psychiatric symptoms so that the person can be more quickly brought to trial.

In 2003, the U.S. Supreme Court addressed the issue of whether a pre-trial detainee can be involuntarily medicated for purposes of making him competent to stand trial and, if so, under what circumstances. Charles Sell, an individual with a history of mental illness, was indicted for submitting false insurance claims for payment and subsequently for attempted murder. He consistently refused to take medication, and his condition deteriorated to the point where he was determined incompetent to stand trial. Following an administrative hearing at the facility where he was hospitalized, an order was entered authorizing the involuntary administration of medication. Sell appealed, and the case eventually went all the way to the Supreme Court.

The Supreme Court vacated the order, holding that the involuntary administration of medication for purposes of restoring competence to stand trial was constitutionally permissible only under very limited circumstances. Specifically, medications could be administered involuntarily only if the treatment is medically appropriate, is substantially unlikely to have side effects that could undermine the fairness of the trial, and is the least restrictive alternative available to further important governmental interests (*Sell v. United States*, 2003). The Court also emphasized that the governmental interest in bringing a defendant to trial, while important, may be lessened when the consequence of the defendant's refusal to take medications was lengthy confinement in an institution, as was the case with *Sell*. This, according to the Court, "would diminish the risks that ordinarily attach to freeing without punishment one who has committed a serious crime" (p. 2185).

Interestingly, the Court left the door open to the involuntary administration of medications for the more traditional purpose of alleviating dangerousness to self or others. "A court need not consider whether to allow forced medication for that kind of purpose" (rendering a defendant competent to stand trial), "if forced medication is warranted for a different purpose, such as ... purposes ... related to the individual's dangerousness, or purposes related to the individual's own interests where refusal to take drugs puts his health gravely at risk.... There are often strong reasons for a court to determine whether forced administration of drugs can be justified on these alternative grounds before turning to the trial competence question" (p. 2185).

Applying this decision to the facts in the Weston case, it would be very difficult, following the Court's framework in *Sell*, to justify the involuntary administration of medication to Weston solely on the basis of restoring his competence to stand trial. However, if it could be proven that involuntary medication were necessary to alleviate dangerousness to self or others, this might serve as a valid justification.

Today, eight years after his act at the U.S. Capitol, Russell Weston remains at Butner hospital. In 2001 (prior to the *Sell* decision), a Federal Court ruled that Weston should be administered psychiatric medications over his objections (*United States v. Weston*, 2001). Six years later, his condition has not improved sufficiently to attain competence to stand trial (Fenton & Siegel, 2007). It is not clear that it ever will.

The Right of Prisoners to Refuse Treatment

As in the community, people with serious mental illnesses who are incarcerated sometimes refuse to take psychotropic medications that have been prescribed to them. When untreated, these individuals may create safety and security risks for themselves or others within the correctional setting. The state's interest in administering medication to these individuals centers as much on maintaining security and control within the correctional setting as it does on alleviating the person's symptoms. In 1990, the U.S. Supreme Court directly addressed the issue of involuntary medication in prisons in a case called (*Washington v. Harper, 1990*).

Walter Harper, an individual with bipolar disorder (manic-depressive illness) had a history of incarceration and hospitalizations. In 1981, his parole was revoked after he assaulted two nurses in a psychiatric hospital. He was returned to prison and sent to a special unit for convicted felons with serious mental illnesses. After initially consenting, he refused to continue taking the medications that had been prescribed to him, and the treating physician sought to administer the medications over his objections. The records of the case clearly demonstrated that Harper deteriorated during periods when he did not take prescribed medications.

As in the *Sell* case, the Court began its analysis by acknowledging that inmates such as Harper have a "significant liberty interest in avoiding the unwanted administration of antipsychotic drugs ..." (*Washington v. Harper*, 1990, p. 221). But, this right must be balanced against the individual's medical needs as well as the interest of the penal institution in maintaining safety and security. The state can meet its burden of justifying the need for involuntary medication by demonstrating (a) that the individual represents a significant danger to self or others or is gravely disabled, (b) the drugs are administered for treatment and under the supervision of a licensed psychiatrist, and (c) the drugs are in the individual's best medical interests. The Court also upheld the procedure followed by Washington State for determining the need for involuntary medication, stating that an administrative hearing before a committee comprised of a psychiatrist, psychologist and hospital administrator (none of whom were directly involved in the diagnosis or treatment of Harper) comported with minimal constitutional requirements. An adversarial hearing before a judge is not necessary, the Court held.

This tension between the medical model and the judicial model of decision making is frequently at issue in cases involving refusals to participate in treatment. Proponents of the medical model argue that physicians are most knowledgeable and best able to make decisions that are essentially clinical in nature. Proponents of the judicial model argue that physicians will very likely "rubber-stamp" the decisions of colleagues who recommended medications in the first place and therefore cannot be trusted to make objective, unbiased decisions (Levy & Rubenstein, 1996).

People with Mental Illnesses and the Death Penalty

In recent years, the Supreme Court has held the execution of people with mental retardation (*Atkins v. Virginia*, 2002) and the execution of juveniles (*Roper v. Simmons*, 2005) to be unconstitutional. In the wake of these decisions, questions have arisen about whether it is similarly unconstitutional to execute people with mental illnesses (Hoskins, 2007).

There are no accurate figures on the numbers of people with serious mental illnesses who have been executed. However, there are a number of individuals currently on death row with a documented, uncontroverted diagnosis of schizophrenia or another serious psychiatric diagnosis (ABA, 1986). Virtually every state that recognizes the death penalty identifies in its statute mental illness or some variant of the term among the factors that should be considered as mitigating against the death penalty. However, some evidence has emerged suggesting that mental illness may in fact be construed as an aggravating factor by juries considering the death penalty. In other words, the presence of a serious mental illness may increase the chance that the death penalty will be imposed.

For example, a study of 175 capital cases in Pennsylvania demonstrated that all aggravating and mitigating factors listed in that state's death penalty statute correlated with the eventual sentence imposed in the predictable direction, with the exception of "extreme mental or emotional disturbance", which correlated positively with a death sentence (Baldus, et al., 1998). A Georgia study found a correlation between unsuccessful insanity pleas and the ultimate imposition of the death penalty (Baldus, et al., 1998).

Research suggests two possible reasons for this disturbing trend. The first concerns the perceptions of lay-people that people with mental illnesses are abnormally dangerous. Thus, jurors may view a capital defendant with schizophrenia as beyond redemption—with no amount of treatment likely to reduce that person's violent tendencies. In actual fact, the opposite is true. Psychiatric treatment has been shown to be very effective in reducing risks of violence (Steadman, et al., 1998).

A second reason may be the cynicism of jurors that mental illnesses are real —and perceptions that raising a mental illness as a mitigating factor is a subterfuge designed to enable people to escape responsibility for their own behaviors. Research has shown that mock jurors feel far more negatively towards defendants with mental illnesses than they do towards other types of defendants (Ellsworth, et al., 1984).

The confusion of jurors about severe mental illnesses may not be alleviated by expert testimony presented in the courtroom. In fact, it may be reinforced when competing experts for the defense and prosecution present different conclusions about the nature of the defendant's mental illness and its impact on his or her behavior.

The Legal Backdrop

In 1986, the U.S. Supreme Court ruled that it is cruel and unusual punishment and thus a violation of the Eighth Amendment of the Constitution to execute people who are "insane" *(Ford v. Wainwright,* 1986). The term "insane" as used in this case applied specifically to prisoners determined to be incompetent to be executed. Unfortunately, the Court did not clearly define what it meant by incompetent and thus left it to federal and state courts or state legislatures to develop standards for defining this term (Bonnie, 2005). In a concurring opinion, Justice Lewis Powell stated his belief that the Eighth Amendment "forbids the execution only of those who are unaware of the punishment they are about to suffer and why they are to suffer it *(Ford v. Wainwright,* 1986, p. 422)." Although concurring opinions are generally not binding, many states and courts have adhered to this test (Bonnie, 2005).

Some courts have interpreted this standard extremely narrowly to preclude the execution only of those individuals who are so impaired that they do not understand the nature of execution or the stated reason for their scheduled execution. For example, in the case of Scott Panetti, discussed earlier in this chapter, a federal district court in Texas found him competent to be executed despite his consistent belief that the real reason the state was executing him was that it was in a conspiracy with forces of evil to prevent him from preaching the Gospel *(Panetti v. Dretke,* 2004).

In 2007, the Supreme Court of the United States addressed the question of what it means to be "unaware of the punishment they are about to suffer" when it agreed to review Panetti's case. In a narrow 5 to 4 decision, the Supreme Court rejected the narrow "cognitive" test for determining competency articulated in the District Court's opinion, instead adopting a broader test that takes into consideration the defendant's rational understanding of why he or she is to be executed. Writing for the majority, Justice Kennedy stated:

> The principles set forth in *Ford* are put at risk by a rule that deems delusions relevant only with respect to the State's announced reason for a punishment or the fact of an imminent execution ... as opposed to the real interests the State seeks to vindicate. We likewise find no support elsewhere in *Ford* ... for the proposition that a prisoner is automatically foreclosed from demonstrating incompetency once a court has found he can identify the stated reason for his execution. A prisoner's awareness of the State's rationale for an execution is not the same as a rational understanding of it. *Ford* does not foreclose inquiry into the latter *(Panetti v. Quarterman*, 2007, 127 S.Ct. 2842, 2861–2862).

The decision in the *Panetti* case will have a relatively narrow, although not unimportant impact, since it presumably applies only to individuals who have been convicted, sentenced to death, and are awaiting execution. It may thus have no impact directly on sentencing decisions in capital cases.

Several states, including North Carolina and Indiana, have considered although not yet enacted legislation to eliminate or narrow the application of the death penalty as it applies to people with severe mental illnesses. The ABA has also endorsed a model formulation for eliminating the death penalty for certain individuals with mental illnesses.

One question that must be addressed is how to define "mental illness" in legislative proposals to exempt people with these illnesses from the death penalty. The task force that worked on the ABA's model formulation considered but ultimately rejected an approach that would have identified certain diagnoses —e.g. schizophrenia, bipolar disorder—for inclusion. Instead, the ABA adopted an approach that emphasizes the severity of the impairment imposed by the mental illness. The ABA's recommendation reads as follows:

> Defendants should not be executed or sentenced to death if, at the time of the offense, they had a severe mental disorder or disability that significantly impaired their capacity (a) to appreciate the nature, consequences, or wrongfulness of their conduct; (b) to exercise

rational judgment in relation to conduct; or (c) to conform their conduct to the requirements of the law. A disorder manifested primarily by repeated criminal conduct or attributable solely to the acute effects of voluntary use of alcohol or other drugs does not, standing alone, constitute a mental disorder or disability for purposes of this provision (Slobogin, 2005, p. 1139).

This definition is not all-inclusive. It includes only those with severe disorders that result in significant impairments. Notably, it excludes those with personality disorders that manifest in repeated criminal misconduct and also excludes people whose mental impairments at the time of their crimes are attributable solely to the voluntary use of alcohol or other drugs (with no co-occurring mental illness). Although some on the taskforce would have preferred an even broader definition, it would realistically be very difficult to successfully advocate for legislation that adopts a broader, all inclusive approach in the current political climate.

Conclusion

The Supreme Court's deliberations in the *Atkins* and *Simmons* cases described above were influenced by the weight of public opinion as evidenced by the adoption of legislation banning the death penalty for people with mental retardation and juveniles respectively in a majority of states. Currently, only one state—Connecticut—expressly excludes certain categories of people with mental illness from the death penalty. The Supreme Court will undoubtedly be reticent to exempt people with mental illnesses from the death penalty until it sees a similar trend in legislation enacted in a majority of states.

Legislators are often influenced by an uninformed public. The concluding chapter considers means for implementing informed policies and establishing evidence-based practices in the treatment of persons with mental illnesses.

References

42 USC § 1905(a)(A).

18 U.S.C.A. § 20(a) Supp. (1986).

American Bar Association, (1986) *ABA Criminal Justice Mental Health Standards*.

American Law Institute Model Penal Code, §4.01 (Permanent ed. with revised commentary, 1985).

Atkins v. Virginia, 536 U.S. 304 (2002).

Baldus, D., Woodworth, G., Zuckerman, D., Weiner, N. A., & Broffitt, B. (1998). Racial Discrimination and the Death Penalty in the Post *Furman* Era: An Empirical and Legal Overview, with Recent Findings from Philadelphia. 83 *Cornell Law. Review*, p. 1638, 1688–89.

Bard, J. S. (2005). Re-arranging deck chairs on the Titanic: Why insanity defense law reform is not enough to solve the problem of crimes committed by the mentally ill, 5 *Houston Journal of Health Law and Policy*. 1:37.

Barr, H. (2003). Transinstitutionalization in the courts: Brad H. v. City of New York, and the fight for discharge planning for people with psychiatric disabilities leaving Rikers Island. Crime & Delinquency 49(1), pp. 97–123.

Blackstone, W. (1768). 4 Commentaries on the Law of England, 24.

Blumenthal, R. (2004, February 4). "Insanity Issue Lingers as Texas Execution is Set," *New York Times*.

Bonnie, R. (2005). Mentally Ill Prisoners on Death Row: Unsolved Puzzles for Courts and Legislatures", 54 *Catholic University Law Review* 4, pp. 1169–1171.

Bonnie, R. (2005). Unsolved Puzzles for Courts and Legislatures. 54 *Catholic University Law Review*, p. 1169, 1172.

Bowring v. Godwin, 351 F.2d 44 (4th Cir. 1977).

Brad H. v. City of New York, 712 NYS2d 336 (2000).

Brakel, S. J. (2007). Searching for the therapy in therapeutic jurisprudence. *New England Journal on Criminal and Civil Confinement* 33, p. 455.

Cohen, F. (1988). *Legal Issues and the Mentally Disordered Prisoner*, U.S. Department of Justice, National Institute of Corrections, pp. 54–163.

Cohen, F. (1998). *The Mentally Disordered Inmate and the Law* (New Jersey: Civic Research Institute), pp. 4–33, as cited in Ill Equipped, p. 212.

Collins, K., Hinkelbein, G., & Schorgl, S. (2002). "The John Hinckley Trial and its Effect on the Insanity Defense," *The Trial of John Hinckley*, University of Missouri-Kansas City School of Law, Retrieved August 26, 2007, from www.law.umkc.edu/faculty/trials/hinckley/hinckleyinsanity.htm.

Council of State Governments (2004). *Criminal Justice/Mental Health Consensus Project*, (June, 2002), Retrieved from the World Wide Web on October 11, 2007 at www.consensusproject.org.

del Carmen, R. (1991). *Criminal Procedure: Law And Practice*, 2nd ed. Pacific Grove, CA: Brooks/Cole.

Drope v. Missouri, 420 U.S. 162 (1975).

Durham v. United States, 214 F. 2d 862 (D.C. Cir. 1954).

Dusky v. United States, 363 U.S. 402 (1960).

Earley, P. (2006). *Crazy: A Father's Search Through America's Mental Health Madness*, G.P Putnam and Sons: New York

Ellias. R. (1995). Supreme Court Review: Should Courts Instruct Juries as to the Consequences of a "not guilty by reason of insanity" verdict? [Case Note]. *Shannon v. United States*, 114 S. Ct. 4919 (1994).

Ellsworth, P. C., Cowan, C. L., Bukaty, R., & Thompson, W.C., (1984). The Death Qualified Jury and the Defense of Insanity. *Law and Human Behavior* 8, pp. 81–93.

Estelle v. Gamble, 429 U.S. 97(1976).

Estelle v. Gamble, (2003). Human Rights Watch, *Ill Equipped: U.S Prisons and Offenders with Mental Illness*, pp. 211–214.

Farmer v. Brennan, 511 U.S. 825 (1994).

Federa, L. (1991). A Comparison of the Community Adjustment of Mentally Ill Offenders with Those from the General Prison Population, 15 *Law and Human Behavior*, p. 5.

Fenton, J., & Siegel, A.F. (2007, August 11). Insanity Defense Muddles Case. *Baltimore Sun*.

FindLaw (2007). The insanity defense among the states. Retrieved from the World Wide Web on October 11, 2007: http://criminal.findlaw.com/crimes/ more-criminaltopics/insanity-defense/the-insanity-defense-among-the-states.html.

Ford v. Wainwright, 477 U.S. 399 (1986).

Gutheil, T.G. (1999) "A Confusion of Tongues: Competence, Insanity, Psychiatry, and the Law", 50 *Psychiatric Services* 6, pp. 767–773.

Haimowitz, S. (2004). Slowing the Revolving Door: Community Reentry of Offenders with Mental Illness. 55 *Psychiatric Services* 4, pp. 373–375.

Hausman, K. (2003). Mentally Ill Inmates Win Right to Discharge Planning. *Psychiatric News* 38(6), p. 21.

Honberg, R. (2000). Weston Case Raises Legal Questions Over Forced Medication. *NAMI Legal Letter*, (December, 2000), p. 1.

Hoskins, M. (2007). Interim Commission Studies Mental Illness, *The Indiana Lawyer* 18(12), p. 7

Hull, A. (2001, January 23). A Living Hell or a Life Saved? Capitol Shooter's Untreated Madness Fuels Legal and Ethical Debate. *The Washington Post*, A1.

Jackson v. Indiana, 406 U.S. 715 (1972).

Jacoby J., & Kozie-Peak, B. (1997). The Benefits of Social Supports for Mentally Ill Offenders: Prison to Community Transitions. *Behavioral Sciences and the Law* 15(4), pp. 483–501.

Keilitz, I.,(1987)"Researching and Reforming the Insanity Defense", *Rutgers Law Review* 39, pp. 289–322.

Levy, R., & Rubenstein, L., (1996). *The Rights of People with Mental Disabilities.* American Civil Liberties Union, pp. 116–119.

McNaughton's Case (1843). 10 Cl. and F 200, 8 Eng. Reprint 718.

Panetti v. Dretke, No. A-04-CA-042-SS (W.D. Tex. Sept. 29, 2004).

Panetti v. Quarterman, 127 S. Ct. 2842, (2007).

Pate v. Robinson, 383 U.S. 375 (1966).

Reisner, R., & Slobogin, C. (1990). *Law and the Mental Health System: Civil and Criminal Aspects, 2d ed.* St. Paul, MN: West.

Roper v. Simmons, 543 U.S. 551 (2005)

Ruiz v. Estelle, 503 F. Supp. 1265 (S.D. Tex. 1980).

Sell v. United States, 123 S. Ct. 2174 (2003)

Shannon v. U.S., 512 U.S. 573 (1994).

Should Courts Instruct Juries as to the Consequences of a "not guilty by reason of insanity" verdict? Supreme Court Review (1995). [Case Note]. *Journal of Criminal Law and Criminology.*

Silver, E., Cirincione, C., & Steadman, H. J. (1994). Demythologizing inaccurate perceptions of the insanity defense. *Law and Human Behavior*, Vol. 18, pp. 63–70.

Slobogin, C. (2005). Mental disorder as an exemption from the death penalty: The ABA IRR Task Force Recommendations, 54 *Catholic University Law Review* 4, p. 1139.

State v. Jones, 50 NH 369, 394 (1871).

Steadman, H. J., McGreevy, M. A., Morrissey, J. P., Callahan, L. A., Robbins, P. C., & Cirincione, C. (1993*) Before and After Hinckley: Evaluating Insanity Defense Reform*, New York: Guilford Press.

Steadman, H. J., Mulvey, E. P., Monahan, J., Robbins, P. C., Appelbaum, P. S., Grisso, T., et al, (1998). Violence by People Discharged from Acute Psychiatric Inpatient Facilities and by Others in the Same Neighborhoods, *Archives of General Psychiatry* 55, pp. 393–401.

Thomson, L. (2004, August 29). As defense, insanity is tough sell. *Desert Morning News.* Retrieved from the World Wide Web on October 11, 2007: http://desertnews.com/dn/view/0,1249,595087602,00.html.

Torrey, E. F. (1999). "Reinventing Mental Health Care," *City Journal* 9, p. 4.

United States v. Hinckley, 525 F. Supp. 1342 (D.C.C. 1981).

United States v. Shannon, 981 F. 2d 759 (5th Cir. 1993).

United States v. Weston, 255 F. 3d 873 (D.C. Cir. 2001).

Wakefield v. Thompson, 177 F. 3d 1160 (9th Cir. 1999).

Washington v. Harper, 494 U.S. 210 (1990).

Weil, M. (1998, July 25) Gunman Shoots His Way Into Capital; 2 Officers Killed; Injured Suspect Held. *The Washington Post*, A1.

Winerip, M. (1999, June 3). After Years Adrift, Treatment in Jail; Advocates Seek Another Chance for a Schizophrenic Inmate. *New York Times*. Retrived from the World Wide Web on April 27, 2008: http://query.nytimes.com/gst/fulpage.html?res=9A07D81E30F930A35755C0A96F958.

CHAPTER 12

CONCLUSION: STRIVING FOR INFORMED POLICIES

"For these are all our children. We will all profit by, or pay for, whatever they become."

—James Baldwin[1]

"The coin of honor is always inexhaustible and fruitful in the hands of one who distributes it wisely."

—Beccaria (1764)

Since its inception the criminal justice system has worked to establish and maintain relationships with communities. Variations in the quality of law enforcement across jurisdictions are contingent upon community involvement. The same is true for mental health treatment. Attitudes held by police officers, correctional officials, community leaders, and citizens, have shaped responses to mental illness. A largely uninformed, misinformed and apathetic public has contributed to the criminal justice system becoming the de facto mental health system. As Mark Twain once said, "We are all ignorant; just about different things" (Koppel, 2000, p. 33).

News coverage of events involving the mentally ill often brings to the public's attention the complexity of dealing with mental illness. Answers to issues facing the mentally ill lie in the development and sustenance of collaborative relationships. Bureaucracies by their nature inhibit communication and collaboration and the sharing of information. We hope the information in this book will help inform decisions, motivate policymakers and citizens, and provide an opportunity for positive, collaborative change.

---

1. National Center for Schools and Humanities at Fordham University, Independent Parent Survey, Retrieved January 27, 2008 from the World Wide Web: http://www.ncscat-fordham.org/pages/home.cfm.

In the long run providing appropriate mental health care for all will save money. It is the right thing to do and worth the investment. We are not merely talking about providing persons with mental illnesses get-out-of-jail-free cards. In fact, some individuals perceive it as easier and less of an infringement to just do a short stint in jail without the intrusive linkages to community treatment. Such a response involves providing persons with mental illnesses that come into contact with the criminal justice system with voluntary treatment options. Treatment, when possible and appropriate, should not be connected to the criminal justice system or associated with confinement. It appears that we have moved away from the least restrictive environment rule established by earlier court decisions.

It is important to stop the maddening recycling of mentally ill offenders through the criminal justice system and to develop effective intervention strategies. The loss to individuals, families, and communities from failure to respond to this growing crisis is incalculable. It is imperative that our society go beyond the power of shame so long associated with mental illness and become proactive in the management of our individual and collective mental health.

Which Way Will the Virginia Tech Crisis Drive Policy?

In December 2005, Seung Hui Cho sent messages to two coeds that resulted in police contact with him and a warning to cease and desist from contacting them again; Cho, in turn, expressed suicidal ideations to a roommate, and the police re-contacted Cho and escorted him to a mental health facility where he was referred to the court for a commitment hearing (Schulte & Jenkins, 2007). As noted by Schulte and Jenkins (2007), the following day a judge determined Cho to be an imminent danger to himself due to his mental state and ordered him into involuntary outpatient commitment; however, there was no follow-up. In retrospect, under intense scrutiny, the mental health treatment or lack thereof leading up to Seung Hui Cho's massacre at Virginia Tech appears to be a comedy of errors. The problem is no one is laughing now.

A Virginia judge maintains that the court's responsibility ceases at the courtroom door, as the court has no authority to follow up; mental health officials contend they are never advised if referrals are made to them by the court (Schulte & Jenkins, 2007). In other words, the common belief and practice is that when the court mandates that someone get treatment, the order is to the individual in need of treatment to seek treatment, not to the mental health agency to en-

sure that the treatment occurs (Schulte & Jenkins, 2007). Of course, this reliance on persons with mental illnesses to be responsible and obtain treatment,
when it is considered that many individuals with mental illnesses in crises lack
insight into their illnesses, seems ludicrous. Lack of follow-up is also blamed on
a lack of resources, and typically judges in Virginia find out a problem has
emerged with their referral to mental health treatment when an individual winds
back up before them in court after acting out (Schulte & Jenkins, 2007).

The law in Virginia is clear: mental health agencies "'shall recommend a
specific course of treatment and programs' for people such as Cho who are ordered to receive outpatient treatment. The law also says these boards 'shall
monitor the person's compliance'" (Schulte & Jenkins, 2007, p. A01). When
confronted with the wording from the statute, an employee of a mental health
agency in Virginia replied, "'That's news to us.'" (Schulte & Jenkins, 2007, p.
A01). Lack of communication and lack of clearly delineated responsibilities
between the mental health system and the courts, as well as a lack of mental
health resources, appear to rule the day. Of course, courts are not enforcement bodies and must rely upon other entities, such as the mental health system, to carry out their dictates.

Multi-agency memorandums of understanding entered into by the courts,
mental health providers, law enforcement agencies, and any other involved
parties could serve to ensure comprehensible specification of roles and responsibilities clearly outlining who is responsible for what actions. Such agreements would go a long way towards overcoming custom and practice, for
example as seen in Virginia, and would seek to ensure accountability.

Since family members are often the primary caregivers for loved ones with
mental illnesses, Levit (2005) discusses means by which family members can
understand and navigate HIPAA requirements. She also notes that 29 states
do not have in place any legislation in addition to HIPAA governing the release of medical information to families, and she designates a couple of websites for consideration.[2]

In the aftermath of the Cho incident, the Report of the Virginia Tech Review Panel (2007), including its recommendations, has been released. The
panel investigating the shooting at Virginia Tech made over seventy recommendations (Virginia Tech Review Panel, 2007). The panel in their analysis
dedicates an entire chapter to privacy laws such as HIPAA (see discussion by

---

2. http://www.cdc.gov/privacyrule/privacy-links.htm provides a link to each state's
HIPAA site, and http://www.healthprivacy.org/info-url_nocat2304/info-url_nocat_search.htm
provides a summary of each state's privacy law.

Petrila in earlier chapters) and the Family Educational Rights and Privacy Act
(FERPA) due to the inherent confusion and erroneous beliefs regarding restrictions on sharing information about Cho exhibited by professionals leading up to the tragedy. A tell-tale observation of the panel that could apply to
almost any jurisdiction in the United States is:

> In the wake of the Virginia Tech tragedy, much of the discussion re-
> garding mental health services has focused on the commitment
> process. However, the mental health system has major gaps in its en-
> tirety starting from the lack of short-term crisis stabilization units to
> the outpatient services and the highly important case management
> function, which strings together the entire care for an individual to en-
> sure success. These gaps prevent individuals from getting the psychi-
> atric help when they are getting ill, during the need for acute stabiliza-
> tion, and when they need therapy and medication management during
> recovery (Report of the Virginia Tech Review Panel, 2007, p. 60).

While the Virginia Tech campus was designated as a gun-free zone, meaning
even those with concealed weapons permits were not permitted to bring guns
onto the university grounds (Barone, 2007), and Cho reportedly was already
legally prohibited by federal law from purchasing a firearm (Luo, 2007), recommendations from the Virginia Tech panel investigating the Cho incident included
tighter restrictions on gun purchases by persons with mental illnesses (Virginia
Tech Review Panel, 2007). Congress, in turn, recently approved legislation supported by both the Brady Campaign to Prevent Gun Violence and the National
Rifle Association to supposedly more expediently and precisely recognize likely
gun purchasers who have mental health issues that would be restricted from
firearms ownership under federal law (Williamson & Schulte, 2007). Echoing
how crisis drives policy, United States Senator Charles E. Schumer remarked:
"'We can never know if we could have prevented the shootings' at Virginia
Tech[.] ...'It is a shame that we're again called to act on ... legislation in the face
of tragedy, but now it is Congress's moment to take a huge step toward fixing a
broken system'" (Williamson & Schulte, 2007, p. A12).

While the verdict is still out on which recommendations of the Virginia Tech
Review panel will be implemented, we are cautiously optimistic that this ter-
rible crisis can result in an opportunity for positive change. Perhaps parity in
the funding between mental and physical illness will be part of that equation.

Some mental health providers are pleased with the status quo. Some criminal justice practitioners do not feel it is their responsibility and some judges

do not feel it is their role to intervene. Meanwhile legislation continues to be passed and policies implemented that contribute to the criminalization and recycling of persons with mental illnesses through the criminal justice system. What is needed is education of everyone: from a citizenry that is bombarded by media sensationalism, to lawmakers that are influenced by an ill-informed citizenry and driven by perceptions of short-term savings that actually have long-term costs, to the legal community, criminal justice practitioners, and mental health providers. Enhanced sensitivity to mental illness would go a long way toward the eradication of stigma, as would the passage of federal parity legislation,—whereby insurance coverage for mental health would be on par with that for physical health, sending the message that we each have one body and our health should be treated accordingly. It is also critical that assessment strategies be developed that provide more reliable and valid determinations of the role a particular mental illness plays in a specific criminal act.

At the federal level efforts are underway to pass parity legislation to provide funding for mental illnesses on par with all other illnesses. This could greatly assist in eradicating stigma by sending a message to the general public that mental illnesses are essentially no different from physical illnesses. The illnesses emerge from one body, and we don't, for example, blame someone for being diabetic, which results from a chemical imbalance, nor should we blame someone for having bipolar disorder, which results from a chemical imbalance in another area of the body: the brain. Furthermore, parity would insure greater access to mental health treatment and lessen the burden on the criminal justice system, allowing criminal justice professionals to focus on their roles as crime fighters.

Congressman Patrick Kennedy, who acknowledges that he has bipolar disorder, and former first lady Rosalynn Carter, who has written a book on care giving for persons with mental illnesses, appeared on Wolf Blitzer's Situation Room on July 12, 2007, discussing their campaigning on capitol hill and advocating for parity, whereby mental health would be covered on par with physical health (see CNN Transcripts, 2007). On September 18, 2007, the U.S. Senate passed the Mental Health Parity Act of 2007 (S 558), legislation requiring health plans to cover treatment for mental illness on the same terms and conditions as all other illnesses, and the bill was sent to the U.S. House of Representatives for consideration (NAMI, 2007). On March 5, 2008, the U.S. House of Representatives passed parity legislation. While there are differences in the House and Senate versions of the bills, it is hoped that a satisfactory compromise can be reached (American Psychological Association, 2008).

Discussions of outpatient treatment often focus on tragic incidents carried out by individuals such as Andrew Goldstein and Julio Perez. Even in the case of these perceived notorious individuals, as previously discussed, it is not as if they never asked for treatment. There were numerous missed opportunities to provide each of them treatment. These missed opportunities prompted Kim Webdale, the sister of Kendra Webdale, in Congressional testimony to tell members of Congress that the more she and her family delved into Kendra's tragic death, the more Kim found her sister to have been the "unsuspecting victim of a sick man and an equally sick system" (Webdale, 2000). Instead of focusing so much on forcing individuals into treatment, we ought to hone in on forcing providers, armed with adequate resources, to provide appropriate treatment.

Who Wants to Take Responsibility for Ending the Needless Recycling of Persons with Mental Illnesses in and out of the Criminal Justice System?

It appears that there has been a lot of shifting of responsibilities from one entity to another. The states have been all too happy to shift the financial responsibility for persons with mental illnesses to the federal government via its provision of benefits, while the federal government has refused up to this point to pass parity legislation, and to cities and counties through such mechanisms as preferred drug lists that serve to restrict access to medication and can send persons with mental illnesses spiraling out of control.[3]

Mental health providers have been quite content to have someone else handle the job that the providers are supposed to do. This handling has occurred

---

3. When should the legislature get into the business of prescribing psychotropic medication? For example, Orlando Sentinel reporter Stephen Hudak is currently investigating a story regarding Keith Howard, a man with schizophrenia, who, after having his medication changed in compliance with preferred drug list requirements implemented by the Florida legislature, killed his mother and is currently institutionalized having been found not guilty by reason of insanity (S. Hudak, personal communication, September 20, 2007). As Slate informed the Florida Senate Committee on Health Care in his 2005 testimony, their policy would be driving crises see Chapter 3. Also, Sgt. Jack Richards of the Ventura Police Department in California fully understands the importance of CIT training and its emphasis on de-escalation techniques. Having been involved in a fatal shooting of a person with mental illness earlier in his police career, while not equipped with such training, Sgt. Richards also points to the failure of the system to provide adequate access to mental health treatment as a significant contributing factor to creating unnecessary situations that lead to hostile confrontations like the one he encountered (J. Richards, personal communication, April 30, 2007).

via the criminal justice system that has its doors open 24 hours a day, 7 days a week, 365 days a year in the form of criminalizing persons with mental illnesses via police encounters that result in the further status-degrading process of not just being mentally ill, but of arrest and often times conviction, jail, or prison. Contrary to many treatment entities, criminal justice facilities do not place any restrictions or stipulate any prerequisites for entry (Abram & Teplin, 1991). Thus, persons with mental illnesses are often locked up simply because more appropriate treatment settings are not accessible or agreeable to providing treatment (Lurigio, Fallon, & Dincin, 2000), as the community mental health system has abdicated its responsibility in treating persons with mental illnesses who encounter the criminal justice system (Solomon & Draine,1995a). Who can blame the mental health providers, particularly if they are designated as accountable yet not equipped with adequate resources to meet such responsibilities? It is not uncommon to find treatment providers opposed to such interventions as mental health courts because such entities will strive to hold them accountable while their resources will likely not be enhanced. Designating accountability without resources and ensuring follow-up is irresponsible. Of course, policymakers must ensure that proper resources are in place to provide appropriate mental health treatment to the citizenry.

For example, Florida, the third most affluent and fourth largest state, is 48th in mental health funding (Editorial Board, 2004). However, Florida was 12th nationally in spending for forensic mental health services in 2006, and that ranking is likely worse today (Transforming Florida's Mental Health System, 2007). It is the politicians that fail to adequately fund the public mental health system. All the while, many lawmakers, like the Wizard behind the curtain in Oz, continue with their supposed cost savings measures, such as implementing preferred drug lists and not passing parity legislation, contributing directly to the criminalization and further stigmatization of persons with mental illnesses. In spite of the apathy or greed of some politicians, informed citizens are beginning to get the message. This is evinced by the fact that "some innovative mental health program financing has been adopted by [some] states, … such as California's Proposition 63 initiative in 2004, which provides a stable, significant source of revenue for mental health services through a so-called millionaire's tax" (Daly, 2006, p. 8).

The System That Wouldn't Say No Is Beginning to Say No

This is not just about making persons with mental illnesses responsible through treatment for their actions. It is also about making actors within the criminal justice and mental health systems responsible for their actions or in-actions as well. This is about everyone and every entity being accountable. As reflected in this book, most of the research publications regarding the inter-face of the mental health and criminal justice systems are occurring within the psychiatric journals. Perhaps there is promise in the criminal justice sys-tem working collaboratively with the mental health system if mental health providers are willing to seek funding for mental health treatment. However, the mental health system, perhaps because it lacks the influence or the will, maybe both, to intervene, has in many respects taken a back seat to efforts to reverse the criminalization of persons with mental illnesses. If mental health providers are not willing to do so, they might as well step aside, as criminal justice authorities have clout and leverage with policymakers and the com-munity to pursue alternatives to the criminal justice system for persons with mental illnesses. Most grants aimed at stopping persons with mental illnesses from recycling through the criminal justice system are spearheaded by crim-inal justice entities. Also, sheriffs, police chiefs, judges and the associations they belong to have been quite influential in bringing about meaningful change and influencing lawmakers.

At least some of the criminal justice professionals who have long been in the dumping grounds for society's ills have begun to stand up collectively, and sometimes in multi-system collaborations, to stop the revolving door of the crim-inal justice system for themselves and for persons with mental illnesses. While there are indeed differences between the actors from the various entities in-volved in the interface of the mental health and criminal justice systems, they share a lot of common ground. It seems that what has worked best in fighting against the criminalization of persons with mental illnesses is collaboration: bringing together law enforcement, judges, prosecutors, public defenders, cor-rections officials, mental health clinicians, mental health advocates, consumers of mental health services, family members with loved ones with mental ill-nesses, and victims' advocates to craft workable, meaningful solutions in ju-risdictions across America. If additional mental health treatment services are needed, then such multi-system collaborations can be quite formidable in lob-bying lawmakers to address needs. The beauty of multi-system collaborations is finding the issues and approaches that everyone can agree on and putting aside differences, e.g. building consensus. Sterling examples of such collabo-rations can be found in panels assembled to testify before Congress as spear-headed by the Council of State Governments (CSG), and also the CSG's Criminal Justice/Mental Health Consensus Project—an ongoing process, not just some report stuck on a shelf collecting dust, and Florida's Partners in Crisis [FPIC].

Florida Partners in Crisis

Michele Saunders, Executive Director of Florida Partners in Crisis offers the following information about this organization (M. Saunders, personal communication, August 1, 2007):

> Recognizing that the criminal justice system in Florida had inappropriately become the state's primary mental health and substance abuse receiving system, a statewide coalition of criminal justice, mental health and substance abuse stakeholders formed Florida Partners in Crisis (FPIC). Their mission: improve and reform Florida's mental health and substance abuse delivery system by ensuring access to treatment for those served by the publicly funded systems. To accomplish this mission, FPIC promotes the funding of adequate state and local resources for the prevention, care and treatment for those living with mental illness and/or substance use disorders along with criminal justice and law enforcement diversion programs which help make jail the last resort.
>
> In doing so, FPIC is giving a voice to those whose calls for help have gone unanswered. What makes the organization unique is the diversity of its partners, and its criminal justice emphasis on local and statewide reform. Members include judges, law enforcement, correctional officers, prosecutors, public defenders, service providers, hospital administrators and people recovering from mental illnesses and substance abuse disorders and their families.
>
> Background
>
> Traditional advocates, such as providers, family members and consumers, have had little or no influence on or access to the legislative process. The only way to change the paradigm was to change the advocates and change the message. Advocating for social programs by traditional advocates was no longer sufficient. Law enforcement officials, along with criminal justice officials, advocating for more treatment programs rather than incarceration under the premise of public safety and wasted tax dollars, got the attention of Florida Lawmakers.
>
> What began as indescribable frustration by the Chief Judge of the 9th Judicial Circuit of Florida because he was unable to access treat-

ment for an individual in jail with serious mental illness,[4] has led to a national movement of criminal justice stakeholders partnering with mental health and substance abuse providers, family members and consumers to reverse the criminalization of mental illness. Judge Belvin Perry, Jr. brought together the criminal justice stakeholders, including law enforcement, correctional officials the state attorney and public defender along with the traditional mental health and substance abuse stakeholders. Together, with one voice, they educated and successfully lobbied the Florida Legislature for millions of additional dollars for mental health and substance abuse treatment for the Orlando area. In 1998, recognizing that they could only duplicate their success by expanding this model statewide, Florida Partners in Crisis was born.

Unlike other advocacy organizations, the make-up of FPIC affords its members easier access to policymakers which allows them to help fashion appropriate solutions to these difficult and complex issues. All of the Directors of FPIC continue to be elected officials from the criminal justice system. Florida Circuit Court Judge, Mark Speiser recently became the State Director/Board Chairperson of

---

4. Judge Perry had a young woman in front of his court that had a serious substance abuse problem and was under a court order through the Myers Act (what is now the Marchman Act). Judge Perry ordered the woman for substance abuse treatment into residential treatment. At the conclusion of that hearing, Sally Wolfe, the court's mental health manager went to the Judge's chambers to inform the Judge that the woman he just ordered to treatment would not be going. Sally Wolfe told the judge that there were no beds available at the treatment facility. Judge Perry questioned her about why there were no beds available and she explained the problem the community was having related to mental health and substance abuse treatment beds. In addition to so few substance abuse treatment beds, three (3) inpatient mental health units closed and over 400 people with mental illness were in the Orange County jail. At that point, the judge decided the best way to better understand the issues and to find solutions was to get everyone to the table that was involved in the mental health and substance abuse community.

Judge Perry called together the Clerk of the Court who happened to be the former County Chairwoman, Linda Chapin, along with the providers, the Department of Children and Families, law enforcement, the State Attorney, and the Public Defender. He determined that there truly was a mental health crisis in Orange County and that is how Partners in Crisis began. Shortly after the first meeting of the group, Deputy Eugene Gregory, a Seminole County deputy was killed by a person with paranoid schizophrenia who had fallen through the cracks of the mental health system (previously discussed). This event also added an urgency to address the issues. The membership of the group grew as the issues were discussed and strategies developed to solidify the relationships for shared advocacy on how to increase resources for the system.

FPIC. Past Directors/Board Chairpersons include the Chief Judge of the Orange County area Circuit, Judge Belvin Perry, Jr., Seminole County Sheriff Donald Eslinger and Duval County Sheriff John Rutherford and Circuit Judge Nancy Alley of Seminole County.

Structure

Currently, FPIC is a 501 (c) 3 charitable tax-exempt organization and has a full time Executive Director. FPIC is organized in three levels: general membership, Statewide Board of Directors and Statewide Board of Trustees (Advisory). A general member is a person or organization that has made a commitment to support the mission and goals of the organization. The Statewide Board of Directors consists of 30 members (2 from each geographical region) who coordinate activities locally and represent their districts at the statewide meetings. The Board of Trustees is the advisory body of the organization and is mostly made up of elected officials. The State Director/Board Chairperson of the FPIC is elected to a two year term.

The development of legislative priorities, educational materials and advocacy strategies, growing the partnership base and increasing funding for the organization is accomplished through four committees: Legislative Committee, Education Committee, Partnership Committee and Development Committee.

Outcomes

Over the years, Florida Partners in Crisis has played a key role in achieving significant increases in funding, as well as in preserving access to treatment by helping defeat fail-first and restricted formulary legislative proposals. In the 2007 legislative session, Partners in Crisis took the lead role in advocating for a new law that would create a state-local matching grant program to help fund local counties in planning for or implementing or expanding "best practice" programs focused on jail diversion, court intervention and/or successful re-entry to communities from jail or prison.

Through the use of successful billboard campaigns, public service announcements, effective press conferences during legislative sessions, and local advocacy by "partners," FPIC has continued to focus the attention on resolving the ongoing crisis in Florida's mental health and substance abuse services.

Current Focus

The current focus of FPIC remains each year tied to its mission which is to promote state and community collaboration across the mental health, substance abuse and criminal justice systems, to reduce contact of people with mental illnesses and substance use disorders with the justice system and support their recovery. FPIC promotes the following goals and activities to further its mission.

Goals

Florida Partners in Crisis strives to achieve the following goals:

1. Promoting education and fostering awareness of mental illnesses and/or substance use disorders and effective treatments
2. Advocating for appropriate and adequate resources for prevention, care, treatment and follow-up services for those who have a mental illness and/or substance use disorder
3. Encouraging community collaboration to promote and implement best practices around effective police response, jail diversion, court intervention programs and re-entry programs that reduce the criminalization for those who have a mental illness and/or substance use disorder
4. Encouraging accountability of providers across systems

Activities

Education—activities are designed to foster awareness of mental illnesses and/or substance use disorders and the needs for an improved system of care. This is accomplished through the distribution of reports, surveys, statistics and data to lawmakers, policymakers, key community leaders and the general public.

Advocacy—activities revolve around community and state forums, press conferences, media contact, testimonies and distribution of literature. Florida Partners in Crisis uses the **One Voice** campaign as its mantra. (Thus, stances on controversial issues such as outpatient commitment have been avoided, as consensus building and agreement on issues, speaking with one voice on issues is the aim of the organization).

Technical Assistance—activities include assisting communities in building effective community collaborations for strategic system changes and assisting communities in the development and implementation of Crisis Intervention Teams (CIT).

A recent member of the Partners "family" is the Crisis Intervention Team (CIT) Coalition coordinator. This informal organization advocates for the expansion of the CIT model to law enforcement agencies across Florida and promotes the use of core model elements to foster excellence.

Best Practice Summits/Conferences—activities are designed to bring communities together to share and exchange knowledge and information about best practice programs and initiatives around effective jail diversion, court intervention and re-entry.

Essentials for Building Effective Partnerships

Florida Partners in Crisis has been successful with its partnership and therefore with its advocacy work primarily because it has followed some key essential elements for collaboration. These key elements include:

Strong leadership—Partners primary vehicle to carry the messages lies with Judges, Sheriffs, Police Chiefs, and other leaders within the criminal justice system.

Commitment to the cause—although Partners does not have a formal Memorandum of Understanding or Agreement among its members, by virtue of signing up as a member, being elected to the Board of Directors or agreeing to serve on the Board of Trustees demonstrates each partners commitment to the mission and the organization's efforts.

Ability to develop consensus with all the stakeholders—Partners' legislative priorities are agreed upon by all stakeholders before session, and the group speaks with one voice around a single message and the defined priorities.

Ability to create a shared vision, mission and goals for the system—Partners develops this as a team.

Communication tools and feedback loops—Partners uses email, phone, mail, meetings and visits to keep its membership informed, prepared for action and to communicate with legislators.

Recognition—Partners not only recognizes key lawmakers who are supporters of the mental health and substance abuse issues but also among its members, Board and committee chairs are acknowledged for their work. Members and the Board are all volunteers, and their participation in this advocacy work is invaluable and priceless.

Funding Sources for Florida Partners in Crisis

FPIC as a 501 (c) 3 corporation can solicit and receive charitable contributions. Several funders have provided resources for the activities of FPIC. Pharmaceutical corporations have provided funding, as well as grant money from the JEHT Foundation, and contributions and in-kind services from partners and partnering organizations have been procured.

Summary

The unique partnerships that make up Florida Partners in Crisis, the strength in numbers for its **One Voice** campaign and the credibility of the criminal justice leaders has led to Florida Partners in Crisis being a viable force in the state capital with lawmakers and our invitation to the planning and policy tables of several state agencies. The Florida Partners in Crisis model of advocacy truly makes a difference in influencing policy in the State of Florida for reducing contact with the criminal justice system for those with a serious mental illness and/or substance use disorder.

Through the efforts of hundreds of "partners" statewide, Partners in Crisis has become a national model for effective advocacy on behalf of people with mental illnesses and substance abuse disorders. Similar organizations have been founded in three states: Washington, South Carolina and Oregon (M. Saunders, personal communication, August 1, 2007).[5]

The establishment of Florida's Partners in Crisis provides another example of crisis driving policy and exemplifies seizing upon an opportunity for positive change. Judge Perry's actions here demonstrate, whether they want to or not, judges are uniquely positioned to bring together stakeholders and seek meaningful alternatives to the criminalization of persons with mental illnesses. As noted by Miami Judge Steven Leifman : "When I was a public defender try-

---

5. Websites for Partners in Crisis organizations can be found at: http://www.flpic.org/index.php Florida Partners in Crisis; http://www.wapic.org/home/ Washington State Partners in Crisis; http://www.scpartnersincrisis.org/ South Carolina Partners in Crisis; See http://www.lpscc.org/docs/mh_wkgrp_rpt_2005.pdf Oregon Partners in Crisis; http://www.picusa.org/content/view/13/26/ Partners in Crisis of America

ing to address this problem, I called a meeting of all the key stakeholders, and no one came. When I became a judge I called the same meeting. Everyone was five minutes early" (Council of State Governments, 2007a). Seizing upon the pivotal role that judges can play in this process, funding has been established for State Supreme Court Chief Justice led task forces in seven states (California, Florida, Georgia, Missouri, Nevada, Texas, and Vermont) across the country to promote partnerships between the criminal justice and mental health systems (Council of State Governments, 2007b).

Testimony

One of the masterminds of behind the scenes consensus building and impacting criminal justice/mental health legislation is Mike Thompson with the Council of State Governments in New York. He operates much like a director/producer, as he orchestrates working with various organizations to select the slate of individuals who will testify on a particular issue and ensure their statements are in agreement and on point.[6] In addition to the previously discussed congressional testimony of Kim Webdale, what follows is the testimony of Risdon N. Slate.

---

6. Here is an example of a series of panelists he worked with other organizations to convene for testimony before Congress that ultimately led to federal funding for mental health courts across the country. Testifying before the congressional subcommittee were The Honorable Mike DeWine, (R) U.S. Senator, Ohio; The Honorable Ted D. Strickland, (D) U.S. Congressman, Ohio; Dr. Bernard S. Arons, Director, Center for Mental Health Services, Department of Health and Human Services; Chief Bernard Melekian, President, Los Angeles County Police Chiefs Association, and Pasadena Police Department, Pasadena, California; Ms. Kim Webdale, New York, New York; Michael F. Hogan, Ph.D, Director, Ohio Department of Mental Health; Steven Sharfstein, M.D., Medical Director, Sheppard Pratt Health Systems, Baltimore, Maryland; Mr. Donald F. Eslinger, Sheriff, Seminole County, President, Stanford, Florida; The Honorable Michael Schrunk, District Attorney, Multonomah County, Portland, Oregon; Risdon N. Slate, Ph.D., Florida Southern College; The Honorable James D. Cayce, Judge, King County Courthouse, Seattle, Washington; Reginald A. Wilkinson, Ed.D, Director, Department of Rehabilitation and Correction, and Vice President, Association of State Correctional Administrators, Columbus, Ohio; The Honorable Robert J. Thompson, State Senator and Chair, Law and Justice Committee, Harrisburg, Pennsylvania. (Witness List, 2000). (Slate, 2003, p.25). http://judiciary.house.gov/judiciary/3.htm. This is representative of individuals from diverse backgrounds and points of view in agreement on requesting intervention to stop the recycling of persons with mental illness through the criminal justice system.

One-Page Summary Statement of
Risdon N. Slate, Ph.D., Nami-FL Board Member

For Judiciary Committee, Subcommittee on Crime,
September 21, 2000

In June of 1986, I had earned a master's degree in criminal justice, had two years of experience under my belt as a correctional official, and was just beginning my career as a United States Probation Officer. That promising career soon came to a screeching halt when, within a two week span of time, I was diagnosed with manic-depressive illness, forced to resign my dream job for medical reasons, and I was left while hospitalized and ultimately divorced by my wife. It truly felt like my world had ended.

However, I was encouraged by treatment professionals, and the prescribed medication—lithium (an element on the periodic chart) —worked for me. As a result, I was able to put my life back together, went on to the Claremont Graduate School, earned my Ph.D. in criminal justice, took a job in 1989 as a full-time criminal justice professor in Maine, and then moved to Florida in 1993, where I currently reside and work, taking a job as a criminology professor at Florida Southern College.

Upon my arrival in Lakeland, I located a new physician so I could continue my medical prescription for lithium. Unfortunately, this psychiatrist decided that I was not mentally ill and convinced me to stop taking the medication that I had been taking for eight years. I complied with his advice, and my condition soon deteriorated.

During a visit to South Carolina, I suffered the second manic episode of my life. When police were called, although I was exhibiting bizarre behavior and my wife desperately tried to advise them of my illness and show them the vial containing the medication that I should be taking, they took me to jail and put me in a holding cell with approximately fifteen other detainees. Due to my strange behavior, I was first assaulted by an inmate and then by detention officers who ultimately isolated me in a strip cell.

Finally, a federal probation officer with whom I had once worked, Ronald L. Hudson, intervened. Flashing his badge, he convinced my captors to release me. He has since told me that the jailers were glad to oblige him, as they were admittedly at a loss as to how to deal with my behavior. He transported me to a hospital. Ron probably saved my life, as at no time during my stay in the jail, even after appearance before a magistrate who set my bail at $500, did I see any medical personnel or receive any medical treatment.

If such experiences can happen to me, with a Ph.D. in criminology and my background and knowledge of the criminal justice system, they can happen to anyone. I call upon you to intervene on behalf of those who are unable to do so, because it is the right thing to do! By the grace of God and due to the love, support, and encouragement of my wife, Claudia, and my mother, Virginia, I appear before you today to offer the following suggestions:

In terms of recommendations, persons with mental illness and the practitioners they encounter within the criminal justice system should have more options/choices/alternatives available for successful resolution of problems for the sake of all concerned parties, including the public. Certainly, there will be some mentally ill individuals who will require incarceration, but we must ensure them adequate treatment, not only for their benefit, but also for the well-being of correctional personnel and the potential welfare of society when they are likely released.

Continuing Legislation, Testimony, and Considerations

More recent legislation that the Council of State Governments has been instrumental in supporting is the passage of the Mentally Ill Offender Treatment and Crime Reduction Reauthorization and Improvement Act (MIOTCRRIA) which can be accessed at http://frwebgate.access.gpo.gov/cgi-bin/getdoc.cgi?dbname=110_cong _bills&docid=f:h3992ih.txt.pdf (Council of State Governments, 2007c). Demonstrating the criminal justice system's involvement in leading the way in mental health interventions, the National Association of Police Organizations strongly supported this legislation which would authorize $10 million for fiscal year 2008 to encourage mental health and criminal justice systems collaborations to assist persons with mental illnesses (NAPO, 2008).

Even if this aforesaid legislation is passed and funding allocated, it pales in comparison, for example, to expenditures by the United States for the Iraq War. It has been estimated that the Iraq War is costing the United States $12 billion a month (Associated Press, 2008), $100,000 a minute (Mazzetti & Havemann, 2006), and $5,000 per second (Kristof, 2008). In other words, using the more conservative figures listed above from 2006, of $100,000 a minute, in a mere 100 minutes the United States has spent on Iraq the amount possibly earmarked for MIOTCRRIA—$10 million. Unfortunately, Tanielian and Jaycox (2008), in a recent RAND study, predict that the costs related to post traumatic stress disorder and depression to the country will be as high as $6.2 billion in the two years after deployment for returning troops.

The use of an "Iron Fist and the Velvet Glove" approach may well be the best mantra for changing the system (Marx, 1986; Center for Research on Criminal Justice, 1975). Innovations in the recently developed drug and mental health courts reflect themes of accountability and restoration that resound with the notion of tough love. In an era of "zero tolerance" relationships between criminal justice personnel and the public have become strained. In efforts to "get tough" on crime and "clean up America" the criminal justice system lost, temporarily, we hope, its most important assets humanness and civility (Souryal, 1992).

In attempts to overcome years of "iron fisted" approaches to offenders with mental illnesses, partnerships between the key players in criminal justice and mental health systems should be fostered. Better training related to persons with mental illnesses for all parties, particularly within the criminal justice system, should be explored. Promising approaches, such as crisis intervention training for police officers and mental health courts, are already in operation in some venues across the country. Innovative federal funding schemes for such partnerships should continue to be explored which will serve to lend flexibility to the particular needs of local communities. However, solely diverting someone from the criminal justice system should not be considered a panacea in and of itself. Many of those diverted will require follow-up, either pre or post trial, to ensure compliance with conditions which will serve to ensure that they do not put themselves or anyone else at risk and/or they do not recycle through the system. To assure this, sufficient inpatient and community-based treatment structures need to be in place. Today we often institutionalize persons with mental illnesses in jails and prisons, instead of in hospitals. We can ill afford this deinstitutionalization to trans-institutionalization movement any longer.

Lt. Rick Wall (2007), mental illness project coordinator of the Los Angeles Police Department (LAPD), elaborates on the agency's efforts at preventing the recycling of persons with mental illnesses through the criminal justice system in more recent testimony before the U.S. House of Representatives Judiciary Committee's Subcommittee on Crime, Terrorism, and Homeland Security. Wall reports on the predictable monthly behavior that began to erupt from a person with mental illness by the name of "Mike" who repeatedly refused to take his medication and would become violently suicidal at approximately the same times each month. During a year and a half period, "Mike" generated 48 calls for police service, with 22 of these calls resulting in mental health holds. Police responses to "Mike" were frequently met by suicide by cop behaviors, as he expressed desires to have the voices in his head silenced, and his behaviors could prove quite disruptive resulting in displacement of as many as 50 nearby residents when evacuations of the area were required (Wall, 2007).

Several components operate within Los Angeles to try to prevent the recycling of persons with mental illnesses through the criminal justice system. The Mental Evaluation Unit provides a triage desk and is comprised of specially trained officers who respond to questions from dispatchers and patrol officers to assist in identifying incidents involving persons with mental illnesses and providing direction and advice to units engaged with persons with mental illnesses in the field (Wall, 2007). Wall indicates a confidential database is maintained by the Unit to document pertinent information pertaining to previous police contacts with a particular subject in the field and the circumstances of such contacts; if additional follow-up is required, referrals are made to Systemwide Mental Assessment Response Teams (SMART).

Via a partnership with the county mental health department, the LAPD provides citywide mental Health crisis call coverage with 18 SMART teams; recently Homeless Outreach/Mental Evaluation (HOME) Teams have been added to focus on the "Skid Row" area of the city . The HOME teams are comprised of a sworn police officer and a social worker or registered nurse and operate to assist officers who encounter homeless subjects in linking them to appropriate treatment and preventing them from being victimized (Wall, 2007).

The LAPD also continues to incorporate CIT training and currently has over 300 officers trained and represented in all of the agency's 19 geographic divisions as first responders to crisis calls involving persons with mental illnesses. In addition, a mobile crisis team is maintained by the mental health department, known as the Psychiatric Mobile Response Team (PMRT), and is available for interventions and evaluations prior to necessitating an emergency response call (Wall, 2007).

Wall (2007) identifies the Case Assessment and Management Program (CAMP) as one of the most innovative of the programs in operation in Los Angeles. This program is operated by the department of mental health and aims to keep minor offenders in the mental health system and out of the criminal justice system. CAMP investigators identify subjects who pose a high risk of danger to themselves or others and have been the subject of repeated police interventions due to their mental illnesses resulting in numerous calls for crisis services. CAMP investigators also provide follow-up and linkages to treatment services and have yet to have a repeat violent incident with any of their clients. In fact, "Mike," who Lt. Wall began his congressional testimony discussing, became the CAMP program's first client and only required one call for service in 2006, and, via monthly CAMP contact with him and his family, "Mike" has not required a call for police service in over a year (Wall, 2007). This is how the recycling of persons with mental illnesses is prevented, by putting personnel in place who are appropriately trained and know what they are doing and equipping them with adequate resources to thwart the long term costs and human suffering without such interventions taking place. The exemplary, comprehensive approach taken by the LAPD to divert persons with mental illnesses from the criminal justice system is to be applauded. Of course, the LAPD has more resources at its disposal than many law enforcement agencies. However, their model provides an example of how collaborations can work effectively.

The Sequential Intercept Model

The beauty of the sequential intercept model conceptualized by Munetz and Griffin (2006) is that the model visualizes several points for intervention and deployment of the best clinical practices to divert persons with mental illnesses from the criminal justice system and/or to allow them to leave the criminal justice system and re-enter society as soon as practicable with linkages to treatment. The points for intervention include police and emergency services, initial detainment and hearings, "[j]ail, courts, forensic evaluations, and forensic commitments, [r]entry from jails, state prisons, and forensic hospitalizations, [c]ommunity corrections and community support services (Munetz & Griffin, 2006, p. 545).

More problematic is ensuring that employees at each of the intercept points have training in encountering persons with mental illnesses in crises, recognizing the general signs and symptoms of mental illnesses, having the wherewithal and skills to link persons with mental illnesses to needed services that are available. For example, as reflected in Slate's (2000) congressional testimony presented earlier in this chapter, although he encountered three intercept points (law enforcement, detainment and initial appearance before a magistrate, and return to jail), at no time did he receive any mental health treatment. In fact, the magistrate who presided over his initial appearance had a real estate background. As noted by psychologist Fred Frese, Ph.D., who has schizophrenia, unless individuals have a loved one or friend with mental illness, persons with mental illnesses are often viewed as aliens, creatures from outer space (Comptom & Kotwicki, 2007). As we've previously discussed, for criminal justice practitioners their typical familiarity with mental illness is through encounters with persons with mental illnesses in crises. Thus, it is imperative that all criminal justice and mental health professionals who are customarily likely to have interactions with persons with mental illnesses have appropriate training for such encounters—to lessen the possibility for escalation, to remain professional, non-judgmental, and non-stigmatizing and to learn of avenues and resources for linking individuals to suitable treatment. Such personnel should also be exposed to persons with mental illnesses in recovery and be made aware of their significant contributions to society.

In the previously mentioned Florida Supreme Court report headed by Florida Chief Supreme Court Justice R. Fred Lewis, funded and convened by the Council of State Governments, among the numerous recommendations which can be accessed at http://www.floridasupremecourt.org/pub_info/ documents/11-14-2007_Mental_Health_Report.pdf, the involvement of consumers of mental health services in the education and training of judges is included (Transforming Florida's Mental Health System, 2007). Such meaningful involvement of consumers of mental health services is essential for ensuring buy-in and lending credibility to the development of initiatives and policies.

Other Means for Influencing Policy

In the law, duty follows knowledge (del Carmen, 2006). Joseph Mucenski a retired Detective from the New York City Police Department was present when his son was killed by police in what was termed a "suicide by cop" incident. Mucenski and his wife filed suit against the law enforcement agency not desirous of obtaining money, but, instead, epitomizing the spirit of turning crisis into opportunity, seeking assurances that the law enforcement agency would enact more appropriate training standards for their officers. Upon adoption of the CIT training model, the Mucenskis dropped their lawsuit. Now Joseph Mucenski is a leader and proponent of such training in Arizona and will have influence nationally with his recent election to the NAMI Board of Directors. Joseph acknowledges that he is conflicted over what transpired in the incident that resulted in his son's death from his years on the New York City Police force and his role as a father. He admits he isn't certain how he would have handled the incident himself if he had been in charge, but he knows improved training is essential. (Mucenski, 2007; J. Mucenski, personal communication, August 30, 2007).

With a similar outcome, Risdon Slate sent a letter to Polk County Sheriff's Colonel Grady Judd after he had announced his candidacy for Sheriff following a tragic shooting by a person with mental illness by an officer in his jurisdiction in Florida. The letter was not meant to cast blame upon the agency, but its contents indicated that we would never know if specialized training would have made a difference in the matter. The Colonel agreed to meet and made a commitment to implement CIT training as part of his platform for Sheriff. Upon becoming Sheriff, he has stuck by his commitment.

One of the powers of the grand jury system across this country is the ability to launch and conduct investigations. Although infrequently used, the grand jury has, as discussed in Chapter 5, served as a mechanism by which the citizenry can investigate and literally indict the mental health and criminal justice systems in an effort to ensure accountability. How many of these systems in jurisdictions throughout America could withstand such scrutiny?

To influence lawmakers you need to contact them but then Governor of New Jersey Richard Codey indicated that most politicians do not realize how big a problem the inadequate treatment of mental illnesses is for their constituents because people are running from the stigma and are ashamed to discuss the topic. Codey knows firsthand, as his wife has suffered from postpartum depression (Mulligan, 2005a).

In maverick fashion, as a state senator, Richard Codey went into a state psychiatric hospital to do some undercover work. Having discovered that just about 33 percent of those employed in the state hospital system had criminal records, some even for homicide, Codey used the name of a deceased felon and got himself hired as an orderly on the midnight shift at New Jersey's Marlboro Psychiatric Hospital. His first day on the job he was informed that he was fortunate to be working on the midnight shift because it was easier to have sex with the residents; at the culmination of his undercover work, the President of the hospital and some thirty five to forty other workers were terminated for what Codey uncovered, and now criminal background checks are required on all state hospital employees in New Jersey prior to beginning work (Hennelly, 2004).

Immediately prior to signing an executive order to establish a task force to make recommendations on how to improve mental health service delivery and access to services, Governor Codey stopped by to have breakfast with residents at Greystone Park Psychiatric Hospital in New Jersey (Mulligan, 2005a). Indeed, Codey's first official act as Governor was to sign the aforesaid executive order

(Mulligan, 2005b). Governor Codey also signed executive orders and dined with residents of Ancora Psychiatric Hospital as he wrapped up his tenure as Governor and landmark transformation of the New Jersey mental health system (Heck, 2006).

More and more college courses address the issue of the criminalization of mental illnesses and explore means for reversing this trend and honing in on the worth of persons with mental illnesses. For example, Dr. Jacki Buffington-Vollum, a forensic psychologist, at James Madison University, offers a senior seminar course entitled "Mentally Ill Offenders in the Criminal Justice System." In this course she exposes students to the criminalization of mental illness, types of mental illnesses, and the criminal justice process, to include the law enforcement response, mental health courts, confinement, diversion and re-entry into the community, and the use of community corrections. Specially trained law enforcement responders and mental health court professionals make presentations to the class, and students are familiarized with forensic evaluations. Consumers of mental health services presentations have proven extremely enlightening and popular with the students (J. Buffington-Vollum, personal communication, September 9, 2007). Similarly, Michael Perlin, Professor of Law at New York Law School, has established a mental disability law program and offers such courses as "Mental Disability Issues in Jails and Prisons" (New York Law School, 2007).

Conclusion

Accountability can be better ensured when legislators and policymakers make informed decisions. "Lord Kelvin, a Scottish mathematician of the late 1800s, made this astute observation: 'When you can measure what you are speaking about, and express it in numbers, then you know something about it; but when you cannot measure it, when you cannot express it in numbers, your knowledge is of a meager and unsatisfactory kind'" (Power, 2005). As noted by Kathryn Power (2005), Director of the Center for Mental Health Services of the Substance Abuse and Mental Health Services Administration, we need to do a better job of data based decision making. Thus, policymakers need to be provided not only with the reasons for implementing policies but also with the numbers to justify their existence. Experts such as Dr. Henry J. Steadman at the GAINS Center are engaged in assisting agencies in the meaningful compilation and expression of such data.

Guardianships, advance directives, conservatorships, and identification bracelets can provide less intrusive means for attempting to ensure the ethical and adequate treatment of persons with mental illnesses. Furthermore, HIPAA training is needed across agencies to prevent continued breakdowns in communication between fragmented systems. Collaborations between agencies should always include input from consumers of mental health services and from family members who have loved ones that are mentally ill.

"The character Holden Caulfield in *The Catcher in the Rye* envisioned himself standing in a field of rye on the edge of a cliff with the mission of catching all those in danger of falling and saving them from going over the edge of the cliff" (Salinger, 1991) (Slate, 2003, p. 24). "I believe that in a civilized society, we are morally responsible for catching those persons with mental illness that we can and saving them from going over the edge of the cliff into the abyss of the criminal justice system" (Slate, 2003, p. 25), and criminal justice practitioners are logically positioned, whether they want to be or not, as the gatekeepers for salvaging persons with mental illnesses.

As a country we are once again facing the issues contemplated when Dorothea Dix began her campaign to build mental health hospitals. Americans know that prisons and jails are not the proper place to treat the mentally ill.

Beyond the criticisms made by the authors, solutions have been offered where appropriate. In many instances appropriate recommendations have been in place for some time now, and consequently the care of the mentally ill is improving. It is imperative that we carefully monitor those few necessary institutions that have as their primary mission the custody and control of the mentally ill and provide adequate resources and funding to those institutions providing viable treatment options. Critical to this success will be measures and processes of accountability.

There are answers to many of the horrific situations recited in this text. Those answers lie in treatment. Untreated mental illness is like untreated cancer. The failure to detect and treat early sends ripple effects throughout families and communities.

There is no shame in being mentally ill. A person should not have to commit a crime to have a chance at some semblance of treatment in America. The shame is in not receiving adequate treatment, and any entity that obfuscates that treatment should be considered criminal.

While correctional treatment staff are successful in improving the functioning of many mentally ill offenders, prisons remain an inappropriate environment for treating the seriously mentally ill offender. The funding of treatment initiatives have to come from either private sources or public sources. The cost to "do it right" will be enormous, but the cost of not doing so, both in terms of human suffering and financially, is even greater. Innovative funding schemes must continue to be explored with long range therapeutic goals in mind. There are only so many slices that can be cut from the "financial pie." California learned in implementing its Three-Strikes Legislation that getting tough on third time felons is costly. Schools, hospitals and communities suffered (Shicor & Sechrest, 1996).

Mental illness knows no socio-economic boundaries. It affects every segment of our society. As Beccaria stated in 1746, "The coin of honor is always inexhaustible and fruitful in the hands of one who distributes it wisely" (70). It is time to do the honorable thing, to make judicious funding decisions, to rethink priorities, and to provide appropriate community and institutional care for the seriously mentally ill.

References

Abram, K.M., & Teplin, L.A. (1991). Co-occurring disorders among mentally ill jail detainees: Implications for public policy. *American Psychologist* 46, pp. 1036-1045.

American Psychological Association (2008, March 27). Parity achieves historic milestone. Retrieved from the World Wide Web on May 1, 2008: http://www.apapractice.org/apo/in_the_news/house_passes_parity.html#.

Associated Press (2008, March 9). Studies: Iraq a $12 billion-a-month war. Retrieved from the World Wide Web on April 27, 2008: http://www.msnbc.msn.com/id/23551693/print/1displaymode/1098/.

Barone, M. (2007, April 28). Feeling Safe Isn't Safe. Retrieved from the World Wide Web on January 28, 2008: http://www.cbsnews.com/stories/2007/05/01/politics/main2747886.shtml.

Beccaria, C. E. (1764). On Crimes and Punishment, Indianapolis, Indiana: Hackett Publishing Company, Inc.

Center for Research on Criminal Justice (1975). "The iron fist and the velvet glove." Reprinted in Before the Law: An introduction to the legal process by Bonsingore, J., Katsch, E., d'Errico, P., Pipkin, R.M., Arons, S. & Rifkin, J. eds. Boston: Houghton Mifflin Company.

CNN Transcripts (2007, July 12). The Situation Room. CNN. Retrieved from the World Wide Web on July 25, 2007: http://transcripts.cnn.com/TRANSCRIPTS/0707/12/sitroom.01.html.

Comptom, M.T., & Kotwicki, R.J. (2007). *Responding to individuals with mental illnesses*. Boston: Jones & Bartlett.

Council of State Governments (2007c). CSG Justice Center commends U.S. House members for passage of the Mentally Ill Offender Treatment and Crime Reduction Reauthorization and Improvement Act. Criminal Justice/Mental Health Consensus Project. New York: Council of State Governments. Retrieved from the World Wide Web on February 3, 2008: http://consensus-project.org/updates/newsletters/2008-cp-newsletters/2008-jan-newsletter.

Council of State Governments (2007a). Why a JLI? Retrieved from the World Wide Web on October 23, 2007: http://consensusproject.org/JLI/info/jli_about/why_jli.

Council of State Governments (2007b, May 2). National Mental Illness and Courts Forum a Success. Retrieved from the World Wide Web on October 23, 2007: http://www.sconet.state.oh.us/Communications_Office/Press_Releases/2007/mentalIllnessProgram_050207.asp.

Daly, R. (2006). States get disappointing marks on mh report card. *Psychiatric News* 41(8), p. 8, 71.

del Carmen, R.V. (2006). *Criminal procedure: Law and practice* (6th ed.) Belmont, CA: Wadsworth.

Editorial Board (2004, February 15). Dream of dignity collides with reality. *South Florida Sun Sentinel.* Retrieved from the World Wide Web on June 27, 2007: http://www.sun-sentinel.com/news/opinion/sfl-edittdmental1feb15,0,3451912.story?coll=sfla-home-dots-utility.

Heck, K. (2006, January 13). Codey visits patients at Ancora Psychiatric Hospital. New Jersey Office of the Governor Press Releases. Retrieved from the World Wide Web on July 25, 2007: http://www.nj.gov/cgi-bin/governor/njnewsline/view_article.pl?id=2890.

Hennelly, B. (2004, November 14). WNYC News Acting New Jersey Governor Dick Codey. Retrieved from the World Wide Web on July 13, 2007: http://www.wnyc.org/news/articles/40634.

Koppel, T. (Fall 2000). Lulling viewers into a state of complicity. *Nieman Reports* 54(3), p. 33.

Kristof, N. D. (2008, March 23). Iraq, $5,000 per second? *The New York Times.* Retrieved from the World Wide Web on April 27, 2008: http://www.nytimes.com/2008/03/23/opionion/23kristof.html?_r=1&pagewanted=printe&ore.

Levit, L. (2005, Spring/Summer). Families and privacy laws: Understanding and navigating the HIPPA privacy rule. *Catalyst,* pp. 12–14, Arlington, Virginia: Treatment Advocacy Center.

Lurigio, A.J., Fallon, J.R., & Dincin, J. (2000). Helping the mentally ill in jails adjust to community life: A description of a postrelease ACT program and its clients. *International Journal of Offender Therapy and Comparative Criminology* 44(5), pp. 532–548.

Luo, M. (2007, April 21). U.S. Rules Made Killer Ineligible to Purchase Gun. *The New York Times*. Retrieved form the World Wide Web on January 28, 2008 from: http://www.nytimes.com/2007/04/21/us/21guns.html?_r=1 &oref=slogin.

Marx, G. T. (1986). "The iron fist and the velvet glove: totalitarian potentials within democratic structures" in *The social fabric—Dimensions and issues*, edited by James Short. 1986. Sage Publications, Beverly Hills, CA.

Mazzetti, M., & Havemann, J. (2006, February 3). Iraq War is costing $100,000 per minute. *The Seattle Times*. Retrieved from the World Wide Web on April 27, 2008: http://seattletimes.nwsource.com/cgi-bin/PrintStory.pl?document_id=2002780385&zsectio.

Mucenski, J. P. (2007, August 30). Memphis, Tennessee: National CIT Conference Awards Speaker.

Mulligan, K. (2005a). Firsthand experience spurs Codeys' fight to end stigma. *Psychiatric News* 40(10), p. 21.

Mulligan, K. (2005b). New Jersey Governor begins term by naming mental health task force. *Psychiatric News* 40(10), p. 1.

Munetz, M.R. & Griffin, P.A. (2006). Use of the sequential intercept models as an approach to decriminalization of people with serious mental illness. *Psychiatric Services* 57(4), pp. 544–549.

NAMI (2007, September 19). A Major Story. Arlington, Virginia: National Alliance on mental Illness. Retrieved from the World Wide Web on September 21, 2007: http://nami.org/template.cfm?Section=Top_Story&template=/ContentManagement/ContentDisplay.cfm&ContentID=51319&lstid= 809.

NAPO (2008, January 8). The Washington report. National Association of Police Organizations. Alexandria, Virginia. Retrieved from the Wide World Web on February 3, 2008: http://www.napo.org/washington-report/ index.htm.

New York Law School (2007). Mental Disability Law. New York. Retrieved from the World Wide Web on September 21, 2007: http://www.nyls.edu/ pages/166.asp.

Power, A. K. (2005, June 1). Transformation: Moving from goals to action. Joint National Conference on Mental Health Block Grants and National Conference on Mental Health Statistics, Arlington, Virginia. Retrieved from the World Wide Web on July 9, 2007: http://mentalhealth.samhsa. gov/newsroom/speeches/060105.asp.

Report of the Virginia Tech Review Panel (2007). Richmond, Virginia: Office of the Governor. Retrieved from the World Wide Web on September 23,

2007: http://www.governor.virginia.gov/TempContent/techPanelReport-docs/8%20CHAPTER%20IV%20LIFE%20AND%20MENTAL%20HEALTH%20HISTORY%20OF%20CHOpdf.pdf.

Salinger, J.D. (1991). *The Catcher in the Rye*. Boston: Little Brown & Company.

Schulte, B., & Jenkins, C.L. (2007, May 7). Cho didn't get court-ordered treatment. *Washington Post*, p. A01.

Shicor, D., & Sechrest, D. (1996) *Three strikes and you're out: Vengeance as public policy*. Thousand Oaks, CA: Sage Publications.

Slate, R.N. (2000, September, 21). *Testimony before the Subcommittee on Crime of the Committee on the Judiciary, U.S. House of Representatives*. Retrieved October 23, 2007 from the World Wide Web: http://judiciary.house.gov/judiciary/slat0921.htm.

Slate, R.N. (2003). From the jailhouse to capitol hill: Impacting mental health court legislation and defining what constitutes a mental health court. *Crime & Delinquency* 49(1), pp. 6–29.

Solomon, P., & Draine, J. (1995). Issues in serving the forensic client." *Social Work* 40(1), pp. 25–33.

Souryal, S. S. (1992). *Ethics in Criminal Justice*. Cincinnati, OH: Anderson Publishing Company.

Tanielian, T., & Jaycox, L. H. (2008). One in five Iraq and Afghanistan veterans suffer from PTSD or Major Depression. Rand Corporation: News Release, Santa Monica, California. Retrieved from the World Wide Web on April 26, 2008: http://rand.org/news/press/2008/04/17/.

Transforming Florida's Mental Health System (2007). Constructing a Comprehensive and Competent Criminal Justice System/Mental Health/Substance Abuse Treatment System: Strategies for Planning, Leadership, Financing, and Service Development. Florida Supreme Court. Retrieved from the World Wide Web on January 30, 2008: http://www.floridasupremecourt.org/pub_info/documents/11-14-2007_Mental_Health_Report.pdf.

Virginia Tech Review Panel (2007, August). Mass Shootings at Virginia Tech. Report of the Review Panel. Retrieved from the World Wide Web on January 28, 2008: http://www.governor.virginia.gov/TempContent/techPanelReport-docs/FullReport.pdf.

Wall, R. (2007, March, 27). *Testimony before the Subcommittee on Crime, Terrorism, and Homeland Security of the Committee on the Judiciary, U.S. House of Representatives*. Retrieved October 23, 2007 from the World Wide Web: http://judiciary.house.gov/oversight.aspx?ID=291.

Webdale, K. (2000, September, 21). *Testimony before the Subcommittee on Crime of the Committee on the Judiciary, U.S. House of Representatives*. Re-

trieved October 23, 2007 from the World Wide Web: http:/www.house.gov/
judiciary/webd0921.htm.
Williamson, E., & Schulte, B. (2007, December 20). Congress passes bill to
stop mentally ill from getting guns. *Washington Post*, p. A12.

CASE INDEX

Name Index

SUBJECT INDEX